THE CROWD AND
THE MOB

For Anna

THE CROWD AND THE MOB

From Plato to Canetti

J. S. McClelland

Department of Politics,
University of Nottingham

London
UNWIN HYMAN
Boston   Sydney   Wellington

Published by the Academic Division of
Unwin Hyman Ltd
15/17 Broadwick Street, London W1V 1FP

Unwin Hyman, Inc.
8 Winchester Place, Winchester, Mass. 01890, USA

Allen & Unwin (Australia) Ltd,
8 Napier Street, North Sydney, NSW 2060, Australia

Allen & Unwin (New Zealand) Ltd in association with the
Port Nicholson Press Ltd,
60 Cambridge Terrace, Wellington, New Zealand

First published in 1989

British Library Cataloguing in Publication Data

McClelland, J. S. (John S.)
  The crowd and the mob: from Plato to Canetti.
1. Crowds. Political aspects, to 1970
I. Title
302.3'3
ISBN 0–04–320188–1

Library of Congress Cataloging in Publication Data

McClelland, J. S.
  The crowd and the mob: from Plato to Canetti / J. S. McClelland.
  p. cm.
Bibliography: p.
Includes index.
ISBN 0–04–320188–1 (alk. paper)
1. Crowds. 2. Mobs. 3. Collective behavior. I. Title.
HM281.M385 1988
302.3'3—dc19

88–10214
CIP

Typeset in 10 on 12 point Palatino and
Printed in Great Britain at the University Press, Cambridge

CONTENTS

'. . .we have a very imperfect knowledge of the human heart if we do not also examine it in crowds.'

Rousseau, *Emile*

FOREWORD

This book has its origins in some work I did many years ago in Cambridge under the enormously generous and stimulating supervision of George Steiner, and he has been at my elbow ever since. Bill Doyle, David Holdcroft, Keith Jenkins, Dennis Kavanagh, Richard King and David Regan have read chapters in draft, made many suggestions, and corrected many faults. Robert Markus, most conservative and open-minded of men, and Peter Morris, learned and quick-witted, helped me most of all. Miss April Gibbon typed and re-typed the manuscript with the patience of a saint. I cannot end this foreword without a salute to the Unknown Librarian who catalogued a *History of Human Stupidity* under 'Crowds, Masses' in my university library. Whatever else I have said about the crowd, I do not think I have said that.

J. S. McClelland
Nottingham
1.7.87

LIST OF ABBREVIATIONS

The following short abbreviations are used for certain works that are often referred to:

AR	*Ancient Regime*	Taine
CFR	*French Revolution*	Carlyle
CP	*Crowds and Power*	Canetti
CW	*Conscience of Words*	Canetti
DF	*Decline and Fall*	Gibbon
MFR	*French Revolution*	Michelet
SE	*Standard Edition*	Freud
TFR	*French Revolution*	Taine

Introduction:
The Idea of the Crowd in History

There has been a particular way of looking at crowds in every period of history. Explicit, self-conscious, theoretical interest in 'the psychology of the crowd', however, is recent. The attempt to construct an exact theory of crowd behaviour dates from 1870, and crowd theory had to wait until 1960 for its first masterpiece, Canetti's *Crowds and Power*. Histories of political thought concentrate on a succession of justifications for forms of rule. What is to be ruled, the crowd, and what threatens rule, the mob, figure only on the sidelines. If the crowd gets in at all, what a particular thinker has to say about what it is like is either accepted at its face value, or dismissed as bias. Histories of political thought are written from the top looking down; by this I do not mean that historians of political thought are always 'on the side' of rulers, though a case could be made out for that; what I mean is that by attending to justifications for forms of rule, historians of political thought have usually failed to see that justifications for forms of rule are made that much more convincing if the ruled can be made out to be at best a crowd, therefore needing to be ruled, or at worst a mob, therefore threatening rule. This failing in the histories of political thought is surprising, because the compulsion to treat the ruled as a crowd and a mob began very early in the political thought of the West. It could almost be said that political theorizing was *invented* to show that democracy, the rule of men by themselves, necessarily turns into rule by the mob. Athens had been some kind of working democracy for two centuries before Plato invited us to see the Athenian *demos* as an ignorant and irrational crowd always likely to be turned into a mob by its demagogues. Similarly at Rome, where Livy, writing when the republic was over, denies the Roman people a share in Rome's rise to greatness by arguing that Rome would probably have risen to greatness sooner if the wise patrician class had not had to expend so much valuable energy conquering the enemy within – the Roman mob and its agitators, the Tribunes of the People.

If there is such a thing as a Western tradition of political thought, it begins with this profoundly anti-democratic bias, and this bias has crept unconsciously into the histories of political thought. It is probably no one's fault that the history of political *thought* begins with *anti*-democratic arguments, because the tradition of democratic practice in the ancient world never felt the need to arm itself with a theory. While the people were poor, and had arms in their hands, they already possessed the moral claims of poverty and the means to realize and defend them. The activity of political *theorizing* in the sense of 'high' theory, and the activity of reflection on the forms that political rule might take, began as part of the counter-armoury of aristocratic landowners fighting the ages-old plebeian demand for an agrarian law. The *plebs* lost everywhere, and the careful cultivation of patrician contempt for the common people as a spineless crowd or a deluded mob was an important asset on the winning side. Yet the moral claims of the ancient *plebs* kept being made. Christianity reinforced the moral claims of poverty, which proved to be embarrassing when popes and bishops defended the established order against millenarian crowds claiming to be a *plebs dei*, and so the medieval church was always quick to remind itself that the crowd had freed Barabbas and condemned Christ. From the Renaissance onwards, the defence of the idea of the republic was linked to a deconstruction of Livy's account of the Roman people as a rabble roused by demagogues; this tradition is clear through Machiavelli, seventeenth-century English republicanism, through Montesquieu right up to the revolutionary period in Europe towards the end of the eighteenth century, though the story of the transition from King Mob to revolutionary crowd is a complex one.

In the eighteenth century, politicians and political commentators on both sides of the Atlantic shared the fear that the mob would 'get out of hand', by which they typically meant that mobs raised from above to help defend corporate privileges against royal encroachment – Wilkes and the rights of the freeholders of Middlesex, Sam Adams and the Massachusetts Charter – might themselves begin to make revolutionary demands of their own in the name of social levelling, as in Shays Rebellion, sanscullotism after the storming of the Bastille, and the demand for the Rights of Man everywhere. *The Federalist Papers* is the first modern work of political theory implicitly to recapitulate the whole theme of Livy's Roman history by asking its readers to ratify the new Constitution of the United States in order to provide for the strong government necessary to prevent demands for the redistribution of the cultivated land and the abolition of debts from becoming law. The authors of *The Federalist Papers* urge their readers to believe that levelling demands are not plebeian at all, but mob demands, and out of that piece

2

of special pleading comes the slow decline of the Jeffersonian dream of a frugal and virtuous agrarian republic and the rise of the countervailing idea of unlimited economic opportunity. Republicanism is replaced by economic individualism, and finally by Sumnerism.

The mid nineteenth century, perhaps 1848, more probably 1871, is the turning point in the history of the idea of the crowd, because from that time onwards the crowd becomes central to social and political theorizing, or from that time onwards at least any exercise in social theory which did not make room for the crowd at its centre looked makeshift, mistaken or wilfully obtuse. The crowd began to appear in any number of different guises: frenzied mob, misunderstood people, duped politics-fodder, vehicle of an ancient urge for justice, agent of regression to an animal past, threat to the present, hope for the future, but, no matter how it appeared, social theory had to do more than notice the crowd or dismiss it as a passing phase. This important theoretical shift towards the crowd has its parallel in the world of politics. The crowd was claiming more of the attention of rulers at the same time as it was pushing its way into the centre of theoretical concern, and after 1848 a large part of the story of the invention of the modern state, its secret and not so secret police, its laws and its gaols, its lists of suspects and its contingency plans, its first tentative movements towards social welfare as social palliative and its longing for conscription as a way of disciplining the unruly (the English crowd psychologist Wilfred Trotter called the armies of the Great War 'killing crowds') could be written as the modern state's attempt to accommodate itself to and to cope with the crowd. The crowd was fast on the way to becoming a permanent threat to established patterns of social living, to a stable political order, and to a received notion of culture.

It is easy to say that there is nothing particularly new in this. The crowd, it might be said, has been with us since classical Greece. (And perhaps even since Homer. There are hints in *The Iliad* that the war-weariness of the Achaeans threatened to cause trouble for the kings in the assembly ('Who gives a whit who fucks soft Helen?'), though in general we are meant to see the common folk as the great ones' admiring audience when they quarrel among themselves, engage in single combat, or win prizes in the funeral games.) Plato's account in *The Republic* of democracy as mob rule degenerating into tyranny prepares the way for a host of crowd images: the crowd hounding Christ to his death; the crowd bawling for blood in the circus; crowds of mutinous legionaries looking round for someone to raise to the purple; crowds led by wild men in from the desert in Late Antiquity; the Nika Riots which nearly cost Justinian the Empire; later Roman mobs making trouble for popes; medieval crowds volatile at great festivals and fairs; peoples' crusades (Gibbon divides the crusaders into The Chiefs and The Crowd (*Decline and Fall*, VI, p. 50, n. 2)); the barbarism of crowds during the Wars of Religion; crowds at public executions; peasant revolts; Whilkite and Church and King mobs in London; liberty mobs in Boston; the crowd in the French Revolution; lynch mobs; the mobs of industrial discontent; the list is endless. Each particular crowd elicited its own theoretical response, often in the form of politically loaded historical narrative, and these responses are to be seen as cumulative. Later thinkers always had the past's anti-crowd theory to draw on, so that Machiavelli, the crowd's first theoretical champion, has a lot of digging to do before he can get to the root of the main sources of anti-crowd prejudice in Livy's Roman history (see below, Chapter 2).

What is different about crowd theory after the middle of the nineteenth century is that, before, the crowd does not appear to have forced political thinkers to re-examine the assumptions of their own political theorizing. Plato, for instance, has a well-worked-out view of the crowd; and mob democracy, which he blamed for the death of Socrates, was one of the causes of his becoming a political theorist in the first place, but for him the crowd is something essentially negative, to be contrasted with what things ought to be like. The crowd as mob is everything a *polis* should not be, so that the danger of the mob is one more reason for reaffirming and defending his own aristocratic assumptions about desirable social living. The idea that the crowd could itself be a model of social living never occurs to him. There is one type of social living, democracy, which encourages the mob, but the inevitable tendency of democracy to degenerate into mob rule, and then into tyranny, is the cause of democracy's radical instability, and this enables Plato to see mob rule as a fleeting episode in the life of a society, something which cannot last (see below, Chapter 1). Something like this seems to have been the Roman view of the crowd. Livy is full of crowds. His Roman history can be read as an account of the development by the patricians of political skills learned by coping with the people's tendency to degenerate into a mob, and the occasion when Menenius Agrippa persuaded the plebs with a fairy story to return to their allegiance and their labours shows how good they became at it. Later the Empire offered circuses, perhaps the first attempt to institutionalize the business of controlling crowds. The people were allowed to be a mob, but only within strict limits; the circus mob could do almost what it liked in the stadiums, provided it went home quietly afterwards. This required special policing, but not much else, certainly not a new way of looking at society in general. Mobs were just one social danger among others, one more problem that the universal empire ruled by law had to deal with. The christianized Empire had to deal with crowds led by holy men. This created a special problem, to become common in medieval Europe, because more than simple 'law and order' was at issue. Holy men might be acting in obedience to a higher law, so why should they not claim some kind of legitimate obedience from their crowds which was different from, but at the same time a challenge to, the obedience owed to bishops and magistrates? The civil and ecclesiastical authorities had to tread carefully; organized religion and organized society had to make room for the crowd. The crowd's activity became ritualized. Certain things were permitted, on certain occasions, and the signal that the bounds were overstepped was when the crowd refused to go home. The crowd had its own permitted time and space in a society which already recognized a plurality of competing jurisdictions. The holy crowd could not be treated lightly; it had implications for the heavenly as well as for the earthly city, but its religiosity showed that it really presented no fundamental threat to either. The procedures of ordinary theology could cope theoretically with the crowd, and ordinary law-enforcement could deal with its excesses in a society which was not especially orderly anyway. Peasants' revolts came and went, and were dealt with by concession and repression. The urban crowd in the early modern period could be manipulated for religious or political ends that would not have surprised some of the observers of Late Antiquity, and the crowds of 'sturdy beggars' of the English statutes could cause problems for magistrates, but in general there was nothing that the militia could not deal with.

Sympathetic, republican attention to eighteenth-century political riot in Britain and America does mark some kind of new beginning in the crowd's fortunes in social theory. Machiavelli had prepared the way by rescuing the Roman *plebs* from Livy's mobbish smears, and the republican idea of liberty as the action of a virtuous people in arms, asserting their right to land, never died. It turned up in seventeenth-century English republicanism (Machiavelli was a hero to the Harringtonians), and it survived into the ideological armoury of eighteenth-century opposition to monarchical pretension, entrenched oligarchic corruption, and a standing army. Montesquieu, the American Patriots, and eventually the Jeffersonians, were to see 'riot and sedition' as the means to hold free government true to its republican principles, and, in the case of America, as the means to keep government from going down the Hamiltonian path towards corrupt finance and executive aggrandisement (see below, Chapter 4). But this rehabilitation of the crowd was still backward-looking; its images were Roman, and the images of its opponents were Greek; when Alexander Hamilton spoke of the people as 'a great beast', or Hume looked forward to the hanging of the Whilkite agitators so that they could improve English letters with their dying eloquence, they still spoke in and to a mental world which was recognizably Platonic. The crowd could become a mob if the circumstances were right: loss of nerve by local authority; the failure to arrest demagogues; high bread prices, perhaps, or unemployment; then the dormant passions of the crowd would turn into the active barbarism of the mob whose nature could be understood in a way that had not really changed since the trial of Socrates.

This was the perspective that changed after 1789 and which changed definitively after 1848. Europe had been frightened by the crowd long before the French Revolution, but it was the Revolution which, for those who had eyes to see it, ushered in the crowd as a permanent political force. After the Revolution, it became increasingly difficult to see riots as a sporadic series of incidents, which happened to be more frequent in bad times than in good. New, democratic political doctrines appeared, to speak directly to and for 'the people'. Now that the people storming the Bastille had become the central image of crowd politics, those who in the past had been inclined to think of 'the people' as at best the undifferentiated crowd, and at worst an occasional mob, had something more to worry about, and they could easily think themselves into such a state of irrational fear that they could be hoodwinked into thinking that, because the new popular doctrines showed themselves to be remarkably persistent, the revolutionary crowd was equally persistent. If popular political doctrines were permanent, it was plausible to see the threat of popular disturbance as being permanent too. Class war was one of the forms the activity of the mob could take, and Marx was a past master at playing the rulers of Europe at their own game. If there were people foolish enough to believe that it was the Parisian mob, storming the Bastille, that had caused all the trouble in Europe since 1789, they could be frightened into anything. The spectre that was haunting Europe in 1848 was the ghost of the Bastille mob, which now became the mob that had been at all revolutions, failed and successful, past, present and future. The French Revolution showed how permanent and far-reaching the effects of a bread riot allowed to get out of hand could be. Of course, the mob in the strictest sense could not rule for long, but the mob which the Revolution launched into a successful career in the imagination of conservative Europe served as a mentally institutionalized reminder of what the mob had once done and what it could do again. If the mob had once been the expression of the will of the people, it could again and again claim to be the expression of that will, and there was no denying that, looked at from this highly charged perspective, the revolutionary mob had caused a new, hostile world to be born. Translated into less lurid terms, the mob had become a source of political power and a legitimizing source of that power, something it had not really been since the demise of the ancient republics. Popular sovereignty might still clothe itself in the toga, but now there was no looking back over its shoulder for the ancient legitimations which English and American republicanism had looked for before 1789. After Rousseau, just to call sovereignty popular was to give a full account of it.

Now the political opponents of the people were to be made to suffer from the backlash of their own contempt; what they had formerly bracketed together in the same sneer – the people, *canaille*, mob, crowd, anybody except themselves – had now become part of the permanent world of politics and political calculation. Unless the sneerers at the people were to jettison most of their own, self-defining, political vocabulary, they had *necessarily* to believe that any form of popular politics was mob politics. It could not matter how law-abiding a dem-onstration was; it could not matter how respectable the working-class leaders were who asked for the legalization of trade unions; it could not matter that manifestations of popular will took great pains, through self-policing, to show they were not mobs. As soon as a policeman was assaulted, or a cobblestone was thrown, or a property-right was violated, the mob was back and the revolution would begin again if it was not stopped in its tracks at Peterloo.

This is not a very sophisticated perspective, but it appears to be the way in which almost everyone with claims to be a conservative, or who felt nervous, in Europe and America, from the middle of the nineteenth century, looked at any form of popular action. The riot, the lynch-mob, the urban revolt, the *manifestation*, were all seen as the tip of an iceberg or the thin end of a wedge. People had talked themselves into believing that society was imperilled; that settled social living was fragile; that culture was threatened; that civilization was beleaguered. Revolutions proved it, and anything aimed, however lightly, against the established order was revolutionary because the French Revolution had shown how easily the established order could be disestablished by the crowd. The mob had been at the back of everything since 1789, so the mob must be at the back of everything still. Anyone who believed that 'the people' and the mob were the same thing could hardly believe anything else. Perhaps it needs to be said, that this interchangeability of words like 'the people', crowd and mob (and later mass and 'the masses') is necessary only in minds which are already disposed to see the mob everywhere, and perhaps it is also necessary to say that such minds are not likely to be very discriminating. If there are discriminations to be made on their behalf, then 'the people' is what they might call those unlike themselves when they co-operate actively in a common enterprise ('the people' was the common eighteenth-century term for what we would call the 'crew' of a man-of-war; then, when they were called a crew, they were already probably in a near-mutinous state, as in the 'Irish crew' whom King Billy slew); 'the crowd' might refer to those unlike themselves when they are in a passive state, and so requiring leadership if any common enterprise is to be undertaken; and 'mob' refers to them when they create mayhem and are in danger of finding leaders of their own. It will become obvious in the course of this book that other distinctions can be made, as for instance between the mass, supine and culture-indifferent, and 'the masses', 'on the move' and culture-hostile; and even the modest definition of mob given above will not do in the case of the eighteenth-century mob, which was frequently raised by leaders within the world of official politics and was only seen to be getting out of hand when it began to produce its own leaders, by which time it is beginning to look like a 'revolutionary crowd' (see below, Chapter 3). On the whole, I have avoided definitions, preferring to let the sense of what a particular thinker means by terms like these to emerge from what he actually says, though it will be important, from time to time, to point out that the polemical force of what a thinker has to say about the crowd often depends on a too easy elision of terms like crowd, mass and mob (as, for example, in the case of Le Bon (see below, Chapter 7)).

It was for people who were beginning to see the mob everywhere, that Taine wrote his great *Origins of Contemporary France* (1876–94). Taine's intentions were not modest. By contemporary France he really meant contemporary Europe. Like Metternich (and like Marx), he believed that in politics things always happen in France first, and he had no doubt that the French experience since 1789 was bound to be repeated and was actually being repeated in every other European country. To understand what was going on in France and in Europe after 1871, it was necessary to understand what had actually happened during the Revolution. Taine was not the first to challenge the republican mythologies of liberty, equality and fraternity, but the timeliness of the *Origins* goes a long way to explain their phenomenal success. The republican panache of the French armies of 1870 had not been notably successful in defending the *patrie* against Prussia, and the *Commune's* fraternity had left some of the most famous streets of Paris in ruins, so the time was ripe for examining the Revolution which was supposed to be the continuing inspiration both of republicanism and socialism. The *Origins* also came in the right form. Up to the *Commune*, the attack on the Revolution and its legacy in France had been predominantly a Catholic attack, stressing the Revolution's irreligiosity in general, its attack on the Church in particular, and its character as a punishment for the atheism of the Enlightenment which had allegedly been the Revolution's cause. Taine's attack on the Revolution was full-bloodedly positivist, wonderfully attuned to the spirit of the scientific age. Above all it was thorough. Taine did the work, and when he was finished (the last volume of the *Origins* was published posthumously) he had subjected the Revolution to an examination so thorough that there was probably no historical work to date on any subject that was its equal. The mob and the Terror were at the centre of Taine's view of the Revolution, not revolutionary heroism and the conquest of liberty by republican arms. The Revolution's horrors, which the republican view of the Revolution could explain away as unfortunate and secondary when compared with the self-sacrifice of the armies of the Republic and of Napoleon, were now solidly centre-stage, and the revolutionary mob stood as agent and symbol for those horrors. Contemporary France, and therefore contemporary Europe, had its origins in some very nasty riots; contemporary France was either republican or Bonapartist, and after the *Commune*, potentially socialist, so all of these must in some way be connected with the revolutionary mob; the Jacobins emerged as the first leaders of the Revolution in its popular phase, therefore the Jacobins must have been demagogues; socialism comes out of Jacobinism, so socialists must be rabble-rousers too; the Bonapartism of the Second Empire had legitimized itself by plebiscite, therefore the mob must be behind Bonapartism; both Bonapartism and republicanism came out of the Revolution, and the Revolution came out of the Enlightenment, and Rousseau was part of the Enlightenment, so Rousseau must have been a demagogue, or at the very least the inspirer of demagogues; therefore Rousseau was there in spirit every time a château was burned, an aristocrat massacred, or the tumbrills rolled. The illusions which Rousseau spread about the simple goodness of the people – illusions enshrined in Michelet's account of the storming of the Bastille – cannot possibly be sustained after a serious look at what revolutionary mobs were actually like, and these illusions are unthinkable after a serious look at what revolutionary mobs actually did.

But Taine was much more than a good reporter, telling his readers what he saw, with his own eyes, in the documents. The Revolution, in his view of it, was made in the name of a particular view of Man. This man was naturally good, or at least innocent, and he was naturally rational because he recognized that possession of his natural rights implied the duty of respecting those rights in others. In the Revolution this man came into his own; because he knew no frontiers (which were artificial, not natural), he had a message for all other men, everywhere. He said: Do as we have done; Paris is only the beginning; what we do, we do in the name of suffering humanity everywhere. We will soon come to your rescue, for progress cannot be stopped. Taine saw very clearly what that meant. Natural man was being invited to destroy historical man, man as he is, the product of his own time and his own circumstances, man as he is in the street, what Renan was later to call the daily plebiscite, ordinary human living rooted in a particular national life at a particular stage in that national life's unfolding. Taine went far beyond the barbarism of the revolutionary mob to examine the doctrine which encouraged the illusion that the Revolution was

9

the working out in practice of the political aspects of this simple, pure, rational human nature. If, as he believed, natural men were mob men, then the doctrines which encouraged, or supported, or caused, or were caused by the Revolution, must themselves be illusions, so Taine's careful account of the Revolutionary mob is the beginning of a critique of most of the political doctrines of the modern world: the rights of man, democracy, socialism, necessary progress, any defence of popular participation in the business of politics or government. Taine thinks there can be progress, but its nature and its impetus have been misunderstood. It is science that creates progress, but science is the opposite of the consciousness of the mob, and by extension, of the masses who are merely a mob in its dormant form. The role of Reason must be stripped of its progressive, democratizing illusions. These illusions are anti-progressive because the myth of natural, rational man encouraged well-meaning, but mistaken, politicians, administrators and schoolmasters to believe and to teach that the necessary disciplines of the state, the law and the classroom were the means by which the natural, rational innocent nature of man was perverted, corrupted and coarsened. Taine thought history showed the opposite. Men without their chains could be seen murdering in the street, in any great riot. The *Commune* was no different from 1848, and 1848 was a predictable repetition of 1789. Each was a retrograde step, perhaps the beginning of a journey back to primal barbarism down the progressive path that mankind had beaten so laboriously through the ages. Luckily, Taine's Positivism still offered some hope, provided those who understood the dangers had the courage of their understanding, were prepared as rulers to stop the rot, and as propagandists to spread the word among the educated elite that the elite was threatened by the republican or socialist ideas with which it had toyed so disastrously before 1789, and with which it continued to play. Society was to be divided between them and us; they, the sleeping mob, and we, the high-minded keepers of an intellectual and moral culture.

A qualified social optimism was possible so long as that distinction between them and us could be sustained, but when Le Bon brought together Taine's work on the crowd in the French Revolution with other, much more psychologically systematic work on the mentality of crowds in general, that distinction began to look precarious. In *The Crowd*, of which the first of many editions appeared in 1895, Le Bon tried to bring together into a theory all the work that had been done on the crowd since 1870. He was interested particularly in the mentality of crowds. Taine had already pointed out that crowds appeared to think in *idées fixes*, simplistically, in childish images, which could be manipulated to serve murderous ends by demagogues like the Jacobins, and other crowd theorists, notably Scipio Sighele and

10

Gabriel Tarde, had expanded on that theme (see below, Chapter 6). Now Le Bon cobbled together the insights of others, added a few bits of his own, and formulated what he called rather grandly: the Law of the Mental Unity of Crowds. The crowd had a 'group mind', whose workings did not follow the same laws as the workings of an individual's mind because it was unconscious. It was an easy step from this to argue that any group whatsoever in which this 'group mind' could be seen to operate, could be looked upon as a crowd, and because all crowds were potential mobs, any group could become a mob. Some of Le Bon's own observations were of proletarian crowds, but by characterizing the crowd by how its group mind worked, not by where it came from or what it did, he opened up the possibility that any group *at all* could, in the right circumstances, be a crowd: a jury, a parliamentary assembly, an army under discipline, eventually even a whole society, could be a crowd. The crowd then was no respecter of persons; anybody could become part of the crowd if his mind became part of the unconscious group mind. The group mind worked in the way Taine had thought the mob's mind worked, irrationally and stupidly, but Le Bon now said that people who as individuals were neither irrational nor stupid could become part of a group whose unconscious collective mind obeyed his Law of the Mental Unity of Crowds. No doubt, certain types of people were more likely than others to join the group mind and become part of a crowd, factory workers, for example, or peasants, or women, but nobody was in principle excluded.

The group mind hypothesis was very frightening indeed. It became one of the great questions of social theory almost down to our own day, because admitting its validity entailed the modification or outright rejection of a large number of cherished social attitudes and social doctrines. The social attitudes which would have to change would be precisely those whose plausibility depended on a distinction like Taine's between them and us. If *we*, the middle class, the literate, the legislators, the voters, the educated, the faithful, the ruling class, the elite, cannot look down on *them*, the proletariat, the peasantry, trouble-makers, the *canaille*, the masses, the herd, the many-too-many, all of them out there, because they are an undifferentiated crowd, a potential mob, while we are not, then we too are part of the danger to the order, culture and progress which previously we had been able to think *we* defended from *them*. We, in given circumstances, could be a menace too. Our most fundamental claim to superiority has gone. Some at least of the arguments which people like us, or our spokesmen, have always used against the rights of man, or universal suffrage, or socialism, or the parliamentary republic, can now be equally well turned against us. The crowd has been compared to sheep, and the

11

mob to ravening wolves. We, ourselves, can certainly be sheep, and we could now conceivably become wolves.

The implications of Le Bon's unconscious group mind were no less devastating on the level of social doctrine. It drove a coach and four through the assumptions of Liberalism, Idealism, and certain versions of Social Darwinism, and through a theory of history which in its broad outlines was common to all three. Liberals had always seen the rationality in the world as the world's best hope. Whether they traced their intellectual origins to eighteenth-century utilitarianism, or to an idea of rights, or further back to Newtonian or post-Newtonian views of the constitution of the Universe, they all tended to equate human progress with the growth of human rationality. That rationality manifested itself in a number of very diverse, but at the same time, connected ways. Rationality might, as with Kant, simply be the opposite of the irrationality of brute ignorance and superstition; rationality could be natural science, or mathematics, or a correct geography, or an improved agriculture, or a more sophisticated technology; rationality could be improved social theory, or demography, or political economy, or better understanding of the nature of law, or of the processes of social development. Quite how all these were connected was a matter of debate – trees of knowledge with branches for each particular science and twigs for the special subdivisions of those sciences were drawn until well into the nineteenth century – but few denied that everything tended in the same direction, and almost nobody thought that any single line of advance would create problems which would be of more than passing concern for any other line of advance. It was possible to entertain such an optimistic view of the world and its possibilities because for the first time men could be certain that in their own minds they had the right kind of equipment to look the world straight in the face without the uncertainties about the nature of their own minds which had hindered man in less fortunate ages. The Lockian view of mind, upon which all later theories of mind were built, had banished the uncertainties about the nature of mind which had plagued earlier ages. Mind had been emptied of its terrors; it held no secrets; truth was no longer to be seen in visions and dreams. Truth could now be seen with open eyes, and those eyes really did see what they saw, and what they saw was all there was to be seen. The objects of sight were no longer to be seen as symbols and hints of some other, higher reality, of which ordinary men of common sense were privileged only to catch occasional glimpses. And there was no longer a need for a special agency, like a priesthood, claiming the privilege of understanding the whole of God's meaning for the world, or as much of that meaning as it was humanly possible to know. The Enlightenment had started from the beginning; for man to know the world he had first to know himself.

Once he knew himself, the world was unknown only because men lacked the courage to know it further, and out of that understanding would come the technologies of control.

A world that was properly understood was a world that could be improved. The world no longer had to be taken as a given. Nature was no longer implacably hostile. For the first time men could defy the biblical injunction to get their bread in the sweat of their faces. Wild nature could be transformed into a landscaped garden. The political and social worlds no longer had to be accepted as a given. When Hamilton wrote in the first of the *Federalist Papers* that on the success or failure of constitutional government in America depended the greater question of whether the world would continue to be ruled by accident and force, or by reflection and choice, he looked forward to a time, already nearer by the second half of the nineteenth century, when men would live under laws which they had freely chosen, in the making of which they had had some part, however remote, and laws which would be the product of the free workings of the minds of men. This was the great liberal reforming programme of the nineteenth century. Human organizations, states, churches, armies, business enterprises, all public institutions, social, educational and cultural, were to be run on lines that someone, or some body of men, had worked out for themselves. Conscious, rational organization was to replace what had accidentally survived, been inherited, or been foisted upon men by force or fraud.

This view of things would have been impossible without the individual, rational, commonsensical mind which Locke had cleared of all mysticism and clutter, and which Kant had set on the road to Enlightenment with the instruction 'dare to know'. It was this mind which was able to look back to the beginning of its own culture, or to look at other, backward cultures in its own world, with a feeling of superiority. The institutions that in the past had ordered men's lives were inferior because they had not been thought out. Modern monarchy may have come out of ancient or medieval monarchy, but modern kings were constitutional monarchs, and that made all the difference. Constitutional monarchy was monarchy that modern men had thought about, thought through and then thought they wanted. A republic was also a possibility, but the arguments for constitutional monarchy were better, and even republics were presided over by a species of elected kings. The past could be patronized, but it was not necessary to hold it in contempt. The continuity of modern with ancient and medieval institutions was an important part of the story of progress. Liberals did not deal in utopias, so the story of improvement suited their gradualist temper. Things had been worse in the past and would be better in the future.

The idea of the unconscious group mind, whose most obvious manifestation was the crowd and whose most worrying manifestation was the

13

mob, threatened to ruin the whole picture. There could be no denying that there were senses in which the group mind was different from the rational, individual mind. The group mind was fickle; it could not set itself to the long, sometimes tedious, and nearly always slow, business of reform; the group's mind was hardly rational and, being unconscious, there was no knowing what it might contain. There was simply no place for the unconscious mind in the Lockian scheme. If there was an unconscious mind, as there was undoubtedly a conscious mind, then the unconscious mind might play tricks on the conscious and we might never know. We might be seeing things. And Le Bon had shown that everybody's mind could be part of this group mind. How could you tell when your own mind was working as an individual, rational mind, and when it was working as a part of the group mind? Before Le Bon, it had been possible to answer that, of course, minds acted in individual, rational brains when the body it inhabited was not part of a crowd, but Le Bon argued that the physically proximate group of bodies was only the most obvious example of a crowd. If the crowd was characterized as a mentality, then the limiting condition of the physical existence of a crowd was no longer necessary before crowd thinking could be said to be going on. A crowd off the streets, each man in his own home reading a newspaper, for instance, becomes a possibility. And if juries, parliamentary assemblies, and committees could act as crowds, and if these were the bodies which were supposed to make the rational decisions upon which the future progress of society depended, then nothing was certain.

The other worrying fact about the crowd from the point of view of Liberalism was that the crowd was *modern*. Le Bon had said that the modern age was the Era of Crowds. He certainly meant that the discovery of the way the crowd's mind worked was recent; he also thought that in the contemporary world crowds were commoner than they had been, and that more and more of society's decisions were being taken by groups who could easily act as crowds. But when he proclaimed that the modern age was the Era of Crowds he was also attacking the modern age's claim to be modern. Crowd theory showed that modern men were just as unthinking as men had been in the past, and just as unthinking as the men in those societies which Europeans regarded as still backward and primitive. Le Bon was an elitist. There were some men in every society who could understand that this was so, and who could perhaps manipulate the crowd and mitigate the effects of the crowd mentality in social life. But the crowd could not be made to go away. Taine's rational elite, aloof and culture-conscious, leading civilization ever onward and upward in the teeth of the crowd's opposition, was no longer a real possibility. Le Bon thought that the best that could be hoped for was probably a holding operation only, in a bleak future. When Liberalism came to defend itself from the crowd in the person of Sir Ernest Barker, it did very little except moan, concede most of the ground, and put its faith in the Iron Law of Oligarchy and the *embourgeoisement* of popular leaders (see below, Chapter 7).

The Idealist tradition was even more vulnerable to the hypothesis of an irrational, unconscious, collective mind than the Liberal tradition. By the end of the nineteenth century Liberalism and Idealism had made up most of their differences. Idealism was no longer almost exclusively German, and in England some Liberals at least had followed T. H. Green in incorporating into Liberalism the Idealist concept of the social world as World-as-Mind in order to emphasize the wholeness of social experience. Idealists would have no truck with the solitary observing individual whose Lockian mind registered impressions coming from a world 'out there', because that implied that the independent observer could understand a society in the same way that he could understand any other natural phenomenon or process. From the Idealist point of view, a society and its institutions are the product of decisions of the minds of men. That is why Idealist political philosophy since Hegel had been so concerned with the nature and development of law. The act of making laws is a progressively conscious act of will by men who have an intention and a view of the purpose of law, and by extension, a view of the purpose or end of the community whose formal act the making of law is. Not all societies have in fact believed that law can be made. Perhaps only the Ancient Greeks, and modern states since Rousseau, have truly believed that a people can give itself laws as an act of conscious will (and law is only one of the ways open to a community to organize its collective life). The story of the development of a rational system of law unfolds in the company of other stories in a nation's life; some of these other stories merely obfuscate Reason's own story line, while others, the story of clerical ignorance, for example, or of the censorship, or wilful obscurantism, set themselves up in deliberate opposition to it. Only the specially trained mind of the philosopher of history is capable of sifting the gold from the dross.

According to the Idealists, the history of the rationality of law does not, properly speaking, take place in what Liberals call society, if society is conceived of as something separate from individuals. The history of law occurs in men's own minds. Men are part of a collectively developing rationality, and to understand one's own place in the history of the development of Mind-as-Law is to arrive at a genuine self-understanding. Rationality is, therefore, a characteristic of one's own finite mind, my mind, and rationality is also part of the process in the world which my mind seeks to understand. The social world presents itself as mind to my mind, which is itself part of that social world. My mind's rationality is dependent on its being able to grasp and feel itself part of the wider rationality of the State, the legal, moral and constitutional order of a community whose development is advanced when its affairs are increasingly ordered by rationally willed laws, and retarded when its affairs are left to arbitrary, or accidental, or irrational processes, to the whim of a tyrant, for example, or to the grosser superstitions of religion. The Idealist emphasis on this collective nature of mind caused them to suffer some very anxious moments from the hypothesis of the group mind, because the Idealists were already committed to their own idea of a group mind as unfolding rationality embodied in law. The individualism of one version of Liberalism saw society as a sum of individual minds and wills, and the Idealists had attacked them precisely at this point, arguing that men's consciousness must owe much more to society than Liberal individualists were prepared to allow. How could an individual consciousness, which was part of a larger social consciousness, pretend to detach itself from that social consciousness, and constitute itself as the observer and judge of the society which produced that consciousness? The Idealists' larger social consciousness had always been hard to pin down, and it had always been vulnerable to the scorn of the methodological individualism which was the scientific wing of Liberalism. Where, it had always been asked, is the consciousness which is not an individual mind, in which this larger World-as-Mind resides? Collective mind either does not exist, or it is an individual mind puffed up, or it is an image of mind of the kind favoured by a particular kind of Romanticism, not really a mind at all. Now Le Bon's group mind put itself forward as a possible candidate for the Idealist collective mind. It had the advantage of being grounded in the latest psychologically scientific theory, always Idealism's weak point, but Le Bon's group mind had one huge flaw from the Idealist point of view: far from being rational and self-conscious, it was irrational and unconscious, the very last kind of collective mind that Idealism since Rousseau had been on the lookout for.

And Rousseau himself provided another stumbling-block. When English Idealism began to look back for an intellectual ancestry, it recruited Rousseau as the first modern thinker to take seriously the idea that there existed a consciousness which was more than the sum of its parts, or more than an extrapolation from one of those parts. The 'new moral person' of *The Social Contract* was an essential stepping-stone from the ancient Idealism of Plato and Aristotle to the new Idealism of Hegel and the modern world. But Le Bon and the tradition of Taine and Tarde which Le Bon relied on, blamed Rousseau as the progenitor of the French Revolution and the inspirer of the revolutionary mob, which Le Bon invited his readers to see as the fundamental cases of irrational barbarism of the modern era. The crowd tradition by 1895 was inviting anyone who would listen to see irrationality and regression in any

16

form of collectivity, and it caught Idealism between two stools: either Idealism had to believe that rationality inhered only in individuals, something which it had always denied, or it would have to invent a *third* mind for its collective rationality to inhabit which was neither the individual mind of Liberalism since Locke, nor the collectively irrational mind of Le Bon and the crowd theorists which was irrational *because* it was collective. Finding this third mind was theoretically a tall order, and it failed. The Liberal Ernest Barker joined forces with the idealist Bernard Bosanquet (*The Philosophical Theory of the State*) to try to find it, and both ended up in a limp-wristed elitism, no match for systems of politics which took a more robust view of the collective irrationalism of the crowd (see below, Chapter 7). The modern age was Le Bon's Era of Crowds, of collective mental life *par excellence*; substitute the mind of the crowd for the Hegelian mind out of which law as 'the world of Mind brought out of Itself' came, and the whole Idealist enterprise would have to be abandoned. The claims of Hegel's followers that he had 'realized philosophy' by showing Reason at work in the process of history was no longer tenable in circumstances where real collectivities in the form of electorates or assemblies were now being asked to make choices about what the positive law should be, in contrast to societies in the past whose collective rationality had always been created and nurtured by elites. The positive law of Greek city-states, or of Hegel's own Prussia, had been made by special groups acting on behalf of the rest of society, some of whom were capable of appreciating what was being done in their name and others not. Part of Hegel's theory of progress involved being able to show that in fact an increasing number of people in modern societies could appreciate the higher, rational purpose of the state. Hegel was no democrat, but *The Philosophy of Right* (1821) argues that the State should not allow large numbers of its citizens to fall to such a low level of material existence that their concern for where their next meal was coming from blinds them to any view of what the purpose of the State is. When Idealism found its second home in England, where the franchise was being rapidly extended, exactly these arguments were to be used to recommend social reform and social welfare and public education provision. Men had to be worthy of the vote, which meant being rational enough to be able to use it. But if Le Bon was right, real collectivities were being asked to decide upon questions of real political importance at the very time that it had been discovered that the collective mind was incapable of acting rationally at all. The mind of the crowd, which in Le Bon's hands had become the group mind, could now be seen as the mind of a whole society. The crowd had come a very long way from the time when it could be considered as an occasional social phenomenon and a peripheral concern of social theory. The crowd could now be seen as a model for a whole society, and it might even *be* that society.

If Idealism was threatened by the crowd, so was a particular version of Social Darwinism. Darwin's influence on social theory was enormously diffuse. Some of that influence was based on an understanding of the *Origin of Species* and the *Descent of Man*, but much of what passed for Darwinism had only the remotest connection with anything Darwin ever said; much of it came through popularizations of evolutionism, and especially through Herbert Spencer. Evolutionist concepts became catchwords which could lend a biological, and so scientific, gloss to the most disparate of social doctrines. The 'struggle for life' fitted in well with the extremer versions of individualism, particularly a 'rugged' individualism; the 'survival of the fittest' had a fine ring to it for elitists; 'adaptation' and 'evolution' suited both the mildly reformist doctrines of progressive conservatism and the more adventurously progressive doctrines of liberalism; 'favoured races' encouraged racists and imperialists; 'species evolution', as the evolution of collectivities, lent credence to socialist ideas about class solidarity and international brotherhood; and the fact, above all, that evolution had not yet stopped reassured everyone who was prepared to believe it, that evolution *was* progress. But there was another, darker, side to Darwinism. It was easy enough in the second half in the nineteenth century to take a sanguine view of the future, but there were always some who saw in 'the deadly, but true, nihilism of Darwin' (the phrase is Nietzsche's) a sanguinary challenge to the doctrine of necessary and inevitable progress which Darwinian biology could be used to support. Where, it began to be asked, is the place of mind in the doctrine of evolution as progress? The Positivist version of the Enlightenment's promise of rational progress had always stressed that reason as science as technology was the royal road to human happiness. Rationally planned societies, ruled by those who understood the special social science which makes a planned society possible, would replace the ramshackle apologies for societies which men happened to find themselves living in. The progressive consensus was not a consensus about who should do the planning. It might be done by the State, or by private associations or by private individuals, but plans there had to be. A rationally organized society would produce rational men in greater numbers, who would in their turn be able to devise more rational plans, and at the same time more men would be more amenable to the exigencies of plans, the necessity for which larger numbers of men could now understand. Dissent could be written off as social Luddism, teething troubles, obstetric pains, or as a secularized version of Hegel's Cunning of Reason, testing man's belief in the attainment of a now temporarily obscured future good. But there was nothing in the

Darwinian perspective which corresponded to the rationally planning mind. Unless you were prepared to see the hand of God in evolution, or any other hidden hand, what was immediately striking was evolution's randomness. Evolution was chancy in ways which were not dissimilar to the chanciness of the development of those societies in the past in contrast to which modern societies were supposed to be progressive.[1]

Herbert Spencer's reputation as a biologist could obscure for a time that social evolution was only *analogous* to biological evolution. Darwinian evolution was the story of species, not of groups or of individuals within the species. Man was a species, but social theory dealt with much smaller groups: societies, states, nations, classes, families, and what biological evolution had to say about them was never clear. Even less clear was what part particular subgroups had to play in the evolution of the groups themselves. Biological evolution had a good deal to say about what effects the social organization of animal groups had on their chances of survival, but nothing at all to say about how this could be best *managed* in the future, unless men were to copy what animals did, or had done in the past, but this could hardly be called progressive. Loose talk about evolution acting on human groups in different ways from the way it acted on animal groups, or the idea that organized human societies adapted better than individuals, or the idea that conscious social organization was another, and more successful, example of adaptation, could not long survive the straightforward objection that Darwinian evolution was not talking about these things at all. Most obviously, the time-scale of Social Darwinism was wrong. Its attempts to speed-up the process of evolution in the case of human societies was an affront to the new awareness of how long the world had been here. Social theory now had to take account of a past which was almost unimaginably longer than men had hitherto been prepared to believe. Prehistorical, anthropological, zoological, biological and geological time-scales now overshadowed the pygmy time-scales of the recorded histories of human societies. In this new, infinitely longer perspective it was absurd to pretend that an 'evolutionary' advance could happen within a historical scheme which could not even be extended much beyond the Flood. The speed of the decline of Spencer's own reputation served as a warning of how quickly these human illusions could come and go.

The crowd helped speed Spencerism on its way out, and in its turn encouraged a different, more pessimistic, social Darwinism. Followers of Spencer looked round for some explanation for the binding of groups which were able to adapt to prevailing conditions and survive them because of their cohesiveness. The crowd, held together by Le Bon's group mind, seemed to be an obvious candidate. Crowds 'kept together'; 'had an instinct for survival'; 'huddled together for protection';

produced what Le Bon called 'an illusion of invincibility'; men lost their identity in the crowd, so the crowd could survive, and the individual within it; there was safety in numbers. But the same objections could be made to this style of argument as could be made against Idealism. If Le Bon was right, human adaptation and survival was being secured at the price of a lowering of consciousness; a retreat from reason was the price men had to pay for their sense of safety in groups. Crowds, perhaps groups in general, seemed to be more primitive than the individuals who made them up. This 'primitiveness' had very definite resonances in an age when evolutionary analogies were commonplace. Evolutionism had encouraged the view throughout the human sciences that to explain something was to show how the 'lower' led to the 'higher'. This was true in biology, and it was also held to be true of all development, and especially of social development. This in turn could lead to the view, explicit or implicit, that all the really important events, or series of events, had taken place in the past, so that to ascribe a remote cause to a present happening was to give a convincing explanation of it. Long-term explanations were better than short-term explanations; the remoter the explanation, the more learned and more sophisticated it was. The prevalence of this view can be judged by the frequency with which it was attacked. Liberals and Idealists patiently pointed out that to trace the origins of a society was not the same thing as proving the primacy of origins, and it certainly did not account for changes in the quality of social existence. Unless some allowance was made for qualitative changes in the nature of social life, there was a danger that the view that life now was not all that different from what it was like in the remote past would become the consensus view. The doctrine of the importance of primitive states of things would imperceptibly become the doctrine of the inescapability of the primitive state of things. If they were not careful, Europeans would begin to look at themselves as primitive men with a gloss of civilization in the way they were beginning to look at Westernized blacks as savages in white men's clothing.

The crowd seemed to have characteristics which minds trained to evolutionism were quick to associate with earlier stages of social development, so giving a positivist gloss to the ordinary vocabulary of civilized outrage already available to greet the mob at its every appearance: barbarians, animals, a disgrace to their species, not deserving human, and certainly not humane, treatment. (Captured *communards* were put on show, and were shown as monkeys in cartoons in the government press, leaving no one in any doubt what kind of treatment they could expect in an age which had yet to hear of 'cruelty to animals'.) The victory of the Darwinians over the Lamarckians added further to the gloom. Any change laboriously contrived for the better by one generation would not be passed on automatically to the next, whereas the animal nature of man which had been there at the beginning was always handed down in the unconscious mind, a *damnosa haereditas* which each new generation had to cope with in the cause of civilized living. In the modern idiom, no new generation ever came genetically programmed with the social advances of its predecessors, while each new generation came complete with a programme from the remote animal past into which the crowd could hack at will.

Pessimistic evolutionism was simply progressive biologism in reverse. No sooner had the human body itself come to be seen as a miracle of multicellular co-operation, and therefore as an ideal model of social integration, than it began to be suggested that the dissolution of a body into its component cells was the ideal model of social disintegration, with the crowd to pick up the pieces afterwards. Everyone agreed that the dissolution of a society meant the undoing of the patient work of the social division of labour over centuries, or even over millennia, and everyone agreed that the crowd was an undifferentiated aggregate of monotonously similar individuals, so why not say that the crowd was both the cause of the dissolution of a society and its chief beneficiary? When men became part of a crowd, they no longer fitted their normal social categories. A crowd was a group which was not constituted of other groups; it was not plural, but *sui generis*, an outstandingly simple and isolated social fact which fitted into no greater whole. It was this very simplicity which made the crowd so puzzling to thinkers like Scipio Sighele who had been brought up in the tradition of Spencerian social evolutionism, and the conclusion they were bound to come to was that, if the crowd fitted in anywhere, it fitted in right at the beginning of evolution, where all was undifferentiated matter. It need hardly be pointed out that a conclusion like this was obligatory only for those thinkers who took their evolutionism very literally. A thinker like Gabriel Tarde, whose social theory sat well with evolutionism but did not depend on it, could accommodate the crowd with none of the theoretical twistings and turnings which bedevilled the more evolutionarily minded (see below, Chapter 6).

If it was true that each generation had to relearn the arts of civilized living, then it followed that the agencies which did the teaching were entitled to a new respect, especially as now they began to look very fragile when threatened by the barbarous energy of the crowd. Repositories of ancestral wisdom like the family, systems of education, settled socializing institutions in general, could now appear to be much more precarious than conservatives like Burke had thought a century before. In his *Reflections on the Revolution in France*, Burke had warned against frivolous radical tampering with settled ways, because what had taken centuries to build up could be torn down in a moment and would take centuries to build up again. Now political radicalism still

21

had to be reckoned with, but much more threatening was the weight of an anthropological and animal past which no amount of socialization could definitively erase. Conservatives had always looked to the past for comfort, but the new time-scales made available by the evolutionary sciences, of which crowd theory was one, did not present a reassuring picture. The past was much older than Burke could possibly have realized, and behind the historical past lurked other pasts which still spoke directly to men in crowds, an animal past beyond barbarism, and perhaps even a vegetable past beyond that. The ordinary metaphor of a civilization 'vegetating' could take on at least a thin coating of scientific respectability. The endless round of existence, from which the only escape was nirvana, pure inertness, still held the East in thrall, and might now be seen to be nothing more than the expression of a yearning for the simplicities of the vegetable existence which all living matter had once lived. As it came to be obvious just how exceptional civilized existence was when compared to the sum total of all existence, and how great the effort was which had to be put into living a civilized life, then a return to vegetable existence might be an attractive, even a rational option. If civilized life was shown not to be worth it according to some kind of emotional calculus, then a return to a vegetable existence, to life lived not according to Nature, but *as* Nature, a life which asked no questions and stood no test, made a kind of sense. The idea may be fanciful, but something very like it could be entertained by thinkers like Freud, and it gained a worldwide hearing.

This pessimism about a world threatened from within by the unconscious and from without by the crowd was at first shared only by a few who could be written off as the age's share of Jeremiahs, tolerated, but unheeded. The very act of tolerating them could be part of the argument against them. Here, if anything, was the proof of modernity. The age's confidence in itself allowed it to believe that good arguments would drive out bad. Dissenters no longer had to be led to the stake and their opinions censored. Public debate was a surer way of weeding out. An enlightened public opinion would fulfil the programme that Mill had sketched out in *On Liberty* now that Mill's own fears about the spread of bigotry could be safely set aside. The fears that the crowd aroused could be allayed by the invention of new techniques of crowd control. Crowds could still be manipulated. Not everybody had to share Le Bon's pessimism, and Le Bon himself had spoken of the possibility of a new technique of mass manipulation, and there was every reason to suppose that the science of crowd psychology would, like other sciences, produce its own technology of control. And perhaps Le Bon exaggerated; he was a popularizer; he was interested in effects, in making a name for himself. Wiser counsels would prevail.

The pessimistic message about the Era of Crowds could be taken much more seriously after the Great War had made the idea of a European 'fellowship in civilization' seem an exercise in fatuous equanimity. By all the canons of rationality the war should never have happened, or, if war was an acceptable instrument of policy, *that* war should never have happened because there was no account of the ends of human action which could justify those means. No rational calculus – not the Liberal version of utilitarianism; not Idealism; not the need for national self-expression; not the preferability of a war of nations instead of classes; not even the need for a civilization gone soft to be shaken out of its torpor – could cope with the scale of the violence and destruction. (President Wilson's belated attempt to attach a set of war aims grand enough to have made the war worth fighting – a war for democracy, for national self-determination, a war to end wars – was a brave try at doing what President Lincoln had done in similar circumstances for the American Civil War, which may have begun as a war about tariffs but ended as a crusade against slavery. Similar attempts were made after 1945 to say the war was worth it because it stopped the Germans massacring Jews.) Only a very obdurate spirit could see the Great War as a stage in the rational progress of mankind. Nationalists in Eastern Europe, and Bolsheviks in Russia, did well out of the war; but modern Europe, which had taken pride in its progressive civilization, did not. After 1918 Europe was forced to see the less agreeable aspects of its political life before the war in an accentuated form, but without that cultural optimism which had once made it possible to see through the disconcerting present to the assured future beyond. The war itself had been half-welcomed by some statesmen as a somewhat drastic way of coping with the political problems which increasingly claimed the attention of governments at the end of the nineteenth century. Problems of national separatism or social revolution could all, at bottom, be looked at as problems of civil order. Governments began to feel that they were losing control of their populations, and in a period where the advance of mass democracy was part cause and part effect of this process, democracy could easily be seen as the crowd come into its own. The enthusiasm for conscription, at which even Liberal England jibbed only for a time, is evidence that governments welcomed the opportunity to put the masses into uniform and under discipline before they became a mob who would carry all before them. Drill-sergeants all over Europe would drill some sense into the masses and make them into a disciplined army, the very antithesis of a crowd. The 'killing crowds' as Wilfred Trotter called them, proved so good at killing that the scale of destruction they accomplished made the war a failure in the purpose of controlling the masses, as it was a failure in almost everything else.

This sense of failure was almost universal; it was the failure of all the great historical systems that Nietzsche had predicted, of all the universal schemes of human progress which had been the pride of nineteenth-century civilization. It was not possible to regard the Great War as a minor set-back in the march of civilization. European dreams of a fellowship in civilization were no longer dreamable, and were replaced by much grimmer intimations of the future, based on a view of the present as the age of the masses. There was a remarkable consensus about this. Before the war, the masses and the crowd were different aspects of the same thing coming to the attention of social theorists and rulers. Each was a cause and an effect. After the war there could be no doubt that the age of the masses had arrived, and that the form its politics would take would be crowd politics. Everybody was prepared for the politics of the mob. This easy sequence of ideas, or shift of expectations, was part of a more generalized pessimism. Before 1914, it had been possible to see the masses as a crowd which might occasionally turn into a mob. The mob was a part of the mass which had got out of hand, similar to the sort of incident which occurred frequently at a time when a runaway horse was an almost daily event in the crowded streets of a large town, a part of Nature that had got away, or had not been adequately tamed. (Every decent man carried within himself the fear that he would skulk into a doorway and shirk the duty of controlling the runaway before somebody got hurt.) In the age of the masses, when democracy institutionalized the crowd, when the crowd occupied the centre of the social space, it was no longer the crowd that was to be feared, but the mob. Democracy had institutionalized the crowd which was now part of the given world of politics to which rulers and social theorists had to give their first attention, and there already existed a body of theoretical literature to show that there were ways of coping with the crowd out of which the Iron Law of Oligarchy and the theory of *embourgeoisement* came to reassure the fearful. But just as out of civilization came the masses, so out of the masses would come the mob. Out of the masses came one form of politics, the parliamentary republic and its variants. The remaining question for the 1920s and 1930s was: What form of politics would come out of the mob? There was no reason in principle why the mob should not be institutionalized in its turn. The fact that fascism caused no surprise *then* should cause *us* no surprise. Europe was psychologically and politically well prepared by 1920, by which time the institutionalization of the mob into the fascist party had begun.

Part of that psychological preparation was the normalization of violence. From Plato onwards, observers of the crowd had been frightened by the crowd's violence, but the emphasis had always been on the destructiveness of crowds, not on the violence itself.

At some time between the Enlightenment and the First World War, there had developed a squeamishness about violence which Sorel had commented on in the *Reflections on Violence* before 1914, and which Nietzsche, in his eccentric way, had become aware of thirty years earlier. This squeamishness was evident at all levels of social practice and theory, from a concern for the beating of children, to distaste for the barbarous rituals of public execution; from the arguments about the wastefulness of war, to the hope that peace might be a permanent condition and not just an interval between wars. Being a civilized man came to mean ordering one's own life without having recourse to force except as a last resort, and then only in self-defence against the violence of others; being a member of a civilized state meant that the agents of that State were authorized by its citizens to use violence only when the attempt to regularize men's relations with each other through the public reasonableness of law had manifestly failed; being civilized meant taking pleasure in observing how violence, which in the past had regulated the affairs of nations, was now giving way through the mechanisms of free-trade and international co-operation to a European fellowship in civilization which would in the near future become the fellow-feeling of all mankind. This attitude was almost impossible to maintain after 1918, at least on the level of theory. Of course there was a reaction to the horrors of war, but the fact of the matter was that millions of men had participated, and millions who survived had lived with those horrors daily, as a matter of course. Some, no doubt, had never overcome their initial revulsion at the sight of blood, but most, apparently, become inured to it, or found ways of coping with it.[2] Indeed, in the democratic age, all male citizens of a certain age were expected to be violent when conscription required it of them. This violence, which was real violence, violence to the point of sticking a bayonet into someone, was supposed to be *controlled* violence – a man was expected to kill someone hand-to-hand one minute and to submit to the ranting of his superior officer without protest the next. But each man was required not just to be capable of doing it, but to think it was his duty to do it, a duty which took precedence over his obligations to any other group to which he might feel a loyalty. Nothing could come between him and that duty except conscience: not family, friends, class, church, not even his intelligence, even if it told him that the war was stupid, immoral, or wasteful.

The duty to defend one's country was drummed into men by the propaganda of the First World War as duty pure and simple, duty *as such*, the highest duty. All other duties were subordinate, all inferior, all seen as pale reflections of the supreme duty. With the idea of duty went the idea of sacrifice. All duties mean some sacrifice of inclination, but this duty meant blood sacrifice, and it carried the presumption with it

25

that those who were the first to make that sacrifice were the best. The volunteer was a better man than the conscript, and those who deliberately courted death were the best of all. Those in danger were a shame to those still at home and the dead were a shame to the living. Men could be ashamed to be alive. Those who came back, who had lived through it all and who had become accustomed to the sight of blood, were capable of feeling guilty, of having let down those who had died, and those who survived and continued to live could be counted in millions. Men like these could not be counted on to be squeamish when mass politics became mob politics, when violence, or the threat of violence, or even a cult of violence, became part of the political programme of fascist parties. Nor was this simple fact lost on aspiring political leaders like Mussolini and Hitler. The least they could count on was that most ordinary men would look on a few broken heads and broken windows, a fire or two, a quiet beating-up in a cellar, a political assassination or private purge, as pretty small beer. They could not count on approval or support, but a horror of the *fact* of violence was unlikely to arise in the minds of those who had been part of the great killing crowds of the war. These crowds had been made up of all sorts and conditions of men, so that the fears of the theorists of the crowd before 1914 that all men in the right circumstances were mob men were triumphantly confirmed.

In the period between the wars, under a specific set of pressures, fears about the crowd could be turned into hopes. The peace settlement was to make the world safe for democracy, the form of crowd politics which offered most hope for the future in a world whose existence had been threatened by a war of mass armies. That part of human optimism which the war did not destroy survived in the hope that democrary was the way to stop the war happening again. Men's expectations of democracy shifted fatally from the position where the democratic republic was the end to which human progress was moving, to the position where the democratic republic was a means to other, very generalized ends. In the future, the democratic republic would not just have to *be*, it would have to deliver. It would have to provide prosperity to please social democrats, and peace to please everyone else. What was forgotten was that democratic republics had not been conspicuously successful in providing either prosperity or peace before 1914, when the democratic republics had gone to war as blithely as the autocracies (one democratic republic, Italy, had entered the war with no very clear idea why it did so, and another even came all the way across the Atlantic to join in). This was not how the victors saw things at Versailles. 'War guilt' meant blaming the war on what appeared to be the undemocratic aspects of the societies of the Central Powers. They chose to ignore the fact that some of the politics of the democratic republics before the war had been disagreeably mobbish and violent. The mob had been a part of French politics since the *Commune*, and had been called out by both sides during the Dreyfus Affair; British politics had seen the mob in various forms – workers, women, even members of the House of Lords; and, obviously enough, whatever democracy existed in the Habsburg Empire had produced the Viennese anti-semitic Christian Social mob, led by Hitler's political teacher, Karl Lueger, against whom the only weapon seemed to be the Emperor's veto on his becoming the popularly elected mayor of Vienna. (Emperors had now disappeared from continental Europe, though in Germany the hope that Hindenburg would do to Hitler what Franz Josef had done to Lueger did not die easily.)

The democratic republic in Germany and Austria came into being in impossible conditions. It was imposed by the victors, and so had to live down its past. It had to establish itself and solve great national problems at the same time, a time when it was easy to see the republic as a betrayal of everything that was best in the past. The defenders of the Weimar and the Austrian republics did not have the advantage that the defenders of the Third Republic had, of being able to argue that the republic was the culmination of a democratic, revolutionary tradition which, since 1789, had become a vital part of the nation's life; the French Republic might have its faults, but an anti-Dreyfusard like Barrès could still argue that it was a part of *us*; changes might be necessary, but the Republic could accommodate them. No such residue of implicit loyalty was available to German democrats. It was not enough that the German republics just existed, and the German democrats could not just be content to occupy power. If they could not solve problems, they would come themselves to be seen as a problem. If leaders elected by lawful universal suffrage could not solve the nation's problems, then there were other leaders, who would emerge from other constituencies, who could. If the organized masses, safely tamed by their political rights in their legal political parties, could not produce the kind of dynamic leadership that circumstances required, then a new force would have to emerge out of the constraints of an order which was itself insecure and produce a leader of a very different type. The question was: What was the source of the leader's authority and power to be? Obviously, not the formal/legal legitimacy of a republic based on electoral law. The political arrangements of the present were useless precisely because they could not produce a leader who would really lead. The alternative was to look at things the other way round. The relationship between the leader and the led became the beginning, not the end, something from which everything else followed, not, as in the case of the democratic republic, something which emerged at the end of the day when the votes had been counted. The intensity of the relationship between the

27

leaders and the led was to replace the arithmetical formality of the relationship between democratically elected leaders and the citizens of the
country they were called upon to govern. Eventually, everyone was to
become a follower, and to that end the mechanisms of democracy were
useful, but these mechanisms were not what conferred legitimacy. That
was provided by the direct, felt relationship between leader and led.

The model for this relationship was provided by the crowd theory
developed by 1914. The Iron Law of Oligarchy only told one side of
the story of political leadership in a mass age. The ultra-respectable
leaders of European mass parties with Marxist or socialist doctrines
were not really frightening because leaders distance themselves from
those whom they lead. Involved here was not just the watering-down
of radical doctrine into Revisionism, as leaders had to balance the
possibility of adding more to already solid gains against a wild throw
for the whole revolutionary future by storming heaven, though that was
comforting enough. More reassuring still was *embourgeoisement*, the tendency of mass leaders to distance themselves from what we would now
call the life-style of the kinds of people their followers were. The charm
of political life, the sense of socialization into a club, parliamentary
magic, the feeling of being an insider, smoothed very rough diamonds
until their very photographs showed them as indistinguishable from
the ruling elites whose existence their own professed doctrines were
supposed to threaten. They seemed to have come a long way from their
rabble-rousing days, and so they had, and so had their followers. But
there were still direct, violent crowd incidents taking place alongside
official politics. Sometimes the mass manifestations of official politics
were the occasion for other, fringe, political activity, and there was
always a 'direct action' group within official political parties. It was
these crowds, and their non-political equivalents, which crowd theorists dealt with. These crowds had their own psychology and their own
leaders. These violent crowds produced leaders of a new type, or, if
they were not a new type of leader, they were the leaders who attracted
the analytic attention of a new type of psychology based on the study of
hypnotism. The hypnotist could recall to the surface things which were
unconscious; he seemed to fascinate his subject; he seemed to be able
to control the subject's own will, and to be able to make the subject do
things which were 'out of character'. If the leader of a crowd could do
all these things too, then the hypnotic model offered an explanation of
how the relationship between crowds and their leaders worked.

Hitler was to give some kind of permanence to the bond which
bound leader and led which would be an alternative to the permanence
of the institutionalization of the masses by the democratic republic.
Nazism and the republic were competing forms of crowd control.
Of course, this was obscured by the street-fighting, thuggish and

threatening aspects of Nazi behaviour, which made it easy to see them as destroyers of the social peace, but that was an extremely superficial view. What they aimed for was a society in which the preliminary destruction of social peace by the mob would create the conditions in which the only safe place to be was inside the Nazi crowd. Recruitment by violence could persuade people that a Nazi was a fine thing to be, or the only safe thing to be. Out of disorder would come a new order, which would be a real order because its basis was a felt relationship to a leader. The images of party-as-army of Leni Riefenstahl's *Triumph of the Will* represented what the street battles had been fought *for*. The fighting crowd had been turned into an army again, whom the 'official' army of the republic was forced to salute. (One shot in the film shows a group of regular army officers looking on at the marching columns of the Nazi Party with diffidence and *envy*.) The 'official' army, and by extension, the ordinary forces of law and order, which in old Europe had been the last defence against the crowd rising to destroy civilization, now becomes an onlooker, while the leader of the crowd shows the mastery of his will over the crowd which is now back where it belongs, in an army whose controlled aggressiveness shows that the war to end wars, and make the world safe for democracy, has failed. The scene represents the undoing of history, or of a version of it, in which the aim of civilization is the democratic order based on the individual and his rights, enshrined in a publicly conceived system of law guaranteeing equality of legal rights. This formal equality is shown to be nothing beside the real equality of the comradeship of men under discipline in close ranks, touching, all the distance which the individual's rights create between one man and another removed. The party was a permanent crowd which could take over, or control, or manipulate, a whole society, and its propaganda and activity (there was hardly a difference between the two) was intended to make a whole society into a crowd (see below, Chapters 9 and 10).

The purpose of this crowd was to unravel history. The crowd-army was a direct defiance of the Treaty of Versailles's restriction on the size of German armies, because the victory of the leader's will showed that the whole nation would soon become an army which the official, Versailles-permitted, army could only observe and eventually join, but behind the purpose of undoing the damage which the *Diktat* caused lay the more serious purpose of unravelling the theoretical and practical histories of which Versailles could be seen as the outcome. The hopes for universal peace through the establishment of democratic republics were the old dream of the Enlightenment, institutionalized in a settlement at a time when the First World War made those hopes more vulnerable than they had ever been before. The war of the killing crowds had shown how precarious a civilization based on the idea of rational progress was. Versailles was a Voltairean solution to the problem. If the same has failed in the past, the answer is more of the same. If reason fails, it fails because there was not enough of it. But there was the alternative history which had been quietly making its way underground in the second half of the nineteenth century, and which could now be brought to the surface by the crowd. This counter-history opposed every central category of the Enlightenment's view of history with a category of its own. To reason it counterposed the passions and the will; to civilization it opposed vitality; to progress it opposed development; to co-operation it opposed struggle; to civility it opposed heroism; to the rights of man it opposed the values of the tribe; to the citizen of the world it opposed the *enraciné*; to the quiet progress of reason it opposed the pursuit of a dimly perceived but deeply felt destiny. This alternative version could find its own line of counter-heroes stretching back into the Enlightenment itself. It could recruit Rousseau, Herder and Vico; it could include the Romantics and Nietzsche, and it could include anyone who had ever contrasted the enervating qualities of contemporary life to the rude, vibrant, energies of a real or imagined past. In this view of history, the authorized version of the history of civilization had produced rotten fruit, and civilized man had either forgotten what fresh fruit was like, or had begun to enjoy the smell of corruption. What was needed was a new irruption of those healthy barbarian energies described by Tacitus in his *Germania*, which had rescued Europe from the decadence of the Romans. The crowd was the bearer of those energies which had been tamed by progress traditionally conceived. Progress was already old; it was holding back the new world, just as the bonds of an old civilization were holding back the crowd, which was the bearer of the new. But this 'new' was new in name only. It was the resurgence of a primitive past, even of a primitive man who would sweep away what was left of an old order which had manifestly failed, and create an order of his own. The crowd becomes the agent of its own liberation.

This perspective, or something very like it, informs much of what Canetti's great *Crowds and Power* has to say about crowds. The modern world has to confront crowds with ideologies, or ideologies which have views about crowds. No age ever confronted the crowd simply as a throng of people doing something or doing nothing, whose behaviour could be treated with the seasoned indifference that magistrates have always cultivated in the face of ordinary criminality. Mobs had never been treated simply as criminals doing crime together. There had always been more to it than that. Even when there was nothing more to it, officials had always tried to prove the existence of some form of criminal conspiracy in the heart of the mob, to show that something important enough to justify their fears was going on. These were fears of a very generalized kind, fears for order, or for 'the world as we know it', threatened by subversion. After the French Revolution those fears could be of a much more specific kind because a particular ideology could be tied to the crowd. The crowd became less mysterious, but more frightening. The Rights of Man, or Jacobinism, or socialism could be seen at the back of the crowd. After 1848, it came to be recognized that the crowd had a mind of its own, 'mob mind' or 'group mind', which, being unconscious, could be understood as the opposite of all that was rational, civilized, advanced and progressive. This was the mind that had to be controlled or repressed, if civilization was to advance, or even to maintain itself. This was the mind that ran riot in mass disturbances and in wars, and it was this mind that the progressive theory of history supposed could be led to rationality and to its place in the democratic republic as the mind of the citizen who recognized that his own enjoyment of rights entailed the recognition of the same rights in others. It was for this mind that there was a battle. But those who chose to see in the crowd the hope for a new kind of future did not want the crowd mind to be contained. They wanted it liberated, emptied of what it contained as a new form of social living, more primitive perhaps, but more *real*, a return to origins which the world of modernity had all but obliterated, so that the unconscious mind was their last refuge.

Two ways of looking at the crowd, the mob, and the riot, came out of these two histories of the crowd mind. The first would have us restrain the crowd and repress the urges which keep the crowd in being and which are given their head in riots. The mob, like our own savage selves, must be kept down; its energies must be channelled and its activities ritualized, by well-tried occasional festivals and shows which the forces of law and order can develop techniques to control – 'riot control', 'crowd control'. Mechanical metaphors inform this style of thinking. You cannot press down on the crowd indefinitely, because the head of steam becomes too powerful, and society will eventually blow its top. The solution to this problem is not a dam, but a channel; control and manipulation, not prohibition; containment, not containing. The mob and its riot will always be dangerous because the mob can be used, manipulated by ideologues, can become 'political'. And the mob is not a pretty sight. It contains echoes of a buried, barbarous, animal past which must occasionally be heard, but never allowed to dominate the conversation of mankind; that way lies madness, brutalism, an end to civilized living. Alongside the mechanical metaphor of the crowd lies the counter-claim for the crowd as the source of a revolutionary energy, whose primitiveness is its virtue, not its vice. This energy civilization wastes, and the social order which this energy could

31

create were it to be released would be the social order of the tribe, or the gang, or an army.

Canetti's *Crowds and Power* is an attempt to find a way out from these two alternatives. *Crowds and Power* is a complete masterpiece because Canetti is able to look back on the whole crowd theory tradition as that tradition has worked itself out in the practice of the politics of the twentieth century, and especially in the Third Reich. Canetti sets out to disentangle the different crowd themes of Nazism as they relate to the horrors, because the horrors were not accidental but the result of the commands of superiors. Crowd theory's reliance on the hypnotic model of leadership created the expectation that a leader would one day come out of the crowd whose commands would be obeyed even in defiance of the most fundamental dictates of his followers' own conscience, so that there was literally nothing they would not do for him. Canetti realizes that received crowd theory encourages the tendency to see the same psychological mechanisms at work in Hitler the spell-binder of crowds and Hitler the commander of military and murderous subordinates. Canetti knows that no man is immune from the crowd, but he is unwilling to concede that therefore there is no defence against each of us becoming one of history's butchers, so he takes the obvious way out of crowd theory's theoretical impasse here by denying that the leaders of crowds are necessary, or even all that important. The crowd in Canetti's *Crowds and Power* is man's last refuge from command. He sets his face against everything that crowd theory had been saying about the crowd and its leaders since Plato. Canetti's is a heroic attempt to write the demagogues out of crowd theory by denying that they do in fact command the crowd. This is a thesis which any other crowd theorist would have found very startling indeed, because, since Plato, a crowd without a demagogue was either a contradiction in terms, or nothing, not a crowd at all in any sense that was worth worrying about, and certainly not worth a theory. Canetti not only believes that the crowd is a defence against command, but he also believes that the effects on personality of previous commands can begin to be erased in one type of crowd, the reversal crowd. The psychology of being commanded and the psychology of men in crowds are set one against the other. Canetti knows that the crowd can show an ugly face, but he does not regard it with contempt, and he is the only crowd theorist who does not look at the crowd to define the elite to which he thinks he belongs.

Notes

1 People did in fact continue to speak about evolution as if a creator planned it. Creationists and children still speak that language: *That* species

was made to have *that* character to make it survive *because* it is favoured by a creator. (The teleological flavouring to evolution is encouraged by the fascination with freaks: *that* species cannot have been meant to survive; therefore it was lucky; it must have slipped through when someone was not looking.)

2   It has always surprised me that no crowd theorist ever made anything out of shell-shock which is just the kind of morbidly nervous condition which, widely spread in a population, might account for some of the more wayward characteristics of crowds.

1

The Crowd in the Ancient World

Philosophers and historians in the ancient world took a great deal of interest in the crowd, and although this interest lasts from the beginning to the end, from Plato to Procopius, only Plato ever worked out anything approaching a theory of the crowd. Plato's serious theoretical interest reflects the seriousness of the crowd's claim to be able to rule a society successfully, because it is only at a fairly elevated level of theorizing that he can in fact find really damaging things to say about the rule of *demos*, and even at that level some of his criticisms of democracy, for example, his claim that the democratic man is unhappier than the timocrat or the oligarch, are difficult to sustain. The Roman historians, Livy and Tacitus, wrote when whatever pretensions the *populus* ever had to consideration as a force in the State were a thing of the past. They can afford to shed a generous tear for the brave days of old without any risk. Livy's account of early Roman history is interesting because it became one of the great Renaissance and modern sources of republican inspiration because it provided a finished account of the only republican government about which enough was known to make it worth talking about. That was certainly Machiavelli's view, so that even if Livy's own reflections about the republic never reached the level of high theory, his account of its early history did get into high theory, if only at second hand. And there is a good case for saying that the most celebrated theory of liberty in the modern world, that of Montesquieu, has its origins in Machiavelli's critical reading of Livy's treatment of the Roman crowd in the first *Decade*. Tacitus and Procopius see the crowd off the stage of Roman history. Procopius sees it making a world of its own. In Tacitus, the crowd is so sated with theatrical shows that it ends up by being unable to distinguish between a show and a desperate battle where the blood that is flowing is real blood. In Procopius, the circus crowd lives in a world of its own making, a fantasy world in which all the rules of ordinary living are turned upside-down, a nightmare utopia at which the ordinary sane spectator can only gawp.

The Mob and its Leaders: Plato on the Institutionalized Crowd

One problem that Plato did not have to face was the problem of who the crowd was and where it came from. The crowd of Athenian democracy was official. The Assembly, the Council and the Jury were made up of men whose names were on the citizen rolls, and who meant to keep them there because that meant they could enjoy the privileges which made being a citizen worthwhile. The critics of democracy said the lists were so long that privileges shared by so many were not worth having, but that is not what the citizens thought. The privileges were modest enough: citizens were different from women, slaves and foreigners; they received a small *per diem* for offices open to everyone by lot; there was pay for rowing on a trireme and an occasional distribution of grain or loot; citizens could own land (it may be that one of the reasons why Aristotle did not succeed Plato as head of the Academy was that Aristotle as a foreigner would not have been able to take over the property). However, the privileges seem to have been enough to make Athenians proud of their democratic constitution and to spread its fame. When there was trouble at Rome between the plebs and the patricians at the time of the Decemvirs, it seemed natural to send envoys to Athens to find out how the Athenians ran their affairs, a thing the Romans would have been unlikely to do if the Athenian democracy had not caused a stir in the world, and even a prejudiced critic like the Old Oligarch admitted grudgingly that although there were strong grounds for objecting to democracy on principle, the Athenians seemed to be able to make a go of their democratic constitution and even to prosper under it (Moore, 1975, p. 45). By the time he was writing, the Athenians had had a democratic constitution of sorts for nearly a hundred years, and was to have one, except for a few minor oligarchic deviations, for another hundred years after that.

What seemed peculiar to contemporaries about Athenian democracy was the choosing of men by lot for offices (though not the highest 'executive' and military posts), payment for public service, and what we would call a democratic way of life. Selection by lot from the whole citizen body was the assertion of legal equality over inequalities which were plain for everyone to see. Not everyone was equally competent to exercise state power, so it seemed to fly in the face of common sense to allow the operation of chance among the many to decide who should decide on questions which could have very serious consequences for fellow citizens. Payment for public service gave those paid an interest over and above the public interest which everyone publicly agreed was the only thing that should be in the minds of those who were called upon to serve it. The democratic way of life called out the most damning comment, though even Plato is forced to admit that it was

35

attractive, at least at first sight and for those who have not thought the matter out properly (*Republic*, 561). In a democracy, everybody is allowed to live as he likes; there is a bewildering variety of individual characters; this freedom rubs off on women, slaves and foreigners. The Old Oligarch grumbles that at Athens free men are not allowed to hit slaves, because the Athenians dress so scruffily that it is very hard to tell who is a slave and who is a citizen, so a random assault on a slave might be an assault on a citizen instead (Moore, 1975, p. 39). Plato playfully extends this moral and social anarchy to the domestic animals. The only damage any of the interlocutors in *The Republic* admit they have suffered from democracy is that Glaucon was once bumped into by a donkey in the street (*Rep.*, 563). The variety of democratic characters is matched by the variety of democratic constitutions (*Rep.*, 557), and Plato extends the notion to the desires: the democratic character follows the desire of the moment. He fails to order his desires and treats them all as if they were equal; the desires multiply until they overcome the disposition to self-discipline by sheer force of numbers (*Rep.*, 559). Democracy is a mess for its critics; it cannot be a sensible way of doing things.

What the ancients took to be the characteristic features of democracy are not the features which would strike a modern observer, especially if he looks fondly at British and American ideas about constitutionalism. Athenian democracy was direct democracy; there was little of the refining effects of the Iron law of Oligarchy which critics of representative democracy find reassuring. The only representative feature of Athenian democracy was in jury selection, where large popular juries were chosen by lot (501 tried Socrates), but as Finley points out, juries were large to make sure that they represented a true cross-section of the Athenian Ecclesia, and so were representative in the sense that a modern market sample is representative, not in the sense that someone who may be different from you may still represent your views and interests (Finley, 1973, p. 78). Nor was there much of the Whiggish pretence about an ancient constitution which could not be altered easily. The Greeks knew that the antiquity of a constitution was one reason for being loyal to it and wanting to preserve it, and they recognized the value of provisions for making it difficult to alter a constitution, but a free *polis* gave itself laws, and there was no reason in principle why those laws could not be changed. As Rousseau recognized, that is what made a people sovereign. And it is not very clear that the Greeks had an idea of antiquity apart from a feeling for the good old days. Any historical continuity came from the poets' tales of gods and heroes which served for a state religion. Severe penalties could be dealt out for impiety, for religion was a part of public, not private life. The distinction between public and private had very little meaning when the sovereign people could decide about anything, and when it was open

36

to any citizen to lay a charge against any other in the courts. There was no way in which a citizen could protect himself from a majority in the Assembly or the courts short of politicking, or conspiracy, or self-exile. There was a notion of balance in a constitution. Aristotle praises the constitution of Solon for being a mixed constitution with power being shared among the monarchical, aristocratic and democratic principles which gave way under the pressure of increasing public wealth and the growing importance of the people as rowers of the triremes which were the basis of Athenian naval and imperial power, but the critics of democracy saw the subsequent democratic constitutions as victories for the democratic faction at the expense of the rest. Changes in constitutions do not abolish the social divisions upon which the mixed constitution is based, and some balance was preserved. Important offices were not filled by lot, and most of the statesmen and generals came from wealthy families; the leaders who unseated the oligarchic governments in 411 and 403 BC were wealthy, and so was Anytus who laid the charge of impiety against Socrates (Jones, 1957, p. 42). But if a certain political balance was preserved, there was none of the idea of the separation of powers which constitutionalists after Montesquieu have tended to associate with it. The courts were the sovereign people acting in particular cases, the Assembly in miniature, not a separate branch of government.

Athenian democracy institutionalized the crowd and allowed it to make decisions about matters of life and death. The democratic Assembly was not a mob or a revolutionary crowd. The Athenian crowd did not have to resort to violence to make itself heard, like the Roman plebs or the French Sansculottes. All it had to do was to assemble. Perhaps this accounts for the fact that Athenian politics was not especially violent, and it accounts, at least in part, for the longevity of the democracy. If it had had that tendency to violence, its critics would not have failed to point it out, but the criticisms are typically worked out at the level of political and psychological theorizing, and the examples of the democracy misgoverning and degenerating into a mob are examples of the Assembly doing something stupid, or rash, or out of ignorance, following some demagogue or other who manipulates them for his own selfish ends.

Everything Plato has to say about democracy applies to the crowd, and everything Plato has to say about the crowd applies to democracy, because the democratic constitution of Athens made them the same thing. The questions he asks about the crowd are about its character and the kinds of leaders the crowd will follow. For Plato, crowds are always easily led. Like all the ancients, he believes that rhetoric works and necessarily works; the Guardians in *The Republic* are brought up on dialectic, not rhetoric, and their education is a preparation for the victory of the dialectical mind over the falsely persuasive powers of rhetoric. The final test of suitability for Guardianship is the capacity not to be fooled by false arguments of the kind that might have convinced the young men at the beginning of the dialogue if Socrates had not been there to show Thrasymachus up. The Athenian constitution was a standing invitation to demagoguery, so Plato is interested above all in the character of the popular leader.

Plato does not treat the demagogue as if he comes from the crowd itself. He is not worried about leaders who emerge from the common people but about leaders of the people who come from the upper classes. (Aristotle notes that it was not until after Pericles that badly dressed, common leaders like Cleon appeared to shout and use abusive language in the Assembly (Moore, 1975, p. 171).) Plato gives two accounts of the rise of the crowd leaders, first in his account of the corrupted philosopher and second in his account of the corrupted oligarch, but the two accounts can be seen as two different roads to the same end.

The type of the corrupted philosopher is Thrasymachus. The dramatic structure of the first book of *The Republic* allows us to find out a good deal about him. He is a strong character, a natural ruler, persuasive enough to get other characters in the dialogue on his side. His demand to be paid for his conversation is accepted without comment, so we can assume that this is not the first time that Thrasymachus has taken part in a conversation like this, and he expects his opinions to prevail again as they have in the past. He is famous; he comes to the conversation with a good track record; he is overbearing and has to be tamed by Socrates after he starts firing in all directions. Thrasymachus is also worldly-wise; he has been around; he has seen and seen through the world. He lays claim to a genuine political expertise, and this expertise is never challenged by Socrates, whose refutations of Thrasymachus are completely formal. The case against Thrasymachus is that he would only be tolerated in a democratic society, where real philosophers, who are prepared to tell the crowd what it does not want to hear, are despised. The sophist is not just a corrupter, but is himself corrupted by the crowd in democratic societies. It is 'the public themselves who are sophists on a grand scale, and give a complete training to young and old men, and women, turning them into just the sort of people they want'. Young men of philosophical inclinations cannot be expected to resist the plaudits of the mob!

> when they crowd into the seats in the assembly, or law courts or theatre, or get together in camp or any other popular meeting places and, with a great deal of noise and a great lack of moderation, shout and clap their approval or disapproval of whatever is proposed or done, till the rocks and the whole place re-echo, and re-double the

noise of their boos and applause. Can a young man be unmoved by
all this? He gets carried away and soon finds himself behaving like
the crowd and becoming one of them.

(*Rep.*, 492)

The young men are faced with a choice. They can become leaders
of the crowd themselves, when, paradoxically their good qualities help
them to success. They are quick to learn, have good memories and are
brave and generous (*Rep.*, 487), and if they can add good looks and
noble birth they would be natural crowd leaders who, like Alcibiades,
could aspire to lead the whole of Hellas and to conquer the whole
world (*Rep.*, 494). The alternative would be to become a sophist and
aspire not to lead the crowd but train crowd leaders. Plato has no
doubt that this can be done, because the sophists have a genuine grasp
of crowd psychology whose principles are well-enough understood to
be taught. Crowd psychology is not a true science like statesmanship
or medicine, which aim at the good of their subjects. The sophist earns
his living by teaching men how to lead the crowd. It is like learning how
to control a 'large and powerful animal'; you could learn to control the
crowd yourself by carefully watching its moods over a long period of
time, but the sophist can pass his own 'knowledge of the passions and
pleasures of the mass of the common people' more quickly (*Rep.*, 493).
This short-cut to bastard knowledge gets real philosophers a bad name
because they do not deal in easy answers.

Plato gives his second account of the crowd leader in his long
discussion of how the Ideal State degenerated into timarchy, oligarchy,
democracy and tyranny. He imagines the Ideal State as a beginning and
shows how other forms came out of it. It is sometimes said that Plato
does not mean us to take this scheme of things historically, let alone
as a 'theory of history', but if we set aside the existence of the Ideal
State at the beginning, there is a good deal of reconstructed history in
it. Plato certainly wants us to take seriously the connection between
oligarchy and democracy, and the connection between democracy
and tyranny was to become one of the commonplaces of the ancient
world. Oligarchic society collapses when the oligarchs' obsession with
wealth makes the society they dominate unfit for war. The oligarchs,
like all unjust men, compete with each other; they are jealous of each
others' wealth and are not united as a class; they despise the poor and
are afraid to arm them against the enemy, and they are too mean to pay
the expenses of war, but they are few in number and so are forced to
arm the people (*Rep.*, 551). When war comes they can no longer afford
to despise the people, but the people, seeing how few the oligarchs are,
and how unfit their idle and luxurious life has made their sons, begin
to feel contempt for them. The people rise against the oligarchy, kill

or exile the oligarchs, and establish a democracy, with equal access to office by lot (*Rep.*, 557), where everyone is allowed to live the kind of life he chooses (*Rep.*, 557). But democratic society does not acquire its leaders from the poor, but from the corrupted sons of oligarchs. One of the effects of oligarchic society was the corruption of well-born youths by the oligarchs' practice of letting out money at high rates of interest to allow borrowers to pursue lives of ruinous pleasure. Each oligarch saw a profit in the corruption of other oligarchs' sons. These 'thriftless idlers', some 'drones with strings', some without, plotted against the oligarchs when they realized they had been ruined by them, and joined the people when they rebelled against the oligarchy. They survive into the new democratic society as the class from which the leaders come (*Rep.*, 564). Democratic society consists of three classes: surviving drones, out of which the 'drones with strings' emerge as leaders while the rest support them in the assembly, 'buzzing on the benches and not letting anyone else speak'; the mass of the people 'who earn their own living, take little interest in politics, and aren't very well off', and a third class, the new money-makers, who come out of the mass. The leaders of the democracy flatter the crowd and keep them sweet by robbing the rich, keeping most for themselves, and distributing the rest among the poor (*Rep.*, 564–5). These leaders need the sophists' crash-course on crowd psychology to manipulate the people whose character they have come to share. The only difference between them and the crowd is that they are cleverer and have access to the techniques of mass leadership.

A further degeneration of the democratic character produces the tyrants from the sons of corrupted oligarchs. Democratic liberty is attractive only in the short term. The democratic crowd has no high principles and does not look for high principles in its leaders. It cares nothing about their training, and will support them 'provided they profess themselves the people's friends' (*Rep.*, 557–8). The people need something more than flattery to remain convinced that their leaders have a care for their welfare, so the demagogues plunder the new rich and make promises about the cancellation of debts and an agrarian law which they find hard to keep. Oligarchic plots are invented as an excuse for robbing the rich who take to real plotting to defend themselves. Impeachments and treason trials follow, and the democratic leader gets a taste for blood (*Rep.*, 565–6). He is now surrounded by oligarchic enemies and popular rumblings begin over his failure to satisfy popular appetites, which are in principle not satisfiable because the desires like the people themselves, are many. The demagogue-becoming-a-tyrant tries the expedient of war, which reinforces the people's conviction that they need a leader and sends them back to work from their idleness to pay the high taxes which war requires. This gives them less time for plotting (*Rep.*, 567), but they are not altogether fools and begin to realize which way the wind is blowing. The would-be tyrant has no option but to hire a foreign praetorian guard (*Rep.*, 567–8) and these become the companions of his debauches. They make it their business to see that his character continues to be dominated by the desires which they share. The tyrant's character does not go under without a last struggle. He might try to mix debauchery with discipline, indolence with study, so he can get the best of both worlds. This attempt at democratic moderation alarms the desires who begin to despair of their mastery over him. To retain that mastery, the desires decide to sacrifice equality and plot to implant a 'master desire' to rule him completely, while they act as the master desire's bodyguard, making sure that no parsimonious, oligarchic, desires return to overturn the rule of the baser passions (*Rep.*, 571–4). The master passion is the most deeply embedded and secret of all the desires. It is of the kind

that emerge in our dreams, when the reasonable and humane part of us is asleep and its control relaxed, and our bestial nature, full of food and drink, wakes and has its fling and tries to secure its own kind of satisfaction. As you know, there's nothing too bad for it and it's completely lost to all sense and shame. It doesn't shrink at the thought of intercourse with a mother or anyone else, man, beast or god, or from murder or sacrilege. There is, in fact, no folly or shamelessness it will not commit.

The reasonable man goes to bed sober, having satisfied his desires in moderation and with his reasoning element stimulated, and he sleeps untroubled by the terrible desire which disturbs the dreams of immoderate and repressed characters (*Rep.*, 571–2). (It goes without saying that the democratic crowd would go to bed drunk every night if it could.) The tyrant has already got a taste for blood, and this is the master passion which the 'gang of attendant desires' (*Rep.*, 575) strive to protect, just as the tyrant's praetorian guard encourage his descent into corruption. In private life, the tyrannical man turns into a parricide and criminal to support the attendant desires; the tyrant turns his subjects into slaves to support the debauches of his guard. The tyrant himself, under the promptings of his internal master passion and the debauched praetorians, begins to behave 'as badly in real life as we said some men do in their dreams; which is just what happens when a natural tyrant gains absolute power, and the longer he holds it the greater his corruption' (*Rep.*, 575–6).

The condition of the tyrant brings Plato's account of the forms of the State back to a perverted version of its starting point, where the One rules the Many. In the Ideal State Reason ruled through the Guardians and the rest obeyed. In a tyranny, the One rules again, but as the darkest of all passions, the absolute inversion of the Form of the Good which gives Reason the light to see and judge. The just man is the happiest of all men, despite appearances, even in the worst of societies where he will be reviled, tortured and executed (*Rep.*, 362), because only he has managed to achieve that internal adjustment and right ordering of his faculties which can bring the strength and peace of mind which the tyrant lacks. The just man keeps the tumultuous mob of the desires firmly in their place and this entitles him to rule a State where the inferior people, whose life is centred on the satisfaction of appetite, are kept firmly in their place. The tyrant, not the perfectly just man in an unjust society, is the most wretched of men, the slave of a master passion, protected from his enemies by vicious and idle profligates whom he cannot really trust. This provides yet another reason for banning the poets from the Republic. They present tyrants as happy and god-like. No wonder that tragedians like Euripides prosper in tyrannies and democracies (*Rep.*, 568).

If we accept Plato's identification of the just man with the well-adjusted character and the tyrant with the most disturbed character, then it is hard to escape his conclusion that the Guardian is the happiest of men and the tyrant the least happy, and it is certainly true that the idea of mob-leader-turned-tyrant was to have a great future even if it had to wait till the second half of the nineteenth century to come into its own. But there is something too glib about Plato's assertion that the democratic man is less happy than the oligarchic man. He never in fact argues that this is the case. Socrates simply asks Glaucon to rank the types of character he has described in order of happiness and Glaucon, as he is meant to, decides that they are happy in the order that Socrates has followed in his account of their development from the just man, so the oligarchic man comes out as happier than the democratic man (*Rep.*, 580), but no reasons are given, so we are being told that it is obvious from what has already been said that the oligarchic man is happier. On the evidence it is far from obvious. In a sense, Plato recognizes this himself. The picture of democratic life which he paints is meant to look attractive. It is easy-going, versatile, even moderate in its way, but it is attractive only to those who cannot see where it leads (*Rep.*, 561), and of course it leads to tyranny. Only those far-sighted enough can see that democracy will ultimately lead to unhappiness as the tyrant lives out his nightmares in waking life and sucks the people dry to satisfy his and his praetorians' lusts. But to accept this view, we have to accept that Plato means us to take his account of the degeneration of the Ideal State into its corrupt forms seriously. Perhaps he does, but if that is the case, then it can equally be said that the real fault lies not with democracy but oligarchy, because it is the oligarchs who begin the process of the corruption which leads to tyranny. The demagogue, who eventually becomes a tyrant, is the son of a corrupted oligarch who was himself corrupted by oligarchic greed when he accepted one of those 'poisoned loans' that Plato makes so much of. Leaders of the people do not come out of the mob, so the crowd cannot be blamed as the authors of the misfortune of tyranny; they are the accomplices of tyranny, not its instigators. So why not say that only the near-sighted would be foolish enough to believe that democracy is less happy than oligarchy? And the matter could be taken back one stage further still. The rot originally set in when mistakes in the breeding arrangements of the Guardian class allowed some Guardians to degenerate into timocrats, so why not blame those who regard the timocrat as happier than the oligarch for being near-sighted?

The only real crime that Plato can lay at the door of democracy is the judicial murder of Socrates in 399 BC after the rule of The Thirty, and since Plato the trial of Socrates has become something of a test case dividing those who think of democracy as the mob in action from those who have kinder things to say about the political capacity of the people. (Thucydides blames the democracy for the expedition to Syracuse; the democracy brought in The Hundred in 411, and The Thirty in 404, both by a single show of hands. But the expedition to Syracuse failed for ordinary military reasons, and in both the other cases the democracy can hardly be blamed for the excesses of the Oligarchy. Aristotle, for example, praises the moderation of the democracy after the tyranny of Peisistratus (Moore, 1975, p. 165), and the democracy declared a political amnesty after 403. Socrates was charged with impiety and corrupting the youth, though his was clearly a political trial.) In the nineteenth century de Maistre and Sorel thought the trial still had important political lessons to give. Neither Plato's own account of the trial, nor Xenophon's, is a mob account. There are the usual warnings that popular juries cannot be trusted to condemn the guilty and acquit the innocent; there are hints that the members of the jury are jealous of Socrates' superiority in virtue, and a complaint that a day is not long enough to try a man for his life (Lindsay, 1910, pp. 153, 155, 321), but beyond that the jury seems to have behaved itself, listened to the evidence and come close to acquittal. The whole thing might have been fixed behind the scenes, but we are not told that. Socrates' defence rests mainly on distinguishing himself from the Sophists on the grounds that he taught only moderation and virtue, that he has no claims to special knowledge about anything much, and that his only expertise is that of an unpaid teacher (ibid., pp. 5–8). He cannot deny that he had a hand in the education of those who were troublesome under the democracy, especially Critias and Alcibiades, but while they were attached to him they were still moderate. If they came to him for a political education they were mistaken in their expectations, and besides, they were receiving lessons in politics from politicians while they still associated with Socrates. Alcibiades was completing the political education which began with Pericles, so if he was corrupted, he must have been corrupted by someone else (ibid., pp. 8, 14ff.). That Socrates took that line of defence must mean that his accusers and the jury saw him as another Sophist, more persuasive than the rest and so more dangerous, at a time when the Sophists were associated in the public mind with the training of oligarchs when the oligarchy had just been defeated. Perhaps this is what annoyed Plato most. Socrates was being accused of hastening the corruption of the oligarchic character which he argues in *The Republic* is a prelude to demagoguery and to tyranny. (Xenophon points out that one of the most serious pieces of circumstantial evidence against Socrates was his association with the most turbulent spirits in the democracy.) Even though his accusers cannot see it, Socrates is being accused of 'democratic' crimes, whereas the democracy saw itself engaged in a self-protective exercise *against* the potentially destructive powers of corrupted oligarchic leaders, trained in the course of crowd psychology which the Sophist Socrates has already given to Alcibiades and others. For the accusers of Socrates, Plato's *Republic* could only be an *ex post facto* demonstration that the jury must have been wrong to convict *because they were a crowd*, and the proof that they were a crowd was that Socrates could not have been a Sophist because, unlike Thrasymachus, he aimed at the truth which the common people, unqualified for Guardianship, could not see.

That was certainly Sorel's view. It was unfortunate that Socrates was put on trial, and not a real Sophist, because Socrates was formally innocent of the charge of corrupting youth, but he was morally guilty as a symbol of the successful attack on the Homeric values of the old Athenian warrior-democracy in favour of the newfangled professional education from which the people were excluded because they could not pay for it. The Sophists lacked the moral aim of Socrates, but for many of his students 'Socrates was the most admirable of professors and the most convincing of Sophists . . . He had marvellous facility in debate. No Sophist could be compared to him . . . All witnesses agree that he was irresistible' (*The Trial of Socrates*, in Stanley, 1976, p. 64). Alcibiades and Critias certainty attached themselves to Socrates to learn political skills, 'to succeed by demagogic flattery in a democratic society' (Stanley, 1976, p. 64), and there is no smoke without fire. Intellectuals seldom make their contribution to politics direct; they are a behind-the-scenes influence, just like the Jesuits; Rousseau would have tried in vain to explain to his followers that they were applying his ideas badly (Stanley, 1976, p. 66), but it is in ideas that everything begins, so while it was hard luck on Socrates that they picked on him, 'Xenophon's argument does not prove much in favour of his master' (Stanley, 1976, p. 67). (Exactly Barrès' argument against Dreyfus (see McClelland, 1970, p. 167). Sorel, a one-time Dreyfusard, was later, in *La Révolution Dreyfusienne* (1909), to see the Dreyfusards as the new Sophists corrupting the republican *cité morale* (Stanley, 1981, pp. 270–1).

De Maistre, whose *Study on Sovereignty* was not published until 1884, which makes him in a sense Sorel's contemporary, takes the anti-democratic line of a Catholic reactionary. Republics are the least governed of states. They haven't got laws, properly speaking, because law is by its nature divine, so it cannot be made, only recognized. If justice is exercised by magistrates, it is weak, because the magistrate is too near the people and does not believe in his own authority; when the people act as the judge, justice is always 'cruel and irresponsible' (De Maistre, ed. Lively, pp. 121–2). It is absurd for Rousseau to argue that democracy is so perfect in principle that we can afford to overlook its small imperfections when the sovereign people acts. The General Will is always right and tends towards the general good; the people cannot be corrupted, though they can be misled, 'and it is then that they appear to will what is evil. Drink, Socrates, drink; and console yourself with these distinctions: the good people of Athens only *appear* to will what is evil . . . (De Maistre, pp. 125–6).

De Maistre's devout Catholicism led him to see a close parallel between the death of Socrates and the death of Christ, and perhaps that parallel has contributed to the view that Socrates was done to death by a mob, because Christ was hounded to his death by a mob that had been got at behind the scenes by the elders and chief priests to yell for the release of Barabbas and the crucifixion of Christ. (Matthew, 27:19–24; Mark, 15:7–14; Luke, 23:1–25.) Matthew has Pilate throwing the innocent Jesus to the crowd to prevent a tumult become a full-scale riot. Luke is more subtle. He has the chief priests urging on Pilate the view that Jesus is a troublemaker whose death will prevent all kinds of trouble; this persuades Pilate to the extent of making a security alliance with Herod. The chief priests then join with the crowd in the call for the release of Barabbas and the crucifixion of Jesus. One way or the other, the crowd is behind it. This view is sometimes implicit in the way Plato is translated. Lee leaves us in no doubt that we are to think about the crowd's part in the death of Socrates when he translates Plato's picture of the fate of the perfectly just man in the imperfectly unjust society: 'The just man . . . will be scourged, tortured, and imprisoned, his eyes will be put out, and after enduring every humiliation he will be crucified' (*Rep.*, 362–3).

45

Populus and Mob: Livy's History of Rome to 386 BC

Livy's account of Roman history up to the sack of the city by the Goths is a frank account of class war between the plebs and the patricians. The patricians embody the stoical virtues of constancy and self-restraint while the plebs always threaten to turn into a mob if their desires are thwarted. The story has an easily recognizable rhythm. The expulsion of the kings taught the Romans to love liberty, so that rule by Consults and Senate became irksome to the people because the Consuls enjoyed all the powers of the expelled kings (Livy, ed. Selincourt and Ogilvie, p. 105). The people put forward demands: an end to debt-bondage (ibid., pp. 130ff.), a distribution of land (ibid., p. 151), codification of the laws (ibid., p. 192), a restoration of the Tribunate (ibid., p. 241), or access to offices monopolized by the patricians (ibid., pp. 272ff.). The patricians are reluctant to concede, but the people have powerful weapons at their disposal: they can refuse the call to arms at a time when the city is surrounded by enemies who are likely to attack when the city is divided (ibid., pp. 130–4); once in the field, they can mutiny (ibid., p. 236); they can secede from the city, which they did twice (ibid., pp. 141ff, 238) or they could elevate one of their leaders to tyranny or even bring back the monarchy (ibid., pp. 184–6). The obvious remedy of the patricians and the Consuls was to call out the levy and keep the troops out in the field under military discipline for as long as possible in the hope that tempers would cool, because as a last resort the people could become a mob and get their way by violence. The military solution could not be repeated too often; the people became very wary of war scares at times when the passage of an agrarian law was being urged. (In 461 they refused to believe there was danger of war even though the priests claimed it was predicted in the Sybilline Books (ibid., pp. 194–5).) The advantage of solidarity which comes from a small group (there were originally a hundred patricians) which chooses the Consuls was balanced by the institution of Tribunes of the People who could be re-elected and so provide some kind of continuous leadership while Consuls were only elected for a year. The last resort of the patricians was Dictatorship. Cincinnatus was obviously made Dictator to control the people and prosecute the war (ibid., p. 213), but the Dictatorship was as dangerous to Roman liberty as a Tribune of the People who had been made a tyrant by the mob. The Dictatorship was clearly for emergencies only, and the history of Rome to 386 is a story of solid plebeian gains.

For Livy the people are not always a mob, though he always calls them a mob when they threaten violence, and they typically do that when they are roused by a demagogue. Before the Tribunate, they secede to the Sacred Mount under a named leader, Sicinius, 'without orders from the Consuls' (ibid., p. 141); the mob rioting of 461 is led by an extribune, Terentillus (ibid., pp. 192ff.) There are hints of demagoguery even under the kings: Romulus might have been a bit of a demagogue (ibid., p. 50) and the Tarquins certainly were (the first Tarquin canvassed for the future kingship and 'secured the popular vote by an overwhelming majority' and celebrated much more elaborate games than his predecessors, always a sign of currying popular favour (ibid., p. 74); Tarquin the Proud was helped to the throne by the mob (ibid., p. 87), and the Decemvir, Appius Claudius, tried to turn himself into a demagogue to establish his tyranny, even though he had previously been the people's enemy (ibid., pp. 221-2). The led crowd was obviously a danger which the republic would have to live with but it had its equivalent in the feeble-heartedness of the Senate in their failure to stand up to the tyranny of the Decemvirs.

The early days of the republic are its great days; the people have their part to play; occasionally they get out of hand and threaten the balance of liberty, but Livy at least finds their agitations understandable. The story of the Debtor's Plight is feelingly told (ibid., pp. 129–30) so nobody can blame the revolt of the debtors which follows; similarly, the continued agitation over the agrarian law, though it threatens the city by dividing it at a time of danger from outside, is understandable – there is nothing inherently irrational, or even subversive, about soldier-farmers demanding land which they will be willing to defend. And Livy never forgets the origins of Rome. Romulus and Remus first showed their mettle by organizing bands of highway robbers (ibid., p. 38); Rome welcomed fugitives and runaway slaves from neighbouring cities ('That mob was the first real addition to the City's strength, the first step to her future greatness.') (ibid., pp. 42–3); Numa's mumbo-jumbo was needed to tame an aggressive mob of cattle thieves; war was necessary to put some discipline into them (ibid., pp. 54–5); the rabble could only understand authority by 'visible signs' (ibid., p. 42) and they got their wives by rape (ibid., pp. 42–3). Livy refused to cover the origins of Rome with a decent politic veil to emphasize the common, rather squalid origins of both the Senate and People of Rome. The wonder is that such a people were ever tamed at all. This he ascribes to the genius of Romulus and Numa, the first for the discipline of war and the second for the laws of religion. War was a risk for a people who had not acquired 'self-mastery'; Numa greatly elaborated the religious rituals of the Romans (ibid., pp. 54–5) so that the rough mob home from the wars would realize that in peace a different standard of behaviour was required. The laws were so successful that the Roman people was ready for liberty when Brutus expelled the kings. All the kings except Tarquin the Proud are praised as being, in their way, 'successive "founders"' of Rome, and if they had not done their work so well,

Brutus . . . would have done his country the greatest dis-service . . .
One has but to think of what the populace was like in those early days –
and to ask what would have happened if they had suddenly found
themselves protected by inviolable sanctuary and enjoying complete
freedom of action . . . In such circumstances, un-restrained by the
power of the throne, they would, no doubt, have set sail on the stormy
sea of democratic politics, swayed by the gusts of popular eloquence
and quarrelling for power with the governing class of a city which
did not even belong to them, before any real sense of community had
had time to grow.

(ibid., p. 105)

Livy shows us the political maturity of the Roman plebs in his
account of the first secession of the plebs to the Sacred Mount in 494.
There they made themselves a properly fortified camp, refrained from
looting, 'taking only what they needed for subsistence' (ibid., 139), and
waited. No hostile move was made against them (Manlius Valerius,
a moderate, had been made Dictator to avoid the extremist Appius
Claudius (ibid., p. 138). Something had to be done to restore the
harmony of the state, and the Senatorial party chose Menenius Agrippa,
a plebeian, to parley with the people. He treated them to the homespun
wisdom of the fable of the Belly and the Limbs, explaining that if
the members tried to subdue the belly by starvation, the whole body
wasted away to nothing. The belly has no mean service to perform, for
it nourishes the members by sending blood back through the veins, and
upon this blood our life and our health depend. This rather confused
piece of biology convinced the people that the governing class was not
useless; they negotiated concessions with Menenius Agrippa: special
magistrates were to be elected by the people to protect them from
the Consuls; Socinius, who had led the revolt, was elected one of
the Tribunes of the People. (Later, the people under their ex-Tribunes
allied with the Consuls and the Senate to get rid of the Decemvirs (450),
when the price of their alliance was the restoration of the Tribunate
(ibid., pp. 231ff.).) Menenius died a pauper the following year and
was buried by contributions from the people (ibid., p. 143). What
Livy wants us to make of this account is clear. The division between
classes was not complete; the people waited, they knew they were in
a strong bargaining position which they were careful not to jeopardize
by looting; they swallowed a lot from Menenius Agrippa – he was one
of them, and he made no real claims for superiority on the patricians'
behalf – they were not the head but the belly, but they honoured him at
his funeral and so didn't think of him as a traitor to his class. Civil war
did not break out and the people sensibly got the Tribunate as a *quid
pro quo* for their return to the city. Livy does not exactly applaud the

people, but he doesn't condemn them either; even the election of the demagogue Sicinius passes without comment.

Livy does praise the people in the case of the election of the military tribunes with consular power. The election came after a period of party strife which began with a proposal to make it legal for patricians to intermarry with plebeians (ibid., p. 269) which the demagogue Carnuleius made the occasion for a general attack on the privileges of the patricians whom he accused of refusing to recognize the common ancestry of all the Romans in the days of Romulus and Numa. The Senate, therefore, received the news that peace was threatened by the Ardeans, an army from Veii, and the Volscians and Aequians, 'with great satisfaction'. Canuleius then threatened to prevent the levy. The Senate conceded intermarriage between the orders, but this only encouraged Carnuleius, now 'a great man', to push the demand for plebeian consuls while still holding up the conscription. A compromise was reached – military tribunes would be elected, from plebs or patricians, and the matter of the consuls would be left where it was. During the election, all the ex-tribunes and everybody else who had spoken against the Senate and consuls set about canvassing for votes, while the patricians, who at first refused to become candidates because no patrician thought he could work with a plebeian tribune, were at last forced to put themselves forward so as not to lose face. The three candidates returned by the popular votes were all patricians. The mob had become the people; while they fought for their 'liberty and prestige' they followed a demagogue, but when that fight was over, they used their judgement 'unclouded by passion'; the fact that plebeians had been allowed to stand was enough, and no plebeian was in fact elected until 400. Livy comments: 'Such decency of feeling, such fairness and magnanimity characterised, on that occasion, the whole body of the Roman commons – where would you find it today in one single man?' (ibid., pp. 275–7). (Livy was writing in the early years of the empire.)

There is something patronizing about Livy even when he praises the people – it is surprising how well they can act on occasions, all things considered. He is no theorist of the balanced constitution. He has no notion of the necessity of the struggle of plebs and patricians as the condition of the development and preservation of Roman liberty. Brutus and the patricians established liberty, and excessive desires on the people's part, which only another tyrant could satisfy, threatens it. His account of the struggle cannot disguise the fact that the people wrested their concessions from the patricians either by acting as a mob, or threatening to, but the moral he draws is not that liberty is being developed and prolonged by a balance of force. That lesson was left for Machiavelli and Montesquieu. Livy's attitude is that, but for the wisdom and restraint of the Senate, the people would have surrendered their patrician-given liberty to the first demagogue who promised them what they wanted. But for all that, the people become patriots under the good influence of the laws of Romulus and Numa, and under the guidance of the patricians. Despite the fact that the Romans had taken the trouble to inform themselves about the democratic practices of the Greek cities at the time of the agitation for a codification of the laws (ibid., p. 219), it never seems to have occurred to the people to seek help from outside as the Greek democrats did in their struggles against the oligarchs. An outside threat might be the occasion for pressing demands, just as the patricians would use the threat to call the levy to put the people under military discipline, but that was the limit.

Livy's history allows us to see both Senate and People making themselves a constitution and making it work, though we have to wait for Machiavelli, in the *Discourses on the First Decade of Livy*, and following him, Montesquieu, to draw out the lessons for a theory of balanced government and for an account of the essential part tumults of the people have to play in keeping a free government true to its republican principles (see below, Chapters 2 and 3). Livy favours the patricians but he does not treat the people with contempt, and he cannot help letting us see the Roman people making its own history. He died in AD 17, and it was left to Tacitus to chronicle the decline of both patricians and people into mere spectators of the history being made by the degenerate family of Augustus and their henchmen.

The People Marginalized: Tacitus and the Mob of Spectators

The people that Livy's Senate had to stop turning into a mob was predominantly made up of farmers; if they became a mob, their typical demand was an agrarian law. With the expansion of Roman territory, it became increasingly difficult for country people to come into the city to vote. By the third century, many citizens lived more than a hundred miles from Rome. The city itself was getting bigger, and so by the first century the Roman crowd was an urban mob with no ties to the land, slum-dwelling for the most part, wage-labourers, small craftsmen and shopkeepers, freedmen, foreigners and even slaves (Brunt, 1966, p. 6). They had become a real proletariat, with nothing to leave to their country except the memory of their riots and their children. This was the mob of bread and circuses which invited the contempt of Tacitus.

Tacitus wrote a century after Livy. The dynasty founded by Augustus had degenerated into tyranny. Tacitus was born at the end of the reign of Tiberius, and his father had suffered under the last of the tyrants,

Domitian. Tacitus himself fared better. He enjoyed preferment under Vespasian (he was Praetor in 88), received the thanks of the Senate (for the prosecution of Marius Priscus in 99), and spent the last twenty years of his life at the beginning of that 'happy period of more than fourscore years [when] the public administration was conducted by the virtues and abilities of Nerva, Trajan, Hadrian and the two Antonines' (Gibbon, *Decline and Fall*, I, p. 1). He completed the *History* in the reign of Trajan and the Neronian books of the *Annals* under Hadrian (Syme, 1970, pp. 120–9). Tacitus accepts the empire as an accomplished fact. Certainly, it is too well-established to be got rid of (following Syme, 1970, p. 129, rather than Mendell, 1970, p. 68). 'Tacitism' is not a theory of government, but Tacitus has a consistent view of what is important in the government of the empire. What has to be closely watched is the relations between suspicious emperors and their courtiers on the one hand, whose suspicions may lead them into tyranny, and Senators and other aristocrats whose job it is to exercise a watching brief over imperial ambitions to prevent excesses. A wise emperor provides himself with some Senatorial and popular legitimacy (see Galba's speech to the Senate on the adoption of Piso, *Hist.*, 1, 16), though by this time the people's consent is merely assumed by the fact that they do not actually riot. What sickened Tacitus as the unofficial historian of the Senate was the Senate's failure under Tiberius and the tyrants, and with that failure the beginning of the corruption of the whole patrician class. The Senate crawled to Tiberius (*Ann.*, 1, 15), though it was still capable of making virtuous noises (against the luxury of the times, *Ann.*, 1, 33) and virtuous gestures (suspending public business as a protest against the absence of the emperor from Rome, *Ann.*, 1, 35); it joined the 'race of servility' to welcome Vitellius ('Another Senate and another people seemed now to be in possession of Rome' *Hist.*, 1 45); it was reduced to final indignity, regulating the number of gladiators in the games at Syracuse under Nero (*Ann.*, 11, 49), when patricians actually appeared on the stage in the theatre (*Ann.*, 14, 20). No doubt, much could be done by a virtuous Senate under a virtuous emperor, and the Senate's dignity was not lost forever, but the same could not be said for the people who, in Tacitus' account, become completely corrupted and marginalized.

For Tacitus the people are vulgarly credulous (*Ann.*, 4, 2); their support cannot be relied on (*Ann.*, 11, 19); they are no better than slaves (*Ann.*, 1, 45; *Hist.*, 1, 110) or, in their propensity to follow demagogues, no better than savages (*Ann.*, 1, 59); the legions are a mob, 'the refuse of the city', ready to listen to demagogues and incendiaries (*Ann.*, 1, 15; 31), capable of appalling acts of motiveless brutality (*Ann.*, 1, 48–9; a 'dreadful slaughter' of mutineers in Germany, 'no cause assigned, and no explanation given'). In the good old days of the republic, historians had something worth writing about: the 'dissentions between the consuls and the tribunes . . . the agrarian laws . . . the populace and the patrician order inflamed with mutual animosity', not just tittle-tattle about the imperial family and the dismal catalogue of imperial vengeance. He makes it clear that even then the patricians had 'to restrain within bounds a tumultuous and discontented mass', but there is a difference between the republic and the early years of the empire. In the republic, the mob were opponents worth fighting; it was then 'the business of the true politician to study the manners and temper of the multitude', and the man who could combine a grasp of crowd psychology with an understanding of 'the Senate, and the character of its leading members was deemed the most accomplished statesman of his time' (*Ann.*, 32–3). Historians could dignify with eloquence the 'spirit of freedom worthy of the old republic' (*Hist.*, 1, 1); Rome was then a true *res publica*; under Tiberius and his successors it 'differs in nothing from a monarchy' (*Ann.*, 4, 33); under the new constitution men resigned their rights and lived like aliens in their native country while the city itself became 'a theatre of horror' (*Hist.*, 1, 1).

Tacitus means us to take the notion of the 'city-as-theatre' seriously, perhaps even literally. The people made no opposition when they lost their right to elect magistrates under Tiberius (*Ann.*, 1, 15); Augustus tamed them with bread (*Ann.*, 1, 5) and Nero gave them circuses at a time when the demise of popular institutions made the games or the theatre the only places where the people could assemble legally (MacMullen, 1967, pp. 170–3). Games had been customary since the early days of the republic, and might still be managed 'with good order of propriety', but the ancients were wise enough to make the people stand to watch them, otherwise they 'might be tempted to waste whole days in idle amusements'. Now that the people could sit, there was no limit to the time they could spend in idleness interspersed with riot, and 'the new mode of pressing the citizens of Rome into the service of the theatre had ruined all decorum'. The rage for games brought alien customs and riff-raff to the city: 'luxury was called in from every quarter of the globe: foreign nations were ransacked for the incentives of vice; and, whatever was in itself corrupt, or capable of diffusing corruption, was to be found at Rome'. Even patricians took part in games and shows (*Ann.*, 14, 20). Nero led the way in the corruption of manners. The example of the emperor 'brought midnight riots into fashion'. He encouraged riots in the theatre, and 'at length did not blush to appear in the face of the public', so the guard had to be restored and the players again banished out of Italy (*Ann.*, 13, 25).

The people of Rome were being converted into an audience, mere spectators, not actors, at a time when they had no important part in events. They had been pacified by Augustus and turned into an audience by Nero at exactly the moment when 'A new political secret was for the first time discovered. It was perceived, that elsewhere than at Rome an emperor might be invested with the sovereign power.' The Roman people, living like aliens in their own country, were no longer even necessarily spectators at the main events; the theatre was a substitute, where the common inferior populace loitered away their time (*Hist.*, 1, 2). It was now to their advantage that civil wars were fought abroad; peace became an evil where the soldiers ate up everything and behaved riotously in the city (*Hist.*, 1, 89). Tacitus has no doubt that the corruption of the crowd comes from outside itself: the mob cannot even lead itself on the downward path, nor can it follow Nero quickly enough. The first of the quinquennial games passed off decently; 'the rage of the people' did not 'break out into any kind of excess' (*Ann.*, 14, 21); the mob was still capable of showing its disapproval of Nero's treatment of Octavia: Poppea had to warn him that though 'The first alarm was easily quelled . . . a second insurrection might prove fatal. Should the mob have reason to despair of seeing Octavia in Nero's bed, they may, in their wisdom, find for her another husband' (*Ann.*, 14, 50–1). When Nero turned the persecuted Christians into flaming torches as a public spectacle to light his gardens, even 'the rabble' couldn't stomach it: 'Humanity reacted in favour of the Christians . . . it was evident that they fell a sacrifice, not for the public good, but to glut the rage and cruelty of one man' (*Ann.*, 15, 44).

The corruption of the people was completed under Vitellius and Vespasian. They were still capable of tumult, but were incapable of sustained opposition or of distinguishing between important matters and trifles. They had shaken the throne in the last days of Nero, but were now reduced to straining at gnats (*Hist.*, 2, 10). They acquiesced in the rehabilitation of Nero 'like a herd of slaves' (*Hist.*, 2, 95) and pressed the title of Augustus on Vitellius (*Hist.*, 2, 90). Their final moment of degradation comes in Tacitus' great set-piece description of the battle within the walls of Rome between the armies of Vitellius and Vespasian in AD 69:

The people flocked in crowds to behold the conflict, as if a scene of carnage were no more than a public spectacle exhibited for their amusement. Whenever they saw the advantage inclining to either side, they favoured the combatants with shouts and theatrical applause. If the men fled from their ranks, to take shelter in shops or houses, they roared to have them dragged forth, and put to death like gladiators for their diversion . . . these miscreants were employed in plundering . . . Rome presented a scene truly shocking, a medley of savage slaughter and monstrous vice; in one place war and desolation; in another, bathing, riot, and debauchery. Heaps of slain lay murdered in the streets, and blood flowed in torrents, while harlots and abandoned women wandered about with lascivious impudence. Whatever the libidinous passions can inspire was intermixed with all the horrors of war . . . Before this period Rome had seen enraged armies within its walls . . . Upon these occasions the same barbarity was committed; but the unnatural security and inhuman indifference were beyond all example. In the midst of rage and massacre, pleasure knew no intermission. A dreadful carnage seemed to be a spectacle added to the public games. The populace enjoyed the havoc; they exulted in the midst of devastation; and without any regard for the contending parties, triumphed over the miseries of their country.

(Hist., 3, 88)

The whole city has become Tacitus' 'theatre of horror'; the crowd can no longer see the difference between games and the great events of the empire; everything has become a public spectacle. The circus factions at Rome had never divided on public issues as they were later to do at Constantinople (MacMullen, 1967, 170); now they have become completely depoliticized, a lower class or a rabble to be treated with contempt. There is no trace in Tacitus of the Polybian balance between political forces which Livy's account of the struggles between plebs and patricians could not conceal. The Roman people no longer have a part in the making of their history; they no longer compete with the patricians on the equal and sometimes more than equal terms of the republic. They have become the lowest class in a hierarchy; a nuisance when they riot, to be kept in their place and best forgotten; a true urban rabble, and with the city full of foreigners, no longer recognizably Roman.

The Crowd Becomes a World of its Own: Procopius on the Nika Riots

The crowd that Tacitus left gawping at the great events of the Empire could still cause trouble, rabble though it was, throughout the period from the first century into Late Antiquity. All the contemporary sources agree that riots were endemic in the cities of the East, riots during famines, riots got up by monks against the pagans, riots at Church Councils and episcopal elections, riots against rising taxes and unpopular officials, and particularly riots in, or originating in, circuses and theatres (Cameron, 1976, p. 271). Theatres became centres of political demonstration. Theatrical claques could orchestrate rhythmical chanting of political slogans against imperial officials actually present in the theatre, and it was a short step from arranging a protest inside to fomenting a riot outside (Browning, 1952, p. 17). None of this was new.

(Tacitus says that the trouble-making of theatrical claques has spread far enough to cause a mutiny in the Pannonian legions in the reign of Tiberius (*Ann.*, 1, 26).) What was new was that the urban crowd began to divide against itself into a struggle between different factions, and a new kind of rural crowd made its appearance, especially in Syria, in the fourth and fifth centuries. The factions and the rural crowd were crowds with leaders and heroes, charioteers and holy men. 'The Byzantines had two heroes, the winner in the chariot race and the ascetic saint' (Cameron, 1973, p. 3, quoting Baynes), but the crowds that they led, or which formed round them, were very different.

'In every city', Procopius tells us, 'the population has been divided for a long time past into the Blue or Green factions; but within comparatively recent times it has come about that, *for the sake of these names* and the seats which the rival factions occupy in watching the games . . . they fight against their opponents' (italics added) (Procopius, ed. Dewing, 1, p. 219). Something has very obviously changed. The division in the past may have made some sense; perhaps religious or political motives were at the back of it. Recently they have begun to fight (things have become more serious), and 'for the sake of these names'. Beyond that, it is difficult to ascribe causes. The names are enough. The two sides are spoiling for a fight and hardly need a pretext, like enemies on campaign who only have to come into contact with each other for battle to be joined. When Procopius comes to give his very full account of the Nika Riots he is on surer ground after the two factions join together and begin the riot. Procopius, and every historian since, fails to explain the alliance, but, again like every historian since, after the alliance has been concluded he can treat the riot as a 'political' riot, abounding with causes, especially after the crowd, indignant at the sight of officers of the city administration leading some convicted rioters to execution, open the prison and release everyone inside. Desperate men awaiting torture and death (Procopius, p. 221) are ready for anything. The sane-minded flee and the emperor and empress, together with a number of senators, lock themselves up in the palace (Procopius, p. 223). There are demands for the dismissal of two unpopular officials, the praetorian prefect John the Cappadocian and the quaestor Tribonian, and the mob is out for their blood. Justinian dismisses them 'instantly', but that fails to mollify the crowd (Procopius, pp. 223–6). Justinian's dithering causes the throne to wobble. There is a plot to replace him involving some senators and perhaps the nephews of Anastasius (they later denied this) (Procopius, pp. 227–31). The mayhem continues; Theodora rallies Justinian; Belisarius and Mundus lead the veterans of the Persian Wars through the ravaged city to the Hippodrome, attack the 'vast multitude', slaughter 30,000 and the revolt is over (Procopius, pp. 231–7). Hypatius and Pompey, whom the mob had tried to raise to the purple, and the senators who had involved themselves in the insurrection, are then executed (Procopius, pp. 237–9).

What is remarkable about Procopius' account is that there is no attempt to explain how the riot began. He begins with some convicted 'rioters', presumably members of the factions being punished for previous offences, and ends with the slaughter of more than 30,000. He is at no loss for explanation of the *development* of the riot once it has started, but he has nothing *political* to say about the beginning which remotely explains why it should end up in carnage: the factions fight 'for the names'. But Procopius does attempt a *psychological* explanation for the violence of the factions. They have created a world of their own in which they live a life which is as different as it could be from the life around them. In the world of the factions, the ordinary human cares are discounted. Family life ceases to count – the factions are indifferent to what it costs to go to the games; families are divided by faction, husbands against wives, brother against brother. The state of their country doesn't matter to them provided their own faction is winning in the hippodrome. No sacrilege is too terrible in the tumults of the faction fights. Even women, who don't actually go to the games, join with the men 'and even resist them'. And most important of all, the rioters are indifferent to the punishments which they risk, extreme torture and a most shameful death (Procopius, pp. 229–31).

Nothing human or divine counts in this world. Procopius is at a loss to explain how it came to be created. The hostility of the factions to their fellow men 'has no cause', 'and I, for my part, am unable to call this anything but a sickness of the soul' (Procopius, p. 221). There the matter rests. There must be something wrong with these people which is not explicable in political or social terms, so it is almost with relief that Procopius turns to political and social explanation when the factions have joined up to begin a riot which can then be explained. (Libanius and John Chrysostom had already wondered whether daemonic inter- vention had played its part in the great riot at Antioch in AD 387; theatre claques and outside agitators were not enough to account for a riot in which the destruction of imperial statues was bound to call down horrible punishment on the city (Browning, 1952, p. 19.) Procopius is unaware of the similarities between this world of the factions and the world of the primitive church which was to impress Gibbon, but he misses an explanation of the alliance of the factions which is implicit in his own account. The Nika was the moment when the retreat from the *res publica* of the urban plebs was complete, when the process described by Tacitus went on to its culminating stage. The plebs are no longer merely spectators to the games and to the great events of the Empire; they have created their own world, have become actors again, but not in the world which has been left to the emperors and the church to govern. No doubt this is part of that 'leakage of reality' in Late Antiquity which Peter Brown has so eloquently chronicled, and of course it is only a leakage. The factions could not live out the whole of their lives in their self-created world. There were attempts to reintegrate the factions into the social and political fabric of the State. Justinian incorporated the factions into imperial ceremonial (Cameron, 1967, p. 295), and it may even be that the emperor Anastasius had a hand in the creation of the world of the factions itself. Cameron suggests plausibly that Anastasius might have encouraged charioteer worship (the erection of charioteer statues required imperial permission) in the hope that some of the glory of the victorious charioteer might rub off on him. The charioteer was above all things a winner. Charioteers were greeted with the same cry as the emperors, *Tu vincas*, and while a champion like Porphyrius could never be a serious rival, 'the more and greater Porphyrius' victories in the arena, the more and greater the symbolic victories of the Emperor, the louder and longer the cries of *Auguste, tu vincas.*' (Cameron, 1973, pp. 248–9). Far from being in any sense a threat to the Empire, the factions may have become the creatures of the emperor, imperial die-hards, last-ditch loyaltists who could be called upon to man the walls of the city by emperors like Maurice and Phocas when all else had failed (Cameron, 1976, p. 295). Cameron suggests that this shows that the real significance of the riots was that they were not political at all. They did not constitute a growth of some kind of 'popular sovereignty' (how could they, when in the typical riot the factions fought each other?). The Nika Riot was one of the exceptions, and he puts this down to the dithering of Justinian who let it get out of hand so that new emperors had to be found who would do something about it (ibid., pp. 278ff.). Most of the riots were 'what would nowadays be called just hooliganism' (ibid., p. 271). Cameron's 'hooliganism', like Procopius' 'sickness of the soul' still waits for its explanation.

Tacitus' crowd in its retreat into the world of its own presented nothing like the threat presented by Peter Brown's crowds led by holy men in a world where the oracles were silent. The gods had been chased from the poetic landscape and the shrines and temples had been destroyed, so where were men to find that easy and familiar contact with the supernatural in time of trouble which had been so marked a characteristic of the pagan universe (Markus, 1982)? Popular religiosity turned to the saints and their relics, hermits and holy men. No doubt, the official view was that spiritual comfort and guidance should come from the Church and its bishops, but the Church offered its institutionalized help and advice in towns and probably had very little to do with the villages of Syria where the holy men established themselves as leaders in the fourth and fifth centuries. Like the Judges of Israel, the holy man came from nowhere (from the desert); he was without kin, a complete stranger. He needed a crowd to establish his credentials. He ate odd food; he was a miracle-worker whose miraculous judgements were visited on those who refused to believe in him. He was a self-made man who worked hard at convincing the crowd that he was a man apart, and he did this by feats of athletic asceticism which showed he was no fraud. Just as the martyr had borrowed the gladiator's glory, so the holy men claimed some of the popular adulation of the successful charioteer who had only his momentary victories at the hippodrome to set against forty years' residence on the top of a pillar (Brown, 1982, p. 137). The holy men were problem-solvers at a time when the only contact the countryside had with the towns was an occasional visit from a tax-collector. Holy men would help to fix a deal about a tax debt, fix the price of corn or arrange a system of water rationing during a drought (ibid., p. 143). His independence as an arbitrator could be relied on because he was a stranger. Like the ideal ancient legislator, or the Legislator in Rousseau's *Social Contract*, he had no immediate interest in what was being decided, so he could be trusted.

Holy men were looked upon with great suspicion by the bishops and magistrates in the towns. The chronic underemployment and periodic famines of the villages sometimes forced the holy men to lead their crowd to the towns in search of food. The towns closed their gates to them when they could, but sometimes the crowd gained access, to cause great embarrassment to the authorities. The holy man was a char-ismatic leader, touched by God; he wanted nothing for himself and he could perform feats of endurance which even the more sophisticated town crowd would find impressive. The bishops and magistrates could not openly accuse him of being a fraud because who was to say where true spiritual authority lay? (Ayatollahs have always been difficult to resist.) The holy man was a serious rival to constituted authority, and the authorities often had no option but to treat him with kid gloves and hope that eventually he would take his crowd back where it came from (ibid., p. 141).

Holy men seem to have declined in the sixth century, and the truth is that little enough is known about them and the crowds they led, but they did point to the future. If the victory of the holy men was a victory over the institutions of the past, then medieval Christianity was in its turn the victory of ritual and institutions over the holy men, and the crowds they led. A more confident Christianity could accuse the crowd leader of heresy and the crowd of threatening the peace which God had sent kings to protect. A Hume or a Gibbon would see the holy men and their crowds as part of the irrational superstitious mass's refusal to make the intellectual leap from polytheism to monotheism by diffusing the loci of the supernatural in a typically pagan way (ibid., pp. 107ff.). Charles Maurras, searching for the causes of the

French Revolution in remote places and forever sniffing out something Jewish, or at least Levantine, claimed to see in Rousseau just the type of desert-bred fakir who had troubled the peace of the Roman empire, leading his ignorant mass against classical civilization whose protector in France was the Roman Catholic Church (see 'Romanticism and Revolution' in McClelland, 1970, pp. 243–5).

2

Some Medieval Crowds and Machiavelli on the Roman People

In the ancient world, what made the crowd frightening was that there was a *polis* or a *res publica*, a public stage, which the crowd could take over in a sense that is almost literal and call its own.[1] However it was constituted, the publicness of the thing made it worth occupying or possessing. In an oligarchy, like ancient Thebes for instance, the oligarchs did not claim to *be* the *polis*; they claimed to be its guardians, that they knew what was best for it, that it was theirs, but the thing itself was separate from them and in their safekeeping. Possessing the *polis* was worth it. At the very least it conferred prestige, the most public of all virtues, and it brought with it advantages of a negative but not negligible kind, because the class enemy of the oligarchs could not then use the prestige which possession of the *polis* brought as a weapon against the rich, and it put that weapon far from the hands of what all oligarchs feared most, a demagogic tyrant. What the ancients understood very clearly was that legitimacy was power on the cheap, power which does not have to be exercised, or power whose exercise does not of itself require the expenditure of precious resources. Legitimate power was power without the socially expensive use of force. Power could be used to alter what the ancients called the constitution and what we would call the arrangements for holding offices, and it was these office-holders who decided, with the connivance in democratic states of popular assemblies, the business of war and peace, which was the only business that conferred prestige and provided fame. The *polis* existed to make these powers possible, and possessing the *polis* gave the possessors a chance through fame to live beyond their own deaths. What was true of the *polis* was true of republican Rome; legitimacy was crucial to the life of all ancient cities because the city-state was always difficult to rule for long by force alone because the only force available to it that it could easily afford was the force of its citizens. All ancient cities expected to go to war, and this made the enslavement of citizens a very short-sighted policy on the part of rulers. Even in an oligarchy and especially in a tyranny, rulers would need the people in arms one day soon. Legitimacy counted for much in cities where there was not much in the way of bureaucracy or a police, so that citizens had to be relied on to obey the law and keep the peace largely by themselves. Ancient writers emphasize the importance of religion and what we would call public opinion, because these were among the cheapest forms of social control available to cities which often lacked the economic surplus to provide officials with the necessary freedom from getting a living from a craft or from the soil which the professionalization of the function of rule required. The most obvious way to get rule free was to delegate it to slaves, and slaves did act as public officials in some states, but giving slaves even limited rights to interfere in the lives of free citizens was dangerous in time of peace, and to arm them in time of war was to invite one of those slave revolts which all ancient cities dreaded as they dreaded the plague. Hence the to us almost unthinkably amateurish way in which ancient cities conducted their affairs when compared to the civilized despotisms of the East.

Empire changed everything. Imperial decisions, let alone imperial administration, could not be made or done on the basis of discussions for a day in assemblies with little more to rely on than ancestral wisdom or the inspiration of a demagogue. An empire's wars could not be fought by armies of citizens who had to come home the same year to plant or reap the harvest; war ceased to be fought on current income and had to be fought on capital topped up with plunder if the war was successful. All this required full-time officials and professional soldiers who would come to regard crowd control as one of the minor but important arts of government. Much is often made of the victories of the West over the East in the ancient world, but the longest lasting victory of all was the triumph of the ways of Eastern empire over the crowd as armed people in the West. All empires try to centralize themselves, and their longevity depends largely on how successful that centralization is. Centralization in its turn creates the idea of locality; a local revolt can only be local when a centralized administration exists to regard it as merely local, something worth bothering about, but not essentially serious; a provincial governor's problem but not ours. In these circumstances, any riot of the people, against tax-collectors in the countryside, or from the more varied motives of the more complex life of towns, becomes part of the day-to-day agenda of established politics, not part of an attempt to establish another politics in its place. If the centre holds, then so does everything else. Of course, the centre still has its enemies, but the crowd is no longer really one of them. Affairs at the centre become a matter of the stability of a regime, and toppling the regime is a matter of playing on the doubtful loyalties of armies of officials and soldiers, corporations or crowds under discipline. Sheer numbers count for less, organization for more. Contrast the ancient city, where nothing could be local because local discontent was indistinguishable from a conspiracy against the State; it had to go public or die. There, numbers really mattered.

Nineteenth-century crowd theorists were fond of comparing the crowds of their own day to the armies of barbarians which conquered the Roman Empire and established the feudal kingdoms of the West. Le Bon, for instance, saw in the barbarian tribes owing voluntary obedience to a chief the model for the crowds of urban rioters that every state in Europe had to deal with since the Paris riot of 1789 got out of hand and became the French Revolution. The European city mob, in Le Bon's view of it, was a Darwinian survival from, or recapitulation of, the ferocious activity of Huns and Goths. (Nietzsche, prompted by Burckhardt's more refined historical sense, argued more subtly that the *Herdenmenschen* did not come over the walls from the outside, either when Rome fell or in his own day, but were already firmly placed in positions of institutional and cultural power, ready to celebrate the collapse and to profit by it.) But what Le Bon never tells us much about is what happened to the crowd after it had conquered the Roman Empire and before it made the French Revolution. (Clever Georges Sorel was to point to aristocratic Roman prelates lying in wait with their classical education to civilize the barbarian kings and through them to civilize the barbarian crowd.) Le Bon makes passing references to Christianity as a crowd religion and to the Crusades as crowd movements, but that is about all we hear about it, so we are left to assume that the crowd disappeared into feudalism and into the bosom of the Church.

That disappearance is puzzling, because we are used to thinking of medieval societies as violent, and we are used to thinking that where there is violence the crowd cannot be far away. In fact, there was no shortage of great crowds in the medieval period, but what does seem to be lacking is that sense of theoretical panic about the crowd that we find, say, in Plato, or in the social theory of the late nineteenth century. This is not to say that observers of medieval crowds found them uninteresting. Abbot Suger tells us that as a schoolboy at St Denis the brethren used to tell him tales about the crowd that used to flock to King Dagobert's basilica on days when the relics (the Nail and the Crown of Thorns) were put on show to the faithful; he saw the crowd in his youth, 'and in my mature years I strove to correct it' (by enlarging the church). The church would become so full that no one

among the countless thousands of people because of their very density could move a foot; that no one, because of their very congestion, could [do] anything but stand like a marble statue, stay benumbed or, as a last resort, scream. The distress of the women, however, was so great and so intolerable that [you could see] how they, squeezed in by the mass of strong men as in a wine press, exhibited bloodless faces as in imagined death; how they cried out horribly as though in labour; how several, miserably trodden underfoot [but then], lifted by the pious assistance of men above the heads of the crowd, marched forward as though clinging to a pavement.

(Abbot Suger, 1946, p. 89)

The brethren showing the relics 'had to yield to their anger and rioting and many a time, having no place to turn, escaped with the relics through the windows (ibid.). Abbot Suger, ever mindful of the value of publicity to St Denis, invited the great folk from all over France to the ceremony of consecration of the new enlarged church in 1144. Some trouble from the crowd was expected, and Abbot Suger had the foresight to arrange for crowd control by asking the king to provide marshals 'to keep away the impeding crowd from the procession itself'; the king answered that 'he would gladly do this in person as well as through his retinue'. On the day itself, 'The populace milled around outside with the drive of its intolerable magnitude (*pro intolerabili magnitudinis suae impetu foris agebatur*) . . . the King himself and his officials kept back the tumultous impact and protected those returning to the doors with canes and sticks' (ibid., pp. 113–4, 115). Two kinds of crowd control are being exercised here, the long-term by the enlarging of the church, and the short-term by the king and his retinue with their 'canes and sticks'. What is remarkable is how relaxed and straightforward the business is. The Church makes a space for the crowd and the king takes a hand in person, unarmed, in crowd control. No doubt, this was a crowd in holiday mood, but it was also a crowd capable of the violence of religious ecstasy, yet in Suger's account of it there is a complete lack of feeling that anything very out of the ordinary is happening. It is a great day for the crowd, like other great days; the crowd is tolerated and accommodated.

There must have been something about feudal societies which enabled them to find a place for the crowd in the way that the monks of St Denis made room for it by building a bigger church. Certainly, there would have been very little squeamishness about the fact of violence in societies where war was the only honourable profession outside the Church. The French nineteenth-century criminologist Gabriel Tarde wittily pointed out that if the anthropological (=hereditary) theory of criminality was taken literally, you would expect to find most of society's violent criminals – murderers, robbers and rapists – among the upper classes keeping up the traditions of their knightly ancestors

(Tarde, 1912, p. 336ff.). Outside the knightly class, violence would be shameful, criminal violence, the violence of the rabble, not plebeian violence because it would be private violence, and violence without honourable weapons. The only crime deserving of honour available to the people would be crime which imitated what was admirable behaviour in their social superiors, hence the sometimes high prestige of poachers in noble and royal hunting preserves, of kidnappers of wives, and of bandits. The class of warriors had its own forms of permitted riot in battles, or in the sacking of cities, in which the chivalric code was supposed to keep the hierarchical social order intact. The base-born were expected to act as a kind of audience to the honourable and preferably single combat of knights in much the same way that the ordinary soldiers in Homer are spectators of the combats of heroes. Plunder was meant to be shared out according to rank, and even knights could be hanged for keeping back plunder for themselves to which the order of things did not entitle them (see Villehardouin, ed. Shaw, pp. 94–5). Keegan points out that from the chivalric point of view Agincourt was a shambles of a battle because King Henry cheated by allowing archers indiscriminately to kill fallen knights with dishonourable weapons (mallets and knives) and to butcher knightly prisoners (Keegan, 1976, pp. 97–112). In a society like that it is hard to imagine the kind of horror in the face of popular violence which characterizes so much crowd theory from the middle nineteenth century onwards.

How much a society is frightened by the crowd largely depends on how that society is ruled, and on how rule in that society is legitimized. Seen from the viewpoint of the ancient city or the modern nation-state, the government of feudal societies seems overwhelmingly to have been local government, perhaps even local self-government. All the natural tendencies of feudal societies were centrifugal; every lordship dreamt of *de facto* independence in a society which needed a special class of feudal lawyers to keep track of the claims and counter-claims of a myriad of mini-jurisdictions. These jurisdictions were horizontally and vertically integrated only in the systems of formal beauty existing inside feudal lawyers' heads.

Popular revolts were bound to peter out in societies in which rule was so diffused that there was no centre of sovereignty which could be assaulted, even symbolically. Medieval kingdoms had no Bastilles. The only thing that looked like a centre was monarchy, and the only chance a leader of a popular revolt had of succeeding was to pretend to be a forgotten and sleeping king suddenly awakened.

The legitimations of rule in medieval societies were as complex and diffuse as the means by which those societies were in fact ruled. Medieval societies did not need straightforward legitimations for the exercise of their ruling functions because nothing very straightforward was being exercised, certainly nothing that required anything like a modern, or even an ancient, theory of sovereignty. The king's claim to sovereignty was only one claim among many, and that sovereignty was neither claimed absolutely nor from a single source. Ideas of paternity, God's gift, feudal contract, hereditary right and popular election meant that medieval emperors had many suits of clothes. When, in the early modern period, kings began to put all their eggs in one basket, which is what the theory of the divine right of kings amounted to, they covered sovereignty in the flimsiest of all single justifications. Once the claim came to be made that a sovereign centre existed in all states, then the claim that sovereignty was the direct gift of God to kings had to be advanced against the claim that sovereignty lay, however remotely, in the people. Sovereignty became what it had been in the ancient world, something worth contending for, and when a voice cried out that the emperor had no clothes, the only source of sovereignty left was the people.

The theory of the divine right of kings was the easiest to see through of all political absurdities. After the feudal middle had been theoretically squeezed out, kings faced their peoples as direct contenders for the sovereign authority, and it is in this sense that the French Revolution can be seen, as it was seen by many contemporaries, as a contest between the king and the crowd. Medieval kings did not make claims of this kind because they presided over societies which saw themselves as being subject to many different kinds of law emanating from many different sources. Divine law, canon law, natural law, the common law of Christendom, feudal customary law, all acted as constraints on the making of law by kings; so many constraints meant that any law-giver had to cover himself by claiming to be merely the mouthpiece of a law-giver who was greater than he, or at least by claiming to be the declarer of ancient law. Royal justice was one justice among many other justices, which is why in medieval societies political disputes so often took the form of quarrels about jurisdiction. It was probably not until the sixteenth century that it became possible to regard the State as anything like sovereign in the modern sense. Of course, there were exceptions in medieval theory, and many in medieval practice. Kings were expected to be centralizers to some degree; part of being a king consisted of being disagreeable to barons, and the barons did not always win; all kings tried to extend their own domains, tax as many of their subjects direct as they could, invited them to the royal courts with the carrot of quicker and more even-handed justice, and dreamed of a day when their own officials and their own writ would not be excluded from any of the lands which owed them fealty. Kings certainly admired other kings who were able to go some way down that road; the French monarchy was universally admired and envied, and one of the things that made Frederick II the Wonder of the World was that his Sicilian administration was well enough organized that it could produce enough money for Frederick to be able to try to capture the glittering prize of Italy. Roman lawyers were almost everywhere telling kings of the advantages to be gained by rulers who took as their models the great law-giving emperors Theodosius and Justinian, though the time was still far distant when Thomas Cromwell would persuade Henry VIII that England was an empire, where a sovereign king and parliament could make any law it chose, and implicitly invited other kings to deny the universalist claims of the papacy and to take their realms out of Christendom too.

The universal Church, not the kings, was the crowd's real enemy in the middle ages because Christianity's origins as a religion of fishermen made the Church vulnerable to the claims of poverty and especially vulnerable to the claims of voluntary poverty. The ancient crowd had understood very well that it was the arms with which it had defended the public thing and the poverty which was its only reward, which made it a *plebs* and not a rabble. Poverty, or a decent concealment of wealth, were long public virtues at Rome, and when Roman historians looked back to the early republic from imperial days, they looked at their own time, when wealth was in private hands and the public treasury empty, with puritanical condemnation. Its own profession of ecclesiastical poverty was the Church's attempt to pre-empt the moral counter-claims of the real poor, so that between them the Church and the knightly class monopolized both poverty and arms, leaving the poor morally naked, but real destitution continued to clothe itself in the counter-counter-claim that the real poor, and not the fictitiously poor, were the true heirs to the holy and apostolic life. We have already come across holy men and their crowd causing problems for bishops in Late Antiquity when ecclesiastical authority had to tread warily in its dealings with direct-action Christianity because it made sense to regard all Christians as being on the same side when the position of the Church was itself far from secure. The case of the medieval Church was different because it was part of the system, perhaps the most important part, which ruled men's lives. It had a definite centre, Rome, itself a city which had not forgotten the time when the *plebs* had been an estate to be reckoned with, where faction riot could drive out popes to seek the comparative safety of Avignon, and where as late as the middle of the fourteenth century a Tribune of the People could still appear to re-establish more than a parody of the ancient republic.[2] The Church had available to it all that ancient writers had had to say against the crowd, but something more was required to counter the literally anti-papal claims put forward by the leaders of the crowds pursuing the millennium in Cohn's memorable account of them.[3]

Cohn's crowds were millenarian crowds led by prophets (*prophetae*) armed with an ideology derived sometimes distantly from the Book of Revelation, pseudo-Sybilline prophetizing and the twelfth century Italian mystic Joachim of Fiore. They believed that they lived during the reign of Antichrist, that the final struggle against Antichrist was about to begin as a short prelude to the Second Coming of Christ, which would usher in the millennium when Christ and the Saints would rule the earth. Antichrist was variously identified with the papacy, with the organized Church in general (though the mendicant orders were often excepted), or with anyone who lived through greed (*avaritia*), satisfying their lust (*luxuria*) at the poor's expense, which meant virtually all who did no labour. These crowds, whose progress Cohn follows from the eleventh century to the sixteenth, are remarkable for the consistency of the ideas which inspired them: they believed that one world was ending and another was about to begin; they identified a group which caused all the world's ills and a group which would help, with God's grace, to bring in the new world; they were quick to identify internal enemies in Christendom more dangerous than the enemies without, so that the internal crusade became more important to them than crusading in the East (where the poor had been the *real* crusaders); above all, they identified themselves with the elect who would survive the necessary slaughter of the millenarian battles; only the poor, and not many of them, would live to see Christ reign on earth, but it was worth it; and all this was couched in historical language which taught that since the Fall a struggle between the forces of good and evil had been going on out of which good was about to emerge in triumph at last. These crowds, whose leaders were often unlicensed preachers or laymen who found themselves possessed by an extraordinary eloquence, or who went in search of a lost leader, an Emperor of the Last Days (the sleeping Frederick II was always a good candidate), or even Christ himself, were obvious targets for the charge of heresy because their claims were the universalist claims of a rival Church.

These crowds pursued the millennium over centuries, and no single set of causes can explain why they did it; local circumstances – a particularly worldly and corrupt bishop, an oligarchy of foreigners, an outbreak of plague or famine, the appearance as from nowhere of a miraculously eloquent prophet – always counted for much; but it seems to have been the case that it was the urban poor that provided the most likely material for the millenarian crowd. As always, towns were just about the only places where it was possible to be unemployed (in the widest sense) and survive, and only in towns did there exist that marginalized population – artisans excluded from guilds living at or below the breadline, dispossessed or runaway peasants, disbanded soldiers, beggars, failed priests, and prostitutes – who already had very little to lose, and it was in towns that the contrast between the *avaritia* and *luxuria* of the well-to-do, and the destitution of the poor, would be at its most obvious. The settled peasantry, unless they too had been marginalized by wars, plagues, or economic pressures which they could not resist or even understand, contributed much less to the pursuit of the millennium. Peasants' revolts tended to be based on much more specific grievances and to make much more specific demands than the millenarian crowds which always wanted to conquer everywhere and to turn the whole world upside-down.

The distinction, however, did not always hold. In the English Peasants' Revolt of 1381, for instance, realistic and practical demands for the dismantling of those aspects of feudalism which had come to seem impossibly onerous since the Black Death had tilted the balance of economic advantage slightly towards the labourers who survived it, were accompanied by a vision of the egalitarian millennium in the dream of John Ball. There is a sense in which millenarianism and what peasants did during their revolts both show how resilient feudal society was when it confronted the crowd. However 'realistic and practical' the demands of peasants in revolt might have been, the fact that they made so many of them, and the fact that they had so many targets on which to direct their frustration, tell us just how difficult it was to make any kind of successful revolt in feudal societies. Men and women in medieval societies were subject to so many restrictions from so many different sources of rule (and the distinction between 'restriction' and 'rule' does not really apply) that their demands and their targets were bound to be many. The ruled in feudal societies were, like Gulliver, tied down with many cords, no one of which was strong enough to keep them in their place, but taken all together they served their purpose well enough. Any bid for liberation meant flailing about as Gulliver did, and it is easy to see a 'realistic and practical' demand in the moment when each attempt at free movement came up against the particular restraint it happened to encounter. Millenarianism points to the same conclusion; in a society in which each man's body and soul were subject to so many co-operating and competing centres of authority, it made a kind of lunatic sense to want to change everything, utterly, because only by abolishing the whole complex assortment of ways in which people's lives were controlled could men hope to be free in any sense that made sense.

With the taint of heresy on them, the millenarians became the enemies of God and man. The millenarian crowd was riotous in a double sense, a disturber of the peace in both the heavenly and the earthly cities; the millenarians were the first of the heavenly hooligans, rioting in a kingdom whose ideal earthly citizen was probably an anchorite or a cloistered monk. What doomed millenarian crowds was that they chose to play the game of counter-orthodoxy in a moral universe which they still regarded as having a single moral structure; like the Church, they thought in the terms of one orthodoxy and many heresies, so millenarian leaders had no option but to set themselves up as rival successors to St Peter, claiming that they, and not popes, were the true heirs of the apostolic life. Even where millenarian leaders were not as clear-sighted as that, the Church always had eyes to see that every millenarian leader was an anti-pope at heart.

The Church itself was the great agent of crowd control in the middle ages because it *contained* the crowd, hence its hostility to and attempts to control carefully all open-air preaching. Everything about the ritual of the Church was designed to keep unruliness under strict control. In *Crowds and Power* Canetti draws our attention to the deliberate, calm and spacious character of Catholicism; its calmness derives from its aversion to anything violently crowd-like. The ritual 'is of a sustained and unsurpassed deliberation. The movements of the priests in their stiff, heavy canonicals, their measured steps, the drawing out of their words – all this is like an infinite dilution of lament, spread so evenly over centuries that scarcely anything remains of the suddenness of death and the violence of grief.' The equality between members of the crowd in the congregation is diluted by the hindrances put in the way of communication between the worshippers. Worshippers do not preach to each other; the word of the simple believer has no sanctity; everything that comes to each believer comes from a higher authority. The sacred word comes to each man singly, carefully wrapped up and weighed, protected from him in its sanctity so that it is never completely his. Even his sins are not entirely his own; they are not the business of other members of the faithful among whom and against whom they are committed, so that communicating his sins to them brings no relief, but he is still not able to keep them to himself. When he confesses his sins to a priest, the sinner stands alone, confronted by the whole priesthood, which takes from the penitent the necessity of even understanding fully what he has done in return for sin's temporal remission. The way the communion is administered isolates each believer from the rest. The believer approaches the host alone, as an individual; he receives a precious treasure for himself. At the moment he receives it, the communicant feels himself part of the vast invisible Church, but at the same time he feels isolated from the other communicants. The community to which communion points is the 'permitted crowd' of the angels and the blessed. This is the perfectly serene crowd, far removed from the domesticated crowd of the congregation, and infinitely remote from any crowd of which the congregation might be members outside the ordered crowd which the Church's architecture creates by its authoritarian enclosure of human space. The Church is Roman, but the serenity of the heavenly eternal city contrasts sharply with the earthly Rome with its unruly *plebs*. The heavenly host is not active; unlike a crowd on earth, it adds to its numbers only slowly, and it lasts for ever, hardly a crowd at all, but just enough like a crowd for the comparison to be made. The congregation's only unity comes through the priest.

Priests are 'crowd crystals' in Canetti's language, or parts of crowd crystals, highly organized groups around which crowds form but which are not themselves crowds or parts of crowds (what the crowd theorists Sighele and Tarde were to call sects or corporations). The function of the monastic and religious orders is to confront the many who call themselves Christians with the recurring presence of those who truly are Christian. The Church never forgets the turbulence of the early days of mass conversion, and its function as part of the earthly order is to prevent a return to its origins as a rapidly expanding crowd. The Church still wants to increase the body of the faithful, just as it wants to add to the numbers of the blessed, but it wants to do this slowly, deliberately and calmly. It does not want to make converts more quickly than it can build churches to contain them. Catholicism is above all other things an *inside*, though not an inner, religion; the faithful have to be watched. In Canetti's sense, congregations are 'closed' crowds, crowds within boundaries, which sacrifice their chance of rapid growth in return for institutionalized permanence. Of course, the function of the Church's crowd crystals changes when the whole Church feels that it is threatened by an external enemy. Then priests and monks throw over their dignified restraint and become agitators, stirring up the faithful to create an 'open' crowd which can never grow quickly enough or become too large. The most spectacular examples of open crowd formation by the Church are the crusades (Canetti, 1978, pp. 154–8).

What made the crowd frightening to established religious order was the assertion of a rough, natural equality among its members, or, if not exactly equality, then an uncomfortable emphasis on the equal worth of each man's soul. This equality amounted to nothing less than the destruction of the distance which makes one man different from another, and with the removal of that distance, the destruction of hierarchy itself. When this happens, there is nothing to distinguish one man from another, and this tendency for a man to lose himself in a crowd has worried crowd theorists from Plato onwards. The process of losing oneself in a crowd is probably what makes it possible for the crowd to grow: by making everyone the same, the crowd shows that anyone can become a member by letting the same thing happen to him. This is the natural crowd (what Canetti calls the 'open' crowd),

70

which is hostile to all barriers and boundaries and whose strength is always the strength of new growth. Its potential for growth is limitless, but this is also its weakness, because the larger it becomes, the greater the danger of disintegration. It seeks to avoid disintegration by trying to grow even more quickly, but because it grows so quickly it soon falls to pieces (ibid., pp. 16–17). In the end, the crowd's equality is shown to have been fleeting and illusory; the old hierarchy re-establishes itself, men keep their distance from each other and again fear to be touched.

This is obviously a problem which all new religions have to face after the fervour of the early, heroic period of conversion has cooled. In the beginning, all religions want to grow until they include everyone, but the struggle to maintain themselves after they have become established gives them a grudging respect for adversaries. They see how difficult it is to hold their own, so they create religious institutions, a tacit admission that the early stage of rapid growth is over and the later stage of consolidation has begun. Christianity at its origins broke free from the closed crowd of Judaism; the Sermon on the Mount was preached in the open air; Pauline Christianity broke from the tribal confines of the Jews and launched itself as a universal faith. No buildings could contain the new multitudes of the faithful. The history of medieval Christianity is the history of the conversion of the Church from an open to a closed crowd. It built churches to contain the faithful, and there was a strong tendency to collect the faithful in as many separate units as possible, because there is always the danger of disintegration when too many are gathered together in one place after the original, fervent impulse towards growth had been lost.

The congregations, the Church's closed crowds, put their faith in 'repetition' as a substitute for growth; congregations do not disintegrate; they accept the fact of dispersal because they know that they will re-assemble soon. Ritual cannot, and is not meant to, isolate the individual members of a congregation completely. The mass transports the faithful into a 'mild state of crowd feeling', which is fed to them in regular doses so that in the end they cannot do without it. The Church's continuance depends on a nice calculation of the dosage once men have become dependent; any disturbance might upset this 'carefully balanced crowd economy' and lead to the moment of 'eruption' when the closed crowd becomes an open crowd. This is the moment of greatest danger for an established church. Within an established church the equality of souls is never greatly insisted upon in its closed crowds, but the eruption of the open crowd brings, if only for a time, a real equality, and all ecclesiastical authority vanishes. The obsequious flock becomes part of an open crowd of the genuinely converted, a mass equivalent of the religious and monastic orders, every man his own priest, and the Church's institutions become redundant (ibid., 16–17, 24–5).

The Church has to deal very carefully with congregations of the faithful when they burst out of their closed crowds, because its institutionalized memory of its own early history tells it that persecution was a source of strength, not weakness, but it also remembers the defections. The feeling of persecution itself is no more than the recognition of a double threat from enemies within and enemies without. A crowd is like a besieged city; its enemies are to be found hiding in cellars as well as outside the walls. This is as true of millenarian crowds as it is of established churches. The Church has its set procedures for rooting out its internal enemies, while the millenarian crowd tries to survive by reaching out to everyone and by keeping on the move. The Church must not persecute the open crowd of the millenarians too harshly, because that might strengthen it, or too quickly, but it must also not give it time to turn itself into a closed crowd with institutional structures to rival its own. The ultimate horror would be of a church outside the Church which had found ways of making itself so permanent that it could threaten to invade churches themselves, though such an invasive church would, if it was to be successful, probably have to persuade secular authority to break its ancient alliance with the established Church and ally itself with the new. This, in its turn, would presuppose a secular authority confident enough in its own powers of crowd control to be able to dispense with the crowd-controlling apparatus of the old church, at least in the period of transition. Afterwards, the secular authority could rely on the gratitude of the new established church for it to control its own closed crowds in the same way that the old church had done. A secular authority willing to ally itself with heresy would have to be something resembling the modern State, secure enough in its ability to rule its own territory and people and beginning to be jealous of rival claims to jurisdiction either from its own nobility or from the Church. The most obvious case of this is the English Reformation, where the break with Rome and the rise of the modern State went hand in hand. Reformation in general can be seen as a process in which converts to their own religion cut the ground from under the feet of the priesthood and so frighten bishops and churchmen into an alliance with the secular State often on the State's own terms.

Machiavelli Rehabilitates the Crowd

Machiavelli recognized that the most secular of medieval governments, the most State-like in the modern sense, were the governments of the city-states. Crowds, as we have seen, could cause more trouble in city-states, or in states dominated by great cities, simply because there a marginalized population existed which could become a crowd much more easily than discontented peasants in the countryside. In rural areas, which meant nearly everywhere, it required extraordinary events for crowds to gather which had any hope of lasting, and it could not have been very obvious what a crowd of the rural discontented could actually do except move on a town which could always close its gates against it. Crowds in from the country for great fairs and festivals would always have to go home again, no matter how alarming their behaviour might be while the occasion lasted. Towns were different; there a way had to be found of coping with the crowds which were always more or less a permanent feature of their existence. This was especially true of northern Italy, where city governments had survived and maintained a degree of secular and even ecclesiastical independence by playing off Guelph against Ghibelline, and where Renaissance humanism increasingly taught men to compare their governments with the republics of the ancient past. In these cities, it was again possible to conceive of a status for their people which was neither noble nor base, but public; there men could walk in the *piazza* and imagine themselves in the *agora* or the Forum, and think of their city's laws as their laws. Law itself would come to have a different meaning. It was a Paduan, Marsilius, who tilted the balance of law away from its association with the idea of a universal justice towards the idea of law as the guarantor of the peace and prosperity of a people as law-makers. So sure was Marsilius that this new assertion of the ancient idea of sovereignty would startle even those contemporaries who were likely to be sympathetic to it, that he was careful to point out (in the *Defender of Peace* (*Defensor Pacis*), 1324) that the idea of a people as legislators was not to be taken quite literally. Marsilius knew his Aristotle and his Roman history well enough to fear the unsettling effects of factions of the Few and the Many in republics. His republic was to be aristocratic, where the patricians would effectively make law and the people obey; his was to be no invitation to the demagoguery of Tribunes. But however his republic was in fact to be governed, there was no disguising the fact that a people was to make law for itself independent of all outside claims to jurisdiction, whether from emperors or popes, and that the legitimacy of that law depended on the explicit or tacit consent of the people. The peace and prosperity which the law was to secure were no doubt godly ends, but Marsilius argued that any rational man, provided he had read his Aristotle and knew his Roman history, could work out for himself, independent of papal guidance or divine revelation, what the means to those ends should be.

The re-invention of the idea of a people as law-makers, or as the source of a sovereignty which they could not permanently alienate even with their consent, revived all the ancient caveats about the unruliness of the people and their unfitness to exercise in person the sovereignty which was ultimately theirs. The old arguments against the people as crowd were available, ready-made, to add to the Church's hostility to anything violently crowd-like. By the end of the thirteenth century, most Italian cities had abandoned their republican institutions and accepted the rule of powerful *signori*, and most observers attributed the demise of those institutions to the faction-fighting between people and nobles which all the best authorities agreed were the bane of republics. Some cities, notably Florence, which prided itself on its pre-imperial foundation by Sulla's veterans, held out, and the champion of its republican liberties was Machiavelli.

The sheer intellectual weight of anti-popular argument available at the time makes the republicanism of a thinker like Machiavelli all the more remarkable, and it explains why Machiavelli has to follow the trail of the anti-crowd argument to its origins in the depths of Livy's Roman history. In his *Discourses on Livy*, Machiavelli has to create a virtuous popular past to vindicate the Roman people, and by extension any *populus*, against all its detractors, ancient and contemporary. Machiavelli is shrewd enough not to deny that the Roman *plebs* was turbulent; what he does brilliantly is to turn the turbulence of the Roman people into a source of Rome's strength, not weakness, by making that turbulence one of the countervailing forces in the Roman republic's balanced constitution. Machiavelli is careful not to romanticize the people; they can be easily led, fickle, vicious and short-sighted,[4] but he tempers this by pointing out that these are not faults which belong to the people alone; princes are no strangers to the vices of mankind, and neither are aristocracies. *The Prince* and the *Discourses on Livy* are meant to show how men's vices can be used to cancel each other out, so that only their virtues remain to serve the public good.

Machiavelli's reading of Roman history through Livy convinced him of the obvious truth that no state can *begin* as a republic. His is a mind Christian enough to want to think things through from a beginning, classical enough to imagine that all beginnings are chaotic, and realistic enough to see that if men are to move out of their original chaos they must have the good fortune to find themselves a leader. At the beginning stage, necessity does not operate; some peoples are fortunate enough to find princes and others are not. Once a people has found a prince – a Lycurgus, a Moses, or a Romulus – the rules of necessity begin to operate, and *The Prince* is a guide to those rules by showing new princes exactly what the choices open to them are, and what limits those choices. All princes want to survive and to acquire the esteem of other princes, and all princes want to found dynasties; this is a general principle of human nature as it applies to princes, and it requires no special explanation. If the new prince is to survive, there are certain things he *must* do first; only later is he confronted with alternative courses of action. A new prince trying to consolidate his position in an old state must first destroy the family of the prince he has supplanted; he must humble powerful nobles even though they have helped him to power, because he cannot hope to satisfy all the hopes they have placed in him, and he can only reward them according to their expectations by disinheriting others and so creating new enemies; much better to reward those who do not expect it, because receiving rewards from those from whom one expects injuries magnifies the gift. Having removed the obvious sources of danger, the new prince must cultivate the people by acting like a king. The prince does this by appearing to be just and liberal; he lets his agents do the dirty work, and they must do it quickly so that the people do not have the spectacle of the prince's cruelty daily before their eyes; the good he does he must do piecemeal, dragging the business out for as long as he can so that the people are always aware of the prince's goodness so that each man can live in the daily expectation of reward. At the beginning, it is probably enough for the prince not to raise their taxes, keep away from their women, and ensure that they have easy access to his person, because the people expect him to be avaricious and haughty; this is another negative reward, but it is magnified to a people who expect the worst; it costs the prince nothing and it binds the people to him. In this, the prince has no choice; either he does it or he loses his state, which no prince wants. Once he has settled himself in, the prince begins to be faced with genuine choices.

The choices now facing the prince are about how he should treat his people. He might settle for the people's sullen acquiescence in his rule; he would disarm them if they were used to arms, abolish their old laws, and take the risk of being hated by them so long as they feared him. At worst, this would turn them into a rabble, but provided there were no surviving nobles the fame of whose ancient names might serve as rallying cries for popular insurrection, the prince could probably survive. This policy, though attractive at first sight, Machiavelli thinks is short-sighted, because the prince must never forget that he has to survive in a world which contains other princes, and a rabble will be of no use to him in war. War is the trade of princes; it is in war that they acquire new states and lose old ones; those states are indeed called fortunate which have been given such advantages by nature that for them war is not a matter of necessity but of choice; Sparta, perhaps, miles from anywhere, or Venice, safe among her lagoons. A prince might try to avoid war, but this is another of those short-sighted policies that Machiavelli warns princes against; by putting war off, a prince loses the opportunity of fighting at the time and place chosen by himself; when war is forced upon him he will fight when the enemy, not he, is fully prepared, and he will fight in his own country, so that even if he wins his own lands will be devastated. If a prince must fight, and fight on his own terms, then how are those terms to be arranged?

The prince can either fight with his own arms, or with the arms of another, with a citizen militia, or with mercenaries and allies. As in all things, so in this, the example of the old Romans is to be followed. A citizen militia is by far the best; allies fight for themselves and not for you, so that what you gain by them you hold of them; mercenaries are ruinously expensive, consuming as pay in time of peace what they do not take as plunder in war; they are easy to acquire, but hard to get rid of, and the state that relies on them lives in the constant fear of a military *coup*; to pay them you have to tax your own subjects to the point of beggary, and when there are battles to fight and the pay is uncertain, they melt away. None of these objections can be made against a citizen army, but a citizen army cannot be conjured out of a sullen rabble suddenly bawling for war just because it knows its prince wants it. War fought by citizens requires training in both peace and war, in laws and in arms. The wise prince will train his subjects to become citizens; he wants them to feel that the laws are their laws, and that the city is their city. The prince must be interested in what kind of men they are, for just as there is a virtue proper to princes so there is a virtue proper to citizens. Machiavelli's reading of Roman history and his own close attendance on the great events of his own day gave him a very keen sense of how easily a people could be corrupted by tyrants, and he means by corruption what the ancients had meant. He is no admirer of Julius Caesar's, not because of what Caesar did to acquire his state, but because of how he used the state's power afterwards to corrupt the people with bread and circuses; Machiavelli's admiration is reserved for the Antonines from Nerva to Marcus, because they tried to teach the people what it was to become Roman again. Machiavelli sees the Italians of his own day as Romans without *gravitas*, a view he shares with Mussolini in his day; they need princes to teach them their ancient manners.

The cure has to be drastic where the disease is far gone. The medicine (Machiavelli is fond of the medical analogy) must be surgical, not prophylactic; republican Florence, for so long the glory of Tuscan liberties, will have to endure the ministrations of a Medici prince if that is the only way out of her present troubles. It is good fortune, not necessity, which produces the right kind of prince, but a people in chaos would be well advised to try any prince who comes their way. Trusting to fortune is not, however, as chancy as it might at first seem. Fortune, being a woman, favours the young and the brave, those who seize the day and yet know when to keep their powder dry.[5] Burckhardt taught us long ago that the Renaissance prince saw his state struggling to get out of the block of marble; the prince was its sculptor with nothing but his inner eye and the skill of his own hands to accomplish the work. Machiavelli's prince has his work cut out; he has to make his own people in the image of the old Romans, but at the same time he has to create his own legitimacy in a world where legitimacy is still thought of in the terms of traditional Christian kingship, and he has the added problem that some of his enemies will be Christian kings. (Benvenuto Cellini remarks, with his characteristic mixture of glee and awe, that most of the princes of Italy were born out of wedlock.) The princes whom Machiavelli is addressing had none of the legitimizing qualities available to kings who had inherited the kingdoms over which it was their duty to preside. Machiavellian princes had to create their own states almost from nothing, and had then to preserve them as best they could; legitimate kings had only to 'keep up their state'; Machiavelli's princes had first to create their states, and the creation of legitimacy was of the first importance if they were not to rule them by the resource-consuming means of force alone. However well the new prince acted out the role of king, every man who bent his knee before him would be saying to himself: There, but for fortune's grace, go I. Such a prince has only fortune's smile to distance himself from ordinary men. If he acts well, and if fortune continues to smile on him, he may be able to establish a kind of dramatic distance between himself and his subjects, so that they look upon his glory and bask in its rays without thinking that it might have been theirs. The prince's luck is not, after all, entirely fortuitous; successful princes are larger than life, Homeric heroes in whose fate the gods take a constant if sometimes treacherous interest, and it is that which is their substitute for the annointed legitimacy of a hereditary king; the Renaissance princes still command out of their portraits while the medieval kings, their swords sheathed, take their rest upon their tombs. It was this quality, which we now call charismatic, which led the late-nineteenth-century crowd psychologist Gustave Le Bon to call Machiavelli the greatest crowd psychologist before Le Bon himself. The princely man alone can make a crowd out of a rabble, and then make them into a people. His success becomes his people's pride, in the way that the ancient crowd took pride in the feats of its athletes and its demagogues, or in the way that the Achaeans prided themselves in the killing feats of Achilles, or in the way that a football crowd now takes pride in the feats of a striker of goals. Nowhere is Hobbes' dictum that the unity of a thing consists not in the thing represented, but in the representer, more apt.

This sense that, under the tutelage of a well-advised prince, the crowd can become a people in the image of the Roman *populus*, informs the whole of Machiavelli's republicanism. A people will recover its lost virtue if the prince has the sense to give it its own arms and its own laws; this in its turn causes a virtuous intolerance in the people, so that all dynasties eventually fall because of the fatal flaw in the hereditary principle which makes it certain that one of the prince's descendants will sire a tyrant and a loser. That is the moment at which the original prince's education of his people in virtue pays off in the people's favour; they revolt under their chiefs, expel the family of the tyrant, and then live under the leadership of a virtuous aristocracy as the Romans did after the expulsion of the Tarquins. Aristocracy too is vulnerable to the flaw of degeneracy in the hereditary principle. The sons or the grandsons of the virtuous aristocracy forget that it was their ancestors' reputation for justice which made the people call on them as leaders in the struggle against tyranny; the descendants of the aristocrats degenerate into oligarchs, caring only for wealth. The people still retain the pride which arms and laws had given them, and there begins a period of struggle between the poor and the rich; the people claim a share of the *res publica* and produce leaders of their own, the Tribunes of the People, who become magistrates with a constitutionally recognized share in the government of the republic, but that share never goes unchallenged. The people's share in government is never secure, because Machiavelli knows that at Rome, and in the Italian cities of his own day, wealth is the great rival to numbers on the road to political influence and power; his great hero, the Carthaginian Hannibal, came from the most notoriously oligarchic of the ancient cities where offices were put up for public auction, and contemporary Venice, whose constitution was a miracle of longevity, was a closely controlled merchant oligarchy.

The standard taunt against all popular republics was that the tumult of faction would eventually destroy them. The struggle of factions could take many forms and be fought under many different banners, but in the end it always boiled down to the class war between rich and poor, the few and the many. Unlike his contemporaries who were sympathetic to the republic, Machiavelli saw a source of strength, not of weakness, in the tumultuousness of republics. He believed that the only way open to the people to show that they deserved a share in government was tumultuous defence of their liberties. A people who allowed others to exercise their political rights for them, either through laziness or cowardice, was not fit to have those rights in the first place. With the insight of genius, Machiavelli saw that, far from being unconstitutional, popular tumults were what gave a republican constitution its particular animating spirit. A constitution was not something fixed; the laws have their spirit, and the letter of constitutional law can be followed long after that spirit has departed – witness the rise of the princes in Italian cities which still retained the shell of their republican constitutions. The people have only their numbers and their arms with which to assert their ancient rights; they are not a mob, as Livy thought the Roman people were in their struggle with the patricians, but a *populus*. The strength which they bring to a republic does not come only from their own sense of themselves as a people; as a class adversary worth fighting, they strengthen the rival patrician class. The people, like the patricians, have their faults, but in the struggle each side will come to see that its faults will be cancelled out by the faults and virtues of the other; the arrogance of wealth will be checked by numbers, and the arrogance of brute strength will be tempered by wisdom; each side will come to see the guarantor of its own virtue in the other, so that together they constitute a single city.

When Machiavelli's prince is seen in this way as the teacher of virtue in degenerate republics, then there is nothing very surprising that Machiavelli wrote one book, *The Prince*, about how a new prince could make himself secure in a recently acquired state, and another book, *The Discourses on Livy*, praising popular republics. Much has been made of Machiavelli's opportunism in writing *The Prince* and dedicating it to Lorenzo di Medici at the moment when the Medici returned to Florence in 1512 to extinguish the city's republican liberties for ever, but that is the judgement of hindsight. Machiavelli was thinking of the future; if only a prince could see where his own true interests lay he would see that they lay in making his people virtuous through arms and laws. Such a prince would not have to look too far into the future himself, because he might also then realize that one day a virtuous people would rebel against his corrupt descendants. That was the message of the *Discourses on Livy*, which Machiavelli was prudent enough to dedicate to someone else.

The time for popular tumults comes *after* a degenerate prince has been expelled, when the virtuous aristocracy which expelled the kings is itself in the process of becoming corrupted. Machiavelli therefore advises the new prince to rid himself of possible aristocratic centres of opposition while he is consolidating his rule because in the beginning the prince must have a free hand when the state is weak and vulnerable to foreign attack. The prince must expect trouble from the people; Romulus and Numa had troubles enough in their day, but like them, the prince's job is to discipline them into a militia which will be the terror of their neighbours. To achieve that, a prince must use every resource available; he must be cunning as well as strong; he should imitate the fox as well as the lion, and he would do well to adapt these traditional military stratagems to civilian affairs, though the distinction between the affairs of war and peace does not really apply in a state bent on war whose military force is its own citizens.[6] Only after the nobility and the people have expelled the kings do popular tumults have their place in the constitution by establishing a balance between the nobles and the people as happened at Rome after the Tarquins. This Livy could not see, so that ultimately he failed to see the most important truth of his own history. Those who blame the quarrels of the Senate and People at Rome condemn 'the very origin of liberty'. The disunion at Rome made her more powerful as well as more free; the Romans, no doubt, were marvellously favoured by good fortune, but it ought to be recognized that where good order and discipline prevail, 'good fortune rarely fails to follow in their train'. Roman virtue was the result of good examples, but good examples are the result of good laws, and good laws (Machiavelli means the constitution) at Rome sprang from those very agitations of the people which have been condemned by Livy (Machiavelli, 1950, p. 260) and by so many others after him (pp. 119–20). Machiavelli is also at pains to point out that Livy paints an altogether too rosy a picture of the patricians. The patricians, he says, hid their ambitions from the people for as long as the Tarquins lived, laying aside 'all haughtiness' and assuming popular manners, but as soon as they felt safe from the possibility of a restoration, 'they began to vent upon the people all the venom they had retained within their breasts, and lost no opportunity to outrage them in every possible way' (pp. 117–18). The people resisted them in the name of their own ambitions, and so established a free and balanced government. Machiavelli thinks that it is easy to exaggerate the bitterness of the struggle of the factions at Rome; the differences between them from the time of the Tarquins to the Gracchi 'caused but very few exiles, and cost still less in blood' (p. 119). Livy wants us to believe that there is nothing less constant than the multitude, and Machiavelli quotes him on the events at Syracuse after the death of Hieronymus: 'It is the nature of the multitude either humbly to serve or insolently to dominate.' Machiavelli replies that insolence and domination are to be expected of any man or group of men 'not controlled by laws'. Such was the conduct of the patricians after the death of the last surviving Tarquin, and such has been the conduct of princes, ancient and modern, when they have had the opportunity. Machiavelli then uses Livy against Livy to argue that the people of Rome 'neither obeyed basely nor ruled insolently' because they were a people subject to laws, a truth which Livy's own history shows, but which Livy's own prejudices against the people prevents him from seeing. Properly speaking, Livy's condemnation of the multitude must have been meant to apply to 'an unbridled multitude' such as the Syracusans, who committed all the excesses to which infuriated men abandon themselves, and not to 'a people regulated by laws, as the Romans were' (pp. 260–3; Whitfield, 1971, pp. 83–4).

Machiavelli's spirited defence of the Roman *plebs* from the charge that it had been a mob was out of tune with the republicanism of his own day when it was customary for disgruntled republicans to want to imitate the oligarchic republic of Venice. Contemporaries admired

Venice because it had mixed government in a style reminiscent of Plato's *Laws*, but it was mixed government which allowed for only a nominal popular element. The opulence of the merchant oligarchy robbed Venice of any resemblance Venetian government might have had to the republic of ancient Rome. But Machiavelli's concern for what a people with a genuine public spirit might achieve did not die. It kept cropping up, in English seventeenth-century republicanism for instance, despite the victory of the kings almost everywhere, and it is hardly an exaggeration to say that Machiavelli's re-working of the crowd material he found in Livy opened the way for the most celebrated modern theory of liberty under government in the works of Montesquieu. Machiavelli is the crowd's first real champion at the level of theory, and it is through Montesquieu and Montesquieu's influence on the foundation of the American republic that the vindicated ancient crowd makes the transition to the modern world.

Notes

1 Theatrical language has a habit of ceasing to be metaphor when used to describe the crowd. The crowd was 'at the theatre' for much of the late Roman republic and early empire; it was left to the modern world to make the crowd, in the form of the football riot, part of the show itself. The crowd of television watchers is now the crowd of spectators, watching the crowd-at-the-game, as well as the game itself, as part of the entertainment. The only important difference between the game-on-the-field and the game-on-the-terraces is that the game on the terraces *has* to be violent to be worth watching while the game on the field needs only to be ritualistically violent. In the old Roman sense, the game on the terraces is more 'real'. When a violent crowd invades the playing area, ritual gives way to the real thing; dramatic distance between players and crowd-at-the-game is abolished as the bit-part actors make their bid for stardom. What makes this kind of analysis so plausible is that it can be made without stretching the language which is ready to hand.

2 For an account of the tumults of the Orsini and the Colonna, and of the career of the Tribune Rienzi, see Gibbon, *Decline and Fall*, chs 69 and 70.

3 What I have to say about millennarian crowds is taken from N. Cohn, *The Pursuit of the Millennium* (3rd edition, 1970). I have tried to do some justice to part of Cohn's argument, but anyone remotely interested in the crowd in the middle ages cannot do without reading the whole of Cohn carefully.

4 In his *Florentine History*, Machiavelli shows how the turbulence of the people can lead to weakness in a republic which is neither fortunate nor well-ordered like the Roman. In Florence the insolence of the nobles and the licence of the people do not temper each other because neither party is solid, the nobles being divided by the ambition of rival families and the people being divided into rival factions of merchants and artisans. Florentine politics is therefore a matter of many factions, therefore unstable, while at Rome in her period of republican greatness there were only two parties, patricians and people, which had time to work on each other.

5 That is not altogether an appropriate image to put into Machiavelli's mind. He considers the question of whether it is advisable for armies to use gunpowder, and decides that, if the Romans could conquer the world without it, then there is no reason in principle why a contemporary army cannot do without it too.

6 Commentators eager to find Machiavelli's *Prince* shocking have always seen as particularly shocking the famous passage in Chapter 18 where Machiavelli urges the new prince to imitate the lion and the fox. There is in fact nothing very remarkable about that advice; its origin, though this is a matter of some dispute, is probably Plutarch's *Life of Lysander*, where Lysander tries to temper the traditional bone-headedness of Spartan generalship of his colleague Callicratidas by remarking that 'where the lion's skin will not reach, you must patch it out with the fox's' (Plutarch, *Lives*, ed. Clough, II, p. 120). Similarly, when it is said of Antoninus Pius in the *Augustan History* (ed. Birley, p. 105), that he allowed the children of officials convicted of malpractice to inherit their fathers' wealth, praise is being given to that emperor's extraordinary nobility and clemency. When Machiavelli says that the sons of destroyed enemies must be allowed to inherit to keep them quiet, the advice is devilish.

3

The Crowd and Liberty: Machiavelli, Montesquieu and America

It is scarcely an exaggeration to say that Machiavelli's re-working of the crowd material in Livy opened the way for the most celebrated theory of liberty under government in the works of Montesquieu, and it has never been seriously doubted that Montesquieu was one of the most important intellectual influences on the writing of the Constitution of the United States, though the precise nature of that influence has often been disputed. There has been a tendency to see Montesquieu as the theorist of a very orderly liberty, a liberty under law, where law means that any man may do what the law does not specifically forbid, and where law also shades into law-and-order: a man will be protected by law-enforcing agencies while he does what the law allows him to do. In this view of the matter, Montesquieu is seen as emphasizing above all the security which the law provides for actions not contrary to law; under law, men know where they are, and so can plot the course of their future conduct to avoid known legal obstacles and arrive safely at their own self-chosen destinations. This view of Montesquieu fits well with the 'government of laws, not men' which the Constitution of the United States was designed to provide. The Constitution's declaration that it was the fundamental law of the land so that any ordinary law which contradicted it was not law at all, and the doctrines of separation of powers and checks and balances which put strict procedural constraints on the business of law-making, make up a recipe for a polity which was going to be law-bound in all its essentials.

No doubt this 'orderly' Montesquieu exists, even if there seems to be a shade too much of J. S. Mill about him, but Montesquieu's own sympathetic reading of Machiavelli on the Roman crowd points to another, much less orderly, Montesquieu, who admires the turbulence of the people as a safeguard for liberty and as a means of periodically returning corrupted popular governments to the purity of their republican first principles. The connection between Livy, Machiavelli and Montesquieu on the crowd is worth spelling out because it raises questions about what Montesquieu actually thought preserves liberty in republics, and it certainly raises questions about how this other, 'turbulent', Montesquieu came to be lost from view. What is argued below is that in America, around the time the Constitution was being written, some sleight of hand was going on with Montesquieu's name; that the orderly Montesquieu was being cried up and the turbulent Montesquieu was being played down. This was done for a purpose. Montesquieu, for all the celebrated talk in *The Spirit of the Laws* about the separation of powers, may in fact have believed that what preserved liberty and good government was the check of the threat of popular turbulence on *mixed* government. It may be that the Founding Fathers, and almost certainly Hamilton, Jay and Madison who wrote *The Federalist Papers*, thought that they were founding a *mixed* government from which they wished to exclude the possibility of popular tumults. Popular insurrection had been justified in the period of the revolutionary struggle with Britain but was to be out of place under the new government where the substitute for popular insurrection was to be the widespread and orderly exercise of political rights. The new government under the Constitution was to develop into a version of Whig oligarchy whose stability was to be provided by an alliance of wealth and government on the English pattern. In this scheme of things, popular turbulence would be at best a nuisance, and at worst it might unfasten the links between wealth and government by a return to republican first principles. So the new Constitution, in *The Federalist Papers'* gloss on it, carefully excluded any hint about the legitimacy of popular clamours. The *Papers* invited Americans to see the Constitution as a safeguard against popular insurrection and to see the threat of popular insurrection as a threat to the bonds between wealth and government upon which the future political and economic prosperity of the Republic was to depend. This view of the people as a turbulent crowd goes back beyond Montesquieu, and even back beyond Montesquieu's own source, Machiavelli, to Livy.

Montesquieu takes Machiavelli's line on the Roman crowd in his *Considerations of the Causes of the Greatness of the Romans and their Decline*, which he wrote under Machiavelli's influence.[1] 'While Rome conquered the world,' he writes, 'a secret war was going on within its walls.' When royal authority passed undiminished into the hands of the Consuls after the expulsion of the kings, 'the people felt they lacked the liberty they were being asked to love'. The patricians gave way to popular demands, because at Rome poverty was public virtue, and opened certain magistracies to the people; the Senate feared that the Tribunate would produce a demagogic tyrant, but that did not happen, and Rome had wise and balanced government (*Considerations*, ed. Lowenthal, pp. 83–4). The plebeians pressed their claims so successfully that by the time of Gracchi the ancient distinction between plebs and patricians had become almost meaningless now that all could receive offices and honours. From then on the only distinction that mattered at Rome was the distinction between rich and poor. With the decline of the old morality, wealth became the means to political power, so the nobles could resist the people with confidence and even with arrogance, as when they went outside the law to murder the Gracchi and their friends, but in the best period of the Republic Roman government had been wholly admirable because abuses of power could be checked within and by the Constitution, 'whether by means of the spirit of the people, the strength of the Senate or the authority of certain magistrates' (ibid., p. 85). Being 'constantly subject to agitation' is the hallmark of a free government, and the Republic was able to last for so long because it was able to correct itself 'by its own laws' (pp. 85–7). 'Popular tumults' are bound to agitate free governments, 'for warriors who were so proud, so audacious, so terrible abroad could not be very moderate at home'. The condition of a tranquil republic would be no better than the 'concord of Asiatic despotism', whose peace disguises 'real dissension'; Asiatic despotisms are quiet only because some oppress others without resistance, and 'if we see any union there, it is not citizens who are united but dead bodies buried one next to another'; the genius of republics produces harmony between opposites, 'as dissonances in music co-operate in producing overall concord' (pp. 93–4).

It is obvious from the closeness with which Montesquieu follows Machiavelli in his account of the dissensions between Senate and People at Rome that one of the principles of Montesquieu's theory of liberty is already there in Machiavelli's own commentary on Livy. Of course it is possible that Montesquieu came to his own conclusions about the connection between the public spirit of a people and liberty, and about the desirability of balancing wealth with numbers, through his own reading of Livy, and only later found it confirmed in Machiavelli's *Discourses*, but this seems unlikely. It is much more likely that Montesquieu used Livy as the source for his chapter on 'The Dissensions that always Existed in the City' because Machiavelli had already used Livy for his own account. Montesquieu does not in fact use Livy much as a source except when discussing the internal war between the patricians and the people. Livy is certainly no favourite of Montesquieu's. He typically only uses him in the *Considerations* as a source for factual detail and minor embellishments, preferring Dionysius of Halicarnassus for the legendary period of Rome's history and the more 'philosophic' Polybius for the period of the war with Hannibal (Mason, 1971, p. 128). Livy alone of the ancient historians

comes in for some fairly tart criticism (e.g. for his woodenness in failing
to imitate Homer who made those 'enormous colossus of antiquity'
come alive (*Considerations*, p. 55), yet Livy is almost his only source for
the chapter where Montesquieu draws the same conclusions about the
connections between virtue, turbulence and liberty which Machiavelli
had already drawn in the *Discourses*. It seems very likely indeed that
Montesquieu read his Livy through Machiavelli's eyes, and that Livy's
crowd, its significance altered, lives on in one of the principles of
Montesquieu's theory of liberty.

Machiavelli may even have had a hand in the most celebrated
principle of Montesquieu's theory of liberty, the idea of the separation
of powers. The conventional view is that Montesquieu derived the
doctrine of the separation of powers from Bolingbroke and from his
own rather myopic observations of English government, expressing
it in language which derives ultimately from Locke (Shackleton,
1949, *passim*; 1961, pp. 286–7, 298–9), but a remark at the end of
the chapter 'On the Dissensions that always Existed in the City' in
the *Considerations* about English liberty shows that Montesquieu was
thinking about English liberty and Machiavelli's critique of Livy at
the same time, and we also know that it was in England during his
visit of 1729–31 that he had his conversation with Arbuthnot about the
republicanism of Machiavelli while he was working on the *Considerations* and preparing to write the *Spirit of the Laws* (for the chronology,
see Shackleton, 1961, p. 405). At the end of that chapter, Montesquieu
praises the part that the English parliament plays in the preservation
of English liberty. In contrast to ancient Carthage and Athens, and to
the modern city republics of Italy (he is probably thinking of Genoa
and Venice), England is fortunate to have a body which 'continually
examines' English government and 'continually examines itself'; as a
consequence, the errors of English government never last long, and
they are useful 'for the spirit of watchfulness they give the nation'
(*Considerations*, pp. 87–8). What Montesquieu is plainly pointing to here
is parliamentary opposition to the executive which typically clothed
itself in the rhetoric of the separation of powers; all opposition in
Walpole's England lived the dream of excluding the placemen as a
way of stopping the management of the legislature through executive
patronage; only a separation as to persons and powers, as far as was
compatible with government by a ministry responsible to the House of
Commons, between executive and legislature would restore the purity
of parliament and preserve liberty. The ministry's case was always
based on the plea for mixed government; English government was
a partnership between king, lords and commons, whose sharing of
power in a sovereign legislature meant that government itself was a
co-operative enterprise in which everyone, either direct or through

their representatives, had their say. In comparing England with less fortunate states, Montesquieu is thinking of the oppositionist platform and the 'popular agitations' against Walpole which it was occasionally able to raise. It might be that part of what turned Montesquieu's mind towards the separation of powers idea was his reading of Machiavelli on Livy's crowd, with the people jealous of their liberties urging their representatives in parliament as Tribunes to oppose the corrupting arrogance of the Walpole oligarchy and through it to curb royal power itself.

When Montesquieu came to write *The Spirit of the Laws* with its famous statement of the doctrine of the separation of powers in Chapter 9, Book 6, the connection between Machiavelli's critique of Livy and English liberty, was still going through Montesquieu's mind, because shortly after the separation of powers chapter (ch. 6) there follows (chs 12–14) a recapitulation of the account in the *Considerations* of the foundation of Roman liberty after the expulsion of the kings, again using Livy, a source he does not often use in *The Spirit of the Laws* either. If this direct line of descent from Livy's crowd to Montesquieu's *Spirit of the Laws* holds good, then it has profound implications for any view one might care to take of the foundation of the American Republic and of its Constitution. The definitive eighteenth-century commentary on the Constitution, *The Federalist Papers*, makes it clear that one of the chief things that the Constitution has to recommend it is that it will make internal tumults of the people in the individual states easier to deal with. With the recent example of Shays's Rebellion in Massachusetts in mind, Hamilton points to the inadequacy of the old arrangements under the Articles of Confederation for dealing with attempts to usurp the authority of state constitutions by 'malcontents', who, if they were to find a Caesar or a Cromwell for their leader, might establish a 'despotism' which would threaten the liberties of neighbouring states while the 'national government could legally do nothing more than behold its encroachments with indignation and regret' because under the Articles each state retained the right to settle its own affairs within its own borders (*Federalist Papers*, Hamilton *et al.*, XXI, p. 99). A new national militia, commanded by the President, its discipline regulated by the future act of a prudent Congress and its officers appointed by the individual states, would be able to nip such domestic insurrections in the bud (ibid., XXIX, pp. 139–40). This looks very like a repudiation of Montesquieu's principle that 'popular agitations' are necessary to preserve the liberties of free republics, yet Montesquieu's name is banded about pretty freely in the *Papers* in the name of the liberty guaranteed by the separation of powers (e.g. ibid., IX, pp. 38–41; and the whole of XLVII, pp. 245–51), and the separation of powers doctrine is itself recommended on the grounds that the most democratic part of the legislative, the House of Representatives, will have its wings clipped. Madison regards it as an axiom that 'power is of an encroaching nature' and, no doubt with the traditional Whig doctrine of the supremacy of the legislature in mind, he observes that 'The legislative department is everywhere extending the sphere of its activity, and drawing all power into its impetuous vortex'. The experience of the Revolution has had an unfortunate effect on the way Americans have come to see the dangers to their liberties, for it has led them to concentrate their attention on the threat posed by kings and has diverted their eyes from the dangers threatened by popular assemblies (ibid., XLVIII, pp. 251-3). This is true both at the national level and at the level of individual state legislatures. It begins to look as if one of Montesquieu's principles of liberty, the separation of powers, is being used against another of his principles, the necessity of 'popular agitations' in a free republic. Yet Madison claims (ibid., XXXIX, pp. 190-2) that the Constitution conforms to what are generally agreed to be republican principles. Something odd is happening here; perhaps Patrick Henry was right to 'smell a rat', and we are certainly entitled to ask again what kind of republic it was that the Founding Fathers thought they were constructing which could exclude the 'popular agitations' which Machiavelli and Montesquieu both thought were essential to a republic's strength and liberty; it might be that the Founding Fathers were going, albeit unconsciously, back beyond Machiavelli and Montesquieu to a view of the people as mob which has more in common with Livy's view of it, thereby unravelling the republican reading of the early history of Rome.

The question of what kind of republic the Founding Fathers thought they were founding can best be approached on two levels, on the level of theory and on the level of their own revolutionary experience, though of course the two are closely connected.

On the level of theory, *The Federalist Papers*[2] make much of the fact that they are recommending a constitution for a large republic. They cite Montesquieu with relief on the unsuitability of direct democracy in large republics (IX, pp. 38–9), and they cite him twice with glee on the advantage in a confederate republic that, should a 'popular insurrection' take place in one of the states, the others are able to quell it (ibid., IX, p. 39, XLIII, pp. 223–4), but this tells much less than the whole story of Montesquieu's own view of what constitutes a republic, what constitutes liberty, and the place of popular tumults in both. The Founding Fathers conveniently forgot what Montesquieu had to say about the beneficent effects of popular tumults in the preservation of the liberties of that republic with monarchical forms, England.

There can be no doubt that Montesquieu admired the degree of liberty enjoyed by Englishmen in their republic 'disguised' under the form of monarchy (*Spirit of the Laws*, V, p. 19), but when one begins to ask what Montesquieu's explanation of the basis of that liberty was, then all certainty ceases. It is not clear, for instance, in what sense he regarded England as a republic; it does not fit with his classification of republics of the ancient type as being either aristocratic or democratic, Roman or Spartan, because these were small; the Roman example does not fit because the Roman republic had no king and was animated by a spirit of 'equality and frugality' while England has a hereditary king and is commercial and opulent; Rome and Sparta had mixed government, even balanced government, and Montesquieu sometimes talks as if England had mixed and balanced government, but the problem is that the idea of mixed and balanced government, and the idea of the separation of powers, which Montesquieu also says the English have, do not quite fit together (Vile, 1969, pp. 83–5), though they are not as far apart as Shackleton would have us believe (Shackleton, 1961, pp. 298–9).

The question centres upon the problem of sovereignty. The theory of mixed government frankly acknowledges the existence of sovereignty and worries about how sovereignty is exercised; the theory of mixed government also carries with it a straightforward sociology: society is divided into three estates, king, lords and commons, each with a legitimate claim to a share in the exercise of sovereignty. Mixed government solves the problem of the exercise of sovereignty by giving each estate a share in it, and provides the institutional arrangements which make this possible, which just happen to be the English king-in-parliament. The emphasis is on co-operation and interdependence of the parts in legislation, and in the provision of the money which makes government possible. Who actually exercises the various functions of government is of lesser importance; there is no reason in principle why the executive, legislative and judicial functions of government should be separate as to persons and as to powers, and there are good reasons in practice why they should overlap, because anything that ties the parts together makes the sharing of government that much easier. Plainly, this scheme has much to recommend it as a description of English government in Montesquieu's day, and in fact the mixed-government thesis was always how the ministry defended itself (see above, p. 86–7).

Separation of powers is different. In principle at least, it has nothing to do with class; it holds that liberty can only be secured 'by dividing political authority (which being divisible cannot be sovereign) into its three constituent functions, who will exercise their powers separately and without collusion' (Shackleton, 1961, p. 299). The mixed-government theory has a good deal to say about good and lasting government, but not necessarily anything to say about liberty; the separation-of-powers theory has everything to say about liberty but has nothing necessarily to say about effective government, and as Montesquieu himself hints, the parts may be 'naturally' in repose, which might mean that there was no government at all. This is the system which Montesquieu thinks is provided for in England 'by their laws', though he allows himself to doubt whether it exists in practice, which in its pure form we and James Madison can see (*Federalist Papers*, XLVII, p. 246) it did not. Perhaps it would be best to conclude with Vile (1969, loc. cit.) that Montesquieu's importation into French of the term 'constitution' without a qualifying adjective as a neologism (instead of *la constitution du gouvernement* or *la constitution de l'Etat*) (Shackleton, 1961, p. 284) might be meant to tell us that.

But what will not do is to think that Montesquieu could not tell the difference between the theory of mixed government and the theory of the separation of powers; his reading of Bolingbroke and his observation of the party battles in England would have been enough to tell him that (and we know that the part of *The Spirit of the Laws* which deals with the separation of powers in the English Constitution was probably the first part of the work to be written, being complete by 1734, soon after his return from England, though the whole work was not published until twelve years later (Shackleton, 1961, p. 151)).

The one thing that is certain about these two theories of government is that the theory of mixed government is the older. It is the account of government given by Machiavelli of the Roman Republic, and by Montesquieu; it is the account of English government given by the standard authorities since the beginning of the sixteenth century; Charles I argued it against parliament, and it survived, by then very old, into Blackstone's *Commentaries* to be ridiculed definitively by Bentham in the *Fragment on Government* (1776). The theory of the separation of powers, on the other hand, had the stamp of modernity on it, especially in its indifference in principle to class. Its classless character made it particularly attractive during the Interregnum, when the abolition of the monarchy and the House of Lords put the theory of mixed government, temporarily as it turned out, into abeyance. In England, the Restoration of 1688 succeeded in reconciling the idea of the supremacy of the legislative branch of government both with the idea of the separation of powers and with the idea of mixed government. What the supremacy of the legislative meant was that everybody, the king included, was subject to the law. In Locke's version, the legislature – of which the king is a part – must be superior simply because what 'can give Laws to another, must needs be superior to him' (*Second Treatise*, XIII, para. 150, cit. Vile, 1969, p. 63). This trivially verbal assertion of the supremacy of the legislative having been made, Locke can go on to say that in fact the king can reasonably be said to be supreme in another, more real sense, because being part of the legislative and also undisputed head of the executive, he is simply more powerful, or at least more important, than anyone else. This is especially true not only because his power of veto means that he cannot have laws forced upon him, but also because the executive has the 'federative power' – the power of the sword of war – to defend the nation, and a residual power in the prerogative of all power to act in emergencies for which the law 'can by no means provide'; in emergencies the executive must act, and act quickly, in a way that no other branch of government can, for the public good 'without the prescription of the law, and sometimes even against it' (ibid., XIV, para. 160, cit. Vile, 1969, p. 65). That this is a partial separation of powers in Madison's sense is obvious; equally obvious is the fact that, as it was meant to, it left mixed government intact; king, lords and commons were still there, as they were meant to be, except that now kings were not to act outside the law.

All this Montesquieu could no doubt accept, but it still does not explain English liberty. What, for instance, was to prevent king, lords and commons, each with a due regard for the rights of the others, and with the co-operation each with the others in the true spirit of mixed government, making and executing law which threatened the liberty of the citizens of England, those liberties which Montesquieu so admired?

If we are to believe Dickinson (*Liberty and Property*, 1977), not very much, if the idea of liberty is to be extended beyond the mere defence of property right. Self-congratulation for the bloodlessness of the Glorious Revolution set in very early, but part of the self-congratulation was also reserved for the speed with which the crisis of vacant sovereignty was resolved. James II threw the Great Seal of England into the Thames, but Englishmen found that Hobbes was not true, and that when the sovereign left the realm it did not return to a State of Nature. But Hobbesian attitudes did not die, and a horror of the people as a levelling mob continued to haunt those with memories long enough to remember the experiments with democratic government after 1649. To 'most men of substance democracy was simply mob rule' (Dickinson, 1977, p. 17); most of them would have agreed with the Tory divine Francis Atterbury that 'the voice of the people is the voice of hell, leading to idolatry, rebellion, murder, and all the wickedness the devil can suggest . . . nothing but fire from heaven can stop the cry, nothing but sulphurous flames can quell the voice of the people' (cit. Dickinson, 1977, p. 45). No doubt this is less than generous to the militia, but Dickinson argues that it explains why the Tories stuck to Divine Right before the Revolution and why many were so quickly reconciled to the Revolution afterwards. The 'willingness of men of substance to put their liberties at the mercy of an absolute king can only be explained by their horror of the "mob" and their fear of social revolution' (ibid., p. 16); after 1688 they simply transferred their loyalty from kings to the sovereign legislature of which the king was a part (ibid., p. 47). The Whig argument in defence of 1688 was only marginally more favourable to the mass of the people whom the speed of the Revolution had deliberately excluded. Very few of the Whigs mentioned Locke and his idea that the origin of government was in a contract which the king had broken; they preferred to talk the language of ancient rights and liberties because these could be defended without having to refer to any notions of equality of rights or to an ultimately popular sovereignty which, however attenuated Locke wants them to be in practice, are certainly to be found in the *Second Treatise* (ibid., pp. 76–7). Rather, like Burke in his *Reflections* on another revolution, the Whigs stressed that resistance to government was justified only in cases of dire necessity; it certainly was not justified to make routine improvements in the Constitution; 'many Whigs suggested that resistance should only be offered by the nobility and gentry, and not by the people at large', or would have agreed with James Tyrrell when he said that 'I by no means allow the rabble or mob of any nation to take arms against a civil government, but only the whole community of the people of all degrees and orders, commanded by the nobility and gentry thereof' (ibid., p. 78). A supreme legislature, a balanced constitution, and a king with considerable powers reconciled nearly all the Whigs and most Tories to an ideology of order. Now that things had been settled in England, the party battle should be fought within a constitutional settlement with which nobody now had good reason to quarrel. It was the beginning of that mysterious constitutional fetishism which was to last almost indefinitely in England. One of the most important effects of 1688 was that popular tumults were even less justified than before. As Swift pointed out in his *Discourse of the Contests and Dissension between the Nobles and Commons in Athens and Rome* (1701), those for whom the constitutional settlement was made should moderate their dissensions among themselves and concentrate on the real job at hand, which was to display 'a steady constant resolution . . . never to give way so far to popular clamours, as to make the least breach in the constitution' (cit. Vile, 1969, pp. 67–8).

Swift's injunction to the political nation to defend the constitutional settlement against the people as mob was to find more than an echo in *The Federalist Papers*, which were themselves intended to explain and recommend a constitutional settlement which would make government more effective against popular agitations and also rob those popular agitations of their justification, but what the English defence of 1688, and the Federalist defence of the American Constitution both leave out of account, is Montesquieu's consistent claim that, whatever else helps to preserve liberty in republics, agitations of the people are *essential*. That is Montesquieu's view of England in the *Persian Letters* (1721) ('England, where liberty continually emerges from the flames of discord and sedition; a nation impatient, but wise even in its distemper' (Letter

136)), of Rome and England in the *Considerations* (see above p. 87), and of England again in *The Spirit of the Laws* where the preservation of English liberty through 'a certain impatience of temper' is famously connected to the foulness of the English weather; the English nation is 'so distempered by the climate as to have a disrelish of everything, nay even of life' (the English disease is suicide); this 'impatience of temper' is not very considerable 'of itself', nor is it to be confused with levity, which makes people undertake or drop a project 'without cause'; when it is allied to the courage which is a characteristic of all northern peoples, it becomes a formidable force for liberty. England is indeed fortunate that its government is such that 'they cannot lay their uneasiness to any single person's charge'; it is only because English government is 'under the direction rather of the laws than of the prince' that enables England to have government at all. 'This temper in a free nation is extremely proper for disconcerting the projects of tyranny', and a note adds 'Here I take this word for the design of subverting the established power, and especially that of democracy; this is the signification in which it was understood by the Greeks and the Romans' (*The Spirit of the Laws*, XIV, p. 13). Montesquieu seems to think that agitations of the people are necessary to the preservation of liberty no matter whether the nation concerned has mixed government, or the separation of powers, nor, one might add, could it possibly matter if the nation concerned has a partial separation of powers with checks and balances, like America. Popular tumults are useful for the preservation of liberty in all governments with any tinge of republicanism to them.

This seems a reasonable conclusion, if only for the very simple and very general reason that Montesquieu is interested in both the institutional arrangements and the spirit of a people as bases for the preservation of liberty, and it seems only sensible that each should, in the right circumstances, support and be supported by the other. This makes the case for the American Constitution, as expressed in *The Federalist Papers*, even stranger, because on the one hand Montesquieu's authority is eagerly canvassed for the partial separation of powers, and on the other hand, the Constitution is recommended to the state ratifying conventions for the specific reason, plainly hostile to Montesquieu, that the government which the new Constitution will make possible will be able to deal effectively with popular tumults like Shays's Rebellion. One part of Montesquieu's theory of liberty in republics is being used against the other, institutional arrangements are being recommended as an antidote to the spirit of a people. But Montesquieu had taught the whole eighteenth century that laws (that is, forms of government) which were not supported by the appropriate spirit of a people were doomed. Montesquieu followed Machiavelli, the seventeenth-century English republicans, and Bolingbroke in believing that any form of government that was incapable or returning to its first principles from time to time was bound to change, by degrees, into a different form of government (Shackleton, 1961, pp. 268–9; *The Spirit of the Laws*, VIII, p. 12). Such a return to original principles in a republic could only come about if the spirit of the people remained uncorrupted, and the only form it could take would be insurrection or the threat of insurrection. By 1787, when the American Constitution was written, speculation in America about the nature of the 'American character', and about the laws which that character demanded and could sustain, were already far advanced (for example, see, Crèvecoeur, 'What is an American?', in *Letters from an American Farmer*, where very early on the miraculous change which America produces in a man's character is already being celebrated; by degrees he begins 'to forget his former servitude . . . to become a free man, invested with lands, to which every municipal blessing [that is, political rights] is annexed' (*Letters*, pp. 82–3)), and all the accounts of the American Revolution stress that great strides towards an idea of republican equality were made during the revolutionary period, and most of the accounts argue that these strides were what made the period revolutionary. Madison accepts this in *Federalist* XXXIX, where he sets out to show that the new Constitution conforms to republican principles, because 'It is evident that no other form would be reconcilable with the genius of the people of America [and] with the fundamental principles of the Revolution' (ibid., p. 190). Madison recognizes that in making their Revolution, the Americans have done something so remarkable that the corrupt republics of recent experience can offer nothing like a precedent for judging whether the purer American Constitution conforms to the best republican principles. Nothing except a return to the basic principles of republicanism will do to decide the matter. (In fact, Madison's definition of republicanism is either very generalized or very negative; it is *essential* that a republican government is 'derived for the great body of society' and not from an inconsiderable proportion, or a favoured class of it'; it is *sufficient* that 'the persons administering it be appointed, either directly or indirectly, by the people' (p. 191, italics in original); beyond that, he is content to point to the 'absolute prohibition of titles of nobility' (p. 192), and to show how the principles on which the Constitution is based are similar to the principles on which various state constitutions are based (p. 192); there is no gloss at all on what the 'genius of the people of America' might be.) Yet for all this show of returning to the basic principles of republicanism, *The Federalist Papers* make it clear that the new Constitution is designed to prevent a return to republican origins once the Constitution's new government is established, both in general – there is to be an end to tumults of the people, or if they occur, they are to be dealt with quickly before they have time to spread – and in particular – there is to be no institutionalized means by which the people are going to be able to correct their government if it strays from constitutional propriety, and they are going to have no direct say in the fundamental question of alterations to the Constitution.

In *Papers* XLIX–LI Madison tries to demonstrate why it is that to subject the workings of government to constant institutionalized popular scrutiny is to extend an open invitation to the mob. In answer to Jefferson's proposal in the projected Constitution for Virginia (appended to the *Notes on Virginia*) that breaches of the Virginia Constitution should be corrected by a convention of the people, Madison goes to Plato, of all places, for his counter-arguments. To call on the people frequently to judge their government would weaken all respect for government itself; the 'reason of man, like man himself, is timid and cautious when left alone, and acquires firmness and confidence in proportion to the number with which it is associated'; men need to be convinced by ancient precedent and numerous associates in the rightness of their own opinion respecting government. This is no doubt a melancholy truth: 'in a nation of philosophers' it might be disregarded. A reverence for the laws would be sufficiently inculcated by the voice of enlightened reason. But a nation of philosophers is 'as little to be expected as the race of philosophical kings wished for by Plato'. In every other nation the most 'rational' government will not find it 'a superfluous advantage' to have 'the prejudices of the community' on its side (p. 258). Not only are most men incapable of judging matters relating to the constitutional propriety of government but, when gathered together in a convention to judge these matters, they would turn into a mob. 'The *passions* . . . not the *reason* of the public would sit in judgement. But it is the reason, alone, of the public that ought to control and regulate the government. The passions ought to be controlled and regulated by the government' (p. 260). Referring questions of constitutional propriety periodically to popular conventions had already been tried in Pennsylvania, where the Council of Censors met in 1783 and 1784 to enquire whether the constitution had been violated (p. 261); the Council immediately split into two violently contending factions. 'In all questions, however unimportant in themselves, or unconnected with each other, the same names stand invariably contrasted in the opposite columns'; two crowds confronted each other, in rival unanimity: 'Every unbiased observer may infer . . . that, unfortunately, *passion*, not *reason*, must have presided over their decisions. When men exercise their reason coolly and freely on a variety of distinct questions, they inevitably fall into different opinions on some of them. When they are governed by a common passion, their opinions, if they are to be so called, will be the same' (262). We have to wait till Madison describes the 'anarchy' in the state of Rhode Island to find out that what really worries him about returning republican government periodically to the judgement of the people is the danger of a majority faction which would make rights, by which he means property rights, insecure (p. 267). But why should we not say that the unanimity of a majority faction is the 'spirit of a people', or even 'virtue', in the sense that Machiavelli, the English republicans, Bolingbroke and Montesquieu had always understood it? Madison obviously thinks that there is something *there*, that it is unruly, and that it has to be put down.

The Constitution was intended to produce a government (in the ordinary sense of 'a system of government') which could never return to its supposedly republican origins, partly because the Constitution would not let it (no constitutional amendments to be referred to popular conventions, arrangements for election to and composition of the legislature, etc.), and partly because this return to origins was to be made doubly difficult because in the future American government was intended to develop in a particular direction – towards a Whig oligarchy – and the Constitution was supposed to make this easier. In this sense, the Constitution is not to be regarded, with Montesquieu, as the act of a virtuous and free people giving itself laws, but as a definite exercise in *social* engineering as a way to securing a very definite political end, political stability, by allying the moneyed class in America to the new federal government in a way that is entirely analogous to the binding of mercantile wealth to the Revolution Settlement in England after 1688. The Founding Fathers were not just writing a Constitution at Philadelphia in 1787; they also had a very good idea of what kind of *political system* they hoped the new Constitution would make possible; they did not go to Philadelphia just to talk about the separation of powers, but to talk about power; they wrote a Constitution which would be hard to alter, but they had a very shrewd idea of how the power relations within the political system would develop. This binding of wealth and government could only be embarrassed, if not actually threatened, by periodical returns to ideas of republican virtue and popular clamour. They were Whigs in a sense that Burke would easily recognize when he said that all talk about the *origins* of government was bad for the future of established government.

That is probably as far as the matter can be taken on the level of theory. What now has to be explained is what the Founding Fathers were afraid of in all this republican talk about a return to origins, and in particular, it has to be asked what kind of unruliness it was that made the new Constitution necessary. Historians are still arguing about what kind of revolution happened in America after 1776; that there was a political revolution nobody doubts, but there seems to be considerable doubt about whether there was a social revolution on anything like the scale of the French Revolution. America got rid of its Loyalists and their estates were sold up partly to pay for the war with England, but this can hardly be compared to what happened to the French aristocracy after 1789 because these estates went to men whose class position was not very different from those whom they were expropriating; everything depended on which side one chose to be on after 1776 when it was by no means obvious which side was going to win. Besides, any revolution which began as a tax-revolt of merchants and landowners could not be expected to be radical in a sense that would become increasingly familiar in Europe after the French Revolution. Hence the tendency of historians to describe the American Revolution as being in important ways backward-looking, Whiggish, even conservative. Two things make that view of the early history of the American Republic especially plausible: first, the fact that the American rebels had no central government to take over in 1776; if there was a centre of American government in the eighteenth century it was London, where the special concerns of individual colonies were pursued by their agents lobbying parliament and the Privy Council. The Continental Congress which met at Philadelphia in 1774 and which was to declare independence, was, from the point of view of later revolutions, a very odd gathering because if there was to be war with England, the Congress would first have to create a government, or to become one, and this it eventually did through the Articles of Confederation, under which America fought the War of Independence and governed herself until the new Constitution was ratified in 1789. The first impulse of the American revolution was, in this sense, governmental. (And it is remarkable that it succeeded; the Frankfurt Parliament of 1848 failed because it failed to do for the German states what the Americans did at Philadelphia for the thirteen colonies.) The American revolution was always going to be a revolution of order. The second thing that points up the orderliness of the American revolution is the ease with which the Americans were able to obtain the help of the greatest of monarchies of the *ancien régime*, France. Of course, France was pursuing a traditional policy, on the basis of which anyone anywhere making trouble for the English ought to be encouraged and helped, but even so the ringing Declaration of the Rights of Man that came from Jefferson's pen only thirteen years before the French Revolution does not seem to have disturbed the French monarchy, or have hampered Jefferson himself when he became American minister at Paris. Whatever the perceptions of the French of Jefferson were, he was not regarded as the dangerous radical he appeared to be to some of the federalists at the time of Shays's Rebellion and the making of the American Constitution ten years later.

At the same time, there was a considerable degree of popular partici-pation in the American revolution right from the beginning particularly in the New England seaboard towns, and above all in Boston, which made most of the running in the dispute with England up to 1776. If there was an incipient radicalism in the American revolution, we would expect to find it in the Boston Sons of Liberty mob manipulated by Sam Adams. Brogan remarks that the 'crowd in the American Revolution badly needs a historian', by which he means that the traditional picture of a 'uniquely discriminating, moderate, politically motivated mob, led or manipulated by, if not consisting entirely of the middle or even the upper classes (one hears repeatedly of workmen's clothes and blackened faces serving as ineffective disguises), has been discredited, but as yet no complete substitute has been provided' (Brogan, 1985, p. 128). The closely controlled Boston mob, whose famous Tea Party was a triumph of logistical planning, undoubtedly existed, and we have a marvellous account of it in J.C. Miller's *Sam Adams: Pioneer of Propaganda* (1936). What more recent historiography has brought to light is a rather different crowd, which does not share the 'monolithic ideology' of the Patriots whose crowds were 'conservative, often extra-legal, but not anti-institutional, except against foreign (British) institutions, and seldom embodied class or any other form of intra-mural conflict'; this *other* crowd was violent, anti-institutional and class-conscious; it did not enjoy the tolerated, extra-legal status of the Patriot crowd; it alarmed the governing elites who always put them down vigorously where they could. The classic cases of this crowd are Shays's Rebellion in 1787 and the Whiskey Rebellion of 1794 (Slaughter, pp. 1–6).[3] Slaughter's detailed examination of the recent historiography leads him to distinguish between 'consensual' and 'non-consensual' crowds, and he concludes that in the 1780s and 1790s even the tolerated crowd was becoming a thing of the past as the political elite developed an increasing intolerance 'for all kinds of crowds', including 'basically pro-institutional mobs' (ibid., p. 18).

Brogan and Slaughter concur in the opinion that no generalization about the crowd in early American politics will fit all the cases, but Slaughter suggests that around the time when the Constitution was being written the governing elite itself was beginning to abandon its own distinction between crowds which could be tolerated and crowds which could not. *Any* crowd was a danger. Why? The reason is that in America crowd politics old-style, a style that was common both to England and the American colonies, was beginning to give way to a new style of crowd politics, but a style which was not yet the politics of the revolutionary crowd of the French Revolution. Shays's Rebellion, which so alarmed the Founding Fathers and the authors of *The Federalist Papers*, was the work of a very ancient kind of crowd, mainly rural, making the age-old demands of farmers who have returned from wars for 'land and freedom' and attacking the age-old enemies of farmers: lawyers, tax collectors and landlords (Slaughter, p.

23). It takes no stretch of the imagination to see in the demands made by the Shaysites a recapitulation of the whole theme of Livy's Roman history where the plebeians always demanded abolition of their debts and an agrarian law when they came home victorious from Rome's wars with their arms still in their hands. Shays's veterans of the War of Independence were replaying the drama of the agrarian republic and casting the federalists in the role of patricians as viewed by Livy. This is certainly how Jefferson saw it when he made what are usually taken to be some rather intemperate remarks from Paris about 'the tree of liberty' being 'refreshed from time to time with the blood of martyrs. It is its natural manure' (*Papers*, Vol. XIII, p. 357). Jefferson saw Shays's Rebellion as one of those salutary reminders to governments that the people are not sheep. The curse of all monarchies, except England, and of 'most of the other republics', is that they are governments of 'wolves over sheep'; in England 'to a slight degree, and in our states in a great one' the will of everyone 'has a just influence', so that there the mass of mankind 'enjoys a precious degree of liberty and happiness'; this brings with it necessary 'evils', 'the principal of which is the turbulence to which it is subject', but this is as nothing compared with 'the oppressions of monarchy'. And this turbulence, evil though it is, 'is productive of good. It prevents the degeneracy of government, and nourishes a general attention to public affairs.' Jefferson does not see popular insurrection as the curse of republican government alone: in England they happen every half-dozen years, in France there has been one every year for the last three years and in Turkey they happen every day. There is more than a hint in what Jefferson has to say about Shays's Rebellion that republican America has let its republican origins down by the infrequency of its insurrections: 'Calculate that one rebellion in 13 states in the course of 11 years, is but one for each state in a century and a half. No country should be without one for so long' (*Papers*, Vol. XI, pp. 22–3). There is room for beginning to wonder how far America has deserted its origins when even Turkey does better for rebellions. Jefferson's mind was plainly running on Roman parallels ('The people are the only censors of their governors') and he makes it clear that censorship means giving government very sharp reminders of 'the true principles of their institutions'. Once the people has become indifferent to these principles, 'you [he is writing to Colonel Carrington] and I, and Congress, and Assemblies, judges and governors shall become wolves'. He ends with an injunction straight out of Machiavelli and Montesquieu: 'Cherish therefore the spirit of our people' (*Papers*, Vol. XI, pp. 48–9).

Jefferson's view of Shays's Rebellion is the view of a man who is worried about the way government in the United States is going, and that partly accounts for his obvious attempts to play Shays's Rebellion

down. (Shays had 9,000 men under arms at one time, a number comparable to the armies which fought the War of Independence. The number
of the Whiskey Rebels in 1794 is put at around 7,000 and the number of
militia sent by the (by then) President, Washington, to put them down,
at 12,000, a number almost certainly larger than any army on either side
in the War of Independence.) Jefferson's other motive for playing the
rebellion down is that he plainly thinks that the rebellion was being
played up for the benefit of the Founding Fathers at Philadelphia. In his
letters from Paris Jefferson is careful to point out that the rebellion has
not made much of a stir in Europe, certainly nothing like enough of a
stir to make Europeans begin to doubt whether America is capable of
governing herself under her new republican institutions. To Jefferson,
it seems that all the rather loose talk about anarchy is coming from
the American side of the Atlantic. Even in England, where there is
more reason to gloat over the ungovernability of the ex-rebels than
elsewhere, the Ministry has had to hire hacks to convince the English
that America is in anarchy; the ministers have come to believe their
own propaganda, 'and what is more wonderful, we have believed it
ourselves'. This 'anarchy' exists only in Massachusetts, and he doubts
whether history can produce another instance 'of a rebellion so honour-
ably conducted'. Patrick Henry had smelt a rat about the Constitutional
Convention at Philadelphia; Jefferson's reaction was ornithological: he
suspected that the blowing-up out of all proportion of the 'anarchy'
in America caused by Shays's Rebellion was a deliberate attempt to
persuade the Convention into 'setting up a kite to keep the hen yard
in order' (*Papers*, Vol. 12, 356–7). The kite is presidential power under
the new Constitution, especially presidential control of the new militia,
and that was the power which was to put down the Whiskey Rebels in
1794. Jefferson sees Shays's Rebellion as one of the necessary returns
to first principles whose institutional form he had originally sketched
out in his draft constitution for Virginia which Madison attacks in *The
Federalist Papers* (see above, pp. 95–6). Shays's Rebellion is no doubt il-
legal, and the loss of life is unfortunate, but what worries Jefferson is that
any republican government which closes down extra-legal manifestations of the spirit of the people must be turning into a government whose
form is republican but whose spirit is not, and this was happening at
the very time when he suspected that the Founding Fathers were writing
a Constitution under whose government returns to the first principles
of republicanism would be put altogether out of the question.

America's republican plebs was to live out a short, unhappy life
between 1787 and 1794, but it did get a theory for itself in Jeffersonian
republicanism, a counter-theory in *The Federalist Papers*, and a kind of
obituary in the Constitution of the United States. By contrast, it was
easy to see the permitted, Patriot crowd of the American revolution

as just another eighteenth-century mob out to make a name for itself. The mob, Wilkite, Patriot, or Gordon-rioting, did not *need* a theory because every one recognized that it was part of the accepted pattern of opposition. This is not to say that the eighteenth-century mob could not be frightening; it could always 'get out of hand', as it did in the case of the Gordon Riots, and where there is fear there is also the search for precedents (Gibbon saw in them a recrudescence of Puritan fanaticism (see below, p. 113)), but they singularly failed as crowds to produce anything like their own theory. Their admirers simply chose to see in them the embodiment of something they admired and their enemies saw embodied in them something they detested, but the thing they saw did not come out of the mob itself. The case of the Boston Patriot crowd is instructive. It was controlled by opposition politicians like Adams and Otis to keep the pot boiling for a cause; this was recognized by its Tory opponents – however much Governor Bernard might fulminate against them as 'rabble' and 'scum', he knew perfectly well that Sam Adams was at the back of it. In Miller's view, the mistake the Tories made was to assume that, as with other eighteenth-century mobs, the authorities would eventually put the Boston mob down when it began to go too far (Miller, 1936, p. 113). The Boston mob demonstrated; it manifested itself; any occasion (like school holidays; but there was no rioting on Sundays in Puritan Boston) and any issue (like 'No Popery') would do. Miller remarks shrewdly that Sam Adams showed his real power in Boston as much by being able to turn the mob off as by being able to turn it on. Royal government was government by his permission, so that when Adams made his famous declaration on 18 March, 1768: 'No mobs – no confusions – no tumults', the Governor and the Customs Commissioners were probably just as frightened by the absence of riot as they had been by the 'tar-and-feather' mobs. It was this proof that Adams ruled Boston that finally induced the royal government to quit, which in its turn led to the garrisoning of Boston by the British (Miller, 1936, p. 140). When the British occupied Boston without a shot being fired, Sam Adams bided his time, then took to organizing against the British the same kinds of demonstrations he had already organized against the king's governor, while assiduously spreading horror stories about the licentious soldiery all over Puritan Massachusetts. At the same time, Sam's cronies dominated the Massachusetts House of Representatives as surely as his caucus had dominated the old Boston town meeting. It was one of Sam Adams's mobs (cousin John Adams said it was a 'motley rabble', not fit to be called a 'mob') which British troops fired on in what came to be called the Boston Massacre, and another which invited the British to the Boston Tea Party (ibid., pp. 163–82). What Sam Adams did was to use the mob, like the caucus, as a political base to defend the Massachusetts Charter against the royal prerogative. His was a typically

Whiggish defence of corporate rights like Wilkes's defence of the rights of freeholders of Middlesex and the Charter of the City of London, using the only forms of democratic politics available.

The Boston Patriot mob was a version of the mob as fourth estate which was a part of English politics in the eighteenth century. Henry Fielding remarked in 1752 how strange it was that writers on the English Constitution should take notice of only three estates of the realm, King, Lords and Commons, 'all entirely passing by in silence [he might have made an exception for Montesquieu] that very large and powerful body which form the fourth estate in this community, and have been long dignified by the name of The Mob' (cit. De Castro, 1926, p. 249). Swift had earlier taken issue with the neologism 'mob' itself (a contraction of 'mobile'), preferring the truth-telling of the ancient name 'rabble' (Beloff, 1938, p. 9) and Defoe, in his *Hymn to the Mob*, was still keen to conflate the rabble and the mob: 'The Reason and End, for which all Government was at first appointed was to prevent disorder and Confusion among the People; that is, in few words to prevent Mobs and Rabbles in the World' (cit. Beloff, 1938, p. 129), but by the middle of the century the term 'mob' had acquired a special meaning which was by no means straightforwardly abusive. As early as Queen Anne's reign, a mob which had the temerity to attack queen and parliament (though only figuratively) called forth the rebuke from one pamphleteer: 'You a Mobb! You are the Scum and Dregs' (cit. Beloff, 1938, p. 51). (The spelling of Mobb perhaps shows that the writer, or his printer, was using language which was still experimental.) If you could insult the mob by calling it the 'scum and dregs', as John Adams was to do again later in Boston, then there were recognized limits to what the mob could properly do, and the fact that there was a language of invective available for use against the mob shows that just to call a mob a mob did not exhaust the vocabulary of contempt. Beloff (1938, pp. 50–1) agrees with Montesquieu that free-born Englishmen were expected to, and expected to be able to, riot when the occasion suited, and it was recognized that in England riot posed particular legal and even constitutional problems. Beloff's chapter in *Public Order and Popular Disturbances, 1660–1714* on 'The Machinery of the State' is remarkable for being unable to discover any machinery to speak of, certainly nothing to shake the conviction of foreign observers that by eighteenth-century standards England was badly policed. There were practically no professional officials and no professional soldiers; parish constables, the Justices and the militia were all amateurs in a country where everybody was supposed to be an upholder of the Law (and where the mob was even institutionalized as the *posse comitatus* and authorized as the 'hue and cry') and where a standing army was thought of as the first step towards the establishment of a Jacobite tyranny modelled on France.

The Duke of Newcastle got it exactly right when he said that when the mob exceeded its permitted limits 'We must be either governed by a mad, lawless Mob or the peace be preserved only by a Military Force (that is, a standing army); both of which are unknown to our Constitution' (cit. Rudé, 1962, p. 55). When Lord Shelburne suggested to the House of Lords during the Gordon Riots that England might do well to copy the professional police of France he shocked most members present, even though he was careful to say that he was not blind to its dangers (Hibbert, 1958, p. 54). Reading the Riot Act (1714) as a prelude to ordering the militia to fire on the mob was all that eighteenth-century government in England had in the way of community policing.

Mobs could always 'get out of hand', but even to use such a phrase is to presuppose that the mob was always raised by politicians with causes to promote who used the crowd as one of their power bases. No doubt in England, as in revolutionary America, the 'other' crowd existed too. By the 'other' crowd I mean something like what has come to be called the 'revolutionary crowd' with aims and leaders of its own, and which was not a part of ordinary politics, making its orchestrated voice heard on some of the items on the political agenda of the day. Perhaps that is the possibility that contemporaries meant to refer to when they acknowledged that popular tumults had their place, but a limited place. By referring to a permitted crowd I wish to make no judgement about what all eighteenth-century crowds were actually like. (For what it is worth, I think that Edward Thompson is probably right that the English working class was made in the 1790s, and that they had a class-conscious ideology based in part on Tom Paine's *Rights of Man* (Thompson, 1968, *passim*); apart from anything else, Burke's *Reflections* would not seem to make much sense if what Thompson says about the 1790s isn't true. Burke has a great and justified reputation as a predictor of events in France, and even in Europe as a whole; why should he not have been right about England too?) I merely wish to insist that the crowd that Sam Adams led in Boston was very like the permitted crowd in England; Wilkes was just as much a hero in Boston as he was in London. I also want to insist on the essentially Whiggish, back-ward-looking nature of the Boston Sons of Liberty, backward-looking in the sense that there was at least three-quarters of a century's worth of English precedent for what they did, and backward-looking in the sense that they were raised and led to defend established incorporated rights against the royal prerogative. Neither the Adams crowd nor the Wilkes crowd was in any sense revolutionary. Of course Sam Adams seemed im-possibly demagogic to the aristocratic planters of Virginia, even though they too became rebels in the same cause, just as Wilkes seemed impos-sibly demagogic to Dr Johnson (though the remark that Johnson would rather dine with Jack Ketch than Jack Wilkes is an invention of Boswell's);

Wilkes was eventually reconciled both to George III and to Johnson, and almost the last glimpse we have of Wilkes is of him as a Buckinghamshire Militiaman (he had been MP for Aylesbury) shooting rioters while defending the Bank of England during the Gordon Riots (and if his *Diary* is to be believed, he killed two of them) (De Castro, 1926, p. 142); 'mobbish' Sam Adams, the 'Jacobin' Governor of Massachusetts, the 'baleful demagogue', reacted to Shays's Rebellion in a way that the old Wilkes would have understood. Adams failed to understand how men could be freer when the struggle with George III for the sanctity of the Massachusetts Charter was over and now that all Americans lived under laws that they had established themselves: 'the man who dares to rebel against the laws of a republic ought to suffer death' (Miller, 1936, pp. 373–4).

Death was precisely what could not be dealt out to the Shays Rebels because there was no national force to deal it, but the federal militia provided for in the new Constitution of the United States existed by 1794 to deal it out to the Whiskey Rebels (not to many of them, as it happened, because most of the Whiskey Boys had the good sense to fade away at the approach of federal troops). There is a notable irony in the fact that it was not a standing army that put down the Whiskey Rebellion, but that most republican of institutions, a citizen militia. A militia had been recognized as a litmus test of republicanism at least since the Renaissance; Machiavelli had tried to get the Florentines to establish their republic on the sure footing of a militia of its citizens, and when that militia failed, the republican liberties of the city were lost for ever; fear of a standing army and faith in a virtuous and godly people in arms was at the centre of English republicanism in the seventeenth century, and that fear of a standing army remained part of Whiggery for as long as Whiggery lasted; Montesquieu knew the value of citizen armies to the preservation of Roman republican liberty through the tumults of a people who could not be docile at home after they had been terrible and victorious abroad. Pocock has traced the connection between the idea of republican liberty and the idea of a militia all the way from Renaissance Florence to the American colonies on the eve of the Revolution. Standing armies were seen to be partly the agents, and partly the cause of, the corruption of a civic and patriot ideal which stressed active citizenship and which saw any institution which took the business of war and government out of the hands of citizens as destructive of republican virtue (Pocock, 1975, p. 507). During the War of Independence American patriots saw themselves as freemen in arms fighting corruption's standing army (ibid., p. 513). Pocock calls this (and much more besides) America's 'Machiavellian moment', a re-enactment of part of a republican tradition which goes back to Florentine civic humanism. What Pocock does not emphasize nearly enough is the importance which Machiavelli and Montesquieu attached to the necessity of popular tumults as a way of getting back beyond the corruptions of republics by returning them to the invigorating springs of their popular origins. Just as the Founding Fathers used one part of Montesquieu against another, so the Constitution, in its provision for a militia, enabled the federal government to use one part of Machiavelli against another. Pocock speaks of a Machiavellian moment, but he should more properly have spoken of two, because when the federal militia met the Whiskey Rebels, one part of Machiavellianism, the militia, met another, the popular tumult. Machiavelli himself thought that he was bound for Hell after his death, where he hoped to enjoy the conversation of Plato and Aristotle; little did he know that his shade was to meet his ghost in the valleys of western Pennsylvania in 1794.

The Constitution of the United States was intended to be the founding charter of a Hamiltonian oligarchy, not a Jeffersonian republic of yeoman farmers. Commerce and opulence, not virtue and frugality, were to be its watchwords. Recent scholarship (e.g. Wills, 1978) has begun to cast doubt on the pervasiveness of the influence of Locke on the mind of America on the eve of the Revolution as argued by Carl Becker (1922) and Louis Hartz (1955), yet it seems to me that the Hamiltonian vision of tying wealth to government through a Bank of the United States, which would create a class of fund-holding creditors who would be directly interested in upholding the government of the Republic, is impeccably Lockian. If Locke's *Second Treatise* teaches us anything, it is that any government which alienates wealth cannot survive long; the history of America's own revolution teaches the same lesson, and that lesson was taught in reverse by the history of English public finance in the first half of the eighteenth century, when the genius of Walpole discovered the simple truth that taxing wealth causes trouble but borrowing from wealth on the security of stable government gives lenders a vested interest in keeping government stable. It is hard to see how the leaders of a revolution which began as a revolt of taxpayers could come to anything but Hamiltonian conclusions, unless they were to settle for the frugality of Jeffersonian democracy. Of course, writing a Constitution is not the same thing as creating an oligarchy, but it can be the basis for the public credit without which no oligarchy can hope to prosper (in this sense I follow Charles Beard). Again, of course a Constitution does more than establish public credit; it also becomes a battleground, providing both the institutional setting and the rhetoric for political battles to be fought out. Jeffersonian republicanism did not lose the moment the Constitution was ratified. Nor was the Whiskey Rebellion the end of American unruliness; far from it, but it was almost the end of that particular form of popular tumult. Shays's Rebellion and the Whiskey Rebellion were both rebellions of the frontier when the frontier was very near the Eastern cities, rural crowds in a society which lacked feudal controls on popular disturbance and therefore a threat to the towns from which government came; that is one of the things that made them different from the city mob of the eighteenth century. It was Jefferson himself who banished the rural mob to the wilderness when he bought Louisiana from the French in 1803, but he banished it theoretically as well by providing the basis for unlimited economic opportunity, so that in America the moral claims of poverty could always be put down by the counter-charges of shiftlessness and failure to seize opportunities which were there for everybody.

The permitted crowd was supposed to disappear at the same time, partly because under the new Constitution, and under the new state constitutions, there were enough political rights to go round; mob-bishness had been justified during a revolution in which desperate times required desperate measures and when one of the reasons for that revolution was that the British were denying Americans their political rights. But now that everyone, or everyone that mattered, had political rights, the time for the mob was over. The Constitution-makers were still afraid of the mob, and the federalism of Constitution can be seen as a way of making sure that if the mob was going to make itself felt in politics in the future, it would be banished to the individual states. Of course, the mob has always operated in the individual states (everything that happens in America which does not happen in Washington DC happens 'in the individual states' because there is nowhere else for it *to* happen). One of the things that made the mob uncongenial to constitutional sensibilities in the eighteenth century was its tendency to mob representative assemblies. The mob had to mob something, and it was natural that it should mob those assemblies where a semblance of democracy was decently cultivated; in that sense, mobbing was a substitute for the regular exercise of democratic rights. Sam Adams was the master at making sure that representatives did inside assemblies what the mob outside wanted them to do, and he did this twice, once in Boston, and again at Philadelphia in 1776, when the mob outside the Pennsylvania legislature had the double job of persuading the Pennsylvanians, who were sitting upstairs, to indicate that they were in favour of declaring independence to encourage the members of the Continental Congress, who were sitting downstairs, to declare independence, and vice versa (Miller, 1936, p. 342). The permitted crowd was supposed to be an adjunct to politics, but it was not supposed to call the tune. What horrified contemporaries about the Gordon Riots in 1780 was that Lord George Gordon gave the mob a running commentary on the debate on the petition inside the Commons chamber by addressing them through an open window from the chamber itself ('Lord North calls you a mob!'; 'The Member

106

for Bristol is now speaking. He is no friend to your petition' (Hibbert, 1958, pp. 43ff.)).

For the Founding Fathers, mobbishness was the most direct manifestation of the direct democracy which the representative principle was meant to blunt. The mob was meant to seem very far away, and the movement of the federal capital away from the scene of Sam Adams's triumphs in Philadelphia (at the time the largest city in America) to Washington DC (which wasn't even a town yet, let alone a city) must have made the mob seem even further away. That only left the state legislatures to be mobbed, but that possibility was taken care of by the Constitution, which, in Article IV, Section 4, commands the federal government to protect each state against 'domestic Violence' (this was the Section under which the Whiskey Rebellion was put down) at the request preferably of the state legislature, but at the state governor's request 'when the Legislature cannot be convened', that is, if the mob so interrupts the legislature's business that the state governor begins to panic.

What the Founding Fathers could not predict, perhaps the one thing which they got spectacularly wrong, was the democratic development of the presidency. Jefferson read their minds correctly when he described the presidency as a kite to keep the hen-yard in order. The president was expected to preside over the government of the United States, not to be its vital spring; he was to be its chief executive, but an executive in the seventeenth-century sense of one who executes laws which are the will of another, and not in the modern sense of the active manager of an enterprise who makes its day-to-day decisions and plans for its future. The president was meant to be above the hurly-burly of politics, especially of party politics, perhaps not a politician at all in the ordinary sense; he was meant to be like George Washington, who sat in Independence Hall in Philadelphia in the summer of 1787 while the Founding Fathers tailor-made a presidential office specially to suit him. During the War of Independence, it had been the Continental army, and Washington at the head of it, which had been the centre and symbol of national unity, and the presidency of the Constitution was designed to be the centre and symbol of national unity in the hoped-for years of domestic peace that lay ahead.

What the Founding Fathers had not counted on was that such a high and glittering office would become the prize of party, and that it would be the prize that would make national parties possible. The office of the presidency drove a coach-and-four through Madison's 10th Federalist because, being the only great national office, it was worth founding national parties to capture it. Madison's version of America as a republic so large, and with such diversity of local interests, that national factions would be impossible, began to look shaky by Washington's second term as president. (One might add that the Constitution itself was the single great document, dispute about whose meaning was capable of providing the ideological divide between national parties.) The presidency could not be kept long from the people in a country where there was widespread, if patchy, enjoyment of democratic rights, and something like a meeting between presidency and people happened in Jacksonian democracy. By 1828, the choice of presidential electors was in the hands of a mass electorate in every state in the Union except South Carolina, and so presidential elections became recognizably modern. This was not to everyone's taste; the incumbent John Quincy Adams remained true to the old Federalist view of party as faction, and faction as mob and refused to go looking for popular votes; besides, Jackson was from the West, at least in the popular imagination, where unruliness was supposed to wait for decent statehood before it showed its face in the nation's capital; yet when Jackson was elected he brought a triumphant mob with him to his inauguration; it took over the White House, tucked in to the food and drink provided for the gentlefolks, and could only be induced to leave when someone had the idea of putting out tubs of punch on the White House lawns. Daniel Webster spoke for an earlier generation of America's leaders when he exclaimed: 'I never saw such a crowd here before. Some have come five hundred miles to see General Jackson' (cit. Brogan, 1985, p. 280). That crowd, some of whom had come five hundred miles to see General Jackson, negated the physical and political distance the Founding Fathers had so carefully put between the president and the crowd.

Notes

1 Shackleton, 1961, p. 269: 'The train of thought which led to the formation of the doctrine of the principles of government [the spirit of the laws] seems to have started with Montesquieu's reading of Machiavelli.' See also Mason, 1971, 134, where she argues, citing Levi-Malvano, 1912, ch. iv, that Montesquieu's source for the connection between 'the spirit of a people' and the constitution of its government 'is almost certainly Machiavelli's *Discorsi*'. Shackleton in fact distinguishes between two periods of Machiavelli's influence on Montesquieu: an early period, up to about 1716, which led to the *Politique des Romains dans la religion*, and a later period, dating from his travels in England, 1729–31, which led to the *Considerations* (p. 269). It was while Montesquieu was engaged in this second, 'more thorough study' of Machiavelli that he learned from the Tory wit Arbuthnot (the inventor of John Bull, a spirit of the laws if ever there was one (*Dictionary of National Biography*, I (p. 535)) that 'the great republican Machiavelli had only spoken of princes as Samuel had spoken of kings, without approving of them' (Shackleton, 1961, p. 142). In

The Spirit of the Laws, 6, v, Montesquieu calls Machiavelli 'this great man', whose judgement, albeit with qualifications, he is prepared to accept.

2 I am only too aware that to assume that Hamilton, Jay and Madison speak for all of the delegates at the Constitutional Convention at Philadelphia in 1787 is to walk into a minefield of learned controversy; I just assume they do, but if they don't, then my arguments apply only to them. Part of my reason for assuming this is that the expression 'Founding Fathers' has entered the language, which the expression 'the authors of *The Federalist Papers*' can never hope to do.

3 For what I have to say about the other, non-Patriot, crowd in America in the revolutionary period, I rely heavily on the long, meticulous and extremely useful (but as yet involuntarily unpublished) historiographical essay 'Mobs and Crowds, Riots and Brawls: The History of Early American Political Violence', by Professor Thomas P. Slaughter of Rutgers. References are to pages in Slaughter's typescript.

4

Some Historians on the Crowd before and after the French Revolution: Gibbon, Carlyle, Michelet and Taine

The great crowd scenes of the French Revolution made the crowd a force to be reckoned with both in political theory and political practice. After the Revolution, it was no longer possible to see the crowd, as Gibbon did, as an occasional nuisance, on which contempt could be poured from the heights of Augustan detachment while the State, if it stood firm, could be relied on to deal with it. Gibbon's own account of the Nika Riots in the fourth volume of the *Decline and Fall* can be seen as a reflection of an enlightened, aristocratic view of the Gordon Riots which occurred when he was preparing to write his account of the reign of Justinian. That was just nine years before the fall of the Bastille. A similar equanimity was not to be possible in the nineteenth-century historians who were to write accounts of the crowd in the French Revolution. For Carlyle, the revolutionary crowd is the vehicle of World-History, and he is careful to keep it free from as much of the guilt as he can for the horrors of the Revolution. Sansculottism is predestined to destroy the hollow shell of French society and bring a sense of reality into French life. The crowd is bound, in the end, to be defeated because it cannot produce a Great Man, and will not accept the leadership of a Hero, but it does pave the way for the next best thing, our last Great Man, the flawed Hero, Napoleon. Michelet's view of the revolutionary crowd is less metaphysical. His crowd is the whole people, with the Rights of Man written on their hearts, storming the Bastille for all mankind. His crowd is less abstract, showing that real, living men can make their own history. The revolutionary crowd is the people, the people is the revolutionary crowd, and Rousseau is their hero. It was this view of the Revolution that Taine set out to destroy, and, by implication, to destroy what he took to be all the illusions which

110

had allowed the Revolution to happen. These illusions continue to feed democratic and socialist ideas and practice in contemporary France, and in contemporary Europe, and Michelet's view of what happened in 1789 is the greatest illusion of them all. Taine begins at the beginning, thinking that if he can show that the Revolution was an outburst of primal barbarism, people will come to their senses and reject all the political and social doctrines which either prepared the way for the Revolution or which rely for their plausibility on the view of the Revolution presented by Michelet and his kind. In the process of showing Frenchmen what their grandfathers were like, Taine develops at least the outlines of a genuine theory of the crowd as a psychopathology of politics, and out of that psychopathology of politics he developed an eclectic theory of history. Unlike Michelet, who had a theory of history before he began to write the history of the Revolution, Taine developed a theory of history out of his account of the Revolution, the centrepiece of which was his analysis of revolutionary crowds.

An Enlightened Account of the Crowd: Gibbon on the Nika Riots of 532 and the Gordon Riots of 1780

Gibbon was preparing to write his admirably succinct account of the Nika Riots (*Decline and Fall*, IV, pp. 160–7) in the aftermath of the Gordon Riots (Swain, 1966, p. 137; Craddock, 1972, p. 314) and he tailored his account of the Nika to point a moral about Gordon. To do this he has to omit Procopius' suggestion that the Nika was led by people in high places so he can show that the riots were simply the product of Eastern religious fanaticism and faction. Gibbon can then pretend that all mobs are really *canaille*, that upper-class involvement is merely incidental, and that the only proper attitude to the crowd is enlightened patrician contempt.

   Gibbon's account of the Nika Riots can be brief because his treatment of the early Eastern Empire has already prepared us for the riots, or for something very like them. The Eastern Empire has had to cope with the fanatical zeal of the Christians in the same way that the old Empire had to cope with the fanaticism of the Jews. Gibbon the anti-semite feels he can say things about the Jews which he cannot quite bring himself to say about the Christians. That 'race of fanatics whose dire and credulous superstition seemed to render them the implacable enemies not only of the Roman government, but of mankind' (*DF*, II, p. 3) is Gibbon's model for the Christians in the Eastern Empire with the difference that theological controversy has divided them into factions, orthodox and heretic, so that they disturb the peace of the

111

Empire even though Christianity has become its official religion. The emperors themselves are not blameless. The rival religious factions have colonized the circus, dividing the audience into orthodox and heretic, Blues and Greens, and in the reign of Justinian the Blues have come to enjoy a certain imperial patronage which made them 'insolent with royal favour' (*DF*, IV, pp. 161–2). In the Nika Riots, the ordinary faction game is played right up to the moment, left unexplained by Procopius and by Gibbon, when the factions unite and the real trouble begins. Gibbon is oddly silent on how that could be.

The obvious answer is that the mob found leaders or a leader. That answer was certainly available to Gibbon. One of the things he says made Christianity dangerous in the Empire was the success of famous preachers who are to the Empire's Christians what the demagogues were to Athens and Rome, and some remarks about demagogic preachers keeping the fanaticism of the factions going is just the kind of thing one would expect of Gibbon, but he does not even suggest this though he is bitter elsewhere about the insolence of preachers even daring to invade the 'ears of monarchs' with the 'harsh sound of popular eloquence' (*DF*, II, p. 256). The other possibility, also available to Gibbon, is that the mob found leaders from the senatorial class. Two of the standard ancient accounts of Nika, those of Procopius and Marcellinus, mention senatorial involvement in the riots (Bury, 1897, p. 93). Procopius refers to a meeting of those senators who had not fled to the palace, and he makes it clear that the mob had at least some degree of senatorial leadership. Some senators urged the mob to attack the palace and seize the emperor, but instead the mob was persuaded by another senator, Origines, who obviously knew his Justinian but not his Theodora, to let Justinian flee and his authority would simply melt away. Origines tried to persuade the mob to set up a proper headquarters and to play a waiting game, but the mob, 'as a mob is accustomed to do', wanted some kind of immediate action and made straight for the hippodrome to crown the rival emperor Hypatius (Procopius, ed. Dewing, I, p. 231). None of this is mentioned by Gibbon, though he generally prefers Procopius to any other Byzantine source. Instead, Gibbon prefers to follow John Malalas (and Theophanes and Zonoras who themselves follow Malalas (Bury, 1897, pp. 93, 101)) who, like Gibbon, but unlike Procopius and Marcellinus, only mentions 'eighteen illustres and senators' being executed as accomplices of the mob, not as its leaders. Gibbon seems intent on excluding the counterpart of Lord George Gordon and his friends from his account of the Nika.

That this is a deliberate omission is made much more likely because Gibbon's letters of the period, while they show Gibbon as much concerned with the gout as with Gordon, contain the same general explanation of the Gordon Riots as he offers of the Nika Riots in the

Decline and Fall. Religious fanaticism of an anti-Catholic kind is at the root of Gordon: 'forty-thousand Puritans, such as they might be in the time of Cromwell have started out of their graves, the tumult has been dreadful . . . that scum which has boiled up to the surface of this huge cauldron [of the city of London] . . . the month of June, 1780 will ever by marked by a dark and diabolical fanaticism' (*Letters*, ed. Newton, II, pp. 243–4). Some of the points of detail which Gordon picks out of the ancient sources for the Nika have their parallels in Gordon: the mob may have friends in high places; the prisons are opened; high authority connives in the rioting in its early stages before the mob gets out of hand. Even the lucky chance of the presence of the veterans of the Illyrian and Persian wars who eventually put down the Nika insurrection have their counterparts in London in the 15,000 regulars who will 'do the trick' (ibid., II, p. 243). Gibbon's refusal to acknowledge the possibility that the 'eighteen illustres and senators' might have played a significant part in leading the Nika rioters is plainly meant to avoid awkward questions being raised again about the connection between the Gordon rioters and parliament. Of course Gibbon knew what these connections were. Gordon was an MP and so was Gibbon. Gibbon was reluctant to concede that the Gordon mob was not mere *canaille* (he wrote somewhat disingenuously to his mother that 'every Gentleman' in London was turning out to put the riots down (ibid., II, p. 243)); that would have spoiled his own enlightened view of religious mob fanaticism as proper only to the unphilosophic lower orders of mankind who could believe so unthinkingly and so literally in the truths of their religion that they felt they had to do something collectively and immediately about it. We can now see why Gibbon introduces those 'eighteen illustres and senators' at all. They appear only to be executed as a not very veiled hint about what would be the proper treatment for other would-be Gordons.

It may even be that an earlier mob, whose effects Gibbon felt by ancestral proxy, lies at the back of his account of the Nika. Gibbon was Boswellian about nobility, and in the *Autobiography* he is proud of being able to trace his descent from the Lord Say who is killed by the mob in Act 4 Scene 7 of Shakespeare's *Henry VI, Part 2* after having been arraigned by Jack Cade on the grounds that he had erected a grammar school, caused 'printing to be used', built a paper-mill, knew the difference between a noun and a verb and, most damning of all, could speak Latin. Perhaps Say's descendant, committed if any man ever was to a correct Latin style and to the publishing of books, saw the Gordon Riots as a repetition of Jack Cade's rebellion and felt the noose tightening round his neck.

The Nika Riots, like the Gordon Riots, came and went. The mob in Gibbon's account of it does not threaten anything very seriously, though there is a hint of revolution in the mention of Cromwell's time. The Nika did not threaten the Empire. The most that could have happened was that one emperor could have been changed for another. The mob was regrettable, but there had been mobs before, and Justinian did not even try to abolish the factions which were the mob's nucleus and inspiration. Gibbon's account of the Nika ends with the laconic observation that the mob continued to cause trouble in the future, a sure sign that he means us to consider it a slightly abnormal aspect of normality and certainly not as a revolutionary crowd.

A Pre-psychological Account of the Leaderless Crowd: Carlyle on the French Revolution

Carlyle's view of European history since Luther as the Spirit of Reformation working its way through European Society and politics enables him to treat the French revolutionary crowd on a similarly abstract level. The French Revolution, after Luther and Cromwell, 'is properly the third and final act of Protestantism' (Carlyle, 1888, p. 363), the attack in France against old popery and hollow aristocratic and monarchical pretension, the victory willed by God, of 'disimprisoned Anarchy' over 'worn-out Authority'. Sansculottism is therefore 'transcendental', not to be explained by experience, almost without precedent, a miracle sent to expose and destroy the lie in French society which is not 'real'. French society consists of 'Phantasms of realities'; some men are 'partly real and human', but most are 'buckram masks' (CFR, I, pp. 170–1). The Sansculottic crowd is a preternatural force which cannot be explained in ordinary historical and psychological terms. Insurrection, Voltaire had said, is the only invention of the French, and the French are undoubtedly better at forming crowds than anyone else, especially crowds capable of acting with a single purpose. 'That talent, were there no other . . . distinguishes . . . the French People from all Peoples, ancient and modern', and its typical expression in quiet times is the French genius for forming queues (Belloc appears to be right when he says (CFR, I, p. xv) that Carlyle was unacquainted with the French character), but beyond these few remarks the crowd cannot be explained. Our interest in the mob is understandable enough in an age which has no comparable spectacle now that war has become 'wearisome', devoid of 'individuality and spontaneity', not worth watching half so much as the battles of Homer's day when the armies were 'fighting mobs'. Beyond that explanation cannot go. Mobs are like 'the inflammablest immeasureable Fire-work, generating, consuming itself. With what phases, to what extent, with what results it will burn off, Philosophy and Perspicacity conjecture in vain' (CFR, I, pp. 201–2). Yet the Sansculottic mob is 'the crowning Phenomenon of our Modern Time' (*CRF*, I, p. 171).

This disembodied, abstract quality of Sansculottism is preserved by Carlyle's emphasis on the anonimity of the crowd. The crowd consists of 'unknown Tatterdemalion Figures' or 'Brigands, or whatever they may be' in the Réveillon riots (*CFR*, I, pp. 104, 105); when the Estates General meet, the Third Estate is lifeless, waiting for the mob's force to gather round it (*CFR*, I, p. 125); everything else is inertia. The Clergy and the Noblesse are both internally divided. The only action comes from the duc de Broglie who begins to move troops into Paris (*CFR*, I, pp. 125–6); we hear of starvation, nameless Palais Royal orators and pamphleteers, Rumour and crowds in the galleries of the Estates. Paris is bewildered and paralysed. Even the Tennis Court Oath and the Third Estate's conversion of itself into the National Assembly are the results of inertia. The Third Estate simply refuses to be moved. The only movement, apart from Broglie's troops taking up their positions in Montmartre, comes from the carpenters who move the Third Estate out of their meeting place to build a daîs for the king to sit on in the forthcoming *séance royale*. The carpenters, not the Third Estate itself, decide the course of events (*CRF*, I, pp. 134–5). Food shortages become an accomplished fact; Broglie is digging in in Montmartre but there are doubts about the loyalty of the troops; there is brigandage in the countryside; Broglie's intentions are not clear; nobody knows what is going on, not the Court or the National Assembly; 'preternatural Rumour' is 'driving most hearts in France mad'. A crowd of a few thousand, but getting larger the whole time, appears from nowhere to rescue eleven soldiers who have been imprisoned for refusing to obey orders. 'So hangs it, dubious, fateful, in the sultry days of July' (*CFR*, I, 134–7). The weather is sultry. The tension is becoming unbearable. Carlyle knows that we know that the crowd is about to storm the Bastille, but he holds the crowd back, anonymous, amorphous, but threatening, until the 12th of July.

When the revolutionary crowd does make its appearance, it comes almost out of the blue, *de novo*, without provenance, fully-armed. It is Camille Desmoulins who calls it to arms, but the cry is not really his. The call comes from 'the throat of a whirlwind'; France has been dried to tinder by its force, and now catches fire (*CFR*, I, p. 141). From this moment Carlyle takes off into his own whirlwind of mixed and contradictory metaphor: the mob becomes 'a living, foaming sea, chafed by all the winds'; while Broglie remains passive, 'mad Paris is abandoned to itself' (*CFR*, I, pp. 143–4). It soon becomes clear why Broglie can do nothing. He was only a force while his cannon could be aimed at a named target, the National Assembly, but he cannot threaten, let alone contain, a fire or a storm at sea. But these natural phenomena are as nothing compared with the assaulting host of abstract nouns: Patriotism, Sedition, Sansculottism, on one occasion a whole Suburb moving like Birnham Wood to Dunsinane. We are only allowed to see faces in the crowd when the crowd is centre-stage – Tournay, Élie, Hulin, Cholet, Georget, Bonnemère, Réole, Santerre, Maillard and, slightly sinister, a glimpse of Marat – but we see them *in* the crowd. They are not the crowd's leaders, because the World-Bedlam, World-Chimera needs no leaders. It is itself. To show us that the faces in the crowd are not the faces of crowd leaders, Carlyle emphasizes that after the Bastille has fallen, named individuals are powerless to stop the atrocities despite the terms of the surrender sworn on Hulin's word of honour. On that day, men are named only to show how little individual human will counts in the face of a world-historical phenomenon. De Launay perishes; Broglie and Besenvel are helpless (*CFR*, I, pp. 154–8). The naming of the figures of 'outworn Authority', apostrophized in their impotence, highlights the leaderless imperiousness of the crowd. The only led crowd that Carlyle mentions is the crowd of women which brings back the king from Versailles. 'Cunning' Maillard's dispositions are obeyed (*CFR*, I, p. 209), but Carlyle makes a good deal of Maillard's profession as an usher. Maillard arranges things but does not make the arrangements. No doubt, Carlyle's jaundiced view of women led him to emphasize the fact that a crowd of women had to be led by a man, but he makes it clear that it is Maillard who helps to organize the expedition to Versailles, and not the obvious leader-figure, the man on the white horse, Lafayette: 'The great Scipio-Africanus can do nothing' (*CFR*, I, p. 208).

The Sansculottic crowd is a vehicle of World-History. Sanscullotism rises 'unexpectedly' (*CFR*, I, p. 167) to judge Berthier and Foulon. Its justice is rough justice, but justice all the same. It is capable of atrocity, but its atrocities are not hidden. Its justice is seen to be done, and Carlyle lets Barnave's question: 'Le sang qui coule, est-il donc si pur?' pass without comment (*CFR*, I, pp. 167–8). The Sansculottes are not the scum of the earth and there is no mention of the bribery that was to feature in later, hostile accounts of the revolutionary crowd. The crowd of women are 'Judiths', 'all Eve's daughters, mothers that are, or are to be' (*CFR*, I, p. 206). There is a hint of coercion in Camille's phrase 'the Universal Press of Women', otherwise 'ancient Virginity tripping to matins' might not have joined the march to Versailles (*CFR*, I, p. 202), but there is none of the whores-dragooning-decent-women theme that figures so prominently in Taine. Carlyle is careful to absolve the Sansculottes from atrocity guilt where he can. Sansculottism is only indirectly responsible for the Jacobin dictatorship and so only indirectly responsible for the Terror. He seems to be aware that his account of the crowd as leaderless will raise some eyebrows, so he raises the question himself of how the Jacobins came to power: 'But speaking of an amorphous Sansculottism taking form, ought we not, above all things, to specify how the Amorphous gets itself a head?' Carlyle's answer is vague: 'by fortune, by internal Jacobin energy'. The Jacobins emerged as an effective clique capable of making the Constitution work, and as the only force capable of defending the Revolution against the Duke of Brunswick. The Committee of Public Safety, formed 'as it were, for miscellaneous accidental purposes requiring despatch', took over the other agencies of government but never subjected Sansculottism to its will (*CFR*, II, pp. 244–5). The Jacobins do not lead Sansculottism, they 'lean on' it (*CFR*, II, pp. 77–8). Sansculottism prepared the way for Jacobinism, and it acquiesced in the Jacobin exercise of power, but the Jacobin conquest of power was a matter of high politics where it was their 'energy', not their claim to lead the crowd, which led to their success. The Terror is explained not as the systematic extension of the rough justice of the *lanterne* but as the outcome in practice of almost every doctrine and attitude which preceded the Revolution: 'Catholicism, Classicism, Sentimentalism, Cannibalism . . . What the French National head has in it comes out' (*CFR*, II, pp. 294–5). By blaming doctrine, Carlyle shifts the blame for the Terror away from Sansculottism, because in his account of the revolutionary crowd, doctrine, like leaders, plays a very minor part. The Evangel of Jean-Jacques has had a part to play earlier in the Revolution, but mainly as an influence on the Third Estate and the National Assembly who, under the influences of the Contrat Social and 'public opinion', would not cede precedence to the Nobles and Clergy, and hardly even to Majesty itself (*CFR*, I, p. 123). Sansculottic justice appeared suddenly; the Terror is thought out, deliberately planned by a doctrinaire leadership, though the doctrine is, in truth, something of a rag-bag. Of course, Sansculottism acquiesces and so is probably an accomplice to the Terror, but the Terror also needed the acquiescence of the French National head, which enables Carlyle to say what he has been wanting to say all along, that the Terror is a peculiarly French piece of nastiness in which French Catholicism is partly to blame. (There is no mention of Jean-Jacques's origins in Calvinist Geneva.) This distances the Terror from the world-historical role of Sansculottism. Having done what he can to clear Sansculottism from the guilt for the Terror, it is plain sailing for Carlyle to show that the September Massacres have no connection whatsoever with the revolutionary crowd. The massacres are not the work of a mob, but of criminals, 'say a hundred or more', probably paid assassins of the kind who take such a delight in murder that they would do it for nothing. Carlyle reserves for the *Septembriseurs* that kind of Calvinist reflection on human nature at its worst that Taine was later to apply to the revolutionary crowd as a whole: 'of such stuff are we

117

all made; on such bottomless guilt and criminality – "if God restrained not" . . . does the purest of us walk. There are depths in man that go to the length of lowest hell' (*CFR*, II, p. 150). He cites verbatim the accounts of witnesses to the massacres to put the *Septembriseurs* on trial to emphasize that here it is a question of *real* criminality, not criminality by analogy, not even justice at its roughest. To put the matter beyond all doubt, he tells us that opinion at the time had no difficulty in distinguishing between a *Septembriseur* and a true revolutionary hero: the *Septembriseurs* enjoyed 'a name of some note and lucency – but lucency of the Nether-fire sort; very different from that of our Bastille Heroes, who shone . . . as in Heavenly light-radiance' (*CFR*, II, p. 162).

It is only in its decline that Sansculottism becomes less abstract. By 1795 the revolutionary crowd has become 'the Unruly', the Paris sections organized by Lepelletier in the last insurrection of the people against the Convention, doomed to fail, as we already know, in the Napoleonic whiff of grapeshot (*CFR*, II, p. 385). Now that it is a spent force, Sansculottism can be identified and its leader named. It is no longer the stuff of which History is made. It becomes a specific target, as the National Assembly had been for Broglie's guns in 1789. Broglie could have destroyed the National Assembly but was powerless to stop the people once they had seized their world-historical role. Now that the revolutionary crowd has emerged from its historical anonymity, Napoleon can easily do for the Directory what Broglie could not do for the Monarchy. The era of world-historical changes is over. Changes now happen by degrees, 'by intriguings, caballings and then by orderly word of Command, almost [Carlyle's contempt is magisterial] like mere changes of Ministry' (*CFR*, II, p. 388). Napoleon will arrange his dictatorship in much the same way that the Jacobins had arranged theirs. With the defeat of Sansculottism and the advent of Napoleon, the revolutionary crowd in France no longer has a wider significance; it becomes a French crowd, not a world-crowd. The revolutionary mob is still 'the crowning phenomenon of our modern Time', but it will have its day in other countries. Chartism in England is only one example (Carlyle, 1888, pp. 26–7).

Sansculottism was defeated because it made the understandable mistake of thinking it could do without Great Men. In an age of scepticism, it assumed that, because constituted authority was false, all authority was false (ibid., p. 337). Sansculottism would not accept leaders from outside itself and it could not produce leaders of its own because no true leader ever comes out of the crowd; Frederick the Great did not come out of the crowd, and neither did Cromwell. Part of Cromwell's greatness was his aloofness and his contempt for the crowd. God had noticed him and was in him, so 'what good could it do him to be "noticed" by noisy crowds of people?' God's word was in him, so he could afford to ignore 'huzzaing mobs' (ibid., pp. 352–3). Carlyle even defends Cromwell's notorious windbaggery by claiming that he 'despised' eloquence. He was always 'sincere'; his character had nothing of the 'theatricality' of the 'Fanatic-Hypocrite' type of pseudo-hero, the 'empty, barren quack, hungry for the shouts of mobs' (ibid., pp. 349–50, 353). He was one of 'the great *silent* men' (ibid., p. 353) – an odd judgement when Carlyle's own edition of Cromwell's *Letters and Speeches* runs to five volumes. Sansculottism paved the way for Napoleon, 'our last Great Man' (ibid., p. 367). Napoleon was able 'To bridle in that great devouring, self-devouring French Revolution; to *tame* it, so that its intrinsic purpose can be made good, that it may become organic' (ibid., pp. 365–6). Napoleon was able to make the French Revolution capable of sustained life and development, but even he has something of the Quack-Hero and Fanatic-Hypocrite about him (ibid., p. 364). At first he was a sincere democrat, defeating reactionary, popish Austria and opening up the career to the talents, but the fraudulent concordat with the papacy and the foundation of the phantasmagorical dynasty are serious flaws, so that while Napoleon is our last Great Man, he is not quite the genuine article. This may not be Napoleon's fault, because the modern age is peculiarly unsuited to heroes. The modern age is the age of the mob, 'the crowning Phenomenon of our Modern Time', but Carlyle thinks that the only justification for the mob is that it prepares the way for heroes whose rule is 'the ideal of Constitutions'; otherwise Sansculottism is 'a sort of madness' (ibid., p. 333), attended by 'horrors and crimes' (ibid., pp. 26–7). Chartism, for instance, is the continuation of the French Revolution in England, so what are the prospects for English Sansculottism? In the modern age it cannot produce a Great Man, not even a flawed hero like Napoleon, so Carlyle is pessimistic and his pessimism leads him to soften his own earlier account of the revolutionary crowd to tone down what he fears might be the impact of the Sansculottic mob in England. In *The French Revolution* it is 'violent Rebellion . . . Victorious Anarchy, Jacobinism, French Revolution, Horrors of French Revolution . . . destructive wrath' which amount to 'the crowning Phenomenon of our Modern Time' (*CFR*, I, pp. 170–1). Sansculottism and the mob are inseparable. Yet in *Chartism* he can write off the Chartist riots as mere 'symptoms on the surface' (Carlyle, 1888, p. 4), and there 'the crowning Phenomenon of our Modern Time' is simply 'The French Revolution' with no mention of Anarchy, destructive wrath or the horrors. He now wants to *explain* the mob which in *The French Revolution* was not explainable. In England things might be different because we 'with our better methods, may be able to transact it by argument alone!' (ibid., pp. 26–7), so there is no real need to recapitulate what has already happened in France. England can go through the modern age without its crowning phenomenon, the Sansculottic mob, Hamlet without the Prince. National character is wheeled in as a desperate attempt at reassurance. In *The French Revolution* Carlyle had contrasted French mobs, 'so rapid; so clear-sighted, inventive, prompt to seize the moment . . .etc' to the mobs of other nations ('dull masses') (*CFR*, I, p. 201), and perhaps he thought that a combination of English parliamentary procedures and a phlegmatic national temperament would save England form the wastefulness of a revolution which would not produce even a Napoleon, let alone another Cromwell.

Carlyle deliberately refused to explain the mob in *The French Revolution* because otherwise it would not have been preternatural or providential. Belloc gets the matter spectacularly wrong when he claims in his introduction to his edition of *The French Revolution* that Carlyle 'comprehended the mob' (*CFR*, I, p. xiv). Carlyle's view of the mob's place in history depends on our never understanding what motivates it. The effect of Carlyle's treatment of the mob would have been spoiled if he had attempted to work out a *theory* of the mob in the way, say, that Taine or Le Bon was later to do, because that would have dragged Carlyle's theory of history down from the heights of abstraction at which he chooses to pitch it. Carlyle understood very well that he could not have a metaphysical theory of history and a humanly understood mob at the same time. That is why in *The French Revolution* the only character the mob has is a national character of a very generalized kind and why we never see *into* the mob. Late-nineteenth-century crowd theory stressed the part that leaders play in the activity of crowds, so that a leaderless crowd became almost a contradiction in terms. The influence of a leader explained how a crowd came to be formed and why it acted in the way it did. Yet this 'dismal science' of crowd psychology would not have impressed Carlyle, because the leaders it showed coming out of the crowd were not of the same stuff that Heroes are made of. One of the ways used to explain the influence of crowd leaders was to argue that the relationship between the leader and the led was the same as the relationship between the hypnotist and the hypnotized subject. Mesmer makes his appearance in Carlyle's history, but only as another quack in an age of quacks and windbags (*CFR*, I, p. 42). Any crowd that allowed itself to be led on by a cheap music-hall trick could certainly not be thought of as playing a role in universal History and no real leader would have to stoop to such trickery. If the techniques of crowd leadership could be learned, so much the worse for the crowd and so much the worse for History.

Dickens unintentionally distorts Carlyle's view of the crowd by letting us into its mind. In *A Tale of Two Cities* we are told far too much about the crowd and the individuals who compose it for it to be a Carlylean crowd. As soon as the crowd stops being abstract, collective, anonymous and inscrutable, the less true to the spirit of Carlyle it becomes. That is why Carlyle's account of the mob is pre-psychological. A psychological crowd could never be the vehicle of metaphysical history.

The Crowd as the Nation: Michelet's 'Whole People' Storm the Bastille

Michelet's famous assertion that it was the whole people, not just a crowd, who stormed the Bastille has let him in for a certain amount of ridicule, and it is certainly true that less enthusiastic historians of the Revolution who want to see something less heroic in the revolutionary people have considered Michelet to be at his most vulnerable when he makes that kind of statement. Yet it is not a piece of wild rhetoric. Michelet is at his most *theoretical* when he speaks of 'the people', and when he does so it is Vico who speaks through Michelet, though a Vico whose voice has been considerably altered by the mind through which it passes. Vico's *New Science* was a revelation to Michelet. It was Vico who taught Michelet that the historian has to understand the culture of a society. History is made by whole peoples, not by great men, or elites, or by the gods. 'Real, living man', as Marx was saying in the *Theses on Feuerbach*, makes his own history. (Michelet remarked that Vico 'contains not only Feuerbach, but Feuerbach's successors' (Pons, 1969, p. 181).)

> He derived from Vico a vision of men as moulders of their own destinies, engaged in a Promethean struggle to achieve their own moral and social freedom, wrestling from nature the means to serve their own human goals, and, in the course of this, creating and destroying institutions in the perpetual struggle to overcome obstacles, social and individual, to the full realization of the moral energies and creative genius of entire peoples and societies.
>
> (Berlin, 1980, p. xx)

Men in primitive societies are only dimly aware, or unconscious of, their collective purpose, whereas a sophisticated society is character-ized by a highly articulate, self-conscious purpose. Michelet sees 1789 as the moment when the French nation shows that it knows it has a collective, self-conscious destiny, which has been long in the making.

France has been a person at least since the reign of Louis XIV, when it was love for the king which showed that the whole nation could share a single emotion. ('Louis XIV, when young, was truly loved by two persons, – by the people and La Vallière (Michelet, *History of the French*

Revolution, ed. Wright, p. 42)'.) The nation was straining to become itself and could hardly wait for the Revolution, but unlike Michelet, who could break off his massive history of France at the end of the reign of Louis XI and jump straight on to the Revolution, the nation had to wait, so, far from having to explain why the Revolution came when it did, Michelet feels obliged to explain why it took so long. Part of his explanation is that the idea of the Revolution, by which he means a desire for justice and liberty, lay too long in the minds of intellectuals ('philosophers, orators and sophists') and only reached the people with Rousseau who urged a return to Nature. Reason 'must descend into the heart'. It was a woman of the people, Madame Legros, and not the *philosophes* or the enlightened nobility, who got Latude released from the Bastille (*MFR*, p. 79). The summoning of the Estates General in 1789 began 'the true era of the birth of the people. It called the whole nation to the birth of their rights' (*MFR*, p. 83). The elections and the preparation of the *cahiers de doléances* strengthen the sense of collective purpose, and when the Third Estate declares itself the National Assembly, it became clear that a will existed in the people to make themselves a Roman *populus* with Mirabeau as their tribune (*MFR*, p. 108). The king's attempts to frustrate the people's will amounted to a *coup d'état*. The people were now on the defensive, with their Assembly being kept like prisoners among the royal troops (*MFR*, 134). The people resist passionately. This has a transforming effect even on the whores of the Palais Royal: 'They could not be virtuous, but they felt themselves heroic, in the name of the liberties of the world (*MFR*, p. 138).' (Not quite Joans of Arc, but patriotic fervour could take them at least part of the way.) Marat makes an appearance (*MFR*, p. 150), not, as in Carlyle, to make events more sinister, but to be noticed as a counter-revolutionary, advising caution, so that when the people eventually storm the Bastille, their motives can be as pure as those of the momentarily cleansed whores. There is to be nothing perverted or unnatural about the crowd which storms tyranny's citadel in the middle of a city that is itself almost in a state of siege.

Michelet makes good use of the fact that some of the royal troops are foreign. The liberties of the whole world are no doubt at stake, but it is the French people who are going to make them secure, so he builds up a picture of Paris besieged by a foreign army. Two days before the Bastille is stormed, a crowd forms from 'quiet people taking their walk, families who wanted to return home early "because there had been disturbances"'; they became indignant at the sight of German troops being moved about the capital by Besenvel. The troops open fire, nobody quite knows why, and the news spreads through the city (*MFR*, p. 152). (Notice, too, how the troops who in the previous paragraph were Swiss, became *German* when they committed the 'outrage' of firing.) Paris begins to arm, because 'nobody was disposed to receive the Croats and the Hungarian Hussars peaceably (*MFR*, p. 154); food begins to run short, but people in search of food are not allowed to leave the city by 'German troops . . . in their Austrian cloaks . . . speaking nothing but German' (*MFR*, p. 157); when the crowd mills about in front of the Bastille, the Swiss engage in 'cowardly warfare', 'little affected by the horror of shedding French blood' (*MFR*, p. 168). These are the same enemies that will invade the soil of the *patrie* in 1792, be defeated by Napoleon, will gloat over a ruined France after Waterloo and, fortunate for Michelet's *History*, will be defeated by Louis-Napoleon in the war for Italian freedom and will besiege Paris again in 1870 to enable Michelet to become the great patriotic historian of the Third Republic.[1]

The people need no justification beyond Justice and Liberty, but the threat of starvation caused by the enemies of the fatherland put the people on the offensive. This happens on the night of 13 July, so that on the morning of the great day, 'a light broke upon every mind, and the same voice thrilled through every heart: Go! and thou shalt take the Bastille!' (*MFR*, p. 161). It is not only Paris that is involved: 'The frightful misery of the rural districts had poured, from all sides, their starving populations towards Paris: it was peopled by famine' (*MFR*, p. 155). The attack was entirely 'the people's'; 'Nobody proposed; but all believed, and all acted' (*MFR*, p. 162). The attack on the Bastille was not rational, but an act of faith. That was why it had no leaders. The Palais Royal orators and the electors of Paris had no faith. 'Who had? They who had also the devotion and the strength to accomplish their faith. Why? Why the people – everybody' (*MFR*, p. 162).

The taking of the Bastille is the people's great moment, not just in French history but in universal history. But Michelet will not let the matter rest there. He is not content for the people to remain a Vichian abstraction, a mere historical cause; it is not even enough that the people should be the Roman people acting through their Tribunes. He wants them to have a real psychological unanimity. His people are not a metaphor. Everybody who took part in the storming of the Bastille felt the same, and the rest of the people felt with them. This was the moment when reason descended into *everyone's* heart, and the later events of the Revolution are judged good to the extent that their actors can re-create that unanimity. The bringing of the king back to Paris is the second greatest of the people's moments because it is 'the most general, after the 14th of July, that occurs in the Revolution' (*MFR*, p. 281). There follows a period 'full of magnanimity, clemency and forgiveness' (*MFR*, p. 322), now that their good king is living among his people and out of the clutches of his wicked advisers, and an extraordinary outburst of mutual love occurs throughout the whole of France. Associations originally formed as a protection against brigands and the aristocracy, when food was scarce, continue 'without any other necessity than that of the heart: To *unite*, as they said, and love one another' (*MFR*, 323). 'There is no longer any rampart between men' (*MFR*, p. 324). The National Guard, which would have become separate from the people but for the providential moment of reunion to bring the king back from Versailles, is now composed of everyone, 'Everybody *without exception* in the rural districts' (*MFR*, p. 324, n.3); 'it is the Jerusalem of hearts, the holy unity of fraternity, the great living city, made of men. It was built in less than a year, and since then has been called *Patrie*' (*MFR*, p. 325). The federations dissolve into one great federation on the anniversary of the taking of the Bastille, and the Republic of brotherly love, one and indivisible is complete. (Compare Taine on the ceremonies of universal federation: nobody quite knew what they were supposed to be doing, felt rather silly and were mostly drunk.) The reports of the provincial federations to the National Assembly are simple, unaffected and Rousseauesque. 'There is nothing official or constrained; it is evidently the language of the heart . . . these enthusiastic documents are love-letters! . . .a unanimous prayer from the heart of France . . . Such is the power of love' (*MFR*, pp. 443–4). It is an extension of the unity of heart and faith which enabled the Bastille to be taken, this time on a national scale. Perhaps it would never be quite achieved again, because 'the grand and national achievements of the Republic and Empire, had nevertheless a partial non-unanimous character', but 'the 14th of July was the day of the whole people. Then let that great day remain ever one of the eternal *fêtes* of the human race, not only as having been the first of deliverance, but as having been superlatively the day of concord!' (*MFR*, pp. 162–3).

Michelet's unanimous people, like Carlyle's Sansculottism, must be absolved from blame. There was a bit of unseemly drunkenness during the Réveillon riots, but most of the people remained honest. The riots were a disgrace not to the people but to the authorities which allowed them to happen. Perhaps this was deliberate. The court had the most to gain because the riots could be a useful pretext for moving more troops into the city and suspending the Estates (*MFR*, pp. 92–3). There was some unpleasantness after the fall of the Bastille, but the judgement of reason descended into the hearts of the people was bound to be swift and terrible after the provocations they had suffered. Only those provocations could explain how the Parisians, who had such a reputation for amiability (*MFR*, p. 157) could become so warlike. What were the sufferings of de Launey compared with those of Latude? De Launey was a 'greedy, sordid soul', made infamous throughout Europe by Linguet's *Memoirs*, who allowed his Swiss to shed French blood (*MFR*, p. 168). Those who massacred the prisoners were not the heroes of the Bastille, but they can be forgiven because that was the only way that they could become part of tyranny's downfall. To dip their hands in the blood of the people's enemies was their act of identification with the heroes, part of unanimity (*MFR*, pp. 177–8). The rough justice of the *lanterne was* justice. Foulon was a part of the conspiracy of famine (*MFR*, p. 206) and a libertine who, though the father of a family himself, 'purchased, on all sides, it was said, little girls twelve years of age' (*MFR*, p. 207), while Berthier had shown 'diabolical activity' in 'collecting arms, troops and the manufacture of cartridges; if Paris was not laid waste with fire and sword it was not his fault' (*MFR*, pp. 208–9). This blood was even less pure than Barnave thought, so they could be massacred without tears. A dragoon did tear Berthier's heart out and eat it, but then he believed that Berthier had been responsible for the death of his father (*MFR*, p. 213). When a woman ate the heart of Major Belzunce, it was no more than he deserved: he was insolent, called the people *canaille*, clearly a *provocateur* (*MFR*, p. 210). Michelet finds it hard to establish who was responsible for the September Massacres, which he sees as a response to the external threat of the armies invading the soil of the fatherland ('the scourge of God, the last Judgement', like waiting for a barbarian invasion or the return of the English in the Hundred Years' War (*Histoire de la Révolution Française*, I, p. 1017)) and to the atrocities committed on patriotic Frenchmen (in the area of Sarrelouis the Austrian cavalry are arresting known republicans and patriotic mayors of communes and cutting off their ears to nail on their foreheads (*Hist.*, I, pp. 1055)). In the near-panic in Paris, nobody was really in control, so that a group of failed actors and poets, of whom the type is Collot d'Herbois, was able to inflame the Paris *Commune* with its taste for tears and the strong emotions and create the right atmosphere for the massacres. They were not actually mad, like Marat, but they shared his madness (*Hist.*, I, pp. 1036–7). The people allowed themselves to be duped by 'three or four hundred' criminals (*Hist.*, I, p. 1093) who did not dare to massacre the prisoners in secret. The prisoners were massacred out in the street so that the appearance could be given that what was taking place was a spontaneous act of popular justice (*Hist.*, I, p. 1054). The real spirit of the people resides in the army, and it is inconceivable that the advance-guard at Valmy and Jemmapes could be murderers. One of the *Septembriseurs* was received with horror by the army and was sabred by his comrades when he was stupid enough to boast about it (*Hist.*, I, p. 1093).

Michelet leaves a good deal of Vico out of his account of the Revolution. Vico's belief in Providence, the cyclical theory of history, the anti-popular prejudice, the clericalism and the admiration for simple-minded societies have no place in Michelet's scheme of things. In fact, there is no attempt in Michelet systematically to apply Vico's theory of history to France. We hear nothing of the progression from the divine state of history to the heroic and civilized states, which Michelet praises Vico for having discovered (Vico, 1963, p. xxiv), though Michelet clearly thinks that other nations will repeat what has gloriously happened first in France. But there is one supremely Vichian moment in Michelet's account of the Revolution. Michelet was fascinated by the idea that a whole society could have produced the Homeric poems. The *poet*, or poets, whom we call Homer, made a whole from the improvised songs and rhapsodic fragments embedded in the popular mind (ibid., p. xxxii). Poetry is collective in the heroic age, which is unconscious of itself; the third, most advanced, age expresses itself through the self-conscious rationality of prose. The third age is not, of course, incapable of feeling, but it can organize that feeling into a programme, a sense of direction, or a declaration of explicit values. Michelet believes that this was done by the National Assembly, under Sieyès' guidance, in the Declaration of the Rights of Man. While the people were realizing Justice and Liberty through an act of faith, the National Assembly, 'without allowing itself to be molested by the noise and clamour was buried in thought and meditation', produced the declaration of the Rights of Man from the authority of Reason (*MFR*, 321). The Rights of Man, 'breathing the sentiment of *duty*' showed 'the true genius of the Revolution, – a Roman gravity and a stoic spirit' (*MFR*, 232); they were worthy of Solon, Lycurgus, or Moses (*MFR*, 235). The whole people storm the Bastille while their representatives declare the Rights of Man which the people already have written on their hearts.

Michelet's account of the revolutionary crowd is vulnerable on two different levels. Empirically, it can be asked: Were the crowd like what Michelet says they were like? Was that unanimity which he is so keen to convince us existed, really there? One recent historian is prepared to give Michelet the benefit of the doubt, at least for the 14th of July (Rudé, 1964, pp. 210–11), but the question can still be asked. Taine took a long, hard look at what those crowds did and came to very different conclusions from Michelet. But there is an even deeper vulnerability, and it stems from a certain republican sleight of hand in Michelet's use of Vico. When Michelet took from Vico the idea that '*a* people' made its own history, whether it was conscious of it or not, he transformed it into the idea of '*the* people', and transformed it still further into the idea of 'the crowd'. Even Vico never pretended that in the most primitive and heroic age '*the* people' sat down one day and wrote the Homeric poems. The Homeric poems were part of a culture in which everyone shared. Michelet now has the revolutionary crowd telescoping the long process of the creation of a culture into a few breathless hours of insurrection. Of course, he points out that the Revolution has antecedents, and in a more advanced age things happen on a conscious level and so can be deliberately hurried, but he makes it quite clear that the assault on the

Bastille is an act of faith, irrational, perhaps unconscious, certainly collective, like nothing so much as the creation of those Homeric poems which attracted Michelet's attention when he wrote his introduction to Vico's *Principles of the Philosophy of History*. It is the National Assembly which, in producing the declaration of the Rights of Man, is acting true to the spirit of modernity. Michelet's opponents were quick to see that the game of sleight of hand could be played in the opposite direction, as Taine does. If the crowd was not as Michelet had described it; if it was barbarous, vicious, corrupt, ignorant and nasty, then 'the people' or the masses, from which it sprung, whose representative it is, must be equally barbarous, vicious, corrupt, ignorant and nasty. Michelet's sequence of *a* people, *the* people, the revolutionary crowd, can easily be reversed, as it is by Taine. The revolutionary crowd is disgusting, so the people must be disgusting too, and that leads Taine on to a critique of the Revolution, the Republic, democracy, and everything for which Michelet stands. Michelet's use or misuse of Vico made his account of the Revolution vulnerable in another way. The implied atavism in Michelet's view of the crowd as a Homeric people left the way open for anti-democratic critics of the Revolution to see in the revolutionary mob the beginnings of a descent into primal barbarism, so that the Revolution itself could be seen not as a *modern* event, but as the event above all others which challenged the idea of modernity.

A Theory of Political Psychopathology: Taine on the Spontaneous Anarchy of the Revolutionary Crowd

Michelet brings a theory of history to the crowd; Taine brings a theory of political psychopathology out of the crowd after the *Commune*. This was a new departure for Taine. His concern with revolutionary politics can be dated with some accuracy from the *Commune* period. By 1870 Taine had a European reputation as a formal psychologist and as a literary historian whose mechanically positivist theory of literature was famous enough for him to be invited to give the Max Müller lectures at Oxford, and it was while he was in Oxford that the Paris *Commune* ran its course and was suppressed. Taine thought that before going to Oxford his life's work was nearly over. The war with Prussia and the siege of Paris left him depressed. He was finding it difficult to work (H. Taine, *Sa Vie et sa Correspondance*, III, p. 30); it was now the time for younger men (ibid., III, p. 30); his one remaining ambition was to write the second volume of his treatise on psychology (ibid., III, p. 30). At Oxford there was a sudden quickening of his interest in politics and a lightening of his sense of resignation in the face of catastrophe. He followed what was going on in Paris as closely as he could. His fear of civil war in France

127

was compounded by anxiety about the safety of his family and about whether his flat in Paris would receive the attentions of the *pétroleuses* (Aulard, 1906, p. 210). Disturbing analogies kept occurring to him: were the June Days to happen all over again? (*Sa Vie*, III, p. 51) or a repetition of the madness of 1793 and the Terror (ibid., III, pp. 91–2)? On the day after he had noted with horror that the Communard newspapers were demanding the return of the guillotine (ibid., III, p. 88), he announced: 'I have sketched out in my mind my future book about contemporary France' (ibid., III, p. 90), a book that was to run to eleven volumes in the standard edition of *The Origins of Contemporary France* of 1899. This vast enterprise would show that all France's troubles in the nineteenth century came out of a misunderstanding of what the French Revolution had been like and an equal misunderstanding of what had caused it. He regarded the Communards as another violent mob – the English newspapers that Taine read at Oxford may have a lot to answer for – of the type which the French Revolution unleashed on an unsuspecting Europe. It would be foolish to pretend that Taine had not thought about crowd politics before the *Commune*. He had suffered from the Napoleonic *coup d'état* of 1851 but had seen mass opposition to the Empire as even worse ('The crowd gives me the creeps!' (cit. Boutmy, 1902, p. 262)). In the *History of English Literature* he had described English society in the eighteenth century as the world of the Beggar's Opera, with the government barely able to keep in the saddle on a huge and terrifying beast (*Hist. Eng. Lit.*, ed. van Laun, II, p. 46). Corruption in high places and Swiftian Yahoos below were not a pretty sight and the Gordon Riots showed what the mob could do if it was allowed to get out of control (ibid., II, p. 46), but these observations are not the basis of any theoretical interest in the crowd. National pride even led Taine to stick up for the French Sansculottes against Carlyle's treatment of them in his *The French Revolution*. The Sansculottes have a claim to be considered as just as purely motivated as the English Puritans in their revolution, and Taine even has a few good words to say about the greatness of Napoleon (*Hist. Eng. Lit.*, II, pp. 225, 472–3, 476). Again, it has to be said that Taine had earlier shown some interest in individual psychopathology. As early as 1855, the madmen of the Salpêtrière and Bicêtre had made him to begin to wonder whether madness had not played an important part in history, and whether there might not be an interesting book to be written on it (*Vie et Corr.*, II, pp. 99–100), and in *De l'Intelligence* (published 1870) there is the suggestion that hallucination, which seems so bizarre, is the connecting link between all our mental processes (Taine, 1948, II, pp. 23–31). What makes his post-*Commune* period so different is his attempt to bring the crowd and psychological theory together into something like a psychopathology of collective behaviour. When the heart of Michelet's people has been examined from this point of view Taine hopes that the concept of the 'noble savage' will be replaced by a savage so ignoble that Rousseau's reputation will never recover.

Taine takes it for granted that the Rousseauist idea of the natural goodness and reasonableness of simple people was the commonplace assumption about human nature at the end of the eighteenth century. It had infected everybody, whether they were defenders of the status quo or not, so that when the Revolution happened everyone was surprised, or affected to be surprised, by the violence and brutality of popular disturbances. How sad it must have been, he tells us, to think you were living in some kind of pastoral idyll, to fall asleep among sheep and, on awakening, to find the sheep transformed into wolves (*Origins.*, Vol. 1, *The Ancient Regime*, ed. Durand, p. 238). Of course men were bound to lose their reason during popular disturbances. The brain is a very complicated organ. The number of cerebral cells is estimated at 1,200 millions and the fibres which bring them together at 4,000 million.

> The simplest mental operation . . . is the play of complicated mechanism, the joint and final result of several millions of wheels which, like those of a clock, turn and propel blindly, each for himself, each through its own force, and each kept in place and in functional activity by a system of balance and compensation. If the hands mark the hour with any degree of accuracy, it is due to a wonderful if not miraculous coincidence, while hallucination, delirium and monomania, ever at the door, are always ready to enter it.

Such a mechanism must clearly have ideal conditions if it is to operate property. Ordinary social living is barely adequate for the operation of what we call the reason, and by this Taine does not mean anything very elevated, but simply not losing one's head. But

> Take women that are hungry and men who have been drinking; place a thousand of these together, and let them excite each other with their exclamations, their anxieties, and the contagious reaction of their ever-increasing emotions; it will not be long before you find them a crowd of dangerous maniacs.

His general conclusion is the reverse of philosophic: 'Properly speaking man is mad,[2] as the body is morbid, by nature; the health of our mind, like the health of our organs, is simply a repeated achievement and a happy accident (*AR*, p. 239). Some men are no doubt capable of the higher abstractions of reason, a Fontenelle, a Hume, or a Gibbon, and some are even capable of looking at political questions with detachment, but it is absurd to expect this of, say, a peasant who only knows physical labour in the open air and who can't keep still indoors for a quarter of an hour, let alone keep his attention focused on questions of a general nature long enough to come to any judgement which is likely to make sense. 'Not only is reason crippled in man, but it is rare in humanity.' It takes a long and specialized education before any man can begin to do anything which could recognizably be called thinking. Even in those who give the appearance of thought, reason is frequently 'a domestic advocate unceasingly suborned', so what can we expect when reason descends, as Michelet says it did, into the heart of the people? 'Reason, in the hands of its new interpreters shall inaugurate riot in the streets and peasant insurrections in the countryside' (*AR*, pp. 239–40).

Taine agrees with Hume that the reason is the slave of the passions. The real masters of man are 'physical temperament, bodily needs, animal instinct, hereditary prejudice, imagination . . . personal or family interest, also that of caste or party'. We would be greatly mistaken if we thought men were good, kind, or generous by nature. They are not even gentle or manipulable, and have little inclination to subordinate their selfish interests to the common good. Of course, this does not apply to everybody, but some men, if left to themselves, would straight away start to create havoc. Taine's vision of man let loose in a hostile world is unmistakably Darwinian in the 'nature red in tooth and claw' sense. Men would never outlive their animal past. In human societies man, unknown to himself, retains a vestige of that animality which fonder observers imagine he has left behind:

> if there is no certainty of man being a remote blood cousin of the monkey, it is at least certain that, in his structure, he is an animal closely related to the monkey, provided with canine teeth, carnivorous, formerly cannibal and, therefore, a hunter and bellicose. Hence there is in him a steady substratum of brutality and ferocity, and of violent and destructive instincts, to which must be added, if he is French, gaiety, laughter, and a strange propensity to gambol and act insanely in the havoc he makes.

The necessity of having to get their bread from an ungrateful soil has left few men with the spare capacity for things extraneous to the land and the plough, hence the peasant vices of avarice and narrow-mindedness. What makes man politically dangerous is that his mental equipment is ludicrously inappropriate to the life which the struggle for existence calls upon him to live. His brain is much too complex for the simple, laborious, repetitive life of peasant agriculture. Because he can't use it properly, his 'delicate mental organization' is troublesome to himself and a menace to his fellow men. He has hopes which cannot be satisfied and fears magnified beyond all reason, while 'an excess of sensibility, sudden outbursts of emotion, contagious transports, irresistible currents of passion, epidemics of credulity and suspicion . . . enthusiasm and panic' from time to time threaten to tear down the stable political and psychological structures which, if he but knew it, are what enable him to cope with life in the first place. They exist to prevent precisely what he uses to destroy them (*AR*, pp. 240–1). These are the psychological phenomena which Taine sees at work in the peasant uprisings and the great mob-scenes of the Revolution.

The great failure of eighteenth-century social theory was its failure to understand the popular mind. Instead, the aristocracy, the whole of the literate portion of the Third Estate, the lawyers and the schools were infected with the doctrine of natural, social man who only wanted his natural rights to begin his necessary and inevitable progress into a perfect social creature (*The French Revolution*, ed. Durant, p. 25). By 1789, it was a commonplace to challenge any form of constituted authority as an affront to the sovereignty of the people until the real, everyday authorities, the *curé* and the *gendarme*, became the objects of ridicule and contempt. The ancient, half-suppressed passions of man can only be kept down. (There is no theory of sublimation in Taine.) Civilization's last argument is physical force, 'the gendarme armed against the savage, brigand and madman each of us harbours, in repose or manacled, but always living, in the recesses of his own breast' (*AR*, p. 242). With that view of the precariousness of civilization, it is hardly surprising that Taine believed that the French Revolution was less a revolution than a dissolution (*TFR*, p. 12). Nor should it surprise us that his account of the Revolution should deal so extensively in atrocity stories, all of which he believes. He has none of the scepticism about what the village boaster might be reported to have said in his cups, which informs the work of Professor Cobb (1970, pp. 86–92). Taine's critics have been unkind about his taste for horror stories. Geyl, for instance, has Taine revelling in the massacres which he related with 'endless repetition of comments of vituperation and loathing' (Geyl, 1963, p. 169), while Cobb, though not naming Taine, wonders whether there might not be something indecent or obscene in the very act of reading the depositions about atrocities, some of which did not stop short of cannibalism (Cobb, 1970, p. 89). This is to be unfair to Taine, or at least to misunderstand why he does it. The views that he is attacking are the eighteenth-century view of man, and Michelet's people storming the Bastille with the rights of man written on their hearts before the National Assembly has had time to get them down on paper. Eighteenth-century social theorists were guilty of a failure of imagination. They could not think themselves into the minds of the people, could not imagine what their minds were like, and so took Rousseau's word for it as the only man of the people whom they had read. (The fact that Taine himself grossly and perhaps deliberately misunderstands the view of man current in the Enlightenment is irrelevant here.) With this failure of understanding went a failure of investigation, almost an intellectual laziness. Eighteenth-century science suffered from an excess of Newtons. Everybody wanted to be the first to discover the few immutable and simple principles of human nature which governed the human world as Newton's Laws governed the physical universe. Eighteenth-century social science was hardly worthy of the name because it was incurably deductive despite its pretensions to learning. Geometry lay at the back of it all. Taine's chief objection against the science of man in the eighteenth century is that only very ignorant men, men ignorant about facts about other men, could possibly been taken in by Rousseau's natural man. Taine is a positivist and an inductivist. Generalizations about man must either come out of a properly scientific investigation of individual psychology, or out of myriads of collected facts about what men actually do when they go about their business in the world. At some happy time in the future, both these fact-finding enterprises will end up by telling us the same thing, and then we will really be getting somewhere. Taine is trying to do both these investigations in *The Origins of Contemporary France*. Peasants have the same complicated brains as anyone else, but the circumstances of peasant life are not ideal for learning how to use them; physiological evidence tells us how complicated brains are, and the realities of peasant life show how perverted their mental processes can be. What the mob in the French Revolution shows is the public effects of that perversion working themselves out when the political and psychological structures which keep them in check have been removed. As an inductivist, Taine has to amass evidence, and that means amassing examples. By the standards of nineteenth-century positivism this is a perfectly respectable intellectual enterprise. No doubt Taine is not keen enough on the collection of counterfactuals to satisfy his master, J. S. Mill, not to mention Professor Popper, but the larger the number of mobs he can find committing acts of unspeakable barbarism, the less plausible the eighteenth-century view of the noble savage becomes and the less likely that they had the rights of man written on their hearts.

Taine's claim that the French Revolutionary mob indulged in collective insanity is not frivolous. Carlyle points out that by 1840 it was a commonplace to observe that during the Revolution the French had 'as it were, gone *mad*; that the French Revolution was a general act of insanity, a temporary conversion of France . . . into a kind of Bedlam' (Carlyle, 1888, p. 335). Taine's insistence on the natural morbidity of mind shows that he means us to take that commonplace literally. The

Revolution's critics have been right all along. The interesting book about the role of madness in history, which he had thought about while a student at the Parisian Bedlam, the Salpêtrière, twenty years before, is *The Origins of Contemporary France*. When Governeur Morris writes to Washington that there is only one sane man left in Paris, or when Mallet du Pan says that everyone had gone mad, they speak truer than they know. Taine saw his work on the revolutionary mob as an exercise in applied psychology (*Vie et Corr.*, IV, p. 57), and that is how the impressive list of his admirers from Lombroso and Tarde to Durkheim, Le Bon and Freud read him (*Reveu Blanche*, 1897, pp. 263–95).

The marshalling of atrocity stories serves another *theoretical* purpose. Taine, if not exactly a Darwinian, is certainly an evolutionist. He regards evolution as a humiliating concept for mankind, because it continually reminds him that he is an animal among animals with no claim to special creation. Even his superior brain, in which man takes so much pride, is made of the same stuff (*matière nerveuse*) as the brains of animals (*AR*, p. 176). This over-complicated organ is far from being a great advantage to most men who have neither the leisure, nor do they live in the appropriate circumstances, to use it properly. Like all evolutionists, Taine is interested in survivals of primitivism and in the resemblance between disturbed behaviour and primitive behaviour. In advanced societies not everything is advanced. There are vestiges of earlier stages of evolution, stubborn survivals from previous epochs in the general history of man, which may reassert themselves if given a chance. Taine tries to document such a process of regression in his account of revolutionary mobs.

The anarchy of revolutionary mobs is spontaneous. By 'spontaneous' Taine means that nobody put them up to it (though he changes his mind about that on at least two critical occasions) and that mobs appeared almost everywhere after the calling of the Estates General. This enables him to see revolutionary violence as an affair of peasants, not townmen, a backhanded attack on Michelet by downgrading the importance of Paris and the taking of the Bastille. The Paris mob is only a special case of a much more general phenomenon. The real immediate cause of the Revolution is the great hope for a nameless improvement which the calling of the Estates kindled in the credulous minds of peasants. The fall of the Bastille is important only because it signalled the final failure of nerve on the part of government, which allowed further disturbances in the provinces. A failure at the centre encouraged tendencies which had begun before the 14th of July. France was fast becoming a people independent of events in the capital; everywhere the ignoble savage was declaring himself; there was a unanimity, but it had nothing to do with the Rights of Man. Rather what was taking place was a return to the barbarism and animalism of primitive ancestors. Men's characters seemed to change; they became suspicious and restless (*TFR*, p. 7); there is a vague feeling that things are going to change for the better (*TFR*, p. 8); there are sporadic atrocities, and men begin to realize that their condition is not very different from living at a time of barbarian invasion (a comparison which Michelet saved for the threat from the army of the Duke of Brunswick), except that this time the Huns, the Heruli, the Vandals and the Goths are not coming from the north or from the Black Sea but are in our midst already (*TFR*, p. 53). The mob begins to act like freed negro slaves (*TFR*, p. 52) and like savages and cannibals. At Troyes they tortured Huez in the manner of Hurons; at Caen they did worse: Major Belzunce (Michelet's *provocateur*) was torn to pieces 'like Laperouse in the Fiji Isles', and a woman ate his heart (*TFR*, p. 67). All the inherited prejudices which make human living possible are giving way. Chastity, the taboo against eating human flesh, toleration for the old and socially useless, a sense of shame, of humanity, of honour, or even of conscience, disappear in the dissolution until men begin to live again at the level of the beasts (*TFR*, p. 208). Man again finds himself an animal among animals, and what men have come to call civilization, like mental equilibrium, proves to have been a temporary and happy accident.

The mechanisms of this transformation of men into brutes are 'vibration of the nervous mechanism' (*TFR*, p. 221), 'contagion' (*TFR*, pp. 36–7, 140), which explains the unanimity of the popular mind so puzzling to the authorities, 'feverishness' which spreads through contact with sufferers (*TFR*, pp. 52–3) and is really contagion by any other name. The result is a 'deranged mind' (*AR*, p. 326), a prey to hallucination and delirium (see *AR*, p. 327, for a very detailed account of a hallucination brought on by an 'orator'). 'Perverted sensations and delirious conceptions of this kind would be regarded by physicians as the symptoms of mental derangement (*aliénation mentale*)'. Over-excited brains are ready to receive and believe anything; they will think in phantoms and distorted images, with everything out of proportion, having little to do with reality. The hideous figures of the aristocrat and tyrant, enemies of the people, and of the patriot, incorruptible and the people's friend, become the standard images of minds no longer capable of thinking, if they ever were. Dream and hallucination take the place of the ordinary processes of perception (*AR*, p. 327).

This groping for a a positivist, technical vocabulary of mass psychopathology has to be dug out of the ordinary metaphors of popular disturbance and social collapse which Taine also uses. Edifices are collapsing, the body politic stops functioning properly because the belly tries to usurp the function of the brain, but the most consistent metaphor which Taine uses is the animal metaphor. A wild beast, incompletely domesticated, goes wild again. Sometimes it is a bull in a market place, sometimes a more exotic creature, 'a tame elephant suddenly become wild again', throwing off its ordinary driver, 'and the new guides whom it tolerates perched on its neck are there simply for show; in future it will move along as it pleases, freed from control, and abandoned to its own feelings, instincts, and appetites' (*TFR*, p. 38). The elephant comparison on the face of it looks an ordinary metaphor, but it is well chosen. Flaubert's *Salammbô* had caused a sensation in 1862, and in one of its most memorable set pieces, the Battle of Macaras, the Carthaginian elephants get out of control, threaten both armies and have to be killed by their drivers by having spikes banged into their brains. Taine's mad elephant has a tame driver, just there for show, carried where the elephant will take him, decidedly not a reassuring image for the law-abiding householder who might have read *Salammbô* and who only had to glance at his elephant's foot wastepaper basket to feel a certain quickening of the pulse. But the metaphor shades into evolutionism. Taine has already reminded us of man's animal past to which social behaviour can regress, so the animal metaphor and the idea of a regression back down the social, anthropological and biological scales, feed on each other in a way designed to be convincing to those whose view of the mob as a wild beast itself feeds on a tradition of animalistic metaphor at least as old as Plato. It may be that to treat Taine as groping for a technical vocabulary of crowd explanation in a welter of metaphor is to look at the matter the wrong way round. Perhaps he embedded the technical vocabulary in the commonplaces of metaphor to make the technical vocabulary more convincing, not the other way round, and it is certainly the case that thinkers like Le Bon, who used Taine's account of the revolutionary crowd as the definitive case study of crowds before the late nineteenth century, had no difficulty in spotting the forward-looking aspect of Taine's collective psychopathology from what merely looked backwards.

Not everything that Taine has to say about revolutionary crowds is new, but his emphasis on the provincial, peasant crowd rather than the Parisian Sansculottic crowd was. Carlyle and Michelet saw the crowd that stormed the Bastille as the paradigm crowd, of which other crowds were the imitation. All revolutionary crowds would have stormed the Bastille if they could, and because the storming of the Bastille needs no justification, the crowd needs no justification. Michelet, for instance, judges all actions of the crowd according to whether what they do, and the spirit in which they do it, resembles what happened on July 14th. Taine regards the Parisian crowd as an exception to the general rule of spontaneous anarchy. For him the typical crowd is the provincial crowd, and the crowd in Paris is the special case. As Professor Rudé points out, Taine's account of the Parisian crowd is backward-looking to the point where he denies that it is a revolutionary crowd at all (Rudé, 1959, p. 283). For Taine, the Parisian mob is an eighteenth-century mob called out by its paymasters for political ends. Money changes hands (*TFR*, pp. 97–8, 99); the dregs of society ('pimps and whores' (ibid.)) and the unemployed are easily bribed; it is all a bit of a muddle because it is difficult to see who the leaders are. Taine has not forgotten his description of eighteenth-century London as the world of the Beggar's Opera. Michelet's people comes out of a lumpenproletarian underworld. There is none of the mothers of Paris persuading 'ancient virginity tripping to matins' to join them in the heroic expedition to Versailles to bring the king back to Paris. Instead we find whores threatening respectable women with having their heads shaved if they resist dragooning into the crowd (*TFR*, pp. 98–9). The bribed dregs of society from the world of Macheath are not the only people to join the crowd. Michelet makes much of the people driven into Paris by famine as evidence that the crowd represented the whole of France. Taine takes a very different view of this. Bands of fugitives from such justice as there was to cope with provincial atrocity camped out in the suburbs 'just as in countries where human society has not yet been formed, or has ceased to exist' (*AR*, pp. 23–4). They made their way into the city to add their primitive barbarism to the mercenary motives of the rabble. When the crowd was actually formed, their behaviour followed exactly the same regressive pattern as the peasant crowds in the countryside, and the fall of the Bastille signalled the end of any effective government in the capital and the provinces. The Parisian crowd is effectively downgraded from its position of leader of world history in Carlyle and Michelet to follower-on of peasant barbarism. Its main achievement is to push France further back down the evolutionary path up which mankind had climbed so laboriously through the ages.

Taine is not just concerned to set a piece of revolutionary history straight after Michelet. The regressive crowd comes out of the French Revolution, and the French Revolution came out of the culture which preceded it. The social theory of that culture left France in 1789 singularly ill-equipped to deal with the Revolution. The ruling class and the revolutionary crowd did not understand what was going on. The Jacobins, if not the first to understand the Revolution, were at least the first to understand enough about it to profit from it. The origins of contemporary France lie in the connection between social theory, revolutionary violence and the Jacobin take-over. The Revolution was the beginning of something which has infected, or threatens to infect, the whole of Europe. Taine uses the analysis of the revolutionary crowd to add to a growing body of anti-revolutionary social theory in the second half of the nineteenth century which puts a theory of the crowd at the very centre of theoretical concern, and which will use his account of the crowd in the French Revolution as the starting point for a coherent and compelling irritationalist and, in some cases, anti-rationalist attack on the theory of progress which was to become one of the characteristic European social theories of the *fin de siècle* and well on into the twentieth century.

Notes

1 Michelet may not be as anachronistic here as he appears to be. He notes (*MFR*, pp. 98–9) that his hero Sieyès was the first to see that the insistence of the nobility and clergy on voting by orders divided France into three nations. Sieyès' pamphlet *What is the Third Estate?* spoke of the nobility as foreigners, 'odious remnants of a barbarous regime', natural enemies of the people. Sieyès turned the Germanicist Thesis of Boulainvilliers on its head. In his defence of the French nobility against the encroachments of royal power, Boulainvilliers had argued that the French nobility was Frankish, had overcome the Romans and established feudalism in Gaul with the natives as their serfs; the Frankish nobles were free and equal men who elected their king, so the rights of the nobles preceded those of the crown. It was easy for Sieyès to turn that argument against the nobility. They had always been the people's enemies; the Revolution was a patriotic crusade to expel foreign invaders; the nation must reconquer its own. If Michelet had this in mind, then his emphasis on the foreign troops is the more understandable. (See J. Q. C. Mackrell, 1973, pp. 21–3, 43.)
2 Durand translates *fou* here as 'imbecile', which loses some of the force of Taine's very direct statement. As a translator, Durand is workmanlike but occasionally prissy, toning down what Taine actually says.

5

The Crowd as the Clue to the Mystery of the Modern World: Taine against the Enlightenment

The period during which Taine's *Origins of Contemporary France* was appearing (1876–94) was also the period in which crowd theory became a recognizable concern for thinkers everywhere. Two years after Taine's death in 1893, Le Bon published *The Crowd: a Study of the Popular Mind*, a skilful compendium of the crowd theory of the past twenty years got up in generalizations so bold and so sweeping that every social group became a crowd, so that all branches of social science became branches of crowd theory. Taine had already taught his readers to look at idealized versions of the storming of the Bastille for the origins of the illusions about popular sovereignty which still encouraged crowd politics, so there was something fortuitous in the fact that Le Bon's *The Crowd* was the first best-seller of social science since Tom Paine's *Rights of Man*. Le Bon's obsession with breaking into the world of official science led him to make ludicrous claims for the originality of *The Crowd* at almost the exact moment when the wrangle between Gabriel Tarde and Scipio Sighele inside the world of official science about priority in crowd theory was about to degenerate into something like a public squabble (Barrows, 1981, pp. 152ff.), and Le Bon patronized Taine in the same outrageous way that he patronized the other crowd theorists whom he plagiarized. He gave Taine quite good marks as a describer of revolutionary crowds, an honest spadeworker whose account of the mob in the French Revolution had to wait for Le Bon himself to give the crowd the theoretical attention which only he was capable of giving it. By assenting with civil leer to Taine's European reputation as the chronicler of revolutionary crowds, Le Bon felt free to gut the *Origins* for crowd material, but that was not the only support that Le Bon got from Taine. *The Crowd* also contained in a simplified form the view of the history of Europe since the Enlightenment which Taine worked out while writing the *Origins*.

The view of the world which Le Bon made available to a huge reading public was Taine's view that something had gone drastically wrong with European society and politics long before the French Revolution, and that 1789 was its inevitable outcome. Taine blamed the Enlightenment for the Revolution, but his attack on it was more subtle than the commonplace Catholic view that the Revolution was God's punishment for the Enlightenment's materialism and atheism. As a positivist who believed that Science, not God, was the Universe's only fixed point, Taine could hardly explain the Revolution as God's punishment for man's impertinence in daring to know more about the mysteries of the Creation than God intended. Positivism owed too much to the Enlightenment for that debt to be repudiated, so Taine has to argue that there was something about the cast of the enlightened mind which necessarily made it misunderstand, or misapply, the science that was available to it.

Taine divides his account of the Enlightenment into two parts, the first of which he calls 'the acquisition of science' and the second, the distortion of that science by the 'classical spirit'. This leaves him free to emphasize the continuities between eighteenth-century and nineteenth-century science, while pouring contempt on the spirit which caricatured scientific discovery to the point where it could become part of the ideology which either caused the Revolution or allowed it to happen. Taine's separation between science and the spirit in which it was received is artificial. Often, those same minds which made discoveries in science were those infected by the classical spirit, and it is hard to see on Taine's account how that could be, but it gives Taine the advantage of being able to say that there was no excuse for enlightened minds not being able to form a true picture of the universal history of man because the materials were readily available to them. If they had read Buffon properly, they would have seen the truths of Darwinism before Darwin, and if they had read Condillac properly they would have realized the true nature of individual minds before the discoveries of mental pathology and vivisection of the nineteenth century (*Ancient Regime*, pp. 172, 181). Instead, a view of human nature came out of the Enlightenment which failed to take proper account of the length of time it took for man to develop from rudeness to civility, and forgot that the same process has to be gone through in each individual man. Taine toys with Lamarckianism (*AR*, pp. 172–3), but he does not think that the advances made by one generation are auto-matically transmitted to the next. The French Revolution is one of the great interruptions of history because it allowed that part of man, and that section of society, which had not progressed to come out on top.

Science should have enabled men in the eighteenth century to guess what the crowd would be like. Now these lessons have to be learned all over again. Science, of which eighteenth-century science is a part, can now teach those lessons because science can be approached in a truly positive spirit. This time the elitist implications of science will not be obscured by pseudo-scientific drawing-room chatter about the Rights of Man as the Newtonian constitution of the moral universe. Real science will show just how hard it is for any progress to happen. It will also show how precarious that progress is, how vulnerable in the face of ignorance and prejudice, how long it will be before the common people deserve, let alone understand, the progress which science itself promises them, so they must be kept away from it for their own good.

Reason was misused in the eighteenth century to teach men the Rights of Man. In the second half of the nineteenth century, reason as science will teach men their place in the scheme of things. Those who understand the science of man have a duty to teach it to rulers, if not to become rulers themselves. Reason will slowly be recaptured by the elite. Science can defuse reason, and save society from rationalist fantasies, and from the radical slogans bequeathed by the superficial mind of the Enlightenment which the crowd continues to chant without understanding them in contemporary riots and demonstrations. Every time that happens, society is in danger of regressing back down the scale of progress. Societies can regress very quickly, and there is no guarantee that, once a lower level has been reached, it can ever be made up again. What is certain is that climbing back up the developmental ladder will be difficult and painful. What causes Taine real anguish is that the ebb and flow of regression and progress is unnecessary because it is predictable. It was predictable even before the Revolution, because all the elements necessary for a theory of regression were already there in the Enlightenment's own science of man, and it is certainly predictable afterwards. The *Origins* shows that the Revolution is the paradigm case of social regression, a case which is only likely to be repeated if the fantasies about the goodness of the people which were the Revolution's antecedent causes continue to bewitch ruling groups who are now in a position to know better. Taine's science of man now teaches the important lesson that a science of man of the Enlightenment type can let the crowd in by putting the elite off its guard.

In the eighteenth century, a whole epoch failed to confront its own world with the necessary humility which its own science should have shown was the necessary preliminary to any understanding of a world outside the self. Taine's account of the *esprit classique* debasing the science available to it is very similar to the account of the Athenian debasement of philosophy into sophistry in Plato. The approval of science's own audience became the test of scientific truth. What had been the merest outlines of the science of pedagogy in Rousseau, of political economy in Quesney, Smith and Turgot, of linguistics in de Brosses, of moral arithmetic and penology in Bentham, became finished systems of truth in the minds of salon amateurs and saloon-bar philosophers. Any kind of erudition smacks of vulgar pedantry; 'good society' alone decides who shall enjoy fame and it is for this 'small group apart . . . rich, well informed and polished . . . the flower of humanity' that great men have laboured. D'Alembert was ashamed of belonging to the Academy of Sciences (Mably claimed 'We, in the French Academy, looked upon the members of the Academy of Sciences as our valets'); only a handful of people listen to a mathematician or a chemist; the man of letters, the orator, addresses the universe (*AR*, pp. 186–7). A gentleman does not have to have read all the books, and certainly not the *Encyclopedia*. He judges with his natural good sense. As Sorel was to remark 'a marquis of the *ancien régime*, is a man who knows everything without needing to study anything' (cit. Horowitz, 1961, p. 232). Science led an underground life, not daring to show itself in good society except as a set of finished truths couched in the language of fashion, not in science's own language. This in its turn affected science itself, especially the human sciences, and particularly history. It would never occur to you (a reader of Hume, Gibbon, Robertson, or Voltaire) that there was any real difference between men of different cultures and epochs. What is peculiar to a civilization seems to them to be superficial, barely skin-deep, accidental (*AR*, pp. 198–9). The French novelists are just as bad. The English novelists of the eighteenth century paint a picture of their society as it really is, 'a complete picture of an entire community, the amplest stock of information to guide me should I wish to write a history of this vanished world'. Historians and French novelists equally failed in the effort of 'sympathetic imagination' (*AR*, pp. 212). They were not interested in men as they really were, but in a kind of abstract man who could be identified behind the accidental qualities which he happened to acquire through living in his society.

The classical spirit was adept at quick and easy generalization. It did not have to look hard at the world, because the same story was being written wherever and whenever men had been exposed to social living. 'Man in general' had been corrupted everywhere by the societies in which he had been forced to live. In some of those societies it was difficult to see his true nature, but the more the apparent differences between men at different times and in different places struck the observer, the greater was the compulsion to think away from men the characteristics which could be attributed to particular circumstances, in order to expose the basic human nature which lay beneath. All that had to be done was to select a very simple proposition, such as an ignorant and inattentive schoolboy could understand, rejecting every

141

difference which sets one man apart from another, call it 'human nature' and use it as the constitution of man to which the constitutions of states must correspond, and the whole programme of the Revolution was complete (*AR*, pp. 232–3). This simple being, who sought pleasure and avoided pain, nothing else, could easily be given the constitution which his nature demanded. The principles of human nature were as simple as the axioms of Euclidean geometry, and the construction of the society of the future was a matter of rigorous deduction from those axioms. The proof that the construction was correct was a matter of logic.

The real culprit was Rousseau, whom Taine blames most of all for the ideology which allowed the Revolution to happen. There is nothing surprising about that in itself; blaming Rousseau for the Revolution had been standard practice since Burke, and was to continue after Taine. What is new is the ambiguity of Taine's critique of Rousseau. As a psychologist, Taine sees the mind of Rousseau as a paradigm of the whole revolutionary experience. He wants to see the connection between the Rousseau of the *Social Contract*, who calculates arithmetically the exact amount of sovereignty possessed by each citizen in his state, and Rousseau the half-mad, *dieu-manqué*, (*Vie et Corr.*, III, p. 290) dreamer of wild dreams, as the connection between the rationalist political theories which preceded the Revolution and the mob barbarism of the Revolution itself. Taine argues what looks like a contradictory case against Rousseau, seeing him as both the archetype of eighteenth-century social theorist, and also as the thinker who points to the future, so that the generalizing, optimistic spirit of eighteenth-century political theorizing, and the political madness of revolutionary politics, of which the *Commune* is the latest example, form a single whole.

Rousseau's rejection of the society around him meant that the truths of nature which he preached could only have come from his own disturbed personality. By his own confession, Rousseau's is a strange, original character. He 'harboured within him a germ of insanity and . . . finally became wholly insane; a wonderful, ill-balanced mind in which sensations, emotions and images are too powerful: at once blind and perspicacious, a veritable poet and a morbid poet, who, instead of objects beheld reveries, living in a romance and dying in a nightmare of his own creation' (*AR*, pp. 221–2). This freak examined his own heart, didn't like what he found there, dared other men to claim they were better than him, blamed all his faults on society, and claimed that his own self-disgust was the universal voice of conscience crying out to be heard in his own breast and in the breast of every man.

Rousseau's rejection of society led him to reject the history which produced that society. If the whole history of man has nothing to teach us except that man's domination of his fellow men leads to the corruption of the moral sense, then the details of that history are not very important. The thumb-nail sketch of the *Discourse on the Origins of Inequality* will do as the history of all hitherto existing societies, so that when Rousseau begins to write the *Social Contract* the previous history of man can be summarized in a single sentence: 'Man was born free and everywhere he is in chains'. If dominion is the cause of corruption, then the dominators must be more wicked than the dominated. They are more sophisticated, further removed from the moral simplicities, which only survive in very primitive societies or in the more primitive parts of advanced societies. Hope must therefore lie in the people, and the political programme of hope is equality, a beginning again from the point where the corruptions of the world originally began. History must be given a fresh start. Men must be treated as if they had no history, and the only way of doing that is to make a social contract on the basis of equality to replace the original treacherous bargain by which the rich cheated the poor out of their birthright (*AR*, pp. 226–30). Even the scientific advances of the eighteenth century, sketchy as they were, are written off as so much wasted energy, and with those advances the civilization which produced them joins every other civilization on the scrap-heap of history. Primitivism is raised to the principle of the highest good over everything that is polished, cultured, or progressive.

So far Taine has done little more than follow Voltaire and Burke, ridiculing the invitation to walk again on all fours, and treating with contempt the idea that men can begin their history all over again. What Taine does is to add a different understanding of that history, and, therefore, a different understanding of culture. Man's past is almost unimaginably longer than Rousseau's pseudo-anthropology of origins would have us believe. For Taine, the past is not just a matter of the history of the progress from rudeness to civility which was the stock-in-trade of eighteenth-century historians. Man has an anthropological past, an animal past, perhaps even a geological past. Certainly, the past has moved with geological slowness, and it has moved very unevenly. In a given society, France in the eighteenth century for instance, different groups of men live at different stages in the history of human progress, and the beginning of the shift of the science of man in the Enlightenment from medieval metaphysics to positive science only took a few *savants*, and the very few who were prepared to listen to them properly, into the modern age.

Most men, in a country where peasants had yet to turn themselves even into Frenchmen, were still living in an age when such generalized conceptions as they could understand had to be couched in the language of the Bible and of Catholicism. The societies in North America and in the South Seas, whose virtues eighteenth-century travellers' tales made so much of, had not even got that far. Yet those were the hearts so simple that they could not be tricked by sophistry, these the savages whose innate, uncorrupted nobility was being held up as the model for civilized men. Their natural reason could equal the discourse of philosophers, and put to shame what passed for polite conversation among the educated classes of the *ancien régime*. 'With Diderot, Otou the Otaheitan, with Bernadin de St Pierre, a semi-savage Hindoo and an old peasant-farmer of the Ile-de-France, with Rousseau a country priest, a gardener and a juggler, are accomplished conversationalists and moralists' (*AR*, p. 236).

If, in the enlightened view of it, there were men living in France in the eighteenth century whose natural reason needed a bit of prodding, society was to blame for having put obstacles in reason's way in the first place. The scholar who scorned a generalization like that voluntarily bridled his own mind, doing to himself what social institutions and customs did to the man of the people. The result of the success of Rousseau's natural man in polite society was a conspiracy of ignorance about what was likely to happen when the social institutions which kept him in his place were attacked. As late as 1789, Necker refused to recognize the imminent danger arising from the usurpation of the Third Estate, insisting that 'reliance must be placed on the moral virtues of man' (*AR*, p. 237). For years the government had spoken to the people as if they were Gessner's shepherds. Now 'The peasants are entreated not to burn *châteaux* because it is painful for their good king to see such sights.' They are exhorted to 'surprise him with their virtues that he may the sooner be rewarded for his own'. At the height of the Jacquerie tumults 'the sages of the day seem to think they are living in a state of pastoral simplicity and that with an air on the flute they may restore to its fold the howling pack of bestial animosities and unchained appetites'. (*AR*, p. 238). The classical spirit and Rousseau left everyone completely unprepared for the mob. Taine's irony is heavy: 'It is a sad thing to fall asleep in a sheepcote and, on awakening, to find the sheep transformed into wolves' (*AR*, p. 238).

Taine's case against the Enlightenment is that the outbursts of primitivism during the Revolution could have been foreseen if only the French ruling class had taken the trouble to understand the regressive implications of the theory of development which had been worked out by enlightened thinkers. He is careful not to blame the Revolution on the direct influence of Rousseau on the people, though no doubt those ideas filtered down from the ruling class who are always the most influential sources of ideas and values in any society. Taine is an elitist, and the Revolution for him is the replacement of one ruling group by another. Rousseau's doctrine of the social contract served a double purpose. It persuaded the elite of the *ancien régime* that it had nothing to fear from the people, and it served another elite, the Jacobins, as the ideology which justified their seizure of power. All simplified doctrines like Rousseau's are double-edged. They can destroy societies in the name of liberty and equality, but they can also, in the hands of ambitious cliques, be used as the basis for a form of rule which makes the old society seem a golden age of freedom (*TFR*, II, p. 20). When the mob rules, sovereignty is scattered about in the streets. This stage of the Revolution is more properly called a dissolution, and is actively encouraged by those who are scheming for the leadership and who, Machiavelli-like, know how to wait. Doctrine is the key to their success, but their use of doctrine takes simplification a stage further. Doctrine becomes a simple slogan, the sovereignty of the people, in whose minds would-be leaders create phantom enemies (Marat, the eternal denouncer is their archetype (*TFR*, II, pp. 5–6)) who can be defeated only if the people delegate their sovereignty to strong and incorruptible leaders who will brook no temporizing with the faith (*TFR*, II, p. 18). The people come to be manipulated by their leaders who eventually take control. The Jacobin conquest is the prelude to the conquest of power by Napoleon, who bequeathed the modern State to France.

The great error of eighteenth-century social theory was its optimism, the assumption that past achievements would inevitably continue as future progress. All that had to be done for the Age of Enlightenment to become an enlightened age was for the discoveries of the *Encyclopedia* to become known throughout Europe. Optimism blinded *lumières*, *illuministi*, *Aufklärer* and the philosophic part of mankind to the very simple truth that what goes up can come down. The possibility of regression was implicit even in the Enlightenment's own psychological theory. The Enlightenment already knew that sensation was absolutely common to men and animals. What kept most men above the level of the brute beasts was the institutions of the society in which they lived. Take those institutions away, and the benefits of civilization, acquired so painfully and over so long a period, could vanish very quickly. Individual psychology for Taine is the enemy of culture. The clue to that simple truth was clearly written in the mind of Rousseau, if anybody had had the wit to see it. Rousseau was unbalanced. He ended up mad. Yet it was the product of Rousseau's own introspection that won the day as the concept of 'natural man'. How could a stable society, a society worth living in, come out of the inmost heart of the most anti-social of all the thinkers of the eighteenth century? Rousseau set up his own personality as the judge of the whole universe. He said: Look what the world has done to me! The world must be all bad to produce the contemptible human being that at least half of me is. Extrapolate from the good part from me, and form a society from the beginning where that goodness can prosper in the new state of the social contract. The world can then remake itself according to the true

145

principles of human nature. The mob scenes of the Revolution were the public acting out of the madness which Rousseau could not control in himself, a collective madness of which Rousseau's own neurosis was the example and paradigm.

These were the origins of contemporary France. The disasters of French politics since 1815 can all be attributed to a failure to understand how things went wrong at the beginning. Just as eighteenth-century thinkers forgot what man himself had been like at his own anthropological beginning and were taken in by the doctrine of natural man which allowed the Revolution to happen, so Frenchmen have continued to romanticize the revolutionary origins of their own contemporary experience. Taine means *origins* in a sense which is more than conventionally historical. Of course, contemporary events can be traced back into the past, but he also thinks that contemporary France has yet to escape from the compulsion to repeat its own origins. The regression of the Revolution threatens to become permanent. Every time the mob is let loose, French society seemed about to return to its origins: in 1848, in the *Commune*, after the return of the *communards* in 1880, yelling for General Boulanger, rioting in the decade of strikes from 1885 to 1895, attacking the government during the Wilson and Panama scandals, celebrating the centenary of the Revolution in 1889, turning out in the great May Day rehearsals for proletarian revolution . . . each more threatening than the last. The Revolution had produced the Jacobin dictatorship and Napoleon, 1848 had produced the plebiscitary despotism of the Second Empire. Now the working classes were taking to syndicalism, Marxism and anarchism, all of them doctrines which were ultimately traceable to the ideas which produced the Revolution, or were produced by it. Each threatened a new dissolution of society, and if the history of the Revolution taught anything, it taught that the regimes which followed social dissolutions were more tyrannical than the regimes which preceded them. Taine is not a reactionary. His positivism gives him some hope for the future, but it is a future in which the values of a high culture have to be protected from the mob who in their turn have to be protected from fallacious sloganizing doctrines (we would say ideologies). When the mob is raised, it hurls itself headlong back towards man's anthropological and biological origins, taking the rest of civilization with it.

Taine was never the best-selling author that Le Bon was to become, but his was the kind of theory of history that his contemporaries were prepared to take seriously because they had been prepared for it well in advance. Studies of the formation of Taine's thought come up with an enormous range of influences. Herder, Hegel, Buckle, J. S. Mill, Comte, Tocqueville, Guizot and Michelet jostle together in Taine's generous eclecticism. There is nothing particularly surprising about the range of sources of inspiration to be found in Taine. Anyone of his intellectual range is bound to owe a lot to others. What is remarkable is that Taine was able to blend together nearly every intellectual trend in nineteenth-century Europe in an eclecticism which had something to offer to all shades of intellectual and political opinion which could in any sense be described as centrist or right of centre. He was able to tie positivism, romanticism, nationalism, evolutionism, elitism, Hegelianism and the emerging psychology of the unconscious to a view of the French Revolution as a relapse into primitive barbarism. The centrepiece of that view was the crowd as the agent of cultural and political regression. Taine was the great synthetic thinker of his generation, a European Herbert Spencer, dominating his own time and like Spencer so exquisitely attuned to it as to be almost forgotten afterwards, except as a figure still to be reckoned with in the debate, largely but not solely academic, about what the revolutionary crowds had actually been like.

The thrust of Taine's argument went in the same direction as nationalist thinking since Herder, which had sought to deny the universal nature of social man in favour of the particular, local destinies of national groups finding their happiness in the development and celebration of their own linguistically defined communities. Taine *has* an idea of universal human nature, but it is an anti-social nature, unconscious, irrational and barbarous, a nature that social institutions are there to tame, not to fulfil. This is the nature which a true reading of Rousseau's *Confessions* helps us to identify, and which we can see in public whenever the crowd makes its appearance in history. Universal, individual nature, and the nature developed in particular national communities, are natural enemies, because the institutions and customs of a people, developed at an anthropological pace, are always vulnerable to the outbursts of atavistic barbarism of the crowd who bring their animal past out into the open in civil society where it has been lying in wait for its opportunity to destroy the existing order of things. This order is complex and therefore fragile, no match for the rude barbarian and animal energies of the mob who can undo the civilizing work of centuries, even millennia, in a moment. Individual psychology is the enemy of collective cultural endeavour. All behaviour which could be in the loosest sense described as instinctual is society's enemy. It is here that Taine's social thought begins to look too much the child of its own time.

There is another line of thought about primitive instinctual behaviour, already there in Le Bon and finding its complete expression in Freud's *Civilization and its Discontents* (1929), which sees the instincts as conservative, not radical; less likely to tear society up by the roots, and more likely to be the source of the energy which goes into the making of a society in the first place. Society begins to be seen as the product of the instincts working out the means of their own survival through the mechanisms of the group; the instincts are no longer egotistical and destructive, but co-operative and productive, and society and the instincts come to be seen as allies, not enemies. If instinct is the friend of the group, then high culture and the effort needed to sustain it can easily come to be seen as the group's enemy. High culture becomes at best a waste of vital energy which could be better spent on affirming group solidarity, or at worst an affront to, or a betrayal of, the group's own life. High culture can even be seen as a threat to the survival of the group conceived of as a class, or a nation, or a *Volk*. If the crowd is thought of as the 'original' human group, as the most 'primitive', as the group of which all other groups are in some sense the imitation, then the culture-hostile mob can see itself as threatened by established culture and established social and political institutions. It is a very short step from there to the crowd's beginning to think that its destiny, and the destiny of the whole people of which it is the vanguard, is to destroy as its enemy those very social and cultural institutions which Taine himself had justified on the grounds that they kept the crowd and its barbarism in check. Nothing could be further from Taine's own high-minded elitism, but the way he thinks about the relationship between man's own primitive nature and a national culture could very easily be twisted to support political positions which are the opposite of his own. All that needed to be done was to put a very different judgement of value on to the rude, barbarian energies of men in the crowd, add a nationalist gloss to those energies as the vital energy of the nation, and it was easy to begin to see those energies as being stifled by the same classical spirit which Taine condemned in the Enlightenment, and by the systems of politics – republican, democratic, or socialist – which continued to look to the Enlightenment for their inspiration. And from there to a programme of fascist politics is no step at all.

Of course, it's not Taine's *fault* if what he thought could so easily be twisted for purposes which he would undoubtedly have looked upon with horror, but his was a name that carried great weight, so that any political doctrine which had as its centre an attack on the French Revolution and all that it was supposed to have launched into the modern world, was bound to find in Taine the kind of scientific support which it might otherwise have lacked. Dimier observed that while the counter-revolutionary movement began with the Revolution itself, 'the counter-revolutionary movement among intellectuals dates from 1876 when the first volume of Taine's *History of the Revolution* (sic) appeared'. De Maistre and Bonald could now be taken seriously again (Dimier, 1906, p. 188), and part of the success of de Maistre's *Study on Sovereignty*, which was published for the first time in 1884, must be attributed to

148

Taine's own attack on the *philosophes* and his exposure of the brutal realities of revolutionary mob violence. Certainly the view of *Action Française* was that Taine showed scientifically and historically that what *Action Française* had to say about the republic, and the tradition on which the republic relied, was true (Bourget, 1900). Aulard knew exactly what he was doing when he devoted two years of public lectures at the Sorbonne (1905–7) to exposing Taine's scholarly errors. (These lectures appeared as *Taine, historien de la révolution française*, Paris, 1907.)

Aulard himself had no doubt that, by attempting to destroy Taine's reputation for scientific accuracy, he was striking at those anti-republican doctrines which fed on Taine's name for their scientific respectability in the positivist age. Taine was treated with great respect even when his opinions were being challenged or rejected. When the young provincials in Barrès' novel *Les Déracinés* reject Taine's scientific elitism on their way to national mysticism, they do it gently and with great regret, and when Maurras argues in *Romanticism and Revolution* that Taine has completely misunderstood the intellectual origins of the Revolution by blaming classicism and not romanticism, he still assumes that what Taine has to say about what actually happened in the Revolution is true. And in the academic mode, historians still worry that Taine's talent (Lefebvre, 1971, p. 247) or genius (Cobban, 1968, pp. 43–4) might dazzle us into thinking that what he said about revolutionary crowds was right.

Taine's English reputation was good enough for him to be among the first continental scholars to be invited to Oxford when that University, in the process of its reform, decided there was a world beyond itself which was worth noticing. His evolutionist approach to the history of human societies fitted in with the evolutionary assumptions of English social theory in the second half of the nineteenth century. Taine was something of a Darwinian, but too much must not be made of this, otherwise it would be easy to fall into the trap of believing that Taine *derived* his evolutionary ideas from Darwin, in the way that some commentators have claimed that Taine must have derived his theory of history from Comte. Darwin made quick headway in France (nine editions of the *Origin of Species* in three different translations appeared between 1862 and 1907, along with two different translations of *The Descent of Man* and three editions of *The Expression of the Emotions in Man and Animals*), but Comtian positivism had already incorporated its own biology into the evolutionary theory of society whose optimism relied in part on the Lamarckianism it shared with Herbert Spencer. Acquired characters were automatically transferred from one generation to the next, building up a constantly increasing supply of successful cultural adaptations, the sum of which amounted to human progress (Simon, 1963, pp. 25–6). Taine shared the evolutionary outlook with nearly everybody else, but his Darwinism led him away from the optimism of the more simple-minded of the positivists. The animal nature of man was not something in the past which men could take pride in having left far behind them in the march of progress. What English evolutionary anthropologists regarded as quaint survivals from a savage past Taine came to see as a permanent substratum of hidden anti-social ferocity which could break out into the open whenever a revolutionary mob was allowed to get out of control by careless authority. Benthamite man would never risk himself in irrational outbursts of collective barbarism, but he gradually lost his central place in social theory in England as the century progressed. J. S. Mill was among the first to realize that the associationist psychology which underlay Benthamite man's claim to be universal man was double-edged, because there was no reason in principle why men should necessarily associate the idea of pleasure with what was progressive according to the Benthamite canon, and pain with what was part of the unreformed world which utilitarianism sought to change (Burrow, 1966, pp. 16ff.). If men took pleasure in non-rational, ceremonial, status-ordered behaviour in preference to practical, calculating, 'useful' behaviour, then who could say that, in the terms of the pleasure–pain calculus, this was not a perfectly rational way to behave? The sovereign masters, pleasure and pain, could still be used to explain *any* human behaviour, but it became increasingly difficult to hold to the position that vested interest and superstition accounted for the fact that not all men regarded it as their primary desire to buy cheap and sell dear as the means of increasing the only happiness which it made sense for a rational man to want. Those village communities in India which James Mill had seen as backward and irrational precisely because they were being prevented from turning themselves into miniature versions of the London Stock Exchange by the superstitious social and religious idolatry of Hinduism, might know a thing or two that was not immediately obvious to Eurocentric observers (Burrow, 1966, p. 74). McLennan, Spencer and Tylor explained the religions and social practices of savages not as mistakes made by the ignorance and credulity of the savage mind, but in exactly the same way that they explained the survival of the pre-modern aspects of their own contemporary societies. Astrology, absurdly exaggerated respect for kings, folk-medicine and old wives' tales, were to be explained no differently from the animism of primitive religion (which McLennan described as 'a highly rational theory for men in a low state of knowledge' because (a shrewd hit at the utilitarians this) the association of ideas was 'the very philosophy of the savage' (cit. Burrow, 1966, p. 249)). Evolutionary sociology was still progressive sociology freed from the constrictions of strictly Benthamite assumptions, but what it lacked was a coherent account of why that progress was necessary now that it had been shorn of its Benthamite imperatives. Take away the Spencerian optimism, and survivals began to look much more threatening. Taine thought that crowds were survivals, but for him they were much more than objects of curiosity, because they threatened everything else. On Spencer's view, crowds should be disappearing from society as rational co-operation between individuals took over more and more areas of social life, but that was a view which it was easier to hold in England than in continental Europe where the rise of militarism in Imperial Germany, *revanchism* and Boulangism in France, and militantly class-conscious politics almost everywhere, showed societies in full retreat from social differentiation into competing versions of group solidarity. Taine's view that the French Revolution and its aftermath made France fit for either despotism or anarchy was not lost on his English readers, especially in the 1890s, when even England had had a whiff of mob politics to compound the general European fears of anarchism. Mr Wilson, speaking up for the gentlemen of England in 1894, got Taine's message exactly right. Things were getting worse than even Taine had suggested in the *Origins*. He praised Taine's 'mental chastity' which shrinks from showing us the full horror of the revolutionary crowds. 'The great distinguishing feature of the Revolution', he writes, 'is that it plucked the muzzle from all restraint . . . The latest and ripest fruit of the French Revolution is, perhaps, the godless bomb-thrower of the distracted hour in which I write.' With a nod towards the new criminal anthropology, he summarizes the lesson to be learned from Taine's view of the Revolution: 'The class which was, in essence, the criminal class became the governing class' (Wilson, 1894, p. 341).

The unifying theme in Taine's eclecticism is his psychology. If Taine had a view of a 'master science', it would have taken the form of generalized psychological laws which would explain all human behaviour, past and present, but his own psychological theories are eclectic in the extreme. Physiological psychology, historical psychology, comparative cultural psychology and the psychology of morbid states of mind (which may have been influenced by the work of his cousin, the distinguished alienist J. G. Baillarger, who was on the staff of the *Salpêtrière* where Taine was a student and who wrote on hallucination and the stupidity of the mentally ill (*La Stupidité des aliénés*)) all testify to the seriousness of Taine's psychological intentions, but they are nowhere brought together into a single psychological theory. Taine's attack on the Enlightenment leads him to stress the non-rational, instinctive, unconscious motivations which prompt human action so that he can ridicule the expectations the *philosophes* had about rational man, but Taine is not quite modern. He has no *theory* of the unconscious mind. All the more bizarre mental states of which men are capable he attributes to a complicated mental machine going wrong, or to a Darwinian instinctual heritage, only partly suppressed, surviving below the surface of ordinary mental life. It should never be forgotten that in the *Origins* Taine is writing a history, not a treatise on general psychology, but, as Le Bon was to realize, all the materials were available in Taine's history for the construction of a theory of unconscious behaviour which would put the final seal on all the rationalist hopes for a society founded on any version of the rational calculus. The psychology of the unconscious, which had been quietly working its way underground since Descartes (Whyte, 1960, p. 63), found its historian in Taine.

Taine's was one of the great characteristic minds of his age. Most of the concerns of the second half of the nineteenth century meet in his view of the revolutionary crowd and its implications for the future of civilization, but there is one extraordinary gap. Le Bon, characteristically, found Taine's weakness as a psychologist of crowds: he had no theory of the leadership of crowds which matches the thoroughness of his account of the crowd's place in history. The *Origins* was unfinished at the time of Taine's death in 1893, and by that time scientific work on hypnotism was being used extensively to explain the relationship between leaders and their followers in crowds. That Taine did not use it is the more surprising because the Salpêtrière was one of the two great centres of research on hypnotism (the other was Nancy). Charcot was famous enough to attract Freud, who knew virtually no French at the time, all the way from Vienna in the 1880s, but Taine made no use of the discoveries about hypnotism. Yet the use of psychopathological material is a characteristic of Taine's method, and he used other material from the Salpêtrière gathered earlier when he was a student there, and his cousin was still on its staff. This is puzzling, and it forms the basis of Le Bon's claim that it was he, not Taine, who first properly understood revolutionary crowds by using hypnotic suggestion to provide a coherent theory of the relationship between the crowd and its leaders. Barrows suggests that the fame of Charcot's experiments on hypnotism came just too late for Taine to incorporate the hypnotic model into his account of the crowd during the Revolution (he had written over half the volumes of the *Origins* before Charcot 'opened the gates' for the serious consideration of hypnotism in 1882) and that, because he regarded the revolutionary leaders as 'dregs who floated to the top of a society in chaos', he was unwilling to attribute to them any 'special skills or charismatic power' (Barrows, 1981, p. 86). This will not quite do. As Barrows is aware, Taine had witnessed hypnotic experiments at the home of Dr Punel and during Baillarger's lectures (though she does not appear to be aware that Baillarger was Taine's cousin), so why should he not have used the hypnotic model before 1882 when he was already using other work on hallucination and the physiology of the brain? Nor can Barrows's surmise that Taine did not want to attribute special skills or charismatic power to the revolutionary leaders explain his failure to use the hypnotic model, because Taine does in fact say that the Jacobins showed they understood the people better than their philosophic predecessors. They were skilful at creating in the minds of the people the sort of phantoms which the psychological state of the people made it likely they would believe in. They conquered power by setting themselves up as the only power who could stand between the people and their imagined enemies. Again, it can be argued that the time for Taine to have used the hypnotic model to the best polemical advantage was *before* hypnotism had received the attention of official science, when it could still be treated as a trick of the music-hall charlatan, probably depending on a fraudulent collusion between the hypnotist and his subject, but capable of rousing the crowd by contagion or by the other psychological mechanisms which Taine believed explained collective behaviour. Taine believed that some members of revolutionary crowds had been bribed, so why should he not have used the paid, hypnotized, music-hall subject as a model for a revolutionary crowd?

Any explanation of why a thinker does *not* think something is bound to be a guess when any explanation of why he *does* think something is still a difficult matter, but it seems likely that Barrows has turned Taine's view of the Jacobin leadership upside-down. Of course, Taine does not like the Jacobin leadership. They are power-hungry, without scruples, the men who did well out of the regressive barbarism of the crowd. They take Rousseau too literally and share his taste for generalization. Theirs is the mind which reasons deductively from axioms, even if that deduction takes them as far as the guillotine and the Terror. But the Jacobins were an elite. If Taine had used hypnotism to explain their hold over their followers, as Le Bon does, then Taine's own elitism would have had to be modified because he would have had to explain how his high-minded scientific elitism differed from Jacobin elitism. In the 1880s there was no general agreement about who could be hypnotized. The Salpêtrière School held that only the mentally ill could be hypnotized, so that hypnotism was a way of demonstrating the existence of mental illness and a way of treating it, but the Nancy School held that anyone could be hypnotized, and it was the Nancy School that was gaining ground. It was on the basis of the doctrine of the Nancy School that Le Bon made his generalization that *all* leadership was to a degree hypnotic. If Taine has used hypnotism to explain the Jacobin conquest of power, he would have had to defend the Salpêtrière School against the Nancy School to preserve the distinction between the irrationalist leadership of the Jacobins against the legitimate, science-based claims that he was making for a new elite whose title to rule was a proper understanding of the science of man and the science of society. If the hypnotic model of leadership that Le Bon derived from Nancy held good, then Taine's elite would be wasting their time constructing a science at all. They would have been better employed learning techniques of hypnotism as Plato had claimed democratic leaders had learned techniques of crowd control from the sophists. It would only have made sense for Taine to have used the hypnotic model if the Salpêtrière School had had the field all to itself. And there was something of the classical spirit in the generalization that because hypnotism was actually a scientifically verifiable fact, then all relationships in which one man automatically did the bidding of another must be hypnotic relationships. This was the method of the eighteenth-century science of man all over again, taking a meagre extract of the science of human behaviour and making it the basis for a whole theory of man and a whole theory of history. Taine had condemned the *philosophes* for that and he was not likely to look with favour on a modern version of the same thing. If all behaviour, normal and pathological, was to be put down to irrational, unconscious mechanisms, then there was nothing to choose between different kinds of leadership. All elites would be tarred with the same brush; all would be groups of sophists on the make. It is a tempting view that Taine deliberately avoided getting himself involved in the snares of hypnotic theory because he could see that it could lead to positions directly opposite to those he wished to hold fast to. Le Bon had none of Taine's caution. The hypnotic model led him to generalizations so sweeping that the operation of hypnotic mechanisms in the crowd came to be understood as the explanation of all human behaviour. The crowd was taking over the whole of modern society, and in Le Bon's hands the psychology of the crowd threatened to take over the whole science of man and the whole science of society.

154

6

From the Criminal Crowd to a Social Theory: Scipio Sighele and Gabriel Tarde

Both Scipio Sighele and Gabriel Tarde approached the theory of crowds from the direction of criminology. Their original interest was in the problem of the degree of criminal responsibility of individuals who had taken part in collective crimes. The range of collective crimes could be stretched very wide, from pairs of burglars to street gangs to conspiracies like the Mafia all the way up to aggressive wars. Both Sighele and Tarde knew the mob passages in Taine's account of the French Revolution, and both saw the Paris *Commune* through Taine's eyes as a crowd event. Their problem as criminologists was to locate crowd crimes somewhere on the scale of collective crime, and then to decide who was, and by what degree, responsible. Sighele and Tarde are remarkable for the theoretically imaginative way they follow clues into territory which lies outside the field of criminology narrowly conceived. I emphasize this theoretical persistence for two reasons: first, to point out that, in the years following the *Commune*, the crowd was not only a 'law and order' problem but was, on the contrary the starting point for the construction of genuinely new and wide-ranging theories of society; and second, to do something to rescue Sighele and Tarde from Le Bon's strictures on them as plodders trapped within the confines of their specialism so that crowd theory had to wait for Le Bon himself to see its wider implications.

Le Bon scooped all the crowd theorists except Taine in 1895, and they were not best pleased (see below, pp. 196–7); Sighele never made it from Italian into English; Tarde, though translated early, has remained a criminologists' criminologist. Tarde has also had to suffer the double indignity of Le Bon's scoop and the revenge of the Durkheimians, who believe that in the debate between Durkheim and Tarde about the nature of sociology, Durkheim won (see below, p. 189). So Tarde lost both ways: from the Le Bon point of view he is a pedant, and from the Durkheim point of view he is a dilettante; but if points had been given for clarity in the debate with Durkheim and for elegance and erudition in the dispute with Le Bon, then Tarde would never have entered the Anglo-Saxon world as a Gallic Casaubon. It is also time to begin to resurrect Durkheim's one-time colleague at Bordeaux, Alfred Espinas. Espinas is only an echo in the English-speaking world, yet he had a clearer idea than anyone of what the theoretical problems were in the evolutionary biology and sociology on which so much crowd theory depended, and his *Des Sociétés animales* had canonical status for thinkers like Sighele.[1]

Though its theoretical ramifications were considerable, the problem which the crimes of crowds originally posed for Sighele and Tarde can be stated very simply: very ordinary people, of previous good character, got mixed up in crowds which committed crimes; there was nothing in their past which could lead a magistrate to predict that they would ever take a hand in crime, and it was equally certain that they would never have done anything remotely criminal if they had been left on their own. They must have been 'carried away' in the crowd. They were not ringleaders; they just happened to be the ones snatched by the police. In court, they made no attempt to deny that they had been part of the crowd, and they could not explain how they had come to be parties to the crowd's crimes. Crowd psychology deals with explanations of exactly that kind of behaviour: exceptional behaviour; automatic behaviour; behaviour that has been suggested to or by the unconscious; behaviour that takes one out of one's self; behaviour that has no relation to previous behaviour; behaviour for which one cannot be, in any ordinary sense, held responsible. This behaviour is not rational because the individual did not *choose* to act, so the individual who took part in the crime did not do it as himself. His crime was part of the crowd's crime. If, as Sighele believes, the crowd's mind operates according to different psychological laws from those according to which ordinary individual minds operate, or if, as Tarde believes, the responsibility of individuals in the crowd is reduced to a point where it is almost negligible, then the only culprit is the crowd. It might make sense to punish the crowd, except that you cannot, partly because it is almost always impossible to arrest the whole crowd, and partly because, once the crowd is separated into its component individuals, the crowd and its mind disappears, so that there is nothing, literally nothing, left to punish. The temporary mind which intended the crime ceased to exist. (Sighele does consider a collective punishment of the whole milieu out of which the crowd and the crime came, which was the custom of the Romans, especially when dealing with foreign peoples, but he rejects collective reprisal as unfitting in the modern age where jurisprudence demands an individual responsible for his own act.) If crowd psychology was true, and if it was also true that anybody could become part of the crowd if the circumstances were right, and if it was also true that there was an in-built compulsion in crowds to create mayhem, then nobody had the right to feel superior. There was no 'rest of society' which had the right to punish, or even to be protected from, the actions of crowds.

When that sense of distance between the crowd and the rest of society had been removed, it was hard to see what could survive from the several versions of nineteenth-century individualism and liberalism. By no means all crowd theorists took the idea of the group or crowd mind as literally as Le Bon did, but they all speak of the present or imminent crisis as a crisis of individualism. This individualism seemed destined to live a short, unhappy life, from the time that Comte and Tocqueville gave it something like its current meaning until the psychology of the crowd, not much more than fifty years. ('Individualism's' life was to be even shorter in England. It only appeared as a neologism in Henry Reeve's translation of Tocqueville's *Democracy in America* in 1862. (Lively, 1962, p. 72).) Individualism went much deeper than economic individualism, or rugged individualism, though it included both. In origin, it was not economic at all, but scientific and historical where science and history meet in the social theories which came out of Darwinian and Spencerian evolutionism. (I say 'social theories' rather than Social Darwinism because the out-and-out, survival-of-the-fittest Social Darwinism associated in America with William Graham Sumner is quite rare in the European social theory of this period, though it does turn up from time to time, for instance in an eccentric way in Nietzsche, in the Le Bon of *The Psychology of Socialism*, and in Sorel's admiration for the Yankee capitalists, fit for any enterprise, a class enemy worth fighting.) It was the basis for a vast scientific and historical enterprise in which all the theorists of the crowd played their parts with the notable exception of Gabriel Tarde.

The original premise of individualism in its scientific version was methodological. Following Spencer, crowd psychologists began by arguing that any biological or social phenomenon could be satisfactorily explained by an examination of the nature of the parts which made up the whole. The whole was no more than the sum of its parts, so there was no difference in principle, and no difference in procedure, between the investigation of how a living body made up of cells worked, and of how a social group made up of individuals worked. Such a procedure for the investigation of social groups had the advantage both of rooting social science in a real science, biology, and of fastening both biological and social science to a tradition of methodological individualism which could trace a very respectable ancestry back through the Enlightenment to seventeenth-century empiricism and ultimately back to Democritus. *Rerum cognoscere causas* consisted of showing that the operation of complex phenomena was the result of the operation of much simpler components which combined with each other in accordance with fixed and knowable laws, so that the composites which components formed could themselves be shown to be acting in accordance with laws which, if they were not exactly the same as the laws according to which their components acted, were at least derivable from them or, at the very least, were consistent with them. This was a methodological scheme of great scope and plausibility. As a procedure, it had genuine claims to universality. The French social scientist Alfred Espinas, who influenced every crowd theorist for the next twenty years, could claim that 'Sociology is a physical science like all the rest' (Espinas, 1878, p. 122), by which he meant that there was no difference between one branch of science and another.

It was even misleading to speak at all of the 'sciences' in the plural. Social science was not science by analogy, adoption, or imitation. The object which social science chose to investigate differed from the single cell which attracted the attention of the biologist only because it was more complex. Many nineteenth-century social scientists looked forward to a time when a complete science – it could be called the Science of Man, but Science would do equally well – would give an account of the whole of life from the cell to the most complex of human societies, with no gaps left in between. Espinas's own *Des Sociétés animales* (1878) contains a brilliant polemic against those who still insisted that sociology should confine itself to the study of human societies. How, he asked, could anyone identify a point on the evolutionary scale above which social life took place and below which it did not? Evolution taught above all else that life was minutely differentiated, so any attempt to draw such a line was bound to be arbitrary (Espinas, 1878, pp. 210–20).

Of course there were great gaps in practice, and what look like wild analogies to us, analogies between combinations of cells and human groups, or between animal societies and human societies, were not analogies to nineteenth-century evolutionists. What we call analogies were working hypotheses to them, attempts to bridge gaps which would be filled as science continued to do its patient work. These short-cut speculations would eventually be tested, reformulated and integrated into a growing corpus of reliable theory. Laboratory improvisations they might be, but they were an essential part of the scientific enterprise, not a substitute for it. It is these bridging attempts which make so much nineteenth-century social science now seem so quaint. Bagehot's *Physics and Politics* (1872) for instance, makes great leaps from reflections on the evolution of the human body to reflections on the development of human societies as if there was nothing in between. The point is that there *was* nothing much in between because the scientific work on the 'in-between' was still being done. Bagehot's was an interim report on a whole scientific enterprise and his use of the word 'physics' tells the whole story. The book is not about physics in any sense that we would recognize, but about evolutionary biology. Bagehot can use the word 'physics' almost casually because almost any other scientific term would do equally well. If what we call the sciences spoke easily to one another, and if all science spoke with the same voice, then why not call all science 'physics'?

Beyond the methodological claim lay an even more ambitious intention. The attempt to explain the complex by the simple, the urge to get at the root, perhaps to the beginning, was an explicit attack on all mysticism. There were to be no mysterious wholes which were greater than the sum of their parts, and there was to be no beginning beyond which all was mystery. If there was a beginning – and this seemed increasingly unlikely as biology and geology developed time-scales which removed the idea of time itself from ordinary understanding – then there would be nothing at that beginning which could not be explained. Besides, enough had happened since that almost unimaginable origin to occupy scientific curiosity for the foreseeable future.

The account that evolutionism gave of the development of life from the beginning was an individualist account. Life had evolved from homogeneity to heterogeneity; from undifferentiated matter to the moment of individualist triumph when man showed himself to be a self-conscious, rational individual capable of making choices about how he should live. The crowning glory of evolution, its special creation even, was man. It was reassuring to reflect upon the enormous distance that separated man from the numberless micro-organisms which had died mindlessly to form the inert land- and seascape in the evolutionary past, and which would continue to die in the same obscurity in the evolutionary future. It was equally satisfying to compare the ordered, but unselfconscious, life of insect societies with the high-degree self-conscious order of some human societies. Real self-satisfaction was to be gained by contrasting the savage, barely differentiated, social solidarity of tribal societies, with the high degree of social division of labour of modern states; and the contrast between primitive men in thrall to their gods and haunted by their dreams, and modern free-thinking men capable of working out the principles of morality for themselves and therefore capable of loving their fellow men independently even of God's command, could lead to positive ecstasy. Evolution meant progress, and progress meant progress towards individuality and individualism. Then, by sleight of hand, or at least by an inversion of cause and effect, it appeared that individualism, the end towards which progress was tending, was also the cause of progress.

Differentiation became the cause of evolution or at least the condition upon which evolution depended.

When applied to human life, the story of progress was always the story of great individuals, inventors whose discoveries were popularized, or of great leaders able to inspire a following, or of elite groups whose lives became patterns for high culture and civility. The necessity for leaders and elites was transformed into a biological imperative. Espinas, for instance, is confident that, since the beginning of the nineteenth century, all the sciences – linguistics, history, palaeontology, economics, biology and zoology – have been telling the same simple truth, that society is a natural organism which develops like any other organism, from being an aggregate of random individuals, to a state where the division of labour is its chief characteristic and the means to its future progress (Espinas, 1878, p. 95). The division of labour is never complete without the essential division between leaders and led. Flocks of birds are not true societies because they have no leaders; swarms of bees are true societies because they are ruled by a queen whose title to rule is based on the defeat of rivals; what makes the domestication of animals possible is that men either control the leader of the herd, and through him control the rest, or men themselves become substitutes for animal leaders; among the higher anthropoids societies develop which approach the sophistication of primitive human societies because the leaders of hordes can establish a paternal authority powerful enough to neutralize the rival authority of natural fathers (Espinas, 1878, pp. 177, 364, 469-73, 484–90, 496–7).

In the human world, natural progress is continued. The savage tribe has its chief; the kingdom has its king whose word is law, and out of the kingdom comes the modern State which is capable of choosing to make law and of choosing what kind of law it will make. As in the animal world, so in the human, the story is not one of *uninterrupted* progress. Societies may regress, and when regression happens, it always happens as a result of the victory of undifferentiated mass over differentiated civility. The barbarous hordes which swamped the Roman Empire undid centuries' work of the social, political and economic division of labour. Society returned to its origins, and the slow work of differentiation had to begin again. What held true for the contrast between different societies – Roman and barbarian – also held true for the contrast between different sections of the same society. Not all the parts of a single society develop at the same rate. That had been a commonplace of social theory since the second half of the eighteenth century, when it became part of Enlightenment to recognize the contrast between the civility of towns and rudeness of the countryside. Belief in Enlightenment meant believing that one day the Scottish Highlands would be like Edinburgh. Progress had come to mean bringing the less socially-evolved parts of a society within the compass of highly evolved life under the wise leadership of an elite. There were obviously dangers in this as an enterprise if it were to be pursued too enthusiastically. Cautious progressives felt that an excess of reforming zeal might give to a State democratic institutions of a kind for which the mass of the people were, quite literally, not ready. Progressive conservatism of Bagehot's kind in England, or conservative liberalism of Taine's kind in France, rested on an awareness of the varied degrees of evolutionary progress in different groups within a single society. It would be folly, in a society where the mass of the people were at a lower stage of evolutionary development than the elite, to require of each individual the exercise of the highly evolved right of rational choice between electoral alternatives. Someone as friendly to democracy as Graham Wallas could begin to wonder, as he saw working-class voters reeling drunk into the polling stations to vote Tory in London School Board elections, whether social evolution might not have so far outstripped biological evolution that the mass of the voters did not even have the mental equipment to make a simple Benthamite calculation of self-interest (Wiener, 1971, p. 40).[2] Responsible political leadership consisted of a principled hesitation in the face of democratic demands which, however well-meaning they might be in the abstract, were not ripe for the time. Attention should instead be paid to the slower work of developing educational institutions which would in the long run – perhaps the very long run – bring the masses up to the level of the classes. This sense of distance between the masses and the classes was the very opposite of reactionary. It was based on the latest, most advanced body of social thought available at the time, and if it was easy to confuse this principled conservatism with older, less scientific, conservatisms, nobody was to blame. Conservatism, at least in principle, could become remarkably forward-looking, but what had never to be forgotten was that the future, like the newly discovered past, could be very long indeed. But the social task was clear. The gap between the more-advanced and the less-advanced had to be filled, and the political debate had to centre round the question of what the best mechanisms were for filling it.

This was a perspective which could accommodate the crowd and the mob without difficulty. The crowd as undifferentiated mass, and the mob as uncivilized violence, were simply primitive. Spencer, Bagehot and Taine taught men everywhere to regard any social unpleasantness as a throwback or a primitive survival. They all speak through Bagehot when he writes:

We see frequently in states what physiologists [he might as easily have said historians, criminologists, social scientists in general] call

'Atavism' – the return, in part, to the unstable nature of their barbarous ancestors. Such scenes of cruelty and horror as happened in the great French Revolution, and as happens, more or less, in every great riot, have always been said to bring out a secret and suppressed side of human nature; and we now see that they were the outbreak of inherited passions long repressed by fixed custom, but starting into life as soon as that repression was catastrophically removed.

(Bagehot, 1876, pp. 153–4)

The crowd was a permanent threat to civilization, and the action of the mob was a crime against it. The crimes committed by crowds could be seen, as they were by Lombroso and by the criminologists like Sighele who followed him, as particular cases of atavism. If, as Lombroso urged, certain sorts of men, born criminals, were physiologically impelled to social wrong-doing, was not the crowd when it committed collective crimes obeying the same imperatives? Society had to be defended against both individual and collective crime, but the theoretical basis for that defence was becoming increasingly difficult to formulate. If the cause of crimes was physiological in some sense, then individualism offered no basis for punishment because it made very little sense to say that the individual was responsible for his own physiology. The born criminal could not be held responsible for his crime as an individual because he had not *chosen* to commit it. The individual in the crowd was in a similar position. All crowd theorists agreed that the chief characteristic of crowds was their unanimity in the literal sense of sameness of mind. Everything that might differentiate one man from another was lost in the crowd. This was also what atavism meant, the loss of the ability to make choices which differentiated one man from another. What happened in the crowd, like what happened in the mind of the born criminal, was the antithesis of what was supposed to happen in the mind of the rational, self-conscious, individual. That is what gave civilized men their sense of distance from the crowd. Not all members of the lower classes were born criminals, though it was easy to elide the lower classes with the criminal classes. What had to be done was to educate the minds of those members of the lower classes who were capable of it to a level at which they could put the danger of social contamination behind them and begin to live the differentiated, individualistic life which nineteenth-century civilization hoped to put within the grasp of everyman.

It was that sense of distance between individuals and the crowd that Scipio Sighele began to erode, and what makes that erosion so poignant is that Sighele fought against it as long as he could. He was an admirer of Spencer, a follower of Lombroso, and was pointed in the direction of crowd theory by the great Italian criminologist Enrico Ferri. His was a characteristically late-nineteenth-century positivist mind, where positivist means evolutionist rather than Comtian. He described himself as 'evolutionist to the root' ('*Evolutioniste dans l'âme*') (Sighele, 1901, p. 85),[3] but it was because he was such a loyal evolutionist that his difficulties over the social message of evolutionism arose. Like Tarde, Sighele was interested in the problem of responsibility for the crimes committed by crowds. The Lombrosian tradition, while offering excellent guidelines for the way the law ought to treat individual criminals, had very little to say about collective crimes. The achievement of Lombroso was to make the law sensitive to the relative weightings of anthropological (=hereditary) and sociological factors in the cause of crimes committed by individuals who were still responsible for their crimes because they at least had some idea of what they were doing. Crimes committed by criminal gangs, like the *Maffia* (sic) and the *Camorra*, fell into much the same category, because born criminals in a criminal milieu engaged in an institutionalized form of criminal conspiracy could hardly complain that they did not know what they were doing, though the law could sympathize with the fact that they were unlikely ever to do anything else (ibid., pp. 29, 159–60, 170). But a problem arises when the magistrate is confronted with an ordinary man, who is not to be feared in ordinary life, who has been snatched out of the crowd which has committed crimes. He deserves more humanity and more psychology from the bench (ibid., pp. 128, 161–2). But what *kind* of psychology? Not Lombrosian anthropological psychology, because he is not a born criminal, and not individualist psychology, because it is quite clear that what he did was unpremeditated. Either the magistrate is confronted with a completely gratuitous act, an act without antecedents, or he needs a very special psychology to explain what has happened *to* the criminal's mind, or perhaps even to explain *what has replaced it*.

The special psychology which explains how human aggregates work Sighele, following Ferri, calls 'collective psychology' to distinguish it from individual psychology and social psychology. Both individual psychology and social psychology obey Spencer's law that the whole can be explained by its parts. Spencer, Comte, Espinas and Tarde are correct when they say that a society should be treated as an individual, and sociology he thinks is psychology writ large. But crowds are different. What they do does not add up. Otherwise how could one explain a particularly hideous crime committed by a small group? Or a stupid mistake made by a panel of learned men each of whom later recognizes the mistake easily? Or an absurdly perverse verdict by a jury? Or lunatic decisions made by distinguished panels of artists or scientists? Or a cabinet making a decision which is much worse than the decision which would have been made by any one of its members by himself? Something must be happening in groups like these to cancel out the good qualities of the individuals of which they are composed (ibid., pp. 1–12). It is this failure to aggregate the good qualities of individuals that makes crowds so puzzling. Crowds do not always commit crimes. On occasion they are capable of heroism – witness the *gamins* of Paris, thieves practically from birth, pimps at sixteen, dying like heroes on the barricades of the *Commune* (ibid., p. 63) – but their heroism is as unpredictable as their crimes. Even a mediocre gathering like the National Assembly could, on the Night of August the 4th, act more nobly than could have been expected from the individuals who were its members (ibid., pp. 61–2). But social science does confirm what the ordinary man already thinks, that we are right to fear the worst from crowds.

What Sighele has to say about the crowd makes it a phenomenon that challenges every evolutionary assumption. The crowd is genuinely new in a way that no other collective phenomenon is. In the ordinary evolutionary sense, it has no past and no future. This is true phylogenetically and ontogenetically. There is no crowd out of which the crowd comes, and there is no crowd-individual before the individual becomes a member of the crowd. When the crowd disperses, crowd-individuals become their ordinary workaday selves. The crowd is in this sense outside ordinary time, and it occupies no obvious social space. It shares characteristics with other kinds of groups, with a criminal conspiracy, say, or a religious sect, or an army, but it is none of these. What makes the crowd different is only partly its impermanence, and Sighele was to change his mind about even that. Its central characteristic is its unanimity. That may not look at first sight to be a very startling thing to say about the crowd, but it is not quite the commonplace that it appears to be. At least at first, Sighele insisted that the crowd was only a moment in the history of a society. As a Spencerian, he thought that societies were indeed becoming more solid, and he hoped that Italy in the *Postrisorgimento* would achieve something like the degree of social solidarity enjoyed by its more advanced European neighbours. But this solidarity had to be differentiated solidarity. What made a society modern was the evolutionary miracle of the combination of a high degree of the social division of labour with a high degree of social cohesion. Anything else was barbarous equanimity. The model of social cohesion was biological. Sighele was an admirer of Espinas, and like him he marvelled at the coherence of living organisms and animal societies, each part of which contributed to the vital life of the whole. That is how Sighele wanted his own society to develop, because, like the good evolutionist he was, progress meant steady, unspectacular advance along the positivist path. Being a positivist in the *Postrisorgimento* meant believing that the new Italian state was best served by putting its energies into a decent postal service, or a comprehensive railway network, regular administration and the integration of the *mezzogiorno* away from Bourbon Africanism into the more advanced life of Italy north of Rome. But Sighele could not help noticing that the crowd stood out as both an impediment and an insult to progress. The crowds that interested him were not confined to Italy. The violence of Italian politics after unification offered examples enough, but Sighele was enormously well-read, and what he found about crowds in Taine, Stendahl, Schopenhauer, Nietzsche, Ibsen, Victor Hugo, Zola, Ibsen, Carlyle, Tarde, Espinas, and eventually Le Bon, made him realize that there was something *modern* about crowds. He began to see that there was an intellectual world beyond Spencerism, and that the key to understanding that world might be in understanding the crowd.

Sighele does not doubt that the crowd has its own special soul ('*âme de la foule*') (ibid., p. 34); nor does he doubt that in the right circumstances any man or woman could become a member of a crowd. (He claims respectable women once ate policemen during a riot in Sicily (ibid., p. 99).) What is it, then, that causes this special soul to appear in the crowd? Sighele's explanation is not very original. He begins from the crimes of crowds, by which he typically means riot, and wonders whether the crimes of mobs might not be compared to crimes of passion committed by individuals. A people in revolt can commit crimes, but he is reluctant to concede that these crimes are the same as ordinary criminality. (Garibaldi and his Thousand plainly lurk behind this distinction.) Ordinary criminality, he wants us to think, is Lombrosian. Born criminals do not commit passionate crimes. Some criminals take to crime as the occasion arises, and others because they are too weak-willed to resist the criminal suggestions of their peers, and yet a third group commit those crimes of passion which arise out of a sense of betrayal, or injured honour, crimes which are, in their way, deeply moral, or which arise from motives which are not bad, or at least not squalid (ibid., p. 29).

Collective crimes are frequently of this last type. For an explanation of what goes on in the mind of the crowd Sighele goes to a famous passage in Espinas about the behaviour of wasps which he quotes in full (Espinas, 1878, pp. 358–9, quoted in Sighele, 1901, pp. 54–6). Espinas, wants to explain how it is that wasp sentinels communicate to other wasps that the nest is in danger. Espinas is very cautious about ascribing all animal behaviour to some vague notion of instinct. Part of the purpose of *Des Sociétés animales* is to show that animal life is intelligent, or at least to show that it is absurd to argue that only human life is intelligent. Animals have an idea (*représentation*) of what other animals are doing. When a wasp sentinel recognizes a danger, it makes a great deal of fuss. That is its form of communication with other wasps who, seeing the fuss, make a fuss themselves. Espinas lays it down as 'a law in the whole domain of intelligent life, that the representation of an emotional state brings on the beginnings of the same emotional state in those who observe it' (Espinas, 1878, p. 359). Sighele says 'That masterful description of Alfred Espinas adequately explains – I believe – the psychology of the crowd' (Sighele, 1901, p. 56). One is tempted to say it doesn't, and Sighele himself almost acknowledges that it doesn't, because he canvasses other ways of explaining the psychology of the crowd. He wonders whether what the wasps do might not itself be the explanation of the more general phenomenon of 'psychical mimesis' (ibid., p. 66), some kind of 'primitive disposition' (he quotes de Maistre and Schopenhauer) (ibid., pp. 56, 68) and he gives the matter an evolutionary twist by adding that in some kinds of crowds the 'good' members are driven to imitate the 'bad' (born criminals who are always to be found in mobs) as part of the 'instinct for survival'(ibid., p. 68). Again, perhaps what the wasp sentinels do is an example of what other crowd psychologists call 'moral contagion', or imitation (he cites Bagehot and Tarde) (ibid., p. 39), or suggestion, which has its origin in hypnotism (ibid., p. 42).

So why is Sighele so interested in Espinas's account of the wasps when it is not in fact the only basis for his own explanation of the crowd? The answer is that Sighele takes a much more general and startling thesis from Espinas, of which the wasps are only a single illustration. Professor Barrows points to this inadvertently in an uncharacteristically hurried judgement on Espinas's influence on other crowd theorists. She writes that Espinas's legacy to crowd psychologists was 'less methodological than anecdotal' (Barrows, 1981, p. 177), and she says this because both Sighele and the French crowd psychologist Henry Fournial (*Essai sur la psychologie des foules*, Lyons and Paris, 1892) both quote the story of the wasps. The word 'anecdotal' does less than justice to the enormous labour that went into *Des Sociétés animales* or to the evident care with which it was read by a whole generation of crowd theorists, and it ignores the problem that Espinas wrote the book to explore.

Espinas wrote *Des Sociétés animales* to show that animal life was social and intelligent, and to do that he has to come up with a view of intelligence, the process of thinking, which was common to both men and animals. He began by denying that all thinking would be syllogistic if it could, because to argue that only syllogistic thinking is worthy of the name would exclude the whole of the animal kingdom and most of the human race from thinking at all. Espinas's set-piece example of intelligence in the lower animals is the process of domestication of aphids by ants (Espinas, 1878, pp. 188–205). Espinas begins by a muted but confident criticism of Darwin, always a sign that he thinks he is on strong ground. Darwin says in the *Origin* that ants began to domesticate aphids out of an instinct for survival; the ants who domesticated aphids survived, the others didn't. Espinas will have none of this, because it cannot be an explanation of the *origin* of domestication, and he always suspects that when Darwin uses explanations based on instinct rather too much of English utilitarianism is being smuggled into the argument. (All creatures would be Englishmen and Benthamites if they could; the sovereign masters, pleasure and pain, somehow work automatically, hence 'instinctively', so ants instinctively domesticate aphids to increase their chances of survival.) Espinas says that if we were to concede that there was an intelligence at work when ants first domesticated aphids, then the circular hypothesis of instinct becomes unnecessary. What kind of intelligence would it have been? Not, certainly, Aristotelian or Cartesian, because animals cannot generalize, but that in itself is not enough to rule out the possibility of ant-intelligence. Spencer himself has established that the most common type of human thinking occurs when inferences are made directly from observation, a syllogism without a middle term. Even science works like that. Syllogistic reasoning is used to examine the findings of inductive enquiry but is not itself a recipe for scientific work. (Darwin borrowed the idea of selection from the pigeon fanciers, not the other way round.) Why not say that ants, like scientists and most human beings, try things out *to see*? (italics in original). Once domestication has been seen to work, all other ants have to do is to repeat it by imitation, and all the authorities agree that to imitate requires no intelligence at all in any recognized sense of the word.

Looked at like that, thinking comes within the reach of most animals and all men. Ants have had millions of years to try things out. The same was no doubt true of the first advances made by man, who must have discovered how to do similar things to aphid domestication before he even had a language sophisticated enough to express the logical connections between the stages of what he had learned to do by direct inference and imitation. This is still probably the case with most men, whose thinking processes are best described as the working of 'an unconscious, or better still, sub-conscious intelligence'. Humanity accomplished *its* first stages of evolution without analytical and explicit reasoning, so why should the same not be true of animals throughout the whole of their evolution? Espinas's conclusion is that it is not very extraordinary that ants do domesticate aphids, and that most men continue to think in exactly the same way as an ant thinks when it domesticates its aphid.

Espinas extends the argument into the single human individual. What particularly interests him is any biological evidence which shows that there are centres outside the brain which are capable of originating physical responses. He cites Haeckel, Virchow, Bernard, Robin, Milne-Edwards and Schaeffle (ibid., pp. 137, 213) to argue against Spencer that the human individual has, like a human society, more than one *sensorium*. Spencer argued in the *Principles of Psychology* (which appeared between the first and second editions of *Des Sociétés animales*) that the chief difference between a single human being and the society he lived in was that there was no real equivalent to do for society what the brain did for the individual. Espinas insists that it has long been a commonplace among physiologists to compare the cells of a living body to the co-operative work of factory workers in a large enterprise, or to the separate but connected lives of the inhabitants of a large city. The arteries of the body have been compared to the canals that feed different parts of a country, and the nervous system has been compared to the system of electric telegraphs which spread information in the form of impulses from the centre to the periphery and vice versa (ibid., p. 214). If there are centres outside the brain which can either originate responses in other parts of the body, or send information to the brain to cause the brain to originate responses which it would not otherwise have caused, then the brain cannot be the only place where nature does its thinking.

It was that argument of Espinas that influenced later crowd theorists, and Sighele in particular. What fascinated Sighele was, quite literally, non-cerebral thinking, if by thinking one meant the causation of physio-logical responses which were both deliberate and unpremeditated. Following Espinas, he makes the rather bold-sounding claim that we don't just think with our brains but with our whole nervous system (Sighele, 1901, p. 55). That is the full horror for individualism of late-nineteenth-century biology and biological sociology. In the body cells suggest behaviour to cells, and in the crowd individuals suggest behaviour to individuals. An emotion transmits itself to everybody in a crowd by the visibility of that emotion in one of its members. This is easily seen in the higher animals, in children, and in savages (Sighele, 1901, p. 55, quoting Espinas), and it happens again in the crowd. The imperatives are therefore biological and neurophysiological, so that to pretend that there are certain kinds of men who are in some sense immune from these imperatives is to maintain a position which is nothing short of ridiculous. This is not to say that all we can do is to sit down and wait to become part of a crowd. Sighele clings as long as he can to the remnants of an individualism which stands out from the crowd now that to say that there are groups which cannot become crowds is a contradiction in terms, and he never quite gives up the Lombrosian hope that those who are not born criminals can somehow be kept out of the crowd, but it is a hope tempered by a deep scepticism, even, until very late, a deep pessimism.

This can be seen most clearly in his treatment of the mechanisms of group contagion.

We have already seen that for Sighele, Espinas's account of the wasps is only one of the possible explanations of the psychology of the crowd. It is certainly an account of what we see when a crowd acts, but Sighele is enough of a Spencerian to know that there must be a great deal of difference between what happens in the mind of a wasp and what happens in the highly evolved mind of a human individual in a crowd. As a criminologist, he knows that it would be absurd for a magistrate to base his treatment of crowd criminals on incidents in the insect world. That kind of criminology would be laughed out of court. What Sighele needs is an account of individual psychology which speaks to what happens to individual minds when behaviour is suggested to them from the outside which they then enact automatically and unconsciously, and, like almost all crowd theorists after Taine, he finds it in the psychology of hypnotism.

Hypnotism carried all before it in its invasion of the scientific world from the music hall in the early 1880s. Hypnotism was very quickly incorporated into crowd theory to explain why the crowd acquired a unanimity which caused it to act as a single individual and in a way in which none of its component individuals would have acted on their own. The crowd's 'idea' of what it must do had to *come* from somewhere, or it had to *be brought* out from something. In either case, why not attribute the agency to hypnotic suggestion? Hypnotic suggestion could come from a crowd leader, or from other members of the crowd ('emotional contagion'), or it could come from both – a leader implanted the 'idea' in some members of the crowd who then infected the rest, so that the crowd behaved automatically in exactly the same way that a hypnotized subject behaved when prompted by the hypnotist. The way hypnotized subjects did in fact behave made hypnotic theory even more attractive to crowd theorists. Part of the charm of hypnotism was that hypnotized subjects could be induced to re-live their childhood experiences, and these childhood experiences were often painful. This was a psychological theory which crowd psychologists could not resist; they responded to the suggestion that hypnotized behaviour was pain-causing, atavistic behaviour, with a positively crowd-like unanimity.

Sighele's reception of hypnotic theory is at least critical. He recognizes that there is not one theory of hypnotism but two, and that each theory does in fact limit its own claims to being a generalizable theory of collective behaviour. The nature of these limitations has not always been well understood. It is sometimes suggested that the difference between the Salpêtrière School of Charcot, and the Nancy School of Liébault and Bernheim, is that the former maintained that only the mentally ill could be hypnotized while the latter maintained that anybody could be hypnotized. The Charcot School is seen as minimalist, wishing to confine hypnotism to psychotherapy, while the Nancy School is seen as maximalist because it opens up a whole range of normal phenomena to hypnotic explanation. Things were not, in fact, that simple. The Salpêtrière School did come round to the view that almost anyone could be hypnotized, but it still maintained that not everyone could be hypnotized equally deeply. Some subjects struggled hard not to submit to hypnotic suggestion, and it is this struggle that Sighele finds interesting because it suggests a struggle between two different personalities, the ordinary personality and an extraordinary personality which is created during hypnosis (Sighele, 1901, p. 131). The normal self struggles with the new self, which is the self to which the hypnotist directs his commands, but the new self does not obey commands to do things of which the normal self disapproves, so the ordinary personality still survives. The Nancy School did not posit this new personality created in hypnosis, but stuck to its position both that all men and women could be deeply hypnotized, though it recognized that in practice it was very difficult with some subjects, and that normal men and women would usually, but not always, obey an immoral command while hypnotized. Sighele recognized that the truly maximalist position on hypnotism was an amalgam of the radical positions held by the Salpêtrière and at Nancy. Add the new personality hypothesis of the Salpêtrière to the Nancy hypothesis that nearly all hypnotized subjects would accept immoral suggestions, and you end up with a very frightening psychology of the individual in a crowd, because that individual could be anyone.

As a criminologist, Sighele fights hard against the maximalist position in order to maintain at least the vestige of criminal responsibility for the crimes committed by crowds. He fastens on to the fact that there are still criminologists who refuse to believe that there is a single case where it can be proved that a criminal committed a crime as the result of direct hypnotic suggestion. If the most powerful suggestion cannot make someone commit a crime, then how can the suggestion that comes from the crowd destroy the ordinary moral personality? He thinks that the crime committed in the crowd by an individual must be a responsible act because some of his ordinary personality, perhaps only a tiny bit, survives to struggle against the immoral suggestion of the crowd. Sighele is plainly hedging here. He goes on to say that while those who commit crimes in crowds are responsible, not all are to be considered real criminals. Chance dictates that there must be some born criminals in crowds, but there are others who are simply 'feeble' (*faible*) and so are incapable of resisting the outside stimulus for long. They are the majority, and they become criminals casually, as the occasion arises, or through passion. In this way, Sighele can retain at least the semblance of the Lombrosian theory of crime. In society, the descent into crime happens as Sighele suggests it happens in the crowd, the only difference being that in the crowd it happens much more quickly, a speeding up of normal social processes. But Sighele's hanging on to the normality of Lombrosian positivism cannot disguise the fact that the crowd is different from a society, where most people do not come into contact with born criminals, and Sighele is honest enough to recognize that groups which are unlikely to contain born criminals – collections of *savants* for instance, or juries – can become crowds (Sighele, 1901, pp. 130–43). These crowds do not commit crimes, but, like all crowds, they are intellectually inferior to their individual members. This is 'the fatal psychological law' (ibid., p. 61) 'which means that when aggregates form in the human world, things go to the bad' (*Se rassembler, dans le monde humain, veut donc dire se rendre pire* (ibid., p. 176).) When human individuals gather, reason is at a discount, and when reason goes, so does individuality, and when individuality goes, morality and everything that is admirable goes with it.

Or does it? Between the first and second editions of *La Foule criminelle*, that is between 1891 and 1901, Sighele had begun to change his mind about crowds. Le Bon's dismissive remarks about the narrowness of the criminological approach to the problem of the crowd in the first edition of the *Psychologie des Foules* (1895) still rankled in 1899 when Sighele lectured at the New University of Brussels on 'The Moral Problem of Collective Psychology' (printed as Chapter 4 in the 1901 edition of *La Foule Criminelle*). In that lecture, Sighele dealt specifically with the 'goodness' of crowds, by which he meant almost anything that crowds did or had done which was not obviously criminal. In the first edition of *La Foule criminelle*, Sighele had said that just about the only good thing ever to come out of a crowd was the repudiation of their privileges by the French nobility on the Night of August the Fourth, and he attributed the moral generosity of the Assembly to the leadership of one of those 'temporary despots' who seem always to be thrown up by crowds (Sighele, 1901, pp. 61–2). To redress the balance, Sighele now emphasized the part played by crowds in creation of what we would now call culture. Crowds are now said to have invented language, writing, poetry and mythology, and he comes to the surprising conclusion for a crowd theorist that the inventions and discoveries of great men are not really individual at all. What the great genius does (he cites Darwin) is to bring to the clear light of day truths residing in ordinary consciousness (ibid., pp. 259–61). He goes on to say that the reason the great beneficent contributions of the crowd to human history have not received the attention they deserve is due to the tendency to explain human progress by the actions and inventions of great men (ibid., p.

265). What is interesting about what Sighele has now got to say about crowds is not the list of the crowd's achievements that he gives, but in the shift in meaning of the idea of the crowd itself. When Sighele first began to look at crowds and their crimes, he was careful to distinguish between crowds and their 'collective psychology', and societies. The crowd was a moment in the history of a society's development. Societies were organic, crowds were static, incapable of development, so they were outside the ordinary processes of social evolution. Now he is saying something radically different, that crowds are capable of doing at least some of the work of civilization. And equally interesting, he says that the 'great man/great inventor' theory of social evolution arises from an idolatry of individualism which the rise of collective psychology and the spread of democratic institutions is beginning to undermine (ibid., p. 265). In this new view of history, crowds and great men are *rivals* for the laurels of progress.

The question is: How could such a view come out of crowd theory? Professor Geiger believes that Sighele's conversion to the crowd did not come out of crowd theory at all. He argues that Sighele changed his mind about the crowd during the period of intense nationalist agitation in Italy which followed the Bosnian crisis of 1908, led to the Libyan War, and which eventually swept Italy into the Great War on the side of the Entente Powers in 1915. In Geiger's view, Sighele's conversion came about despite the scientific pretensions of his crowd psychology, which taught a contempt for the crowd, as a way of reconciling crowd psychology and democracy. Sighele's view of the necessary intellectual and moral vacuity of all collectivities made him contemptuous both of electoral majorities and parliamentary assemblies, and it was only the nationalist revival in Italy which led him to see imperialistic and irredentist nationalism as a way of filling the mind of the crowd with a content which would unite the nation and integrate the Italian masses into the State. (Geiger argues the same case for Tarde and Le Bon during the nationalist revival in France at the time of the Agadir Crisis of 1911; Geiger, 1977, pp. 47–8). Sighele did say some rather over-excited things about the crowd as the nation (*il populo*). In his *Pagine Nazionalista* (1910) he argued a biological case for imperialism ('To live – for the social as for the individual organism – means to expand'; cit. Thayer, 1964, p. 209); he praised the 'action of the people', dying on the battlefields of Africa (ibid., p. 224), and, in a review of D'Annunzio's play *The Fire*, he congratulated the author for having expressed 'in marvellously lucid prose, the unconscious power of the mob' (ibid., p. 215). It is equally true that Sighele had very little time for the parliamentary regime presided over by Giolitti, and after the Bank of Rome Scandal in the 1890s (Italy's Panama) he was positively hostile, comparing the bankers involved in the scandal unfavourably with bandits, because bankers ruin men without risk while the bandit has something of the hero about him (Sighele, 1898, pp. 4–10). Sighele would probably have agreed with Giovanni Bovio, a prominent figure in the bank exposé, who defended the Mafia on the grounds that Schiller, Byron and Victor Hugo had also defended bold spirits (Thayer, 1964, p. 180). But it would be quite wrong to maintain with Geiger that Sighele's changed view of the crowd after 1908 simply comes out of political developments extraneous to the crowd theory which he had worked out before 1900. What Geiger ignores is the effect which Ferri's suggestion, that the crowd was an exception to Spencer's law, had on Sighele. The crowd was in one sense a new individual – it had a mind of its own – but in the Spencerian sense it was also the ideal anti-individual – men in crowds had no minds of their own. In one sense it was typically modern – witness the events of the contemporary world, but in another sense it was ancient – witness the atavism of the crowd. When Sighele tried to make sense of this, and of the added assumption that no man was immune from the crowd, he was rigorous enough to begin to wonder whether there was such a thing as a true individual in either biological or social life. It was here that his evolutionism led him to a profoundly anti-Spencerian conclusion. If the typically modern aggregate was the crowd, and if, as Espinas and the new biology following Haeckel argued, all animal and biological life could be conceived of as the social life of aggregates, then where in this scheme of things was the true individual to be found? Espinas had attributed a kind of absolute individuality to cells because they are the simplest living things about which it can be said that each one is different from the rest of its kind (Espinas, 1878, pp. 220–1), but Sighele pushes the argument beyond even Espinas, by pointing out that there is no reason in principle for stopping at the cell once you have started on that train of argument of evolution in reverse. The only natural stopping place is right at the end, so Sighele comes to the conclusion that the only true individual must be the atom (Sighele, 1901, p. 177: from a reprint of a correspondence between Sighele and Gabriel Tarde in 1893). Sighele is still enough of an individualist in 1893 to begin to wonder whether, biologically speaking, it has been a mistake to assume that the aggregates which atoms and cells form are superior to the individual atoms and cells which make them up. Perhaps the 'psychology of the atom' is in some way superior to the psychology of the human individual, a conglomerate of atoms. Perhaps the individual atom has intellectual and artistic virtues hitherto undreamt of, and he wonders whether there might not be some connection between this psychology of the atom and the psychology of the unconscious, 'still so unknown and so mysterious' (ibid., p. 177). As social theory, this is, literally, a dead end, but its importance lies in the fact that this is a Spencerian positivist speaking. As Enrico Ferri pointed out when he rapped his former pupil very sharply over the knuckles, this was not a science at all but metaphysics. (In a shrewd sideswipe at the French, Ferri assumes that Sighele has been 'derailed – a truly positivist image – by the 'metaphysical vagabondage' of Gabriel Tarde. Ferri's riposte to Sighele's letter to Tarde and Sighele's reply to Ferri, are printed in Sighele, 1901, Part II.) Sighele's positivism was beginning to wear thin by 1894, but it was wearing thin from the inside out, not, as Geiger maintains, from the outside in. Positivist optimism of a Spencerian kind could not cope with crowd theory, if that theory was pushed to the limit, as it was by Sighele.

Sighele's assertion that the atom was the only true individual had important implications for his political theory in general. In 1894 he still believed that there was a particular type of individual who could be called upon in this intellectual emergency, and that was the great man. The atom stood at one end of nature and the genius at the other. Everything in between was subject to the fatal law that to aggregate was to regress. This was a body-blow to the whole enterprise of Spencerian biologism in social theory. Sighele comes close to writing off that whole intellectual enterprise which saw human social progress as a natural extension of biological evolution. The atom is part of physics, not biology, and to argue that the genius is a necessary product of biological evolution is ludicrous. (Sighele *could* have used Condorcet's argument, that because the number of genius births is in a fixed proportion to the number of ordinary births, the number of geniuses born is bound to increase because the birth rate is increasing, but he doesn't.) Geiger would have us believe that Sighele continued to be a great-man theorist until he was thrown off that track by the nationalist delirium of the immediate prewar period in Italy, but again Geiger has failed to understand the direction Sighele was being driven in by the failure of biological life to produce true individuals. By 1894, Sighele had come to see a very clear distinction between the intelligence and the morality of crowds. He was very quickly getting over his pessimism about the criminality of crowds. He had never thought of crowds as being necessarily criminal, but now he began to treat the question of collective crime much more openly than his treatment of it of only two years before. He still thinks that intellectually the crowd is bound to be inferior to individuals, but morally the crowd is likely to be either far better, or far worse, than individuals. The reason for this is that, morally, men are 'additionable', but not intellectually. 'There are collective heroisms, but not collective masterpieces in art or science' (ibid., p. 170). This gives Sighele the clue to what happens when something is actually suggested to the crowd by its leader, or by members of the crowd to their fellows. When ideas are suggested to the crowd, the result is the creation of a group of disciples, but when

174

an emotion like courage is suggested to the crowd, or in the crowd, the result is the creation of a people made up of equals ('un peuple des égaux' (ibid., p. 174)).

It is this equality in the crowd which leads Sighele on to what he was later to call proletarian nationalism, and behind it lies a particular view of the *Postrisorgimento*. Ferri and Sighele clashed about the nature of Garibaldi's leadership, and to take a view of that was to take a view of everything that had happened in Italian politics since 1860. Garibaldi and his Thousand were in some straightforward sense a crowd. But what was the relationship of this most important of Italian crowds to its leader? Sighele seemed to be saying that Garibaldi created his equals in the Thousand, while maintaining that the communication of ideas to any group can only create disciples who are by definition inferiors. A speech by Garibaldi could create a whole crowd of heroes, but a disciple-crowd can never be suggested into equality with a master. Even Spencer cannot make a genius out of one of his readers. Ferri replied to his former pupil by asking the obvious question of how it was possible for a pupil ever to go beyond a master if what Sighele was saying was true, and he cast doubt on what Sighele had to say about Garibaldi. In his reply to Ferri, Sighele hedged about Garibaldi, saying that he did not really mean that Garibaldi in fact create heroes equal to himself; all he meant was that Garibaldi's crowd took Garibaldi for their model 'unconsciously', so that they began to *act* as heroes. (He even admits that there can even be people in the crowd who are superior to the leader (e.g. a better orator listening to Demosthenes), but this he thinks is just coincidence.) But the hedging cannot disguise the main burden of Sighele's argument, which is that if Garibaldi could get men to act as he acted and wanted them to act, there was very little to choose between Garibaldi and one of the Thousand, whereas someone reading Spencer, or listening to an orator telling them some complicated truth, could not be said to be able even to imitate the master (ibid., pp. 177–89).

The equality which happens in the crowd is the key to Sighele's view of the whole *Postrisorgimento* in Italy. Italian politics in the second half of the nineteenth century was cursed by the recent memory of a national revolution which was only half complete. The Roman Question continued to be asked even after most of the Roman territory was incorporated into Italy following France's defeat in 1870, and there were always those who argued that the South had never been incorporated into the new Italian state at all. The *Risorgimento* in the *mezzogiorno* meant the replacement of the old Bourbon officials by Piedmontese-style prefects and very little else, and there was a poignancy in that because Garibaldi had begun his conquest of Italy in the South. The easiest of all styles of opposition in Italian politics was to accuse the government of the day of betraying the spirit of the

175

Risorgimento, or of stifling it, or of being its out-and-out enemy. Against this poetical politics, Cavour, and later Giolitti, opposed a positivist programme of gradualist, evolutionary development for which the models were English constitutional monarchy in the manner celebrated by Bagehot, and English social development as celebrated by Spencer. Italy lacked the degree of social integration which could make such a programme work. The Giolittian programme was bound to fail on the chicken-and-egg principle, though Professor Thayer argues that it had begun to work after 1900 (Thayer, 1964, p. 231). Giolitti's aim was to integrate all sections of Italian society into a single nation, but his programme of gradual change was a possibility only in a society which was already highly integrated. The parliamentary regime with a constitutional monarchy was experimental, and in a sense accidental; if Cavour had not outwitted Garibaldi, Italy might well have ended up with a military dictatorship for which there were Italian precedents without number. The parliamentary regime had to prove itself if it was ever to be seen as anything more than a foreign import, marking the dividing line between a 'legal' Italy and a 'real' Italy striving to realize itself in opposition to yet another system of rule brought in from the outside. If, as the Bank of Rome Scandal of the 1890s seemed to suggest, the parliamentary regime was not only foreign to the real nation, but also corrupt, then it was not clear how parliamentary institutions could complete the work of national integration which the *Risorgimento* itself had left unfinished. It was this perception which was to push Sighele down the anti-positivist path towards anti-parliamentarianism and proletarian nationalism.

The crimes of high politics had a particular interest for Sighele as a criminologist. As a Lombrosian, he had been taught to look at crime as something anthropologically primitive. Lombroso himself had been led into the atavism theory of criminality by his observation, during his time as an army surgeon in the South, that a high proportion of those soldiers who committed military offences were tattooed. Tattooing was the writing of primitive man, so it followed that crime must be a form of primitive behaviour if a high proportion of criminals were tattooed. The criminal was not part of the modern world at all but an ancestral portrait come to life (the phrase is Tarde's). This led to an emphasis on the 'anthropological' factors in the explanation of the causes of crime, where anthropology itself meant physical anthropology with an eye to comparative anatomy and medicine. Some diseases, both mental and physical, were considered to be atavistic, and Lombrosian criminology was at its most rigorous, and most ridiculous, where Lombroso tried to show that all criminality was probably a hereditary form of epilepsy. Sighele had already found that Lombrosian criminology had very little to offer the criminologist who was interested in the causes of the crimes of crowds, and the Bank of Rome Scandal showed him that it had nothing at all to offer the criminologist who wanted to understand the crimes of the world of high finance and politics. That world was supposed to be the most advanced part of Italian life, an overworld as far above ordinary Italian life as the underworld was beneath it. The parliamentary regime was supposed to be Italy's door to modernity, just as the Bank of Rome was to be her passport to a system of sound finance which was the cornerstone of Giolitti's plan to make Italy into a modern state. Parliamentary institutions were new, so Sighele was forced into the position of maintaining that the crimes which accompanied it must also be new, and being new, they could not be accommodated into the Lombrosian scheme of crime as atavism. Sighele decided that crime too was subject to evolutionary change. The Positivist School of criminology in Italy had misled the public into thinking of the criminal as being simple, crude and murderous, but the modern criminal is well educated and well dressed. The prototype of modern criminality is organized brigandage in the South. The Mafia and the Camorra operate like a business enterprise, or like a state collecting taxes; extortion is regularized by a system of contract (offers are made which cannot be refused), and the collection of extra-legal tribute money is not very different from the state raising a revenue; regular payment becomes part of the order of things, and force has to be used only in exceptional cases. Like the crimes of the political world, the organized crimes of the syndicates are collective crimes in which elite brains have replaced the brute violence of the individual criminal. Evolution has worked even in the world of the criminal, but it can hardly be called progress (Sighele, 1898, pp. 4–11).

This increase in collective crimes has important implications for the future of Italian society. The evolutive crime of the higher classes and the atavistic crime of the poor represent two different types of civilization, or two different stages in a single civilization. The Bank Scandal and the peasant revolts are connected because both are particular forms of the 'struggle for life'. What is going on is a class war between two different criminal classes in which the crowd will eventually emerge as the victor. Upper-class crime represents brain in its struggle with the brawn of the crowd. Upper-class criminality may appear to be clever, but its cleverness is the 'senile cunning' of an old and sick society. The collective crime of the lower classes shows that a new era is about to begin. The upper classes exploit their past victories, whereas the lower classes, whose crowds display the virtues and vices of youth – impetuous audacity, impudence and imprudence, still have their victory to win. It is an axiom for Sighele, as it is for the strange bedfellows Spencer and Schopenhauer, that victory leads to weakness. The corrupt upper classes and their allies ('la base sur lesquelles elle repose') represent the majority; the lower class represents the minority whose courage and audacity wins out as the powers that be grow soft. Victory will go to the brave; St Just and Danton were right when they said that daring was the secret of revolutions. This revolution will not be altogether pleasant. Some individuals are bound to be hurt, but then nature is concerned with the species, not the individual. Besides, barbarism is necessary every four or five hundred years to put some life back into decadent civilizations (he quotes the Goncourts on the life-enhancing qualities of *sauvagerie*). Riot is a sign that new life is possible in an old society. Peasants in revolt against tax-collectors, workers on strike, or anarchists on the rampage against all authority, may not be conscious of the new era that they are about to usher in, but an acute observer can see that in the future it is going to be the crowd, and not the will of a prince, that is going to decide the course of events (ibid., pp. 4–33).

Almost all of Sighele's original positivism is lost in the process of his conversion to the crowd. He has deserted most of his Spencerism and at least half of his Lombrosianism. The crowd is now seen not as the cause of the social malady, but as its remedy. Like Le Bon, he accepts that in the period of transition to a new era, when nothing appears to be fixed, the power of crowds is the one power that nothing threatens and whose prestige grows daily. The crowd becomes the one fixed point in an otherwise problematical world. This new crowd of Sighele's is very different from the short-lived, regressive aggregate of his early work on crowds. He now thinks it is an illusion to see the crowd as the enemy of the modern state. The State and the crowd may seem to be very different things, but the modern State is in fact the development of the barbarian crowd over centuries, a single case of the general law that the higher up the evolutionary scale a collectivity is, the stronger the bond of association and the more developed the 'psychological' division of labour becomes. The crowd is the first stage of social grouping, out of which all other groups come. The State is simply a crowd which has institutionalized itself. This is something which Le Bon, in his enthusiasm for calling every human group a crowd, fails to see. Sighele prefers Tarde's classification of groups into crowds, associations and corporations. The movement from one category to the next represents a stage in the process by which the crowd moves from ephemerality to permanence. In the sect, belief provides permanence, in the caste, profession, and in the class, interest. In the State, language and nationality are the bonds which make it possible for some kind of permanent life to occur. Even the State, which Sighele calls the most evolved collectivity, never loses the tendency towards violence which had been the characteristic of collective behaviour which had first interested Sighele in crowds. Sighele is very far from claiming some

178

kind of absolute moral superiority for highly evolved collectivities. (He begins his *Psychologie des Sectes* (1898) by quoting an acid remark made at the first Congress of Criminal Anthropology at Brussels in 1880: 'From the point of view of morality, man could not stand comparison with a horde of anthropoid apes.') 'Evolved' now simply means better organized, so that the State's 'multitudes are called *armies* and their acts of violence are called *wars*, and they have the seal of legitimacy unknown to other crowds. Looked at in this way, we can define war as: the supreme from of collective crime' (Sighele, 1898, pp. 33–51). What the crowd has made it can unmake, and what it has done once it can do again. So what better than the crowd to complete the unfinished work of the *Risorgimento* and make the nation-state?

Sighele never comes quite clean about what crowd he is talking about when he is at his most political. In his early, most strictly positivist, mood, he was careful to isolate the groups which he thought could properly be called crowds. These included rioting mobs, certain kinds of criminal gangs, or specific groups which came under the influence of the collective mentality of the crowd. Sighele's designation 'crowd' becomes more blurred at the edges the further he moves away from Spencerism and Lombrosian positivism. Again, when he analyses society into two criminal classes at war with each other, he stretches the notion of crime to include any individual or collective activity which is extra-legal. Nor is his usage entirely consistent. In his *Littérature et Criminalité* (1908), written when he was at his most nationalist, Sighele reverts to his much earlier view that the crowd, though terrifying when it commits crimes, as in Zola's *Germinal*, is only transitory; it is capricious like a child, and like a child it returns to its ordinary peaceable concerns after its murderous tantrums are over (ibid., pp. 150–1). Sighele says this despite the fact that ten years earlier he had used Zola's *Germinal* and *L'Argent* as paradigm illustrations of the criminal class war as a preliminary to making the very generalized claim that the future would come out of the clash between lower-class violence and upper-class swindling. Perhaps he means that the incidence of temporary lower-class violence will increase, although each incident will not last long, but he doesn't say so. What is certain is that predictions of this kind cannot possibly hold good if the crowd, or crowds, are only episodes in the development of a society, no matter how frequently these episodes occur.

Perhaps it is carping to dwell on Sighele's waywardness as a social theorist when there is something so admirable about the way he thinks himself so reluctantly and so rigorously out of his evolutionary positivism from the inside. Professor Geiger is certainly unfair to Sighele when he says that Sighele finally embraced nationalism as a way of reconciling democracy and nationalism and that this embrace had nothing to do with the scientific pretensions of crowd theory and every-thing to do with the pressures of political events before 1914. Of course Sighele was sensitive to what was going on in the world, but Geiger entirely ignores the parallel development when the crowd made him begin to unpick the apparently secure network of evolutionary social theory which Italy had imported from France and England. Geiger has an eye to the future. He sees in Sighele's nationalism a proto-fascist submerging of the personality of the rational, autonomous individual in the destiny of the nation (Geiger, 1977, p. 67). He finds Sighele's anti-parliamentarianism especially ominous, seeing in it a rejection of the political and economic liberalism which provided the idea of equality on which nineteenth-century justifications of parliamentary democracy rested (ibid., pp. 51–2). In saying that, Geiger wants Italy to be too much like twentieth-century America. The parliamentary regime in the *Postrisorgimento* did not look to America, but to the England of Bagehot, for its inspiration. The parliamentary system and the constitu-tional monarch were meant to produce governments legitimized by the popular will, governments for the people but not of them. In Italy, as in England, democracy was to produce leaders of a class different from the mass of voters. The voters were to be satisfied by the appearance of choice and by the dignity of the monarchy. And in Italy the popular will was not all that popular; squabbles about the electoral law went on well into the twentieth century, and only 3 million Italians were entitled to vote before 1912. The elite that Italian democracy produced was the elite which was compromised in the Bank of Rome Scandal and it was also the elite which was to produce that divide between themselves and the masses which led to the formulation of the classic elite theory of Mosca, Pareto and Michels. It was precisely because the parliamentary regime showed itself to be incapable of representing Italy, except in the most formal sense, that led Sighele into his rejection of it. He was eventually to resign from the Nationalist Association because the nationalists in the Chamber began to move towards an electoral alliance with the clericals and reactionaries. Only the crowd could produce leaders who were able to create equals among their followers. That was what made nationalism so attractive. The leaders of the nationalist movement could, like Garibaldi, create a following of heroes whose deeds would equal the Thousand in the heroism which was still needed to complete the *Risorgimento*.

Gabriel Tarde: Crowds, Leaders and Great Men

For about ten years, Sighele and Gabriel Tarde conducted a coldly cour-teous dispute about who could claim the priority for the invention of the psychology of the crowd. The dispute was in origin methodological, because Tarde was never an evolutionist in the Spencerian–Lombrosian sense. This does not mean that Tarde thought that evolutionism was untrue, but he was extremely hostile to the Lombrosian claim that criminality was to be explained as atavism. Tarde set out to explain why men became criminals in exactly the same way as he would have tried to explain why men took up any other profession, and he did this at a time when Lombrosianism seemed about to become the prevailing criminological orthodoxy. So, like Sighele, Tarde's original interest in the crowd was criminological, and, like Sighele, he went on from there to incorporate the theory of the crowd into a much more generalized social theory. Both Sighele and Tarde were theorists by instinct, making a mockery of Le Bon's jibe that there must be something narrow about the concerns of thinkers who came to crowd theory from the specialized field of criminology, but there is an important difference between the careers of Sighele and Tarde as theorists. Sighele was driven out of Spencerian evolutionism by the crowd into a theory of the criminal class war, and eventually into the theory of proletarian nationalism. His was a case of finding a general sociological theory into which the crowd would fit. The case of Tarde is different. He developed his sociology of imitation and his crowd theory side by side, so that the crowd is only a single, though exaggerated, case of the imitation upon which all social life depends. Unlike so many other late-nineteenth-century social thinkers, Tarde does not rely on biology to explain how it is that societies made up of different parts stick together. His sociology, begun in *The Laws of Imitation* of 1891, and completed in *Universal Opposition* of 1897, is social science in a much more recognizably modern sense, relying as it does on the myriad facts of imitation which are amenable to statistical manipulation out of which come laws of imitation which hold good, at increasing levels of generality, for particular classes of events like murder and suicide, for particular kinds of society, and eventually for the whole of humanity.

Tarde is not especially concerned to prove that men do actually imitate each other. Flatterers apart, they probably do not imitate deliberately; imitation is 'always powerful, generally unconscious, partly mysterious' (Tarde, 1912, p. 323; first published as *Philosophie pénale* in 1892), and the inclination to imitate is a constant, equally strong in the child, the savage, the idiot and the civilized man. Where men differ as imitators is in the obstacles to imitation which they have available to them inside themselves. The most obvious example is the *fou moral* (what we would call the criminal psychopath), who has no 'internal brake' at all (ibid., p. 158). The only proof of imitation that Tarde really offers is a statistical one: it can be shown that there are epidemics of murders and suicides. No one can deny that for individuals these are supremely important events. From the point of view of the criminologist and the moralist they are supremely selfish actions, yet the fact that they can occur like epidemics shows that these actions, far from arising directly from human agency, are the result of imitation. How else could they be explained? If these most individualistic actions come from imitation, who could doubt that all the other actions which go to make up the ordinary life of a society are also the result of imitation? Surely what is true of the greater must also be true of the lesser. Imitation once shown to be the general condition of humanity, Tarde has no need of the elaborate Lombrosian evolutionist theory of crime from which Sighele began, and his critique of Lombroso is devastating. What the Lombrosians could not see was that crime is normal. They want to see something monstrous in crime. A criminal in their eyes is a savage, or a madman, or deformed, or ill. Even in their own terms, this view of criminality is contradictory. The born criminal can't be a savage *and* a madman, because madness and civilization develop together; madness is rare in rural districts, and rare among savages. Lombroso tried to get round that problem in the second edition of *L'Uomo deliquente* by saying that criminality was really a form of epilepsy, either 'manifest' or 'larvated', but this, Tarde thinks, is to make his position simply ridiculous, for it amounts to nothing less than to say that epilepsy must have been the normal state of primitive man (Tarde, 1912, pp. 62–3). The source of this nonsense can be traced to an error in the Darwinian biology on which Lombrosian criminology depends. The Darwinians (by which Tarde means all evolutionists) want to see in the body nothing but the co-operation between members and cells, so they have come to see non-co-operative bodies in the body as *anti*-bodies, elements hostile to a naturally co-operative enterprise whose presence has to be explained by something extraneous to the ordinary life of the living organism. Hence the Lombrosian explanation of crime in the body politic as an atavistic intrusion from an earlier age, and this despite the fact that crime is so common. Tarde chooses to see diseased cells as parts of the body, 'true associates'; like criminals, they are part of what they belong to; crime is not just an anti-social act but an act which takes place within a society and is to that extent as social as the mechanisms by which criminals are brought to justice (ibid., pp. 110–11).

Tarde's theory of imitation meant that he did not have to be surprised by the phenomena of crowds, either theoretically or as a question of politics. Imitation is the central social fact, so suggestibility must be the typical social mechanism. This was no doubt a frightening hypothesis for Spencerian individualists who had come to see the end of evolution as a society of consciously choosing individuals who would increasingly organize their lives according to a plan which was rational because it recognized nature and nature's laws. Tarde could take the idea of unconscious imitation in his stride. All crowd theorists stressed the unconscious mechanisms which operated in the crowd, but they typically did so to emphasize how different crowd behaviour must be from the progressive social life which crowds seemed to threaten. The hypnotic model of political leadership was attractive to crowd theorists precisely because it offered an account of the means by which leaders were able to manipulate their followers in ways that their followers did not understand in order to make them do things they would not ordinarily have done. It was that sense of the hostility of the crowd which made it frightening. When theorists like Sighele began to see that, because everyone could be hypnotized, everyone could become a member of the crowd so that there was no refuge from it, the fear of the crowd began to turn into something like panic. There was no social space that the crowd could not invade, and there was no country in the world in which one could feel safe. Tarde's view of hypnotism was quite different because the perspective into which he fitted hypnotic theory was so different. He sees hypnotism not as the means by which the hypnotized subject is turned into the puppet of his master, but as a kind of persuasion akin to the influence which a society has over its members. He is mildly sceptical about all the fuss that has been made about hypnotic theory in the last ten years. 'Hypnotism', he comments, 'is so hackneyed a subject that we almost scruple to deal with it' (ibid., p. 192). Too much has been made of the hypnotic model, both in criminology and in social theory. He denies that there is a single example well enough verified of a hypnotized subject committing a crime which he would otherwise not have committed, and he wonders whether the supposedly automatic behaviour of the hypnotized subject might not contain an element of 'play-acting' (ibid., p. 194). Hypnotism only really works well when there is a tendency on the part of the subject willingly to go along with it. (Perhaps Tarde means to resurrect here the old suspicion that Charcot's celebrated demonstrations of hypnotism were too well-rehearsed, if by well-rehearsed one means both play-acting and repetition. It is well to remember that repetition and rehearsal mean the same thing in French.) The hypnotized subject is to an extent the accomplice of the hypnotists, and the same is true of the crowd that allows itself to fall under the influence of 'an enchanting man, a fascinator of mobs, a sort of Donato on a large scale' (ibid., p. 194).

Tarde's view that sociability in general is suggestibility means that for him the chief theoretical interest of hypnotism is the light it throws on normal behaviour. Hypnotism is a kind of 'madness at will' (ibid., p. 192) which alienates the subject from his normal self and from his fellow men, and so is a halfway stage between real madness and normality.

It is not real madness, because there is an element of choosing to be hypnotized, and it is not normality, because during hypnotism all the relations of ordinary social life are replaced by the single, exaggerated relationship between the subject and the hypnotist. It is this that makes hypnotism 'the experimental junction point of psychology and sociology; it shows us the most simplified sort of psychic life which can be conceived of under the form of the most elementary social relation' (ibid., p. 192). In hypnosis, a single source of command takes the place of the many, sometimes competing, examples to be imitated in social life, but the mechanisms at work in the mind of the subject are not very different. What is true of hypnosis is similarly true of crowds. The mind of the crowd does not require a very special kind of explanation. All crowd theorists agree that what distinguishes the crowd from other types of aggregate is its unanimity. Why should that unanimity not be a special case of the general principle of imitation? In the *Penal Philosophy* Tarde begins his argument for the social causes of crime as against the anthropological by using the example of the crowd. The crowd is the best example of imitation because 'the great tumultuous assemblages of our cities' strike us so forcibly that their characteristics stand out in a way that the characteristics of a society at peace do not. The process of crowd formation is the formation of a society speeded up. In crowds, imitation happens much more obviously, because more quickly, so it it there that 'this characteristic force of the social world ought to be studied' (ibid., pp. 322–3). The most obvious cases of crowds occur 'in the great scenes of our revolutions', and he refers to Taine's accounts of the September Massacres and of the 14th of July and its effects on the provinces, and to Maxime du Camp's account of the *Commune*. He has no doubt that the mob is a strange phenomenon. It is

a gathering of heterogeneous elements, unknown to one another; but as soon as a spark of passion, having flashed out from one of these elements, electrifies this confused mass, there takes place a sort of sudden organisation, a spontaneous generation. This incoherence becomes cohesion, this noise becomes a voice, and these thousands of men crowded together soon form but a single animal, a wild beast without a name, which marches to its goal with an irresistible finality. The majority of these men had assembled out of pure curiosity, but the fever of some of them soon reached the minds of all, and in all of them there arose a delirium. The very man who had come running to oppose the murder of an innocent person is one of the first to be seized with the homicidal contagion, and moreover, it does not occur to him to be astonished at this.

(ibid., p. 323)

This process is, in embryo, the process of the formation of a society, from the point where it is a random group of people, to the point where it speaks with a single voice in the name of justice. Tarde is well aware of the paradox implicit in seeing the embryo of a society in a revolutionary mob. Taine had taught everybody to regard the French Revolution and the *Commune* not as revolutions but as dissolutions. Tarde is careful to say that the crowd is not the only social embryo. The other germ of society is the family. None the less, the family and the crowd are the primitive, natural groups, and as such, one is not to be feared more than the other. If some societies have their origin in the crowd and if what happens in a crowd is a kind of recapitulation of what happened at a society's beginning, the worst that can be said of the crowd at the level of theory is that it heralds the beginning of a new kind of society, or of a new phase in the development of an old one. Tarde in fact thinks that particular societies alternate between periods of fashion and periods of tradition. By this he means that times which imitate the new succeed times when imitation of the past is normal. The new is ushered in by the crowd, while the past is preserved in the family. Societies dominated by the family spirit, like ancient China and Egypt, change only slowly because there imitation takes the form of custom which is at its most obvious in the repetitive monotony of agricultural life. Crowd society is the society of the city, where imitation-fashion causes rapid transformations among people 'detached from their home and confusedly brought together'. In practice, these two spirits exist in the same society and compete with each other, and Tarde plainly thinks that this is true of France at the turn of the last century.

The political message is not liberal. What Tarde wants to emphasize is that no matter whether a society is a family society or a crowd society, society itself is not a matter of choice. The family and the crowd are similar because neither has its origins in free contract. Of course there is a difference between 'the superstitious and constitutional respect of a son for his father in the ancient household' and 'the infatuation for a day aroused by a leader of riots', but in both cases the group begins with a suggestion and not a contract. The idea that society has its origins in the agreement of independent wills is 'a pure hypothesis'. 'A suggestion is the product of wills which are born agreeing with the superior will from which they proceed; such is the primitive social fact. Every mob, like every family, has a head and obeys him scrupulously' (ibid., pp. 324–6).

The key to the difference between a crowd and a society is the absolute, single-minded conviction of righteousness which members of the crowd feel. This conviction comes from the suggestion which members receive from a leader or from each other, or from a combination of both. The contagion of ideas in a crowd is for Tarde another case of imitation.

This imitation causes reinforcement of the ideas in the minds of the crowd and accounts for 'the multiplication of intensity of belief'. With the growth of intensity goes a tendency towards simplification, because people in similar psychological states exchange similar beliefs, so that the beliefs which become intensified exclude all others. Hence the final stage where one belief is passionately held to the exclusion of all others. In ordinary life things are far more complicated. In society, people do exchange states of feeling, and this creates a bond between them which is similar to the bonding of the crowd, but they also exchange different psychological states because the feeling of intensity is not strong enough to begin the process of belief exclusion which is so obvious in the crowd. When two members of a society exchange, say, a taste for Wagner and a taste for realistic fiction, their inner life becomes more complicated. This *complication of their internal state* is civilizing (italics in original). The exchange of tastes does create a bond, which is a reinforcement of their inner life, because each takes pleasure in the other's culture and is reinforced in the pleasure he takes in his own. But between these two processes of simplification and complication 'there is the musical difference between unison and a chord. A mob has the simple and deep power of a large unison. This is why it is so dangerous to associate too much with minds that reflect one's own thoughts and one's own feelings; in doing this one soon arrives at the *sect spirit*, which is entirely analogous with the *mob spirit*' (ibid., p. 324).

The close comparison that Tarde makes between crowds and sects may seem surprising to us now, but it was a comparison that all crowd theorists made. There might appear to be the widest possible difference between a crowd made up of heterogeneous elements, and a sect. Sects are characterized by their homogeneity, but it is this sameness of mind which makes Tarde compare crowds with great religious and military orders, regiments, workshops, criminal gangs like the Mafia and the Camorra, the Jacobin leadership, and anarchist conspiracies. Sighele had been interested in the same comparison from the point of view of Lombrosian atavism. The crimes committed by sects were part of the general Lombrosian view that criminality was primitive. The crowd was also a primitive social phenomenon, and crowds also committed crimes, so it followed that there must be a similarity between the crowd's collective crimes and those of the criminal sect. Tarde does not share the Lombrosian perspective, but he shares with it the concern for individual responsibility in the commission of collective crime. Like Sighele, he is quick to draw out general social and political lessons from criminology. In a long article in the *Revue des Deux Mondes* in 1893 (references are to a reprint of this article as Chapter 3 of *L'Opinion et la foule*, Paris, 1901), the question of the collective origins of crimes is used as a way into the question of whether any human actions at all can be called individual in the sense that individualism has been understood since the Enlightenment. The eighteenth-century attack on the idea of original sin made the individual responsible for all his own actions, and criminology followed politics, political economy and morality in seeing the individual crime as the most essentially individual act of all. When collective crimes presented themselves to the law there was a rush to break them down into individual offences, but there is now a reaction, both sociological and socialist, to this 'great egocentric illusion', which concentrates on the social causes of action. In the criminological world this takes the form of a special interest in the crimes of sects and in the crimes of crowds, though the way forward was originally shown from outside criminology by Taine's account of the psychology of the Jacobins and of the crimes committed by crowds during the French Revolution.

The socialist and sociological reaction against individualism has turned the tables on the criminologist. He now finds it difficult to find truly individual crimes. A crime can no longer be looked upon as the supremely individual act, so the criminologist is driven out of the world of crime to find any action which comes out of one man's mind without determining influences from the outside. Even the great works of genius are hard to attribute to a single mind. Rousseau understood better than anyone that individual autonomy could only exist in isolation from the social world, and even he admits that isolation is impossible: Emile has a teacher. It is difficult to isolate what is to be attributed to the 'I' in a work of genius, and what can be isolated has no meaning until it comes into contact with the world. What distinguishes the work of genius, and what distinguishes the individual crime, is not that it happens in isolation, but that the outside influences are 'vague, distant, coming from a world outside the self which is un-defined and indeterminate'. Collective enterprises, including collective crimes, 'result from an immediate collaboration of a limited number of co-executants', in other words, accomplices (Tarde, 1901, pp. 159–61). Tarde does not doubt that anything that has ever happened in the world that is worth anything has been the result of the imitation of the work of great individuals, certain moments of moral grandeur in crowds excepted. Collectivities are always subject to the extremes of criminality and heroism, but intellectually they can descend to levels of imbecility unthinkable in any of their individual members. They are incapable of doing creative work. To the terrible things crowds have done, of which individuals would have been incapable: murders, the looting of armed bands, revolutionary incendiarism, September Massacres, massacres of St Bartholemew, 'epidemics of venality', one can cite the heroic things crowds have done of which individuals would have been equally incapable: legendary cavalry charges, patriotic revolts,

187

epidemics of martyrdom, the Night of August 4th, and so on. But there are no works of collective genius to cite against moments of collective idiocy. Perhaps with Sighele's claims for the crowd's contribution to the progress of culture in mind, he finds banal and gratuitous the idea that an incoherent mass spontaneously and unconsciously invented religions and languages. No doubt with Michelet's debt to Vico in mind, he remarks that the idea that the *Iliad* could be the work of a collectivity was only possible in 'a certain epoch of bad metaphysics. Nowadays we laugh at the idea'. The claim that the crowd can make revolutions is equally ridiculous. The crowd is only responsible for the destructive aspects of revolutions. The creative work of revolutions comes not from the crowd but from minds who had thought out the revolutionary work beforehand – he cites Luther, Rousseau, Voltaire and, oddly, Napoleon. No plan of campaign that was good, or even passable, ever came 'spontaneously' out of an army, and there are no collective works of art. What is true of art is even truer of crime. It is a series of master criminals who have brought the arts of murder and theft to their present state of perfection (ibid., pp. 162–3).

The reason why great acts of the intelligence are denied to groups, when they are capable of acts of will, and even of virtue, is that acts of will and virtue are by their nature simple. Acts of genius are complicated. The most universal and seductive of all illusions is that a group is more likely to grasp all sides of a question than an individual. Groups have solved problems in the past, but they have done so as *corporations* which are not simple aggregates (*réunions*), like medieval councils, *parlements* and Estates-General which are 'the panaceas of sick multitudes'. Even corporations – Tarde mentions the religious and military orders – which were on occasions able to solve problems were never able to create anything new. No corporation, however well organized and however well its parts co-operate, can compare 'for complication and elasticity' with a single human brain, 'that incomparable army of nerve cells which each of us carries round in our head'. Ordinary political experience confirms this. Any country, whether its regime is republican, monarchical, or parliamentary, recognizes the need for putting one man in charge in an emergency. This is a custom of great antiquity, a survival, which can only be explained by the fact that mankind, despite its illusions, really knows that one head is better than many (ibid., pp. 163–4).

Tarde's range of reference in the way he deals with crowds is immense, but the connecting thread of his treatment is still criminological. What he is always trying to judge is the question of who is responsible for the actions of crowds. Whatever will and purpose a crowd has always comes from its leader. In this, the crowd is not an exception from other groups. Tarde's general social theory is his theory of the crowd in macrocosm. The source of all social action is in individual initiatives expressed in new ideas or new ways of doing things. These Tarde calls 'inventions'. The essential social and socializing act is imitation, by which inventions become more or less socially acceptable. There are factors which influence the origins of invention itself. Different societies possess different degrees of mental ability, and the social conditions which favour the expression of mental ability are not present to the same degree in all societies, but the theory of invention and imitation at least make it possible to point to a beginning in social processes. Tarde regards it as a general law of imitation that imitations spread outwards from their initial centre in geometrical progression, like reproduction. The rate at which an invention spreads is affected by physical and biological considerations (mainly race) and by social influences, it being another law of imitation that 'imitations are refracted by their media'. These social influences Tarde divides into 'logical' and 'non-logical'. By 'logical' he means the degree to which inventions fit in with inventions already more or less socially accepted, and by 'non-logical' he means to refer to the process by which the invention does in fact spread. Ideas are imitated before the words that express them or before the means to realize them are brought into existence, and in societies resistant to new inventions there can be blockages between the two stages. Imitation proceeds from the socially superior to the socially inferior, and ages of custom alternate with ages of fashion. So the ideal conditions for an invention to succeed would exist if the invention was made in a country whose people had a reputation for quickness of wit, when the invention itself was not very startling and not very difficult to put into effect or into words, and where the upper classes were peculiarly receptive to it. Even if the society was going through one of its periods in which the novel and the strange enjoyed high prestige it would not all be plain sailing even in these circumstances, because ages of fashion are receptive to inventions *in general*. Every invention would have to compete with other inventions as well as with the inventions of the past whose imitation makes up the warp and woof of any society, and in a sense inventions create other inventions because an invention itself is really no more than a combination of ideas which have become current, and therefore commonplace, by imitation. Genius is the ability to grasp the relations between things which have no very obvious connection, like the wheeled carriage and the steam engine which, when combined, produce the railway engine (Tarde, *The Laws of Imitation*, *passim*; and Davis, 1909, pp. 120–1).

Tarde's sociology has suffered long from Durkheim's and others' condemnation of it as 'superficial'. Perhaps it is, but what it may lack in profundity it certainly makes up for in clarity, so that it is easy to see why Tarde, unlike Sighele, did not have to invent a new sociology to incorporate the crowd. The crowd is just another social group which takes its cue from leaders, so the question of the responsibility of the leaders of crowds is no different in principle from the question of the responsibility of leaders of fashion. In the crowd, as in assemblies and associations, the directing idea comes from the leader's suggestion, so he is responsible for its 'direct' effects, but the emotion which accompanies the spread of an idea or plan of action in a crowd is the crowd's own. What may only have been a tentative suggestion by the leader can become, 'by a sort of geometrical progression', a passionate conviction, a deeply felt necessity, and the occasion for hatred and fanaticism. This heightening of emotion is not *caused* by the leader. It is a 'mutual heating-up' among the led, so it would be wrong to attribute to the leader all the crimes which this super-heated emotion causes, just as it would be improper to attribute to a leader alone the great works of national deliverance or great acts of devotion 'sustained by the same fever'. Chiefs are responsible for the 'cunning and cleverness' of successful massacres, robberies and incendiarism, but not always for the violence and the extent of the evil caused by these 'criminal contagions'. A general deserves honour for the plan of campaign, but not for the bravery of the troops (Tarde, 1901, pp. 165–7).

The main difference between a crowd and other social groups is that the crowd is created by an external cause. People in the street become a social group when there is a dynamite explosion. (This is the period of anarchist 'propaganda by the deed'.) The crowd has the same aim – to save itself, and the same emotions – fear and loathing. It represents the first stage of human association, 'rudimentary, fleeting and amorphous', which ascends by stages to the corporation, a crowd with a hierarchy, 'regular, durable and organized'. (He seems here to have forgotten about the family, that other embryo of societies. Perhaps he means that the family can also be the germ of corporations, or a short-cut to them, but he does not say.) All social groups can be located on the continuum crowd–corporation. Corporations are either religious or secular. Their common emotion varies in intensity; the most intense religious corporation is the monastery and the most intense secular corporation is the regiment or workshop (*atelier*). Corporations also vary in extent; the most extensive religious corporation is the Church and the most extensive secular corporation is the State.

Nations in fact swing between the polarities of crowd and corporation; the barbarian kingdom of the Franks becomes the France of St Louis. A modern nation, under the influence of egalitarian ideas, tends to become a crowd, but in these circumstances its need for corporations is increased, not diminished. If it is to survive as a state in peace and war, a nation needs the hierarchical and aristocratic corporations of the army and the administration ('that other huge army'). When wars and war-scares are over, the nation has prepared itself through mobilization for corporatization in its more peaceful form and becomes a giant workshop. All groups on the continuum crowd–corporation have this in common, that they have are led by a chief, 'out in the open, or hidden'. As soon as a group shows that it is united and begins to act purposefully, we can be certain that leaders are at work. This is true of a workshop, a convent, a court, a theatrical claque, or a theatre audience (they submit to the suggestion of the author through the mouth of the actor), so whether it is apparent or not, there is always the distinction between leaders and led (ibid., pp. 167–71).

Tarde insisted, through thick and thin, on the necessity of leaders in the crowd. In a review of Sighele's *The Criminal Crowd* in 1891 he argued that the leader of a crowd could have more influence even than a hypnotist (cit. Barrows, 1981, p. 43), and in *L'Opinion et la foule* (1891) he is obliged to do some intellectual juggling to prove that, appearances to the contrary, there is no such thing as a spontaneous crowd acting with a single will. The occasion for Tarde's juggling was a discussion, at the 1882 Congress of Criminal Anthropology, of Italian and Russian rioting and brigandage caused by famine. These peasant revolts had no obvious leaders, and the fact that there were many separate outbreaks of rioting suggested that there certainly could have been no single leader or group of leaders. In Tarde's language, this appears to be a case of imitation without suggestion, and he will have none of it. He argues that separate outbreaks of rioting must be seen as the work of a single crowd, so that the lack of obvious leaders in a particular mob (*secondary* leaders) does not mean that the crowd in general does not have leaders (*primary* leaders). Besides, every crowd, like every social event, must have a beginning, and Tarde comes close to saying that beginning and leadership mean the same thing: even the man who throws the first stone, shouts, or begins a song, is a leader. And, he thinks, there is no reason in principle why crowds must be throngs. There is such a thing as a dispersed crowd, in which contagion at a distance (*contagion à distance*) can operate. Tarde is obviously struggling here. He knows that a leaderless crowd is an affront to his whole sociology, based as that sociology is on being able to find the origin of social facts in single individuals. All he can do is to heap up striking examples of crowd leadership to show how important leaders are. He even cites an instance of 'leadership after death' in the 'unfortunate case of General Boulanger' as further proof of the necessity of leadership, wishing to imply that if a crowd can still have behaviour suggested to it by a leader from beyond the grave, then if you look hard enough at any crowd you are bound to find a leader somewhere (Tarde, 1901, pp. 171–8).

Crowds, then, are easily led. They are like children, open to the most puerile suggestions and childish images. That is why crowd leaders always exaggerate. Their suggestions are intense, narrow and false, not designed to strike the intelligence. The exaggeration of the suggestions given to crowds by their leaders can be for good or evil. This explains why the very worst types, as well as the very best, so often become the leaders of crowds. Perhaps crowds want to be treated badly; no doubt fear of the crowd leads many to join it, but Tarde wonders whether this fear might be more moral than physical: fear of being left out of the crowd might be as strong as fear of the crowd itself. The alternation of belonging to the crowd and not belonging is at its most obvious in a theatre. Theatre audiences become less of a crowd when they sit. 'To sit down is to begin to isolate oneself within oneself – to begin to retreat into oneself.' Crowds are really feminine. Even in their passion they are docile to the commands of their masters; credulous and over-excited, they swing wildly between fury and tenderness, exasperation and laughter, and this is true even when the crowd is made up of men. Crowds of women would be the worst. *Corruptio optimi pessima.* Taine's and Zola's female castrating crowds tell their own story. Luckily for women (surely he should say men) times have changed since the French Revolution. Now their duties as housewives keep women relatively isolated. All sensible societies in the past have kept gatherings of women to a minimum, and in the modern world women can satisfy their need for some kind of collective life by reading the same romantic novels and poetry. This keeps them off the streets, so crimes like the massacre of Huez and Major de Belsunce are happily of the past. Isolation probably accounts for the lower crime rate in women and in the countryside, but if women were allowed to live a life of daily meetings their depravity would probably exceed that of men, and, given the opportunity, peasants on the rampage are much worse than factory workers. In *Capital* Marx shows that bands of itinerant agricultural labourers in England, men and women, lead lives of debauchery which would excite the envy of Sodom and Gomorrah (Tarde, 1901, pp. 29–30, 52–3, 178–96).

Tarde is so concerned to show that crowds by themselves can do nothing really worthwhile that he reneges even on the heroism which he attributes to them. Anything decent or serious that a crowd achieves really comes from a corporation or a sect. A crowd heroically and spontaneously putting out a fire has an off-duty fireman to lead it; the huge crusading crowds of warriors were sent on their way by Peter the Hermit and Bernadin de St Pierre, members of religious orders; the *levées en masse* of 1792 got their momentum from the political clubs and their discipline from old soldiers; the *jacqueries* and the September Massacres came from the Jacobins (ibid., pp. 196–7).

All political sects have two kinds of leaders, those who lead direct and those who lead 'at a distance'. Political activists, who lead by command, have to be distinguished from political ideologues, who lead by remote suggestion. Tarde's archetype of the leader at a distance is Rousseau. Rousseau was the *incubus* of the Revolution and Robespierre its *succubus* (ibid., p. 212, quoting Sighele). Rousseau's is a uniquely instructive personality of the kind possessed by men who lead the crowd at a distance because we know so much about him, but Tarde's interest in Rousseau is more complicated than that. Rousseau is one of Sainte-Beuve's kingly geniuses who creates his own people (Tarde, 1912, p. 164). Rousseau's people is complete. It consists of a leadership sect, the Jacobins, and the revolutionary crowd which they led. It also contains what Tarde calls a public, one of those watered-down crowds which he thinks will take over the historical role of the crowd in the modern age of popular literacy and newspapers.

What worries Tarde is that the anarchism of his own day only lacks a crowd to become a truly revolutionary force. It has everything else: leaders at a distance, direct leaders, and organization as a sect. When the sect of the anarchists meets its own crowd, then something very like the French Revolution will happen again, a re-enactment of the two characters of Rousseau on the public stage. The anarchists, even anarchism in general, share Rousseau's version of the internal duality of the insane. What puzzled Tarde about the anarchists was the gentleness and sociability of their private lives, something that was also baffling to Lombrosians. Arrested anarchists were by all accounts good, admirable people who happened to be engaged in a murderous conspiracy to destroy the class enemy which surrounded them. This was precisely the contrast to be found in Rousseau, between naturalness, innocence and virtue on the one hand, and vicious paranoia and the urge to destroy named and nameless enemies on the other. The Revolution was the image and child of that contrast, its violent and terrible development (ibid., p. 163). The crowd that Tarde thinks anarchism might capture are the socialists. If they can be persuaded to move directly and violently against the class enemy then they will do so because of one of those terrible simplifications which occur in the minds of crowds. The crowd is simple-minded because it is single-minded, and the world might be in for a new bout of its destructive and collective heroism.

Or it might not be. Tarde is not altogether a pessimist. What he never forgets is that the crowd is only one aspect of a society. He deals very sharply with Le Bon for seeing everything as a crowd, and he turns the tables neatly on those writers who are forever seeing something primitive in the crowd by saying that, if it is really true that the crowd corresponds in some sense to a primitive state in human development, then it is surely likely that the age of crowds is coming to an end and that the function played by crowds hitherto in human history is likely to be taken over by some new kind of collectivity. In a spirited attack on Le Bon in *L'Opinion et la foule* (1901), Tarde suggested that the social group of the future was not the crowd but what he called 'the public'. Just as there were many crowds, so there were many publics, perhaps as many as there were newspapers. Publics and crowds share many characteristics, but the great difference between them is that publics have a permanent enough existence for them to be able to compete with each other. It is also possible to belong to more than one public. Tarde's general contempt for collectivities certainly extends to publics, but in their case a pluralism of opinion and a consequent hesitancy about action gives them a very different mentality from the single- and bloody-mindedness of crowds. Tarde certainly does not think that the crowd will decide what the future will be like; great inventors will do that. He is not even particularly concerned on the level of theory with Caesarism. Boulangism for him is an episode. His marvellous futuristic vision *Underground Man* makes it clear that in corrupt bourgeois republics Caesarism is always a possibility because the centralization of political power makes it a natural object of human desire while making it easier for one man to capture it, but in the imagined future state, as in the Third Republic, crowd politics of the Caesarist kind does not quite come off (Tarde, 1905, pp. 40–1). Caesars come into Tarde's category of fictitious great men, heroes for a day. As the world grows up, so it grows out of crowds.

It was Bergson who pointed out the delightful paradox that the inventor of the laws of imitation was one of the most original of nineteenth-century thinkers (Tarde, 1909, Introduction). Tarde was a solitary, perhaps even a romantic; Lamartine was his special love and his anathema was the positivist dogmatism of Comte and Spencer and the mechanical methodology of Taine. He was a natural provincial swept to Paris and to fame on the strength of the criminological and sociological works he had written in the obscurity of a magistrate's life in Sarlat. The intellectual distance between Sarlat and Paris reinforced a certain mannered hostility to influence in Tarde. His sons tell us that he used to call his ideas his 'inventions' (ibid., p. 39); these inventions did not reach a public in Tarde's own sense until very late. This accounts for something autobiographical, even Rousseauist, in Tarde's sociology and in his theory of the crowd. The inventor of ideas, like other great men, stands slightly apart from his own society. He is 'extra-social', on the borders of society, a 'part of nature' and of 'the other societies which he looks upon with curiosity'. He is not entirely extraneous to the social world, like the madman in his alienation; nor is he in society but anti-social, like the criminal. Rather, 'he keeps close to this world and enlightens it without being a part of it'. Every great man who has enlightened the world – he cites Victor Hugo, Darwin, Spencer (despite his antipathy to him), Plato and Aristotle – is something of a solitary hero. Tarde then adds a piece of pure autobiography:

A learned man who discovers truths contrary to dogma, a traveller who brings with him new usages, an inventor who renders old processes useless, has lived alone, a wanderer, independent of his own sphere; socially he plays the part which the living cells of living bodies play in an organic way, anxious sentinels ready to gather warnings from without in order to transmit them to the interior.

(Tarde, 1912, pp. 164–5)

Tarde is no friend to revolutions, but his love of great men leads him to try to rescue even Rousseau from the revolutionaries. Rousseau's good nature is the true one, and the shame that comes from his evil side, whose product was the revolutionary mob and the Jacobin Terror, 'should but feebly stain his memory' (ibid., p. 163).

Notes

1 Sighele and Espinas are not available in English, and Tarde is not easily available (though T. N. Clark, 1969, is a useful collection), so I have translated them and let them speak for themselves as far as that seemed practicable; the same goes for Lombroso. (I should add that I have translated the Italians out of French editions because I do not altogether trust my Italian.) The fact that no full English translation exists yet of Lombroso's L 'Uomo deliquente is scandalous.

2 A similar perception formed part of the ideology of imperialism. Whites were entitled to rule blacks because whites were higher up the evolutionary scale. Blacks, or most of them, were so far below, that some whites, who were not themselves natural rulers at home, could safely be allowed to rule in the empire. It was easier to become a member of the ruling class in the empire than at home, and the literature of empire is full of the problems faced by upstart imperialists when dealing with genuine empire-builders, and with native aristocrats. See, for example, the novels of John Masters and Paul Scott.

3 The first Italian edition of La folla delinquente appeared in 1891, and a French edition appeared in the following year. I have used the second French edition, which was considerably revised, of 1901. I mention this out of a certain sympathy for Sighele, who would have been pleased to have it emphasized that his book was originally published four years before Le Bon's Psychologie des foules.

7

Crowd Theory Makes its Way in the World: the Le Bon Phenomenon

Gustave Le Bon and Crowd Theory as Conservative Ideology

The part played by the mob in the French Revolution was being drawn to the attention of literate Europe by Taine's great *Origins of Contemporary France* (which appeared volume by volume between 1876 and 1894) at a time when crowd or mass politics appeared to be the developing political style. While the *Origins* was being published, social thinkers in France, England, Italy and America were drawing on them, and on anything else that lay to hand to construct a theory of the crowd which was intended to be as scientific as the theories of biology, physiology, psychiatry and anthropology which they ransacked for analogies or simply lifted whole and applied to the crowd. By 1895, when Le Bon's *The Crowd* appeared, the psychology of the crowd was a recognized intellectual genre with considerable scientific claims which nobody seemed to deny, though there were grumblings about common sense parading itself in doctors' robes (Barrows, 1981, p. 134). Crowd psychology was scientific, even technical, in all the appropriate senses: it had its own special vocabulary; it might be able to provide a technique of crowd manipulation or control, and it fitted well into the evolutionary-scientific view of things which the second half of the nineteenth century had made its own. Le Bon's *The Crowd* was a great publishing success[1] because it was able to summarize what had been worrying the *savants* within the academic world of social science at a time when the literate public were themselves worrying about much the same things. The secret of Le Bon's success was to use science to frighten the public, and then to claim that what science could understand it could also control. His advice to public men about how to deal with crowds, or at least how not to be dominated by them, was put before a public that was quick to

196

make heroes of great engineers, men who had brought technologies out of science to control the waywardness of nature. The technique of crowd control that Le Bon offered was not very impressive, but he saw himself, and was seen by others, as a de Lesseps of social engineering. He sat back, and the plaudits and the royalties came.

Le Bon's career gives the lie to the idea that there is something necessarily furtive about plagiarism. Picard calls Le Bon a scientific guerrilla (Picard, 1909, p. 28), but scientific freebooter would be nearer the mark. Le Bon's technique as a plagiarist was simple. He affected a pose of scientific isolation so that he could claim originality for any thought that came from anywhere into his head. If acknowledgement could not be avoided, as it could not in the cases of his debts to Spencer, Taine, Sighele and Tarde, Le Bon still managed to suggest that it was he who saw the full implications of what they saw only dimly. Le Bon spread himself widely, and when there were public wrangles over priority, as there were over the idea of eternal recurrence and the theory of relativity, Le Bon stuck to his guns and claimed to have thought of everything first. He even had the cheek to write to Einstein demanding public recognition of his own discovery of the relativity principle, pointing out that this was just another example of the Germans' notorious ignorance of French science. Einstein reminded him that stealing an idea amounted not to national but to personal theft, and there the correspondence ended (Nye, 1975, p. 157). But another of Einstein's correspondents, Sigmund Freud, called Le Bon's *The Crowd* 'deservedly famous' and the book continues to be printed. Le Bon was an adept at suggesting that the accusations of plagiarism were caused by professional jealousy, but the very rancour with which, for example, Le Bon and the Italian crowd psychologist Scipio Sighele pursued their respective claims to having been the first to discover the psychology of the crowd, shows what a valuable piece of intellectual property the psychology of the crowd had become. Maxim Revon could write bitterly in 1920, when the twenty-sixth French edition of *The Crowd* appeared, of the imperative of disengaging the study of collectivities from the 'absolute empire' of Le Bon (cit. Nye, 1975, p. 185, n.57), but an impressive list of critics, which includes Durkheim, Alfred Binet, William James and Henri Lefebvre, has never quite been able to efface the signature that Le Bon wrote on the theory of the crowd in 1895.

Le Bon was able to offer a finished version of crowd theory because by 1895 a good twenty years' work on the psychology of the crowd was available to him. It did not worry Le Bon that the psychology of the crowd existed in at least two separate and competing versions in the works of Scipio Sighele and Gabriel Tarde. Le Bon simply took the most pessimistic things that others had to say about the crowd and out of them built a theory which was his own only in the sense that most of the nuances had been lost in the editing. The disputes about priority among the late-nineteenth-century theorists of the crowd make tedious reading now, and we are fortunate to have an excellent summary of them in Professor Barrows's *Distorting Mirrors* (Barrows, 1981, ch. 6 *passim*). What has to be explained is an extraordinary coincidence of intellectual and public concern about crowds; for once, the public got the social science it had been waiting for. The simplest explanation is Le Bon's own, that from some time onwards, say after the Paris *Commune*, Europe was being politically destablized by crowds. A large public became increasingly aware that this was happening, so that any explanation of the mind and actions of the crowd was bound to be reassuring to people who were used to thinking that the first step towards a cure for anything was successful diagnosis. That was certainly what Le Bon said he was doing, and there was something fortuitous in the fact that Le Bon himself was a real doctor, which enabled him to pose as the diagnostician of the crowd-sickness of his own time.

The fact that all crowd theorists depended heavily for their explanations of crowd behaviour on psychiatric medicine, and on the closely related disciplines of biology and neurological physiology, lent a certain plausibility to Le Bon's posturing as a healer of social ills. In France, the study of hypnotism and suggestion, on which crowd psychologists relied for a model of the unconscious behaviour of crowds, was institutionalized in the medical schools. In Italy, where the scientific study of the crowd came out of criminology, criminology itself was institutionalized in the universities where legal and medical studies met in the discipline of public hygiene; crime was to the body politic what disease was to the human body. (The case of England is different. There, the study of the crowd was brought directly out of evolutionary biology and psychology by Walter Bagehot. As a consequence, there was not the same compulsion to treat the crowd as a disease, or as the symptom of a disease.)

But what is lacking in the diagnosis-cum-cure explanation for the public success of crowd psychology is the lack of any real sense of reassurance in the works of the crowd psychologists themselves. Professor Barrows may be right when she says that Le Bon's success comes from his advice to politicians about how to cope with crowds (ibid., p. 173), but Le Bon's advice is not in fact very reassuring, and Le Bon is exceptional even in his massively qualified optimism. Not all crowd theorists are equally pessimistic, but most of them talk the language of apocalypse, of impending doom, of the end of a civilization, or, at the very least, of the ending of an era. The apocalyptic streak was not confined to Europe. Three years after Le

Bon's *The Crowd*, the American crowd psychologist Boris Sidis was to write in his *The Psychology of Suggestion. A research into the Subconscious Nature of Man and Society*:

> When it [suggestibility, what makes the crowd work] rises to the surface and with the savage fury of a hurricane cripples and maims on its way everything it can destroy, menaces life, and throws the social order into the wildest confusion possible, we put it down as mobs. We do not in the least suspect that the awful, destructive automatic spirit moves in the bosom of the peaceful crowd, reposes in the heart of the quiet assembly, and slumbers in the breast of the law-abiding citizen. We do not suspect that the spirit of suggestibility lies hidden even in the best of men; like the evil jinnee of the Arabian tales is corked up in the innocent-looking bottle. Deep down in the nature of man we find hidden the spirit of suggestibility. Man is often defined as a social animal. This definition is no doubt true, but it conveys little information as to the psychical state of each individual within society. There is another definition which claims to give an insight into the nature of man, and that is the well-known ancient view that man is a rational animal; but this definition breaks down as soon as we come to test it by the facts of life, for it scarcely holds true of the suggestibility that characterises the average specimen of humanity, for man is a suggestible animal.
>
> (Sidis (1898), 1927 p. 17)

This sense of crisis pervades the work of almost every crowd theorist. Far from providing remedies, palliatives, or even placebos, they write with the sense of the ending of a world, almost as if they are intentionally trying to create social fear rather than trying to alleviate it. This is as true of Le Bon as it is of the rest, especially true, because Le Bon is a master titillator, who jumps easily from the analysis of the mind of an innocent electoral committee to the comparison of all committees to the Committee of Public Safety, inviting his readers to see the shadow of the guillotine falling over the most innocuous gatherings (*The Crowd*, pp. 169–70). So it would be wrong to see crowd psychologists as providers of the kinds of explanation of crowd behaviour which make crowds easier to live with. They make crowds less mysterious, but by making them more comprehensible they do not make them less frightening. Fear of the crowd, and crowd psychology, feed on each other. Le Bon encourages this; nobody knew better than him what would make a book sell. The more terrifying he could make the crowd, the more his rather feeble advice would be welcomed by the reading public. But what Le Bon has to say about THE ERA OF CROWDS (capitals in original) does not differ substantially from the sources – Taine, Sighele and Tarde – that he plagiarizes so ruthlessly. When the English crowd theorist Wilfred Trotter began to wonder, after the great 'killing crowds' of the First World War had begun their work, whether 'man will prove but one of Nature's failures, ignominiously to be swept away from her work-table to make way for another venture of her tireless curiosity and patience' (Trotter, 1923, p. 65), he summed up the fears which had fed, and fed upon, crowd psychology since the *Commune*.

And the question remains: Fear of what? What was it that people *saw*, and what was crowd theory inviting them to see, when they saw a crowd? Certainly any crowd could appear to be a potential mob, perhaps even a revolutionary mob, but that does not explain why the crowd should have been so particularly frightening in societies where the forces of order always won in the end. What is remarkable about popular disturbances in Europe between the *Commune* and the Great War is how successful governments were at containing them. (It is even possible to see the war itself as a European exercise in crowd-control-by-conscription which went badly wrong.) It might be that it was the theory of the crowd itself which gave to the fear of the crowd its special edge. The psychology of the crowd as Le Bon received it was definitely not reassuring; it challenged everything which the progressive age thought about itself by stating boldly that the crowd was everyone, so that when men looked at the crowd they were being invited to see themselves. The final message of the crowd theory which Le Bon used and modified was that no man was *a priori* immune from the crowd, because crowd psychology had long been chipping away at the sense of distance which ordinary, civilized, law-abiding men had always felt when they looked at crowds with contempt and at the mob with horror. Crowd psychology, as Le Bon found it, was not an invitation to join the crowd (though it came close to that in Sighele's late nationalist phase) – that was to be fascism's particular twist to the theory, but the psychology of the criminal crowd had already begun to provide all kinds of extenuating arguments for those found themselves up before the bench because they had committed collective crimes. Le Bon sniffed out a market among those people who were frightened of the crowd, had begun to wonder whether their world would be swamped by the crowd, and who were understandably reluctant to accept that they, and people like them, were part of the crowd and would end up one day being like *them*.

Le Bon sets out to make the crowd as frightening as possible in order to peddle a particular kind of elitist ideology, and it is a complete ideology in something like the modern sense of the term. Crowd theory in Le Bon is used to offer a theory of history and an analysis of present troubles; crowd theory points to a group which is the cause of those troubles, identifies an elite which is threatened by them, and crowd theory makes predictions about the future by urging the elite to learn the lessons of crowd theory so that the devil does not have all the good tunes; the elite can use crowd theory to outwit the crowd by using the techniques of the crowd's own leaders in order to slip elite leaders into the crowd from the outside. The crowd can then be manipulated in the service of values and aspirations which, if left to itself, the crowd would undermine and eventually destroy. Le Bon's elitist conservatism does not in fact add up to very much and it is not very consistent. In *The Crowd* Le Bon stresses the masses' potential as a revolutionary crowd, but in *The Psychology of Socialism* they have become the listless mass of mass society looking only to the state to solve their problems, while by 1914 'socialism' has made them pacifists. In 1895 the masses were a danger to the Republic because they threatened to take it over; by 1914 they have barely the energy to lift a finger to stop the Germans taking the Republic over. Le Bon, despite the undoubted panache of his publicist's style, is rather a timid thinker, and the value content of his ideology is mostly negative; it can be summed up as an attack on nearly all forms of human collective action, which he lumps together under the name of 'socialism'.[2] But Le Bon is the first crowd theorist to *use* the discoveries of crowd psychology to write a book to frighten readers into an ideology, and he is the first to use the techniques of mass persuasion which crowd psychology laid bare to sell the finished product.

Le Bon's ideological stance is not without its refinements. His attack on the simplicity of the crowd mind, which demands simplifications, disguises his own demagogic simplifications; like Thrasymachus, the original of all demagogues, Le Bon is a simplifier but a simplifier who covers his tracks; but the disguise can wear thin. Le Bon affects a Platonic disdain for the art of the pleaser of crowds; it is 'no doubt of an inferior order' (though inferior to what he does not say), but 'it demands quite special skills (*Crowd*, p. 35)'. The crowd itself is a bit of a Platonist; the ideas suggested to it are either absolute truths or absolute errors (*Crowd*, p. 37); the crowd easily mistakes the unreal for the real, for only the *idea* counts (*Crowd*, p. 53); the crowd likes its ideas fed to it in formulas, 'mysterious divinities', which it devours as a kind of *hors d'oeuvre* before going on to devour what is left of civilization (*Crowd*, pp. 95–6). The way ideas are fed to the crowd matters a great deal, and Le Bon devotes a whole chapter to spelling out how it is done. The leaders of crowds succeed by affirmation, repetition and contagion; the crowd is easily persuaded if the ideas suggested to it are 'pure and simple'; repetition, which works even on 'the most enlightened minds', and contagion, whose power is 'as intense as that of microbes', will do the rest (*Crowd*, pp. 120–2). That is exactly how Le Bon himself operates. He keeps what he has to say about the crowd simple and what appear to be arguments are often no more than tautologies. (On occasions he even writes in capitals for the very simple-minded.) Crowds, he tells us, reason by association; there does not have to be any necessary connection in the flow of ideas presented to the crowd, any more than there have to be any necessary connections between the images in a magic-lantern show (*Crowd*, pp. 47–8). Guilt by association is characteristic of Le Bon's own style – juries and mobs are both crowds, therefore juries and mobs are equally dangerous. And the proof that Le Bon's *The Crowd* is an exercise in crowd formation and persuasion is in what Le Bon thinks a crowd is. All Le Bon's critics have pointed out that he stretches the category of the crowd too wide. What they have not always emphasized is that Le Bon is able to stretch the crowd so wide because he thinks that any group which *thinks like* a crowd is a crowd. Even as acute a critic as Tarde fails to see this when he chides Le Bon for failing to see that the physically proximate crowd is a thing of the past and that the group of the future is going to be the public, which is dispersed, and whose unity is only mental. Le Bon in fact understands this very well. Any group which thinks like a crowd, which obeys what he rather tendentiously calls The Law of the Mental Unity of Crowds (*Crowd*, pp. 1–2), is an organized crowd, where organization refers not to some kind of collective action in the streets but to the mental organization which the Law of Mental Unity demands. No doubt this is massively tautological, but it does make it clear that the crowd off the streets can, in Le Bon's view, be just as manipulable as a mob. It will not do to say that the crowd that Le Bon is trying to create and manipulate is really a Tardean public, and that Le Bon has probably stolen the idea from Tarde, because that is to take the way back to seeing nothing but a talented entrepreneurial vulgarizer in Le Bon, and to miss the ideological thrust. Scholars have always had a field-day showing just how derivative Le Bon's treatment of the crowd is and have tended to dismiss him, but this dismissal diverts attention from the real importance of the Le Bon phenomenon as ideology. By 1895 when Le Bon published *The Crowd* and woke up to find himself famous, crowd theory was complete enough, and generalizable enough, to become an ideology.

Once we begin to see that Le Bon is a new Thrasymachus, then other things about Le Bon which appear at first sight to be puzzling become really quite clear, especially his fame. A recent edition of *The Crowd* published in Dunwoody, Georgia (which is fame of a kind) carries on its front cover the legend 'In all probability the greatest single work ever written on mass psychology'. I'm tempted to say 'Of course it is' because *The Crowd* is not mainly, or even importantly, a book *about* mass psychology, but an exercise *in* mass psychology. (I do not even have to say that Le Bon gets mass psychology right. Le Bon is certainly applying what he takes the principles of mass psychology to be, but it is perfectly possible that *The Crowd's* success as a best-seller is due to causes of which Le Bon never dreamt.) What *The Crowd* plainly is not is just another book about the psychology of the crowd; nor is it, despite its claims, a work of sociology. Le Bon's predecessors like Sighele and Tarde worked hard at trying to distinguish between crowds and 'the masses' in the cause of scientific rigour. In Le Bon's treatment the crowd becomes unrecognizable. For all his parading of his up-to-dateness, Le Bon treats the crowd in a very traditional way, as a synonym for 'the unruly', while being able to claim the scientific status of all the more rigorous work on the crowd that had been done in the previous thirty years. Science and the psychology of the crowd are only banners for Le Bon. Le Bon usually receives honourable, if perfunctory, mention in works of sociology and social psychology, for the acuteness of his social observation and for his prefiguring of the theory of mass society, or, less ambitiously, for exemplifying the 'mass society attitude' (e.g. in Kornhauser, 1960; Giner, 1976; and Stanley, Introduction to Le Bon, 1982).

Le Bon in fact refuses to do sociology at all. Everything that happens in a society which is not a result of a conscious and rational choice on the part of an individual Le Bon lumps into the category of the 'unconscious'. This unconscious is a 'mysterious force'; it is part of the natural world of instinct; it 'acts like a force still unknown' (*Crowd*, pp. viii–ix). This is the same unconscious that comes into play during hypnosis, and in the crowd when the conscious personality of individuals disappears into the 'collective mind' which obeys the Law of the Mental Unity of Crowds. The crowd acquires genuinely new characteristics which each of its members feels. Solely from the fact of numbers, each individual has 'a feeling of invincible power which allows him to yield to instincts which, had he been alone, he would perforce have kept under restraint'. Numbers create anonymity, so all feeling of individual responsibility disappears. A second new characteristic appears, contagion, whose presence in the crowd is easy to detect but hard to explain, though it is certainly one of the phenomena 'of a hypnotic order'. This inclines a man to self-sacrifice, 'an attitude very contrary to his nature'. A third new characteristic is suggestibility, of which contagion the effect. Suggestibility is partly to be explained by the psychology of hypnotism and partly by physiology. The brain of an individual under the influence of suggestion is paralysed and he becomes 'the slave of all the unconscious activities of his spinal cord, which the hypnotiser directs at will', with the difference that in the crowd suggestion acts even more strongly than during individual hypnosis because 'suggestion being the same for all the individuals of the crowd, it gains in strength by reciprocity'. Even very strong-minded individuals, who left alone might be able to resist the hypnotist, cannot always resist suggestion magnified by reciprocity and they are powerless to stop the contagion spreading. All they can do is to make counter-suggestions, and it sometimes happens that 'a happy expression, an image opportunely evoked will divert the crowd from the most bloodthirsty acts'. The whole business can be summed up by saying that 'by the mere fact that he forms part of an organised crowd, a man descends several rungs in the ladder of civilization'. (*Crowd*, pp. 9–13). All this happens in the crowd without any exercise of will on the part of members of the crowd, and it sometimes happens *against* the will of members of the crowd, so it must be caused by a part of the mind which is not conscious, or even by a part of the body which is not mind at all, the spinal column. By an adept sleight of hand, Le Bon then brings into play another commonplace notion of the unconscious which embraces the whole of society. Nobody exactly decides what the values and customs of a society should be, so society too must have been caused by the unconscious. The unconscious is in fact everywhere. Le Bon thinks that any group that thinks like a crowd is a crowd, the crowd thinks unconsciously, so society must also be a crowd. So we are all members of a crowd, whether we like it or not. Whatever that way of looking at social life is, it is not sociology, or, if it is, it is a sociology so simple-minded that it speaks to ideology and not to social science.

Le Bon is deliberately setting out to make the crowd as frightening as it can be. What he wants to suggest is that in the modern world there is nothing to contain the crowd, because the crowd is everywhere, just as on the level of theory there is no sociology which is not itself crowd sociology. That leaves the crowd standing on its own as 'the last surviving sovereign force of modern times '(*Crowd*, p. xiv). The crowd has been sovereign before, notably in those two other great transition periods, the Roman Empire in its decline and the rise of Islam (*Crowd*, p. xiii). There is always a 'period of confused anarchy', a 'barbarian phase', when the crowd comes into its own (*Crowd*, p. viii); the tribes which invaded the Roman Empire were heterogeneous crowds because nothing held them together except the authority of a chief (*Crowd*, p. 157); they possessed no 'general beliefs', and it was only the acquisition of 'general ideas', which are always few in number, which enabled them to transform themselves into the nations of Europe (*Crowd*, p. 45). Race is the only general sociological category that Le Bon takes seriously apart from the crowd. Race is partly biological and partly cultural. Racial characteristics make themselves most obvious

in the belief systems of nations. If there is a containing category in Le
Bon capable of restraining the crowd, it is race. Race and crowd are
sometimes competitors and sometimes allies. Le Bon recognizes that
Anglo-Saxon and Latin crowds act in predictably different ways (e.g.
Crowd, pp. 37, 160), but the cases that really interest him are those
in which the crowd overcomes even the inherited racial characters
which go to make up what social stability there is in human life.
That is why Le Bon is so insistent on saying that when a crowd is
formed its life is genuinely new. Crowds acquire 'new psychological
characteristics, which are added to the racial characteristics and
differ from them at times to a very considerable degree '(*Crowd*, p. v).
In normal times the crowd is not dangerous because its characteristics
are national characteristics exaggerated. The crowd still does display
new characteristics, but these are swamped by traditional ways of
thinking and feeling. Transition periods are very different, because
in these the new characteristics predominate. This, he thinks, is the
case in the modern world, the new Era of Crowds.

The modern State does not help in the Era of Crowds, because
it is both a solvent of racial solidarity and a substitute for it. Racial
solidarity makes possible what Le Bon calls civilization, because it
gives to peoples the 'fixed groundwork' of general ideas which alone
can provide the degree of mental homogeneity without which nothing
of lasting value can be created. The national variants of feudalism,
Christianity, Protestantism (a nice distinction) and, in the present
age, the national principle and 'contemporary/democratic and social
ideals' are examples of general ideas which have either brought races
out of crowds or have prevented races from regressing to the crowd
state (*Crowd*, p. 142). The institutions and customs which a people
gives itself come out of these general ideas, and the 'collective
egotism' of the race breathes life into them. The enemy of the race is
an excess of 'individual egotism' which dominates men's daily lives
and enervates the racial spirit. Something has to take the place of
the racial spirit if collective life is to continue, so the State begins to
regulate men's lives instead. In these conditions, 'the genius of the
race entirely disappears; it is a mere swarm of isolated individuals
and returns to its original state – that of a mere crowd' (*Crowd*, p.
218). Le Bon regards this process of development from a crowd to a
race and back again as the natural life cycle of a people. He thinks
France in his own day is in danger of going through the second part
of the cycle, from race to crowd. The Republic One and Indivisible
is fast becoming what Michelet said it was at the beginning, except
that this time a people is degenerating into a crowd, while for Michelet
the crowd that stormed the Bastille created a people. It is hard to see
how two such opinions about the crowd could be further apart, and

that they are so far apart is a measure of how far crowd theory had come since Michelet.

The spirit of the race leaves behind it the institutions of authority which it created in its heyday, and these institutions are vulnerable to the crowd in periods of transition and disintegration. The natural conservatism of crowds makes them exhibit a 'docile respect for force' and leads them to bestow their sympathies on 'tyrants who vigorously oppressed them'. They crave authority. 'The type of hero dear to crowds will always have the semblance of a Caesar. His insignia attracts them, his authority overawes them, and his sword instils them with fear.' What the crowd cannot abide is weak authority. It turns on a despot when he has 'resumed his place among the feeble'. Its instinct for smelling out weakness is strong, and it destroys institutions which are empty shells which the spirit of the race has deserted. (*Crowd*, pp. 38–9). One of the central illusions in France since the Revolution has been based on ignorance of this simple truth about institutions. The revolutionaries began from the belief that 'natural progress' is the outcome of 'the improvement of institutions and governments' and that belief spawned the illusion that 'social changes can be affected by decrees'. This illusion is not confined to France, but seems to deceive all the Latin countries. Right reason cannot do what only the spirit of the race can do; the proof is that the revolutionaries attacked all government as the product of the past, but the genius of the race forced them to accept centralization of the State and to strengthen it. Some contemporaries want to decentralize the State – a dig at Maurras and *Action Française* – but that would be to repeat the revolutionaries' mistake and try to write off the whole of French history. Institutions do not in fact matter very much because they are the product of national greatness and prosperity, not their cause. Even the celebrated Constitution of the United States cannot contribute much to American prosperity, because the sister republics of South America have very similar constitutions and they are decadent. It is possible for a state to be given a constitution appropriate to the spirit of its people, but that is a happy accident (*Crowd*, pp. 75–80). Only the Romans and the English seem to have hit on the secret of constitutions, which is to let them develop organically (*Crowd*, p. 74).

Race, for Le Bon, is ideally a crowd formed from homogeneous elements. The crowd which succeeds the race in transition periods is heterogeneous because the racial basis of its thoughts has become so eroded that its unconscious no longer speaks with one voice. The racial unconscious is not complicated, though it is far more complex than the mind of the crowd, but the social reality which the racial unconscious sustains can itself be extremely differentiated and sophisticated. Le Bon is uncertain in his treatment of the question of how this can be. At times he talks as if social and political institutions come directly out of the mind of the race, and at other times he talks as if an elite creates those institutions which the mass then become accustomed to, so that acceptance of them becomes second nature. Race is really a limiting condition on social engineering. The institutions of the *ancien régime* were the work of aristocracy. They created a social and political world in which men could live and feel at home. The Revolution was the first serious attempt of individualism to assert itself against a highly differentiated social order. It enfranchised the individual (at least theoretically), but it also isolated him: 'In isolating him from his caste, from his family, from the social and religious groups of which he was a unit, it has left him delivered over to himself, and has thus transformed society into a mass of individuals, without cohesion and without ties' (*The Psychology of Socialism* (1899), 1982, p. 5). By shaking men out of their social categories, the Revolution returned them to a state of nature, and that nature cannot be pleasant now that we know what human nature in the raw has done since 1789 in massacre and riot. The crowd has no ideas of its own. Its members are sociologically heterogeneous and what homogeneity it has comes from the dreary but dangerous sameness of unconscious mind. The racial unconscious is of low reflective capacity, but the new group mind which forms in the crowd is even feebler. Men differ from one another by the degree to which consciousness is developed. This is true of comparisons between races. A race is advanced or sluggish depending on how sophisticated its elites are (Le Bon was the first Frenchman to visit Nepal, where he went with a donkey and a pair of callipers to measure the cranial capacity of the Nepalise elite). The gap between different elites is greater than the gap between different racial masses. The mass in any given society are only capable of thinking in national commonplaces, but when that society is disintegrating and the crowd takes over from the race, the level of thinking of the mass sinks lower still (*Crowd*, pp. 8–9; *Socialism*, p. 25). Anyone who doubts that this can happen in a crowd of ordinary men should recall the collective imbecility of panels of learned men: 'A society directed by an areopagus of scientists, such as August Comte dreamed of, would not last six months' (*Socialism*, p. 55).

It is hard not to use the words 'crowd' and 'mass' as synonyms when discussing Le Bon, and it is important to remember that Le Bon wants to use them interchangeably. Crowd society is mass society, though Le Bon never actually uses the term, so crowd psychology must be the psychology of mass society. In an article on 'The Theory of Mass Society' (1962, reprinted in Shils, 1975) which has become classic, Professor Shils argues that the theory of mass society had to wait until the Weimar Republic to acquire its characteristically modern form. The experience of Weimar demanded a social theory which would explain how the disintegrating effects of an urbanized and capitalist social order left men so alone and helpless that they had to take shelter in the totalitarian party. The mass society theory, Shils argues, was a 'quasi-Marxist' synthesis of a number of the concerns of nineteenth-century social theory which included: reactions to the French Revolution and to the other revolutions which it inspired; the analysis of the demagogic imperialism of Louis Napoleon; Tocqueville's picture of society after 1815 as one that had lost its feudal liberty; the German sociologists' distinction between *Gemeinschaft* and *Gesellschaft*, and 'a certain amount of subsequent embroidery' in the work of Sighele and Le Bon on the theme of the mob and its demagogues. The society of the Weimar Republic 'was declared to be the characteristic pattern of modern society in preparation for its natural culmination'. The theory has gained new strength from 'mass communications' and from apprehension about their effects on the standardless mass.

> The result is the following image of mass society: a territorially extensive society, with a large population, highly urbanized and industrialized. Power is highly concentrated in this society, and much of the power takes the form of manipulation of the mass through the media of mass communication. Civic spirit is low, local loyalties are few, primordial solidarity is virtually non-existent. There is no individuality, only a restless and frustrated egotism. It is like the state of nature described by Thomas Hobbes, except that public disorder is restrained through the manipulation of the elite and the apathetic idiocy of the mass. The latter is broken only when, in a state of crisis, the masses rally round some demagogue. [The theorists of mass society] have stressed alienation, beliefflessness, atomization, conformism, rootlessness, moral emptiness, facelessness, egotism, the utter evaporation of any kind of loyalty – except the passionately zealous attachment to an ideological movement. They point to the indiscipline of youth and the neglect of the aged; they allege a frivolous hedonism and a joyless vulgarity.
>
> (Shils, 1975, pp. 91–2, 105)

Shils then goes on to comment drily: 'There is a little truth in these assertions, but not much' (ibid., p. 105). Shils is wrong on two counts: the mass society theory existed in Le Bon, almost word for word, long before Weimar; and whatever else can be said about Le Bon, he is no 'quasi-Marxist'; the theme of *The Psychology of Socialism* is an attack on all socialism as a primitive illusion and therefore a social danger. A danger to whom? To the elite which liberal society produces despite its pretensions to equality. It spawns a new breed of men, the professional politicians, who will promise anything to get elected and whose self-interest cuts them off from their electors. They are not especially dangerous, though they are almost certainly corrupt, and they are not even in the etymological sense an elite. Le Bon draws on Godkin's *Unforeseen Consequences of Democracy* to suggest that as in America, so in France, the influence of elected representatives is puny when compared to the influence of the hidden elite who operate behind the appearance of democracy. Le Bon also quotes Tarde: behind the formality of democracy the real rulers are state functionaries and the military hierarchy (because of European rearmament); 'prelates, princes of blood, monks and gentlemen, châteaux and monasteries have been replaced by journalists, financiers, artists, politicians, theatres, banks, ministries, great shops, huge barracks' (*Socialism*, pp. 82, 282–3).

This elite is still superior enough to the masses to be worth defending against them. The question then is: How can the masses be provided with a new set of those 'general ideas' which will give society the social cohesion which it formerly had and which it is now losing? The most obvious form that these general ideas have taken in the past is religion. The convictions of crowds have always assumed a religious shape; crowds unconsciously accord a 'mysterious' power to political formulas – this is now true of socialism; the intolerance of the Jacobins was 'as religious' as the Inquisition; the crowd's need for a god is the key to understanding 'the philosophy of history'; Napoleon was a god for fifteen years. This superstition 'of a bygone age' can still move the crowd – General Boulanger might have been one of the great men of history if he had had the strength of character to match his crowd appeal (*Crowd*, pp. 60–3). Real religion is no answer to crowd religion in its socialist or Caesarist form. The bourgeoisie is now eating the bitter fruit of its Enlightenment and its Positivism. There is no going back to the Church on our knees with Péguy. Science has declared its own moral bankruptcy; it can produce only what it promised to produce, truth, not morality; a free-thinking bourgeoisie confronts an anti-clerical mass, and there is no salvation in that (*Crowd*, p. xvii). Solidarism probably won't work either because since the Revolution the French have lifted up their eyes to the State, so there is no tradition of mutual self-help; certainly there is nothing in France to compare with English trade unions and Co-operative Societies, or with successful self-interested pressure groups like the Anti-Corn Law League. There are some hopeful signs in the development of trade unionism in France, but it is too soon to tell (they only became legal

209

in 1884), and even here the Latin tendency towards despotism makes trade union leaders into little Caesars who use their followers as badly as their masters ever did (*Socialism*, pp. 341–55). Decentralization of the State won't work because French history says it can't, so France is stuck with its concentration of power at the centre besieged by a clamouring crowd with no defences in between.

The only salvation is Le Bon's own technology of crowd manipulation. Le Bon's explicitness is bare-faced. 'A knowledge of the psychology of crowds is today the last resource of the statesman who wishes not to govern them – that is becoming a very difficult matter – but at any rate not to be too much governed by them' (*Crowd*, p. xx). The single precedent Le Bon will allow is Machiavelli's *Prince*, the only real treatise of political psychology ever to be published before, and that is four centuries old (Le Bon, 1910, p. 4). Le Bon has no doubt about what league he expects to be in; like Machiavelli's *Prince*, his work is to be a handbook on how new rulers can keep their power or at least survive, because if a way cannot be found for the elite to coexist with the labouring masses who are trying to destroy it with all the fury which the barbarians displayed when they sacked Rome, then civilization might as well shut up shop (ibid., p. 121). When Le Bon actually gets to the point of advising statesmen, the advice has almost nothing of the directness of the Machiavellian original. In *The Crowd* Le Bon does find a loophole in the prevailing gloom for the modern psychologist-statesman. The very heterogeneity of belief which is always the sign of a declining civilization means that crowds are becoming easier to manage. Their irritability and fickleness require careful handling, but 'Crowds are occasionally easy-going masters, as were Heliogabalus and Tiberius'; they are capable of violent swings of feeling and this caprice is what the statesman must work on (*Crowd*, p. 156; Le Bon, 1910, 'The Genesis of Persuasion'). To do this the statesman must learn the lessons of his enemies, the revolutionary syndicalists, who have learned the art of creating and mastering crowds by instinct and by trial and error, and have turned their collectivities into bitter enemies of the established order (Nye, 1975, p. 106). By the time Le Bon came to write *Political Psychology and Social Defence* (1910) he was convinced that only an elite version of Sorel's *Reflections on Violence* could save France from internal chaos and the external threat of German militarism by urging French politicians to try to revive ancient memories of a militant patriotism in the genius of the race; politicians and bosses (*patrons*) 'should promise chimeras, affirm without proof, repeat . . . such is the formula of success' (Nye, 1975, p. 106).

The advice does not add much to what Le Bon had already said in his chapter on 'The Leaders of Crowds and their Means of Persuasion' in *The Crowd* fifteen years before. Perhaps his own publishing successes went to his head, for the advice to political leaders is Le Bon's own technique of persuading his public that what he has to say about the psychology of the crowd is true; what Le Bon could do in books surely France's leaders could do in politics. What is not clear is what Le Bon thought the chances of success were. In *The Crowd* he says that in ages of transition the genius of the race is on the decline; that is true in his terms by definition: a transition period is the breaking up of the homogeneous crowd of the nation into the heterogeneous crowd whose new psychological characteristics enervate the racial unconscious. But it is this racial unconscious which he now asks leaders to revive by using the techniques of crowd demagoguery. This is not necessarily inconsistency in Le Bon. Transition ages can take a long time, and his advice to leaders can be seen as a justifiable last throw of the political dice at a time of national emergency. What *is* glaringly inconsistent is that Le Bon should ask leaders to revamp the racial soul after what he has to say about race in his attack on socialism, where he argues that 'factors of the psychological order, such as race, beliefs and opinions' which have till 'quite lately' had a 'preponderant' influence on the fate of nations, are now giving way to a different set of determining causes which he calls 'the laws of nature', by which he means economic competition. These laws of 'social evolution' are accepted by some nations while others try to hide behind protective tariffs (the Meline Tariffs in France), ignoring the fact that nature's laws 'operate with the blind punctuality of clockwork, and he that offends them is broken by their march' (*Socialism*, p. 2). So now race is being undermined by the two great forces of modern times, the crowd and social evolution, so the chances that race can even survive as an important social force, let alone reunite the nation, must be, on Le Bon's account of the matter, pretty thin.

Protection is another attempt by the State to interfere with the processes of nature, another stage on the way to socialism. Le Bon has got himself into a tangle in dealing with race and socialism. Race is not a predominantly biological category for Le Bon; it looks much more like what we would now call national culture. It was safe for Le Bon to argue for all he was worth that race was the single most important determining force in the history of nations when he was attacking the enlightened and revolutionary illusion that new institutions could create new men. All he had to do was to follow Tocqueville and point out how much of the legacy of the Revolution was in fact a reinforcement of tendencies which were already well developed in the *ancien régime*. The masses were conservative, not revolutionary – witness the Jacobin dictatorship and Napoleonic imperialism in which they readily acquiesced; witness Bonapartist plebiscitary imperialism the second time round. Race impels the French to political centralization; power at the centre confronts a formless mass without those intervening organic institutions which have been dear to the heart of liberalism since Montesquieu. Like his sociology, Le Bon's racial history is history without nuances, but its lack of sophistication makes its direction unmistakable: it should point directly towards socialism in France. Socialist ideas qualify as candidates for becoming one of those historically successful simplifications by all of Le Bon's own criteria. No civilization has ever succeeded in establishing itself without the 'prodigious empire' of the gods. 'The most flourishing civilizations have always been propped up by religious dogmas which, from the rational point of view, possessed not an atom of logic, not a spice of truth, nor even of simple good sense.' Science can only wrestle with the gods, not overcome them. This is true of socialist ideas, which from the point of view of science are so flawed as to be laughable. They are the product of the false fraternity of the Revolution, which sought to deny the obvious natural truth that societies are held together and kept going by elites. Socialism feeds on 'hatred and envy' in the lower classes; the proletariat as socialists would like it to be hardly exists, and the working classes hesitate before socialism even in Paris, which has the most developed tradition of working-class militancy; even Boulangism, which promised improvement to working men, was at heart not socialist but Caesarist; all working men are really bourgeois and sentimental at heart, religious even – they dream of retiring to a little house in the country, followed Boulanger out of a boyish liking for heroes on horseback, and they do not think they are really properly married till they have gone through the ceremony at the *mairie*. Socialist ideas have spread much further among the bourgeoisie, especially among the book-learned *demi-savants* by 'simple contagion'; even some real *savants* have been infected by these ideas, but this was only to be expected: it is notorious that intellectuals have never understood how the real world works. Contempt for the world of affairs which has rejected them has always been part of the stock-in-trade of intellectuals; socialism is their latest way of remaking the world so that they will end up as masters of it just as Marat, Saint-Just and Robespierre did in their day (ibid., pp. xliv, 25–57). And so on, and on. Of course, the world after 1789 has produced its own elite, that aristocracy of financiers which reigns over 'a mob of individuals possessing neither cohesion nor defence' and the masses look to the State for protection from what is only the predictable outcome of the operation of Nature's laws of competition. It is not liberty to which the masses aspire, but collectivism. Unfortunately for France, the machinery of state necessary for the redistribution of wealth has existed since before the Revolution. Since 1870 government has got into the habit of giving way to workers' demands. Socialism will become a reality when government accedes to its demands by using the existing state machinery to 'repair the injustice of Destiny' (ibid., p. 28).

Le Bon seems to make out a case for the inevitability of socialism in France, which is the last thing he wants. In *The Crowd* he emphasized how primitive socialism is when compared to the sophisticated differentiation of modern societies. The undifferentiated crowd threatened to destroy 'society as it now exists' with a view of 'making it hark back to that primitive communism which was the normal condition of all human groups before the dawn of civilization'. Spencerian differentiation would disappear when socialist ideas became 'articles of faith, above discussion'; then they will acquire 'a sovereign force, a "divine right" of the masses, every bit as tyrannical as the divine right of kings' (*Crowd*, p. xvi). By 1899, when Le Bon published *The Psychology of Socialism*, socialist ideas were well on the way to becoming accepted crowd-dogma, and by 1910, when he published *Political Psychology and Social Defence*, Le Bon was close to panic. That is why he began to desert 'race' as a determining social cause in favour of 'the natural laws of competition', which he produces like a rabbit out of a hat. I have said above that there are no prizes for finding contradictions in Le Bon. He is an opportunist, but up to 1899 he clung consistently to race as a general social cause; then he dropped it in favour of competition. It is important to notice that the same thing has happened to Le Bon that happened to Sighele: he has been driven out of one social theory and into another, from his race theory into a last-minute theory of international competition; this change has led him to the position which Sighele eventually adopted, where the crowd and its psychology appears the only way out of present political difficulties. Le Bon's position is different from Sighele's because crowd manipulation based on the psychology of the crowd is to be used by the elite to defend itself, while for Sighele the crowd itself was to be the agent of its own salvation, but the cases of both show how powerful a theoretical force the crowd theory had become by 1900. Any theory which can compel thinkers to these remarkable volte-faces is a force to be reckoned with.

Le Bon urges the French elite to use crowd psychology to prepare the French masses for war in exactly the same way that Sighele thinks that crowd psychology is the means by which proletarian Italy is asserting itself on the battlefields of Africa. What worries Le Bon is socialist internationalism and pacifism. Like Sorel, but from a diametrically opposite political standpoint, Le Bon thinks that 'official' socialism makes pacifists of the French working class. By 1910 Le Bon had come round to the view that what energy the working class had would be expended on the relative peaceful business of finding ways to make the French state redistribute wealth. This was dangerous, especially if the elite lost its nerve, but it was a far cry from what the elite had had to fear from the rude barbarian energies of the masses that Le Bon had warned against in *The Crowd* only fifteen years before. This enervation was exactly what Sorel warned against in the *Reflections on Violence* in 1908.[3] Sorel believed that only the myth of the general strike as Napoleonic battlefield could restore the feeling of class *war* in the proletariat and *also* in the bourgeoisie, who have recently been so gutless as to concede wage increases against their own belief in the iron law of wages. Proletarian violence can 'so operate on the middle classes as to awaken them to a sense of their own class sentiment' (Sorel, 1908, p. 98). For Le Bon, one of the solutions to the problem of the crowd infected by socialism is war. It wasn't Lenin but Le Bon who popularized the idea that the coming European war was going to be caused by international competition, the most important part of which was economic competition. A France rotting behind tariff barriers, progressively giving in to workers' demands, would be living in a fool's paradise. Those laws of nature which compelled nations to compete with each other would win through in the end, just as they would win through in the nation's domestic life. The menace of an economically aggressive and politically militaristic Germany might be the means by which race could win back the ground that it had lost to the crowd when the application of crowd psychology applied by the French elite to the French masses had begun to work.

When the war came, Le Bon showed that he was not all that confident that race would win in its battle to revive the nation. He retired prudently to a remote villa near the Spanish border, and only returned to Paris after the 'miracle of the Marne' (Nye, 1975, p. 123); now there was an end to all the talk of nationalism, militarism and the mystical instincts of the race; France's war aims were directly contrary to the 'instinctual' aims of the Germans; martial France went to war with Reason, Civilization and the Rights of Man on her banners (ibid., pp. 124–5). Le Bon may even have been partly responsible for the way the war was fought. He was proud of the influence that his theory of crowd leadership had on the doctrines and training of the French army, which took his idea of crowd solidarity seriously as a model for attacking infantry. In battle, closely packed crowds acting unconsciously under the direction of a chief could take advantage of that feeling of invincible power which individuals felt in crowds. Crowd psychology could be especially useful with colonial troops who, being blacks, had practically no minds at all, so the orders of their officers could pass almost directly into their unconscious. In 1910 Le

Bon complained his ideas of leadership had not made the same headway in civilian life, and the purpose of *Political Psychology and Social Defence* was to get politicians and bosses to do to the pacifist masses what was already happening to the soldiers (Le Bon, 1910, p. 97, n.1; p. 125; Nye, 1975, ch. 6, *passim*).

Sociology, Marxism and Liberalism Defend themselves against Le Bon and his Crowd

Le Bon may not be the most original of crowd theorists, but he is the most comprehensive. He is good at seeing what the impli- cations of crowd theory are for other social theories. There is not much hope for liberalism, positivism, or socialism if what Le Bon says about the crowd is true. The great catch-all category for Le Bon is the 'unconscious'. His is an attack on all rationalism, and on all political theories which place a high value and high expectations on human rationality. The sometimes highly technical debates which had gone on since the early 1880s about the nature and limits of hypnotism meant very little to him. Hypnotism meant unconscious behaviour, past and present, as either caused by hypnotic influence or analogous to it. Le Bon claims that he is explaining the unconscious behaviour of crowds as a preliminary to offering a way of dealing with it, but he is also frightening his readers with his explanation as well. The category 'unconscious' is not really explanatory in the way Le Bon uses it, and Le Bon comes close to admitting this when he says that the unconscious is still to a large extent mysterious. Like Sighele and Tarde, Le Bon came to see that the distinction between conscious and unconscious behaviour was no clearer than the distinction between sickness and health. An ordinary lived life was not the same as living in a hypnotic trance, or sleep-walking, but there was no obvious dividing line between the more spectacular forms of unconsciously influenced behaviour and the behaviour of daily life. The language of 'more or less' replaced the language of 'either/or'. This in its turn meant that there was no behaviour whose explanation was obvious, and there was nobody whose explanation of his own behaviour one could trust.

This meant that questions were bound to be asked about the rela- tionship between unconscious and conscious life, especially about the relationship between the unconscious and the higher forms of consciousness as they found their expression in morality and law. Central to the modern world's claim to superiority over primitive worlds was that now rational, thought-out conduct would increasingly invade and conquer areas of life still dominated by automatic behaviour inherited from the past. Here nineteenth-century Positivism spoke the clear language of Enlightenment. But if all human conduct could be shown to have an unconscious component, then rationality, however defined, could not be the *cause* of human conduct. The relationship between thought-out schemes of human behaviour and actual human conduct became problematic, cases of Freudian rationalization, Paretian residues, Marxist false consciousness, or Sorelian myth. The message of this was not lost in France. French thinkers had spent most of the nineteenth century trying to understand how the French Revolution could begin in the name of Reason and the Rights of Man, and progress so effortlessly to the institutionalized barbarism of the Terror. The psychology of the unconscious provided one kind of answer. The reasons men give for their actions are never the real reasons, and reason itself cannot be a human motive. The reasons given for conduct are glosses on motives which are often so hidden from the actors themselves that there is no point even in impugning their sincerity. Of course, there are those in all great political upheavals who use slogans consciously to manipulate others, but that was a minor point compared to the possibility that all systems of thought might be the outward surfaces of unconscious drives and wishes. And so on to the typically modern concern of social science to examine all social thought, revolutionary and reactionary, progressive and conservative, for the unconscious determinants lying beneath.

What made Le Bon's line of thought so disturbing was that the category 'unconscious' had in his day no very precise meaning. It could mean 'that which is not thought out'; or 'that which is not intended'; or 'that over which I have no control' (race, tradition, heredity, instinct, custom); or 'that which I would not do if I had thought about it'; but whatever cluster of meanings was attached to it, two ways of looking at the unconscious overshadowed all the rest, the Romantic and the psychiatric. We have long ceased to think that the unconscious was 'discovered', or 'rediscovered', in the nineteenth century. From Plato's account in *The Republic* of the tyrant as the ruler who uses power to act out his dream fantasies in waking life, to Freud's account of the unconscious in the terms of Sophoclean drama, the operation of unconscious forces has been a standard source of philosophical reflection and literary invention. But what characterizes explorations of the unconscious before the second half of the nineteenth century was the lack of any attempt to define precisely what the unconscious *is*; it was Gothic; it was dark, mysterious, perhaps limitless; therein lay its charm. Romanticism had no motive for trying to draw the unconscious in exact contours. To map the unconscious would have been to diminish its fascination as a *terra incognita*, unknown and all but unknowable, into which intense personal journeys could be made and of which travellers' tales could be told. The romantic integrity of the unconscious would be violated by a gazetteer. (The Nile became just another river once its source had been found.) The second half of the nineteenth century saw the beginnings of systematic research into the nature of the unconscious for well-defined medical reasons, and by the time crowd psychologists began to formalize the theory of the crowd the connections between the working of the unconscious and mental illness were well established. Scientifically ambitious plans for physiological and neuro-chemical investigation of the brain were already well advanced, so that some kind of scientifically normal understanding of the unconscious mind should not have been very far in the future. What had been mysterious and chaotic for the Romantics was on the verge of being understood and tamed. The unconscious would soon be safely caged in a scientific zoo which suited an age when zoos were *de rigueur* in every European city with claims to being a centre of scientific life. But the banalization of the unconscious was just too far in the future for it to influence crowd theory before Freud. Freud's attempt to provide a topography and archaeology of the unconscious, and his attempt to explain it through a decoding of Sophocles' own partial encoding of the familiar myth of Oedipus, is evidence of a growing confidence that the unconscious can be confronted head on, and coped with like other puzzles. The results of the physiology- and chemistry-related medical investigations came out only slowly, and Freud was still waiting anxiously for some kind of chemical-biological confirmation of his own theory of the unconscious in the 1920s. The unconscious was still mysterious before Freud, so the medical connection between abnormal psychology and crowd theory was the opposite of reassuring, and the shadow of mental psychopathology hung long and heavily over the whole enterprise of crowd psychology, which seemed to confirm the popular conviction that crowd action was a kind of temporary madness.

Le Bon plays on this popular fear to reinforce the ancient Socratic image of the Philosopher King as the gifted healer whose special skill is to turn pathological states of society into healthy normality. This was especially appropriate in a France which was smarting after the defeat in the Franco-Prussian War and still traumatized by the *Commune*. Various diagnoses were being offered to explain what was seen as a serious case of national decline. Some blamed the egotism of the Jacobin state and its system of education which produced men fit only for state employment or for political agitation; others blamed the corruption of politics by high finance and Jews; others pointed to the effects of alcoholism and neurosis on the birth rate. The sickness of the crowd could be seen at the back of all these, or at least as connected with them. Taine had established the connection between the psychology of Jacobinism and the psychology of the mob, what Sighele and Tarde called the 'sect' and its crowd; corruption in high places was made possible by the gullibility of the crowd of electors; alcoholism and neurosis led directly to the excitability and insanity of crowds. As long as unconscious behaviour was considered to be abnormal, or disturbed, or morbid, then the medical origins of the psychology of the unconscious were bound to cause unease. Crowd psychology compounded this unease even further by continually returning to its medical origins for fresh explanatory categories, despite the avowed intention of crowd psychologists of thinking their way out of the narrower concerns of positivist medicine to the wider field of social theory. They used concepts like *folie à deux* (which sometimes infected doctors who treated the insane), hysteria (an affliction of women, notoriously less stable than men), and contagion, to explain what happened in crowds, showing how difficult in fact it was for crowd psychology to transcend its medical origins. Perhaps the use of the concept of contagion was the most alarming of all. Europe had by no means seen the last of the great epidemics and epidemiology was in the process of turning itself into an exact science. Times of epidemic were also times of panic-stricken mass exodus from cities, so the classic cases of epidemic through contagion were also classic cases of the crowd contagion which crowd theory set out to explain. There were still those who thought that epidemics spread through the air, or by touching, so there was nothing in principle to stop them from thinking that physical contagion and psychological contagion were different cases of the same thing. Investigation into the problems of the exact mechanisms of contagion was common both to epidemiology and crowd psychology. Science had no reason for thinking that these were only analogous problems, so there seemed to be a danger that the crowd could infect a whole society in the same way that a plague could. The crowd was more dangerous than a plague because it did not actually kill its own members. It could become a kind of permanent plague, or society could be seen as a permanent incubatory culture for a virus which could spring into active life at any time in the same way that theorists of class war were beginning to think of it as embers which could be fanned into spreading fire by the winds of discontent. Looked at like that, epidemic could easily *be* the mechanism of class war.

The association of unconscious mental life with psychopathology continued to overshadow crowd psychology and to inform the ambitiously generalized social theory which crowd psychologists drew out of it. By the 1890s, crowd theory was confident enough of itself to advance a serious claim to *be* social theory. Nobody recognized this better than Durkheim. The politeness of Durkheim's debate with Tarde over the place of unconscious imitation in the development of stable patterns of social behaviour and belief barely conceals the growing anxiety that crowd psychology would take over the whole of social science in the same way that crowd psychologists like Le Bon were arguing that the crowd itself was about to take over those very societies whose nature sociologists were beginning to explore. Durkheim explained patiently that sociology could not be 'psychology', because the nature of social groups could not be adequately explained as extrapolations from the psychology of the typical individuals that composed them. Societies did not change as minds changed. The proof of this was that societies could and did survive changes in individual minds, and, through birth and death, individual minds could enter and leave a society while the society itself remained intact. Sociology, in Durkheim's view, should deal with those social facts which existed in finite individual minds but which acted from the outside in, not from the inside out. Durkheim did not deny that there was such a thing as 'social psychology' which properly dealt with the interaction of minds in a given society, and he thought that crowd psychology was one of its concerns, but these were subsciences which had to be kept in their place and prevented from usurping sociology as a whole (Lukes, 1973, pp. 5–13). But Durkheim's attempt to keep the object and methods of sociology separate from crowd psychology was made difficult by his own view of what constituted a social fact. Social facts were not consciously thought out; they existed independently of conscious will and reflection; conscious will and reflection had to make their way in the world against these social facts which acted as constraints. (Witness the resistances to sociology itself.) The culture of a society existed over and above the collection of individual minds in which that culture manifested itself, so the question of how those minds operated when they came together in collectivities like crowds could not be the same question as how that society came to be as it was in the first place. That distinction was difficult enough to grasp in a pre-sociological age, and it was not likely to survive when sociology entered the world of general literacy where it was easy to think that Durkheim's view of social rules as determining behaviour independent of any specific process of human reasoning was the same as the crowd psychologists' assertion that the rules which governed the collective mental life of crowds were different from the rules which governed their mental life as individuals.

Durkheimian sociology was therefore at its most vulnerable in the face of the crowd psychologists' central anti-Spencerian claim that there were characteristics of the crowd mind which had to be treated as radically new, proper only to the collectivity, and which were interesting because they could not be explained in terms of the psychology of the individuals who made up the crowd. It was unfortunate for Durkheim that his sociology was making its own break with Spencerism at the same time as crowd theorists were making theirs, and it was hard for the intellectual public, let alone Le Bon's enormous readership, to understand that these were different anti-Spencerian developments, in different intellectual enterprises, for different reasons. Crowd behaviour was unpredictable in the terms of Spencerian methodological individualism because a kind of group mind came into existence whose workings could not be explained as a special case of the working of individual minds. This distinction, between individual mind and group mind, could look very like Durkheim's distinction between a culture and the individual minds which that culture fills, or on which that culture operates. The crowd mind is not the mind of a typical individual writ large, and neither is a culture. When crowd theorists added that different national crowds acted in fairly predictable different national ways, it was easy to see national culture as group mind.

A measure of the importance of crowd theory outside the world of academic sociology is the extent to which other political ideologies felt bound to take notice of it. Marxism, Idealism, Positivism and Liberalism all tried to cope with the crowd on the level of theory, providing a textbook case of Marx's dictum that, before the real struggle, the contending parties meet and fight it out wearing ideological gloves, so that nobody gets badly hurt first time round; only later do the gloves come off.

Marxism confronted crowd theory through Georges Sorel, whose disillusionment with the moral enervation of official French socialism has already been remarked upon. Sorel's own Marxism was an attack on the spell which evolutionary Positivism had cast over official German and French Marxism since Marx's death in 1883. Belief in the truth of Marxism had come to mean believing that Marx had discovered the necessary laws by which capitalist society moved towards its final and necessary collapse, to be succeeded by a society organized on socialist lines in which the State would wither away. What was not always clear was what part human will had to play in the process. The end could perhaps be hastened by political action informed by correct theory, but there was always the possibility that too hasty action could prolong the very process whose end socialists everywhere waited for so eagerly. Perhaps the best thing was to let capitalist society collapse under its own weight and let the comrades pick up the pieces afterwards. But what if the imminence of the collapse proved to be a chimera? What was a socialist party to do in the meantime? Surely there could be no harm in seeking some changes beneficial to the working class, even though that meant playing the game of bourgeois liberal politics. And so on to what came to be called Revisionism, the domestication of revolutionary Marxism into parliamentary socialism; *embourgeoisement* and the Iron Law of Oligarchy would whip in socialist leaders so that they became indistinguishable from the leaders of the other parties produced by the social and political system which socialists were still in principle committed to destroying. What worried Sorel about Revisionism was that socialists had got into the habit of thinking like bourgeois; Revisionism was very little more than the fashionable evolutionism of the late nineteenth century fleshed out with quotations from Marx. (Sorel in fact admired the inventor of Revisionism, Bernstein, for his honesty because he openly defended Revisionism within the Marxist camp. Those whom Sorel attacks *act* like revisionists while *speaking* like revolutionaries.) Like Le Bon, Sorel could see nothing in this anodyne progressivism which could engage the moral passions. Its socialist version could barely provide a set of cogent reasons why people ought to be socialists. Sorel began to see in Le Bon's crowd the raw material which could merge with the myth of the proletarian general strike to become the motor of a class struggle much more genuine than the shadow-boxing of the parliamentary game.

What Sorel, in his cross-grained way, seized on in crowd theory was violence. Crowd theorists had always condemned acts of collective violence; even Sighele in the period when he was most sympathetic to the crowd felt that the tendency of crowds to violence could only be sometimes justified. He pointed out that not all crowd violence was equally reprehensible; some of it could be heroic and some of it could come out of motives which were deeply moral, but Sighele's tone is nearly always apologetic. In the *Reflections on Violence*, Sorel begins to ask some very searching questions about what made almost all shades of political opinion except direct-action anarchism unite in their condemnation of violence. Sorel believes that this squeamishness about violence is recent. In France, the practice of beating lessons into schoolchildren is decreasing – even Catholic schools are giving up corporal punishment to compete with secular schools where it has been abolished; factory discipline and the increasing sophistication of machinery are tending to eradicate violence, and admiration for brute strength, from the workplace; the defeat in the Franco-Prussian War has made the French think again about the pursuit of military glory while the horrors of the *Commune* make the use of violence in pursuit of political ends almost unthinkable (*Reflections*, p. 189). The tarnishing of *la gloire* since 1870 has altered the way the French look at the whole of their history since the Revolution. Up to 1870, the pro-revolutionary historians had always written its history as the story of heroical revolutionary war. Wars of liberation against Old Europe gave the revolutionary period its continuity and enabled even Napoleon to masquerade as a revolutionary. The political side of the Revolution, its faction fighting, the Terror, the denunciations and show trials, could all be written off as unfortunate, though perhaps necessary, and they were amply compensated for by the thousands of voluntary deaths in the name of liberty suffered by Frenchmen in liberty's crusade. But as soon as people began to doubt the value of battlefield glory, there was a tendency to concentrate on the *politics* of the Revolution, and Sorel admits that, when the wars of the revolution are put to one side, what is left is none too savoury (ibid., pp. 100–1). He admits that Taine's great achievement after 1870 was to persuade Frenchmen that the essence of revolutionary violence was contained in the Jacobin Terror and not in the revolutionary wars. Any attempt to repeat the French Revolution in the nineteenth century was to be seen not as the beginning of European liberation, but as an attempt to re-establish the Robespierrist Terror. That was Taine's view of the Paris *Commune*, and *The Origins of Contemporary France* carried that message to the whole of Europe either direct, or through Le Bon's *The Crowd* (*Reflections*, p. 102). Sorel thinks that there is a danger that a successful socialist party might indeed re-establish the Terror, but he also thinks that the socialist party that is likely to do that is a *parliamentary* socialist party of the kind led by Jaurès in France and Kautsky in Germany. When the parliamentary socialists condemn violence as barbarous, they do so for the same reasons that their bourgeois opponents condemn it, because it is lawless. What they forget is that the violence of the Revolution must have been bourgeois violence because 1789 is, on the Marxist view of it, a bourgeois revolution, The revolutionary Terror was legal violence, violence according to law, designed to protect the republican State from its internal enemies. This is the malicious violence of lawyers trained under the *ancien régime* where the law could also be used ruthlessly against the enemies of the State. Legal violence, what Sorel calls 'force', has an institutionalized existence in the State. In the bourgeois republic it does not operate spectacularly, though it does on occasion, as in 1848 and again in the brutal suppression of the *Commune*. It is this institutionalized force that the parliamentary socialists want to capture for themselves. This legal violence is what parliamentary socialists mean by the 'dictatorship of the proletariat'; the violence they condemn is extra-legal and *anti*-legal violence. Any future violence used by successful parliamentary socialists will be the unheroical, sneaking violence of lawyers, the kind of violence that in the bourgeois order is not *called* violence at all (ibid., pp. 110–11).

Sorel prefers to keep the term 'violence' to describe revolutionary violence which is directed against the State, not in order capture it, but to destroy it. Looked at in this way, violence is greatly at a disadvantage to force, because force has a continuous institutional life while violence has not. Violence tends to be what Sorel calls 'rhapsodic'; it is extravagant, heroical and uplifting, but also episodic, with the separate incidents of violence having no necessary connection with each other, above all without any necessary development towards an end (ibid., p. 49). Now that is precisely how crowd theorists had first begun to look at the crowd. The crowd, like the Sorelian act of anti-State violence, was only a moment, and like a moment, it could not be institutionalized. When crowd theorists like Tarde and Sighele began to wonder whether there were crowds which could have some kind of permanent life, a public, say, or a nation, the permanence of that life was always bought at a cost to the crowd's original life as a crowd. Institutionalized crowds were always real crowds 'watered down'. This is especially true of Le Bon, who wants to see every social group as a crowd, but in fact the further he gets away from what we ordinarily mean by a crowd, the more aware we become that Le Bon is stretching the category 'crowd' to include groups which have only the faintest resemblance to crowds in the ordinary sense. All Le Bon's critics say that, including Sorel, but Sorel was attracted to Le Bon's barbarian crowd. That crowd was a source of rude energy in a society which most of its critics said was decadent.

As a Marxist, Sorel sees evidence for decadence in the increase of social and political complexity. In Marx's own day, when the capitalist class enemy was confident in his own strength and had yet to become maiden-auntish about the use of force by the State, it was reasonable to predict that capitalist society would come increasingly to resemble a battleground where negotiation was impossible and where sides had to be taken. On a battleground there is no middle ground to be held; it becomes quite literally no man's land, the least safe place to be in a war. This did not mean that everybody was, sociologically speaking, either a bourgeois or a proletarian, but it did mean that everybody had to choose which side to be on. Of course, the development of capitalism meant that the sides became easier to recognize as the centres of the polarities 'bourgeoisie' and 'proletariat' hardened, but the mere existence of those polarities was not in itself enough to draw up the lines of battle, though it was probably enough to define the *causus belli* and indicate the place where the battle was to be fought. The division of society into two opposing armies could only be achieved through the agency of the polarities themselves acting on each other. A confident, resourceful and unsqueamish bourgeoisie would create a confident proletarian enemy with the same tactics and strategy. Contrast what seemed to be happening around the turn of the century; government connived at the cravenness of bourgeois surrenders in the face of workers' demands, and the parliamentary socialists set themselves up in the business of persuading the bourgeoisie that the violent tendencies of the proletariat can be contained in return for concessions, and of persuading the proletariat that their exploitation by the bourgeoisie can be softened in return for socialist votes in parliamentary elections. The middle ground, the no man's land of the class war in its ideal form, becomes a complex political mess which expands to take over the whole of the battlefield, so that all its lines become blurred to the point where to speak of sides at all, let alone opposing armies, becomes impossible (ibid., pp. 89–92).

It is in these circumstances that Le Bon's crowd offers a solution to the problem of the blurring of class lines for the Marxist who is prepared to take the crowd seriously. The crowd's violence, which Le Bon had used so cleverly to frighten his bourgeois readers into believing that he had the answer to the crowd problem, could be used to divide society again, but this time from the bottom up; it could do what in Marx's day had been done by the bourgeoisie and their agent, the State, from the top down. The proletariat could become what Marx had always said it would become, truly the historical class, doing in its own time what the bourgeoisie had done in theirs. Syndicalist violence, what Sorel calls 'proletarian' violence to distinguish it from the exercise of State power in its present bourgeois and future socialist forms, forces those members of a society who do not naturally think of themselves as bourgeois or proletarians to choose a side, but for this to happen there has to be something which links separate episodes of violence into a movement with a purpose, and this Sorel calls 'myth'.

Sorel's argument is clever. On the one had, he denies that his advocacy of violence amounts to an orgiastic cult of violence, if by that we mean an invitation to general blood-letting and the consequent raising of the threshold of the toleration of violence to a level where ordinary social life becomes coarsened and unsafe. He means a cult of violence in the sense that a hunter who rarely kills would understand, or a warrior who does not fight battles every day. The cult retains its strength as long as the hunter or the warrior keeps his values pure. (It is in this sense that the hunter asks to be understood when he says that killing is incidental to what he does, or the warrior, when he says that it is fortunate that killing is necessary in wars so that men do not come to love it too much. There is also something here of what de Maistre means when he says that the warrior would be disgusted by what a cook does to a chicken before he puts it in the pot, or that a wife may be chaste amid the transports of love.) The violence which Sorel advocates is violence which does no damage to the morality of its agents. Examples to follow in the modern world might be lynch-mobs in Denver, blood-feud knifing in Corsica, or murder to avenge family honour on remote fjords (ibid., pp. 180–1). This violence is occasional but not rhapsodic, because its connecting 'myth' is the system of values from which it comes and which it reinforces.

The class war for Sorel is the meeting of the violent crowd and its myth of the general strike as Napoleonic battlefield. Sorel regards this as an economical use of violence, almost instrumental. In his appreciation of the value of Le Bon's work, Sorel had still one thing to quarrel with, and that was Le Bon's insistence on the crowd's conservatism, and its consequent tendency to flock to a Caesar. Sorel admits that 'there is a good deal of truth in these judgements' (ibid., p. 133); Boulanger had offered some hope to working men, and the white horse brought back memories of Napoleon and, more distantly, of Lafayette. Le Bon still saw the main danger of socialism in its capacity to split the elite, as Christianity had done in the Roman Empire, and as enlightened ideas had more recently done in the last years of the *ancien régime*. Sorel sees that this is already happening; it produces its own elite of parliamentary socialist leaders and socialist intellectuals who have embraced '*the profession of thinking for the proletariat*' (ibid., p. 138) (italics in original). But Sorel thinks that the tendency of socialism to produce an elite of its own which is gradually domesticated into the elite of the society which it *says* it is bent on destroying, is only a necessary tendency in a society which 'lacks the conception of the class war' as he understands it (ibid., p. 133). Societies where the class war is not properly understood will in fact be the scene of all kinds of social violence, 'revolts of a day' (ibid., p. 133), and as socialism becomes the rallying point of all discontented groups, proletarian and non-proletarian, this sporadic violence might well increase, and it will certainly become messier as society itself becomes an increasingly complex mess. Proletarian violence is a way of simplifying the mess by drawing clearer lines of battle so that the actual incidents of violence will decrease as they become less necessary and more purposeful, a kind of moral training for the great battle that lies ahead. It is this training which will protect the proletariat from exploitation by Caesarist demagogues who stir up the jealousy of the discontented and persuade them that the best way to improve their lot is 'to utilise the power of the State to *pester* the rich' (ibid., p. 164). Sorel thinks that proletarian violence harks back to a version of the class war that the Greeks would have understood, where jealousy is converted into the much stronger passion of vengeance, the pride of free men; 'it forces the desire to satisfy jealousy by malice into the background . . . and thus protects the worker from the quackery of ambitious leaders, hungering for the fleshpots' (ibid., p. 165).

Sorel's defence of the cult of violence is a subtle way of frightening the bourgeoisie by pointing out that crowd violence does not have to be widespread or frequent for it to have revolutionary implications for the society in which it happens. At the same time, Sorel is telling the bourgeoisie that they are right to fear what they fear already. Sorel points to the heart of the matter, and in doing so he exploits Le Bon's own success as an ideologue. Le Bon's *The Crowd* was successful because he was able to play on fear of the crowd in order to sell his own brand of anti-crowd politics. To do this he had to exaggerate the tendency of crowds towards violence, inviting his readers to see every crowd as a violent, revolutionary mob in embryo. What Le Bon never explains is why it was that crowds were so frightening in societies where the forces of law and order always won. He simply accepts that they are, and goes on to compound the fear. Sorel takes the matter a stage further by saying that bourgeois fear of the crowd is rational. It makes perfect sense to be terrified by, say, Zola's account in *Germinal* of the castration of Watrin by a crowd of women during a miner's strike, provided the significance of the Decazeville strike is properly understood. It is not the violence itself which is truly frightening, but the fear that the violence produces in the minds of those who read about it. It is that fear, not the violence that produced it, which divides a society. Once the proletariat itself begins to understand what for the moment it only realizes by a kind of instinct, it will play on that fear, and the division in society will become much more clear-cut. The bourgeoisie, like the proletariat, also realizes the significance of crowd violence in a half-instinctive way. With Le Bon to play on that fear, and Sorel to explain the nature of that fear in the terms of the Marxist theory of class war as *real* war, a picture emerges not of sporadic crowd violence, easily put down, but a threat to the whole bourgeois order. Sorel is playing the bourgeoisie at their own game by compounding the fear of the crowd which their own ideologue Le Bon has already himself compounded. Of course, all this would only be frightening for those prepared to believe that what Le Bon said about the modern age as the Era of Crowds was true. But why should they not believe it? If they were reading Le Bon and Zola, were frightened by Marxism, could remember 1848 dimly and the *Commune* vividly, and had read the highly coloured accounts of proletarian and anarchist violence in newspapers, it is hard to see how they could believe anything else. (And apart from Tarde, there does not appear to have been anyone of sufficient authority to tell them that they had nothing to fear but fear itself.) Fear of the crowd's violence must lead the bourgeoisie to look to its own safety; the bourgeoisie must arm itself, reaffirm its faith in the Iron Law of Wages, and divide society into two warring camps. The Iron Law of Wages and the Iron Law of Oligarchy are seen by Sorel as alternatives; something has to give if the Iron Law of Oligarchy is to work in the case of socialism. (Sorel tends to treat the Iron Law of Oligarchy and *embourgeoisement* as if they were the same.) Socialist leaders have to have something to show their followers in the way of better wages and working conditions if their claim to represent the best interests of the working class is to remain credible; giving up the Iron Law of Wages is the price iron masters have to pay for the Iron Law of Oligarchy to discipline the proletariat. Sorelian crowd violence is the means by which the Iron Law of Oligarchy is suspended in the case of the revolutionary proletariat so that the bourgeoisie is forced back to its other metallurgical principle, sees the proletariat again as the enemy of political economy, and fights the battle out. One or other Iron Law has to be scrapped. Of course, there is no compelling reason in principle why anyone *had* to think like that. The owner of a factory could easily believe that the Iron Law of Wages and the Iron Law of Oligarchy were both true; equally easily, he could have heard of neither, and he could certainly want both to be true. But Sorel did not *begin* the discussion of the crowd's place in social theory; it had been going on for at least thirty years before he added his twists to it, and Le Bon's success as a publicist must mean that the crowd was being talked about outside the walls of the academy.

And it is well to remember that the years of Le Bon's success were also the years which saw the formal working-out of the Iron Law of Oligarchy itself. We could easily guess that Mosca, Pareto and Michels were writing for the same market as Le Bon without knowing that Le Bon arranged for the publication of the French translation of Michels's classic. And it would be Le Bon's market in a very literal sense; he was the market leader; he had created his own mass market for crowd theory; what could be more natural than that writers who were trying to muscle in on Le Bon's act should claim that they were offering a similar product, made in a different way, with different packaging, but for all that not very different from what the public had already bought and found to be good? Hence Michels's own claim that he is only demonstrating the necessity of leadership from another, organizational, point of view. How much of this was flattery to secure Le Bon's endorsement of the product is now hard to say; but in an age when it was customary to believe that what we now call the sciences were different paths to the same truth, it could easily have been the case that Michels's flattery was sincere simply because he had chosen to imitate Le Bon. Nor should it come as any surprise that Michels also admired Sorel, for it was Sorel who from inside the socialist cause fulminated about the *embourgeoisement* of socialist leaders. It would not be stretching matters too far to say that it was Sorel who let the oligarchic cat out of the bag by drawing attention in print to the estràngement of socialist leaders from their following, an estrangement which was the very stuff of the Iron Law of Oligarchy and the theory of circulation of elites. Much good ink has been spilt on the question of the priority of the invention of the theory of the necessity of elites. The consensus seems to give the palm to Gaetano Mosca's two formulations of the theory in the *Teorica dei governi* (1884) and in the *Elementi di scienza politica* (1896)[4] over Pareto's claims for his own *Les Systèmes socialistes* (1903–4) and *Trattato di sociologia generale* (1916), with Michels being given the credit for being one of the first to apply it systematically to political parties. This is no doubt just, if priority is defined narrowly enough to mean 'first between Mosca and Pareto' to the exclusion of a host of other contenders among whom Sorel and Le Bon would certainly be strong runners. But if 'first' means 'first to bring the theory of elites to the attention of the reading public', then Le Bon would carry all before him, with Sorel not far behind.[5] Sorel's *Reflections on Violence* can in this sense be seen as an attempt to go beyond the theory of elites by identifying a tiny part of modern societies, the revolutionary and violent syndicalist group conceived in the idea of the proletarian general strike as Napoleonic battlefield, which is immune from the operation of the Iron Law of Oligarchy provided it understands that law and is prepared to oppose it with its own will of iron.

It is important not to exaggerate Le Bon's influence on Sorel as a thinker. All the authorities on Sorel agree that he is an original because his mind was able to take what he wanted to take from a large number of sources of very different political colours, but they also agree that Marx and Bergson had the deepest and most prolonged influence. No doubt this is true, but it is only half the story. Sorel is remembered best as the apostle of direct action, of a particular brand of propaganda by the deed, and any view of how propaganda by the deed works on those who do it, and those it is done to, must necessarily be founded on a psychology of human individual and collective action, and this Sorel undoubtedly found in Le Bon. Much is usually made of the fact that Sorel was an autodidact. The self-taught read randomly, and it is perfectly true that Sorel might have found the psychology he was looking for somewhere else. But what the autodidact reads he also reads in a kind of isolation, closely, wasting nothing, and that is how I think Sorel must have read Le Bon. And Sorel's staying power as a thinker is in part due to this random single-mindedness; he saw what he saw more clearly than any other thinker of his generation, and he has caused many a man sleepless nights since Lenin.

The psychology of the crowd's antecedents in evolutionism and its dependence on the idea of the unconscious had ominous implications for liberalism right from the beginning. If behaviour, individual and collective, was to be explained in the terms of an unconscious mind which was itself only partly understood, then the self-conscious, rational and autonomous individual had very little space to call his own, and while the close association between unconscious behaviour and pathological behaviour survived, it was difficult to see that *any* behaviour could be considered normal in the old sense, or undisturbed, or even sane. Even the origins of this style of psychological and social theorising in evolutionary biology added to the theoretical gloom. When the psychology of the unconscious threatened to shrink the social space controllable by the individual almost to nothing, it was natural to begin to wonder whether the individualist account of evolution given by Spencer and his disciples was true. Too much of the evolutionary scheme was the story of increasing aggregation for the Spencerian equation: 'Differentiation equals Individuation' to be maintained with the same confidence. Why not draw the opposite conclusion from the individualist one? Why not say: to speak of individuals at all at the higher end of the evolutionary scale is profoundly misleading *because* the story of evolution is the story of aggregation and man is the most complex of nature's aggregates? Individualism is to be found at the beginning of the evolutionary scale, not at the end, in Sighele's 'psychology of the atom'. Nor was there any particular reason to regard man as an 'end' in any sense that had evolutionary meaning. Man might be a biological aggregate whose paradigm form was the undifferentiated crowd conceived either atavistically, as existing at some imagined beginning, or socially, as a moment of atavism in a modern society. The imperatives operating on the crowd could be seen as just as evolutionary in the accepted sense as the imperatives which produced Spencerian individuals. Go one step further, and begin to think of a whole society as a crowd, and add the contention of crowd theorists that any man can become part of a crowd, and you end up with the conclusion that evolutionary imperatives are collectivist, not individualist.

Seen from that perspective, democracy could never be liberal, though it might be socialist. The Italian social psychologist Enrico Ferri was the first crowd theorist to recognize the full collectivist implications of the evolutionary story seen from the anti-Spencerian point of view. In his attack on Sighele's 'metaphysical vagabondage' (see above, p. 174) he had accused Sighele of refusing to see that, once the individualist illusion had been surrendered, then crowd theory was neither puzzling nor threatening. Accept the thesis that all biological and psychological life was the life of aggregates, accept that socialism is the political theory of aggregates *par excellence*, and crowd theory could become the basis of a truly scientific socialism.[6] Le Bon saw what the socialist implications of crowd theory were in France, and he drew out those implications so clearly that *The Psychology of Socialism* can easily be read as a prediction of socialist victory. But crowd theory in fact affected the way people thought about democracy very differently in the Anglo-Saxon countries and in continental Europe.

In Britain and America liberalism and democracy had developed together. Since the ratification of the Constitution in 1789 in America, and since the Reform Acts in England, a combination of political caution and political engineering had found ways of keeping the crowd in its place. Democracies of checks and balances and procedural rigour, backed up with more ancient doctrines of mixed and balanced government, had developed the political skills necessary to curb and blunt the more outlandish and direct demands of the popular will. In societies with traditions of popular representation, the demand for the extension of democratic rights could easily be assimilated into individualism. (Indeed, there was a good case to be made out, as it was, for example, by William Graham Sumner in America, that democracy was a consequence of (economic) individualism, not a cause.) There were problems when non-revolutionary socialist demands began to be made through the mechanisms of liberal democracy, laying bare the hitherto partially concealed tension between the individualism of electoral choice and the collectivism of political parties, political movements, and the aggregations of votes needed to win elections. Crowd theory could easily revive the fear of the mob in its rage for rag-money and worse which the authors of *The Federalist Papers* had used to persuade Americans to ratify the Constitution in the first place. American democracy was based on a civic modesty which invited electors to see their votes as just one vote among many, and to see their right to vote as just one more right among many other rights. The case of Britain was similar; the extension of the franchise added another right to rights already being enjoyed. In Britain, part of the case for extending the franchise was that adult males had already shown that they could exercise rights in the mature knowledge that enjoyment of one's own rights entailed the duty of respecting the enjoyment of the same rights in others. The extension of the franchise could even be seen as a reward for the peaceful and responsible exercise of other rights, a political coming of age. In both the British and American cases, voters were being taught not to expect too much of voting rights, and they were certainly not being asked to use the right to vote to change those societies which had made the right to vote possible. Of course, the voting crowd did from time to time try to bite the hand that fed them, but in liberal societies this could always be countered by the claim that collectivist demands were a threat to the system of liberal democracy which as a system men had already tried and found to be good. Besides, the very idea of liberal democracy meant that there were always mechanisms internal to the system available to those who wished to complete the political education of the masses by thwarting their collectivist aims. Indeed, that those aims could be thwarted was a proof that liberal democracy was alive and well.

The case of continental Europe was very different. In the Anglo-Saxon world, the crowd could be seen as a threat to democracy in its liberal form which democracy itself had to find ways of countering. There was something which could be called 'democratic' already *there* which the crowd threatened. In continental Europe, the history of demands for the extension of voting rights and the history of crowd theory were parallel histories. The questions of a revision of the electoral law, of socialism, and of the psychology of the crowd were all asked at the same time, so it was possible and plausible to see both democracy and socialism as aspects of the same collectivist movement, the mechanism of which crowd theory was beginning to expose. Anglo-Saxon democracy might be threatened by the crowd and its psychology, but continental European democracy *was* crowd psychology. In Europe, crowd psychology was not something which threatened the ordinary processes of democracy from the outside; there, the psychology of the crowd threatened to *become* the 'normal' democratic process.

This mattered particularly in France. Both Taine and Le Bon took the view that, since 1789, the destruction of the great corporate institutions of the *ancien régime* meant that there was nothing left to interpose itself between the individual and the State except the crowd. The revolutionary attack on corporate legal privilege removed Montesquieu's *corps intermédiaires* from effective political life. Contrast Britain, where by accident, and America, where by design, vigorous social and political institutions co-operated in political life, acting as mediators between the will of electoral majorities and the legislative power on which those majorities tried to find a purchase. These competing institutions were a safe refuge for individuals who wanted to pursue their own legitimate (and not so legitimate) interests without being swallowed up in the great democratic mass.[7] Crowd theory was the psychology of the One and Indivisible Republic, of the perfect unanimity which Michelet had celebrated, and which harked back, ominously, to the Spartan monasticism (the phrase is Taine's) of Rousseau's *Social Contract*. But things had changed in one crucial aspect since Michelet's day. Michelet knew, as Rousseau had known, that at best unanimity was only symbolic, a hope for the future. But the crowd's unanimity could be as real as Positivism could make it; as Sighele remarked, 'The crowd is everybody'. If this were true, then the fight for the remnants of Spencerian individualism, and the fight for the remnants of all liberal individualism, could be no more than the death-struggle of a doomed psychological Vendée. Any opposition, any centre of institutionalized mediation between the whole and its individual parts, would have to be internalized, a continuous mental crossing of the fingers, by very strong-minded individuals fighting a rearguard action against an imperious crowd operating with the slow, Calvinist authority of science.

The crowd's last individual was its leader. What no crowd theorist seems to have doubted was that to be a crowd at all, a crowd had to have a leader. Plainly, not all crowd leaders were of the same type. Some crowd leaders were the crowd's own, leaders for a moment, or leaders for a day; other leaders of the crowd found ways of institutionalizing their position, so that crowds became movements; some led crowds direct, others, the ideologues, led from a distance; some leaders came to their crowds from the outside to dominate them in the cause of order, and others came from the outside to manipulate crowds in the service of a cause which they made the crowd's own, but no matter where the leader came from, and no matter what form his leadership took, the leader was the symbol and the cause of the unity of the crowd. With the development of the theory of leadership, so prominent in Le Bon, crowd theory became something like a complete political theory in the old-fashioned sense of the term. Crowd theory identified a human group, explained the origin and nature of the structure of its authority, gave an account of the ethical basis of that authority, explained how the group worked and how it survived, and it explained all of these things in the terms of a methodology rooted in the most up-to-date scientific theory and practice. The English liberal theorist Ernest Barker was quick to spot how crowd theory as political theory differed from traditional political theory in general and liberal political theory in particular: whatever crowd theory was, it could not be a theory of the State as a rational association. Scientific rationality had shown up the limitations of human rationality conceived of in the most general Aristotelian sense.

The extent to which a political theory based on a high expectation of human rationality could be jolted out of its confidence by crowd theory can be seen from Barker's attempt to map out a ground for political theory from which crowd theory can be excluded only to find that political theory's own territory has been reduced to a beleaguered province. Barker's *Political Thought in England from Herbert Spencer to the Present Day* (1915) now reads like the obituary of the Aristotelian tradition of the theory of the State as a rational association. Barker was a sound enough Victorian liberal to believe that Aristotle must have been a liberal because Plato wasn't. Like Aristotle, he believes that the State is the supreme association because its constitution is the product of human will guided by reason, and like all liberals he believes that the State is only one association among many. He knows that many of these other associations – we would call them groups – are not the product of conscious will and reflection. What worries Barker is that since Bagehot's *Physics and Politics* (1872) the methods of evolutionary biology and social psychology have been so successfully applied to the study of social groups that it begins to appear that neither are most groups the products of rational choice nor do they pursue rational ends. Most social behaviour is unconscious, lacking any component of human will and cognition. Ethics and politics, Barker insists, 'belong to the sphere of mind', and after Bagehot, Tarde, Le Bon, Durkheim and William McDougall have finished, there is precious little which is left to mind. Evolutionary biology leads to social psychology, and social psychology, he observes mournfully, leads to sociology, a 'Napoleonic study' (Barker, 1915, pp. 148–57). The study of social irrationality, of which crowd theory forms so large a part, is in danger of rolling up the map of the human sciences to the point where human rationality is called upon to give an account of how it *could* be embodied in social practice. Barker can do little more than reiterate the Aristotelian formula that the body of citizens in the liberal State constitutes an 'association based on intelligent reason' (ibid., p. 160).

What Barker will not quite face is the problem of how it is possible for the State to be a rational association in a society the working of whose groups is by his own account of it largely irrational and unreflecting. This is especially a problem in liberal democracies after Graham Wallas's *Human Nature in Politics* (1908) has shown us the effects of 'emotional symbols' in political life, laying bare the 'psychological substratum of modern elections' as 'psychological orgies', 'exercises in "spellbinding" ' (Barker, 1915, p. 157). In a later work, *Principles of Social and Political Theory* (1951), Barker tries to construct some kind of a solution to the problem of the existence of a rational State in an irrational society by falling back on the ages-old liberal distinction between membership of the State and membership of Society. Citizens are all equal members of the State because they enjoy the same political rights, whereas membership of Society entails belonging to the multitude of different groups of which liberal society is composed. The ideal liberal electorate would be able to shake off the irrational mental characteristics which it derives from its membership of the irrationally constituted groups which make up liberal society and so be able to take part in the process by which rationally willed law is made. Legislation could still be rational, even though the society that legislation operated in was not. Whether that scheme of things is possible is very doubtful; whether from the liberal point of view it is even desirable, because it insists too strongly in the separation of State and Society, is a moot point. What is very obvious is that from the crowd theory point of view it is Barker's account of the State which is most vulnerable. All crowd theorists agreed that groups shaken out of heterogeneous social categories were the most likely to become crowds and to acquire those characteristics of a group mind which showed men at their least rational. The ideal crowd, according to crowd theory, is a group which is absolutely itself; in the modern idiom, a group without subgroups. That description of the ideal conditions for crowd formation comes perilously close to Barker's own account of the ideal condition of a liberal electorate exercising its political rights independent of their membership of particular social groups. The problem which crowd theory poses for liberalism of Barker's kind is that the other groups of which men are members are *less* likely to display the irrational, group-mind characteristics than the electoral crowd. On crowd theory's account of it, spontaneously developed 'natural', corporation-like groups are less likely to descend into that irrational, potentially barbarous equanimity which crowd theorists feared. Barker himself had an inkling of that after he read Wallas's *Human Nature in Politics*, and, looking back, there is something heroical in the way he clung to his liberalism for as long as he did.

What Barker failed to see, perhaps necessarily failed to see, was that it was to the idea of the liberal-democratic State that crowd theory posed the greatest threat. And there is a fatal symmetry to the critique of liberal democracy which comes out of crowd theory; it works both at the level of the electoral crowd and at the level of representative institutions. What is true of the ideal electorate must also be true of the ideal parliamentary assembly when it makes law. This assembly would ideally consist of representatives capable of thinking beyond the interests of the groups which did in fact cause them to be elected. That, in the terms of crowd theory, would make them as heterogeneous as the ideal electorate which might have elected them, so they would be just as likely to become a crowd as the larger crowd from which they came. A parliament could no more be relied on to make rational decisions while making law, than the electorate could be relied on to make rational choices when choosing law-makers. Hence Sighele's disillusioned insight that crowd theory makes parliamentary opposition all the more necessary because it does at least guarantee the existence of a plurality of opposing crowds. Even in England, the Mother of Parliaments, a voice was raised to ask whether Parliament was merely a crowd (Conway, 1905). Of course, there is an account of parliamentary democracy which gets round these difficulties posed to classical liberalism by crowd theory which goes under various names, the most common of which is pluralism. Pluralism's strength as a defence of liberal democracy lies in its low-level expectations of rationality as the self-interest of groups, a recapitulation in a different language of the Benthamite arguments against Tom Paine's *Rights of Man*. On the level of theory, pluralism scores heavily because it is an extrapolation from the practice of democratic politics, but it took a long time coming. The most immediate extrapolation from the practice of democratic politics at the turn of the century was by no means so reassuring. The Iron Law of Oligarchy and the theory of *embourgeoisement* helped (especially if taken together, as they frequently were) to predict that, no matter where parliamentary politicians came from, the parliamentary embrace would homogenize leaders from outside the traditional political class so that parliamentary assemblies would lose the heterogeneity which might cause them to act up as a psychological crowd. But the fascists were to take a very different view of the liberal State. They took literally the idea that the electorate was a manipulable crowd and the parliamentary assembly a crowd of the manipulators, and began to ask how, if this were true, countries came to be governed at all. Then the search began for the real deciders of events, sinister interests operating consistently behind the unruly façades of parliamentary regimes, the money-power, freemasons, communists and Jews. If the crowd could find a real leader, not a sham leader, then the cleansing of the parliamentary stable could properly begin.

Notes

1 Le Bon's *The Crowd* went through 26 printings in French between 1895 and 1920, and the English version was printed 16 times between 1896 and 1926; by 1916 Le Bon had been translated into thirteen different languages, including Arabic, Turkish, Hindi and Japanese.

2 I am continually surprised that the European New Right has not rediscovered Le Bon; he means by 'socialism' what they mean by 'collectivism', and his *The Psychology of Socialism* (republished in 1982 with an excellent introduction by J. L. Stanley) contains the same easy elisions as the New Right's dreary litany: collectivity = collectivism = collective farms = Stalinism = totalitarianism. Perhaps Le Bon's anti-semitism is the stumbling-block.

3 The *Reflections on Violence* is a collection of articles which appeared in *Mouvement Socialiste* from January to June, 1906. It was published in book form in 1908.

4 This work, with a volume appended to it in 1923, was to be translated into English as *The Ruling Class* (e.g. by H.D. Kahn, ed. A. Livingston, New York. 1939), and is the basis of Mosca's reputation in the Anglo-Saxon world; it appears not to have received the title *La classe politica* in Italian until the Laterza edition of 1966.

5 Even this may be too generous to the Italians. If one were to write off the elite theory of the *Teorica dei governi* of 1884 as so sketchy as to *need* reformulation and expansion in the *Elementi* of 1896, then there would be no need to question Le Bon's priority for the elite theory in his *The Crowd* of the previous year. Such wranglings are finally trivial, but the point at issue here is not; Le Bon's influence on the formulation of what is one of the main, if not the main impulses of the political science of the twentieth century can so easily be overlooked that in such a good standard account of the foundation of modern political science as H. S. Hughes, *Consciousness and Society*, New York, 1958, Le Bon does not even appear in the index.

6 Perhaps Sighele's 'metaphysical' doctrine of the 'psychology of the atom' as the absolute individual now seems less 'metaphysical' in the light of sociobiology than it did to Ferri who knew no genetics. Dawkins's 'selfish gene' looks suspiciously like Sighele's atom, and the thrust of Dawkins's argument in *The Selfish Gene* (1976) and *The Extended Phenotype* (1982) is the same attempt as Sighele's to find an absolute individual. By arguing that natural selection works on the gene and not on the species, Dawkins wants to argue an 'individualist' evolutionary case against the 'group selectionist' case. The 'collectivist' case against Dawkins is simple: the

'selfish gene' wants *others like itself* to survive and multiply; the selfish gene is not 'selfish' at all.

7   By a stroke of irony not lost on French liberals, it had been one Frenchman, Montesquieu, who had first pointed to the institutional competition which preserved English liberty and who had inspired the Americans into writing that competition into their Constitution, and it had been another Frenchman, Tocqueville, who had pointed out that, from the beginning, America had been providentially endowed with a class of politicians already skilful in the art of the manipulation of their republican institutions for aristocratic ends, thus enabling them to offset the dangerously levelling tendencies of American democracy.

8

The Leader and his Crowd: Freud's *Group Psychology* (1921)

By the time of the Great War, enough was known about crowds for crowd theory to concern itself with the specialized problem of leadership. The focus of theoretical concern had been shifting away from the crowd, and on to the leaders of the crowds, since about 1890. Of course, crowd theorists had always been interested in leaders, but some measure of how the theory of crowd leadership increasingly became a specialized problem of crowd theory can be seen from the fact that, beginning with Le Bon, each new generation of crowd theorists claimed that its predecessors had failed to understand properly what the mechanisms of crowd leadership were. So Le Bon thinks that Taine failed to understand the psychology of Jacobinism, though he is an admirer of Taine's, while Freud, who is an admirer of Le Bon's, thinks that Le Bon's account of the crowd fails because Le Bon has not gone deeply enough into the question of what binds the leader to the led, and this despite Le Bon's own claim that he is applying the latest findings of depth psychology to the problem.

The context of the enquiry into the nature of crowd leadership was the waning of Continental individualism. That individualism, though based in part on English Darwinism in its Spencerian variety, was never egalitarian and it was scarcely tinged with any feeling of democratic levelling. Great leaders had always been the *summum bonum* of Continental individualism, and after crowd theory had made its considerable inroads into the possibility of an individualism for everyman, as everyman increasingly appeared either to be a member of a crowd or shortly to become one, it is easy to see why the crowd's last individual was its leader. Great leaders were supposed to emerge from the crowd, and their claim to greatness increased with every centimetre of the distance which they could put between themselves and their followers. Carlyle's assertion that the heroes of the modern age were

237

necessarily diminished heroes, or Nietzsche's claim that the heroes of the modern age were pygmies like Wagner ('a splendid miniaturist'), fell on deaf ears at a time when most European countries had only recently acquired new heroes of national liberation and unification. Carlyle's attempt to dismiss Napoleon as the last-ever candidate for true hero status failed completely as Napoleon became the archetypical hero of the nineteenth century. Napoleon was able to become the century's universal hero because he could be the hero of any number of different groups, and the hero of any number of different causes. The 'whiff of grapeshot' made him a hero of order; his wars against the emperors and the kings made him a hero of radicalism; his opening of the career to the talents made him a hero of bourgeois self-improvement; his imposition of his will on a whole nation, and then on a whole continent, made him a great Romantic hero; the formation of the Holy Alliance after Waterloo to extirpate everything revolutionary and Napoleonic from Europe made him a hero of disorder, and after Louis Napoleon and his Saint-Simonian banker friends had tried to turn Napoleon into a kind of socialist hero, the market in hero worship had been completely covered. The Napoleonic legacy to the theory of crowd leadership was thus extraordinarily diffuse. If you took the view that Napoleon stopped the French Revolution in its tracks, then his was the great ordering mission, but if you took the view that he was the Revolution's agent-at-large in Europe, then his was the great disordering mission.

For crowd theorists, the diffuse legacy of Napoleonic leadership narrowed itself down to a single question: Did leaders really control and impose their wills on the crowds they led, or was there in the crowd an implicit contract of depravity by which crowds and leaders went out of control together? What no crowd theorist seems to have doubted was that the crowd had to have leaders to be a crowd at all. We have already seen the lengths to which Sighele and Tarde would go to show that a leaderless crowd is a contradiction in terms. This compulsion to find leaders for the apparently leaderless and spontaneous crowd came part-ly from the criminologist's desire to find someone who could be made responsible for the crowd's crimes, partly from the desire to find some remnant of conscious individuality in the collectively unconscious activity of the crowd, and partly from the hope, expressed most clearly by Le Bon, that, if the crowd could be led from the inside by leaders of its own, it could also be led from the outside by having leaders thrust upon it. Politics in the future was to be a struggle for the leadership of the crowd, so it was vitally important to find out what kinds of leaders the crowd produced as a prelude to finding out what kinds of leaders the crowd would accept, and neither of these things could be known without an exact account of the mechanisms which bound the leader to the led. Crowd theorists hoped that the crowd could be manipulated from the outside by leaders whose values and aspirations the crowd could not fully share, and all crowd theorists shared the fear at some stage of their theoretical careers that, left to itself, the crowd and its leaders would encourage each other into regression towards a new form of collective barbarism. Crowd theorists' hopes for the future rested on the possibility that some leaders of crowds at least could keep their distance from the crowds they led.

The attempt to understand exactly what happens between a leader and his crowd in fact began very early, like so much else, in Espinas's *Des Sociétés animales*. Espinas invents an emotional calculus to explain the often observed mutual heating up which happens when an actor or an orator 'electrifies' an audience. The actor or the orator feels an emotion which he communicates to the audience; let that emotion be, say 10, and let half of his emotion in the first flow of his eloquence be communicated to each person in an audience of, say, 300; then the amount of emotion which the whole audience feels is not 5, but half of 5 multiplied by 300, which is 750. The process works both ways, because the emotion felt by the audience communicates itself back to the orator (the actor gets lost at this point in Espinas's argument), and this fed-back emotion is represented not by the number 5 (the amount which each member of the audience feels), or even by 750 (the amount the whole audience feels), but by 300 times $\frac{75}{2}$ because the orator sees the whole of the crowd's emotion not as an abstract number, but as coming whole from each separate member of it. The orator at this moment is either overcome by the emotion he now feels, or he masters it and recommunicates it to his audience; each member of the audience again feels half of it, feeds it back to the orator, and so on until the numbers representing the emotion felt by the orator and his crowd become exponential (Espinas, 1878, pp. 361–3). There is no reason why this account of the way in which a leader of crowds draws his strength from the crowd should be taken literally, any more than the Benthamite felicific calculus should be taken literally. It seems, like Espinas's famous account of emotional contagion in wasps, to have been taken as read by Espinas's admirers like Fournial and Sighele, but what interested them was less what happened to leaders than what happened to followers, and so this account of Espinas's led nowhere, and even Le Bon, the master plagiarizer, missed it.

Le Bon himself, for all his brave talk about the necessity for leaders to understand crowd psychology in order to be able to divert crowds from their historic mission to destroy civilization, always hedges when he comes to the crucial question of leadership mechanisms by retreating into hypnotism, or into generalized formulas about mysterious and unconscious causes. The theory of hypnotism, such as it was, really put a stop to any further enquiry into the mechanisms of leadership technique because it was so universally persuasive. It became all too easy to say that leaders hypnotized their crowds, and that was that. What no one before Freud seems to have realized was that hypnotism itself had not been satisfactorily explained, and that to explain crowd phenomena by an appeal to the latest psychotherapeutic technique was simply to pass the buck back to depth psychology to give a convincing theoretical account of its own hypnotic practice, but this psychiatric medicine, imprisoned as it was in its neurological and neuro-chemical vocabulary, singularly failed to do. But Le Bon's popularization of crowd theory did have an effect which profoundly influenced all future thinking about the leaders of crowds: in a very general way, Le Bon taught men what kinds of crowd leaders to expect, and what kind of society to expect them in. The theory of mass society which Le Bon, among others, invented and popularized, has now a very dated look about it, but what is not said often enough about the popularization of social science is that the popularization of a theory like the theory of mass society can convince large numbers of people that the society they are living in *is* a mass society, whatever sociologists may say about that society in retrospect. The Le Bon phenomenon is ideology precisely because Le Bon presents a view of a whole society and its troubles, and because he offers a remedy for these troubles: leaders of crowds in mass society can be supplanted by leaders who do not share mass values and who can manipulate the mass to protect the values of a high culture in which the mass has no share.

The common man in Ortega y Gasset's sense was mass society's gift to the modern age; what makes the modern age his is the common man's lack of a sense of his own limitations. After the Great War had banished the kings from continental Europe, or served a warning on them that the world was no longer theirs, the common man would look round for leaders of his own who would be very unlike the departed kings. This was going to be especially true of the Weimar and Austrian republics, where intensely hierarchic societies suddenly had to find leaders to take the places of the vanished Hohenzollerns and Habsburgs in the psychic lives of their peoples. A new theory of ruling and being ruled was needed to explain the implications of the change and all the psychologizing of politics that had gone on before 1914 meant that such a theory, if it was not to be Marxist, was bound to be psychological, and because the latest psychological theory was crowd theory and depth psychology, the new psychology of politics was bound to be mass psychology based on the psychology of the unconscious. The new psychology was not in fact all that new, but the problem it was about to be applied to was.

The fact that the problem was new, and that it was of so general and psychological a kind, meant that the political theory it produced can seem messy to anyone used to dealing with the decently precise categories of 'the history of political thought' whose passing Sir Ernest Barker mourned (see above, pp. 232). What replaced it, for those prepared to take it seriously, was a politics of culture, because the common man's claim to universalize himself came at a time when it was coming increasingly to be recognized that the constraints on the behaviour of individuals living in society were cultural constraints, and that high culture in the possession of a ruling class was one of the means by which the ruled were kept in their place, or, at the very least, high culture mapped out the distance between those on top and those below. What went on in people's minds and how it got there were important considerations for thinkers like Freud who felt a very generalized sense of unease about the future of their societies and about the future of civilization. In Freud's case, that sense of unease went particularly deep, because the bourgeois intellectual Jew who had never felt at home in anti-semitic Catholic Vienna before 1914 was even less likely to feel culturally secure, or even physically safe, in a Habsburgless Austrian republic after 1919 threatened by Marxism, and by some very nasty anti-semitic politics of its own before the *Anschluss* imported Nazism as a prelude to the final horror whose victim Freud very nearly was.

It is tempting to read Freud's account of leadership, *Group Psychology and the Analysis of the Ego* (1921), straightforwardly as an account of the kind of leadership that Adolf Hitler was about to begin to practise, to see in Freud and Hitler the intellectual and practical sides of the same coin, and to use the Viennese connection to tie the matter neatly up. What could be more obvious than that the same city, at the same time, should produce both the theorist of total regressive leadership, and the leader who was to become its most notorious practitioner? Perhaps wishing to cast doubt on that view, or even to modify it, is to fly in the face of the obvious, but one thing does stand four-square in the face of accepting it at its face value, and that is, that to accept it one has also to accept that in *Group Psychology* Freud gives an account of a kind of leadership of which he disapproves. But there is not a word in *Group Psychology* which would lead one to suppose that there is anything special about the *kind* of leadership being discussed. Quite the reverse. The essay is remarkable for the completeness of the generalizations it offers about the nature of the leadership of groups. Freud does claim that the psychoanalytic theory of libido has special insights of a startling kind to offer into the mechanisms of group leadership, but he also makes it clear that these insights apply to all kinds of leaders, and to the leaders of all kinds of groups, from the most formal like churches and armies, to the least formal, like crowds. It is also well known that Freud admired great leaders – Moses, Hannibal, Massena, Napoleon, Bismarck – and identified with them. Freud also regarded psychoanalysis as a movement and himself as its leader, and there is equally nothing in *Group Psychology* which would lead one to suppose that the account of leadership given there does not apply to the leaders Freud admired, or even to Freud himself. So if *Group Psychology* is to be read as a prediction of what Nazi leadership would turn out to be like, one would have to end up by saying that Hitler is just another leader, a bit like Napoleon and a bit like Freud himself, so that any sense of the uniqueness and horror of Hitler's leadership of Nazism would be left out of the account.

Yet it is still the case that the account of leadership in *Group Psychology*, generalized though it is, does fit the case of Hitler remarkably well, and it may be that to be surprised that it does – or even to find in it some kind of miraculous prediction – is to misunderstand the history of crowd theory and the nature of Hitler's leadership of the Nazi Party, and later, of the German state. Perhaps what we should say is that Hitler was exactly the kind of leader that crowd theory had been predicting for fifty years, and that it would have been surprising if Freud's own theory of leadership, heavily dependent as it is on the crowd theory tradition, had not fitted the Hitler case. Freud had read some of the crowd literature, had read summaries of it, and took Le Bon seriously enough to use *The Crowd* both as a finished account of crowd theory to date, and as a starting point for his own work on the leadership of crowds. Freud's entry into crowd theory in 1921 came at a moment when crowd theory, on Freud's own account of it, had been complete enough for thirty years for Freud to see himself as working in a specialized corner of it. Crowd theory's claim to completeness was much stronger than psychoanalysis's own claim in 1921. The classic psychoanalytical trinity of the Ego, Super-ego and Id was still two years in the future (*The Ego and the Id*, 1923), and *Group Psychology* was Freud's route to its formulation. Crowd theory, not psychoanalysis, was the senior and established theory, and part of Freud's purpose in writing *Group Psychology* was probably to advance the cause of psychoanalysis by linking it to a recognized body of theoretical knowledge whose validity no one would deny, and this was part of a general strategy to accomplish the breakthrough of psychoanalysis into the hostile world of gentile culture, a breakthrough which had been partially frustrated by the defection of the gentile Crown Prince Jung from orthodox psychoanalysis before 1914. This widespread acceptance of crowd theory in itself tells us nothing about what kinds of leaders Freud himself approved of, but by the time Freud made his own contribution to it, crowd theory had gone a long way towards teaching people what kind of crowd leaders to expect. Freud does in fact expect the crowd to produce leaders of the kind predicted by Le Bon, though his explanation of what produces them is different, and Freud's *Group*

Psychology, far from being a miraculous prediction of Hitler, makes its own contribution to the self-fulfilment of crowd theory's leadership prophecies of the previous fifty years.

It is in the terms of these prophecies that Hitler's own leadership is best understood. Hitler set out to be the kind of leader that half a century's crowd theory had been predicting would appear in the mass societies that the mass society theorists were telling people that they were living in. It does not matter much whether Hitler actually was that kind of leader, or whether the society he was successful in really was a mass society, but it is enough that enough people thought that both were true. Psychoanalysis made its contribution both to the leadership expectation and to that deeply felt sense of unease about the future which is supposed to characterize a mass society, and it needs no emphasis that these were precisely the themes the Nazis played on. What this view of the Freud–Hitler connection does is to stress the continuity of the theoretical and practical concerns of the European world before and after the Great War. In *Group Psychology* Freud does offer a view of leadership which fits the Hitler case remarkably well, but there is nothing surprising about that; equally, the theoretical basis for the kind of leadership which Hitler announces himself ready to assume in *Mein Kampf* had already been prepared long in advance, though the uses to which he was ultimately prepared to put that leadership were not (see below, Chapter 9).

It is a measure of how far the psychology of groups had come by the time Freud directed his attention to them that he begins *Group Psychology* by wondering whether there *is* such a thing as individual psychology. The distinction between individual and group psychology is not a very real one from the psychoanalytical point of view (*SE,* 18, p. 69).[1] Though Freud was to remain a disenchanted old-fashioned liberal to the end of his life, he does not seem to have shared any of nineteenth-century liberalism's illusions about the autonomy of the individual, and psychoanalysis, in its emphasis on the early development of the Oedipus Complex within the family, does not square easily with an original, atomistic version of individuality. The psychoanalytic equivalent of self-regarding self-interest is narcissism, the inward satisfaction of basic instincts in defiance of the world outside the self; this narcissism is probably neurotic and certainly immature. When psychoanalysis speaks of individual psychology, it refers to a process of the development of the individual's personality in relation to parents and siblings. All psychoanalytic theory, rooted as it is in the family, is in this sense social theory. An adult has had his personality formed for him in the family and in the other groups of which he is a member – race, class, religion, profession. Of course, liberalism had never denied that men were naturally social, but there was a tradition of liberal theory going back at least as far as Locke (and taking more than it cared to admit from Hobbes) which talked *as if* men were not naturally social, that they had to be commanded by God to be social, or that they chose to be social, almost that they had chosen their social personalities for themselves.

The particular force that psychoanalysis gives to the social determinants of personality means that Freud sees the problem of group psychology in a way which is radically different from the way it was traditionally conceived. Freud can agree with Le Bon that it is the nature of the differences in mental life which the group forces on the individual which have to be explained, but he is not faced, as Le Bon is, with the problem of explaining the leap between the discrete, self-regarding individual mind, and a very different, other-regarding 'group mind', because the family and its psychology is the connecting link.

Freud is enough of a Spencerian to want to derive his own explanation of the group mind from the nature of the individual minds which go to make up the group mind, but what those individual minds contain is social, because familial, in a sense that was not available to Le Bon. That necessity of having to explain the jump from the single-minded self-interest of individuals to the group-minded altruism of crowds explains much of the attractiveness to crowd theorists before Freud of the idea of a group mind which looked so different from the minds of individuals that the laws of its functioning could not be explained in any but its own terms. The psychoanalytical view of the individual mind from which Freud begins narrows the gap from the beginning between selfish and self-sacrificing individuals, and so makes the hypothesis of a group mind with its own separate identity, and its own rules, theoretically unnecessary.

What attracted Freud to Le Bon was his insistence on the part played in the group mind by unconscious forces 'as yet unknown and so mysterious'. The unconscious before Freud was so unknown, and, except for moments of illumination, unknowable, because no satisfactory account existed of how the unconscious 'got there'. The unconscious was seen as a permanent substratum, existing in everybody; it consisted of forgotten memories, or instincts, things inherited from the past of a people, or of a race, or from parents, but there was a distinct tendency to regard is as fixed, rocks beneath a sea, dangerous undoubtedly, and probably unchartable. Although the classic Freudian essay on the relationship between consciousness and the unconscious had yet to be written when Freud wrote *Group Psychology*, psychoanalytic usage was already well enough established by 1921 for there to be a very obvious difference between the Freudian idea of a dynamic unconscious and previous ideas of the unconscious. Freud's *dynamic* unconscious is not fixed. It is an unconscious which is more or less successfully repressed and which continually presses its unwelcome attentions on consciousness. Not everything which is unconscious is repressed. Freud uses the term 'pre-conscious' for everything that exists in the mind which is not actually present in consciousness but which has ready and welcome access to it; ordinary forgetting and remembering are the most obvious examples of the pre-conscious leaving and coming into consciousness. Properly speaking, psychoanalysis has very little of its own to say about the relationship between pre-consciousness and consciousness, but it has a great deal to say about the unconscious repressed and the mechanisms of repression. The basic component of the Freudian unconscious is the repressed wish or drive; it is denied access to consciousness by a censor and this censoring mechanism develops through the Oedipus Complex. In the formative and middle periods of psychoanalysis, that is up to about 1920, these wishes and drives were all conceived of by Freud as either sexual, or deriving from sexuality. The very young child is indiscriminate in its sexuality; it wishes to possess its parents; in the boy the strongest desire is for the mother, in the girl for the father. The father's sexual possession of the mother makes him and the boy-child deadly rivals for the mother in a struggle which the father must win; the son is forced to renounce the possibility of possessing his mother and to accept his father's prohibition against incest. The son also loves his father as well as hating him (ambivalence), and he feels guilt for his murderous hatred for his father at the same time as he is forced to accept the ban on incest. This internalized feeling of guilt associates itself with the prohibition on incest as a conscience which represses the son's incestuous drives by denying incestuous wishes access to consciousness. (A parallel development takes place in girls. Because the mother is less fierce in her prohibitions than the father, the Oedipus Complex, and therefore the censoring conscience, is less strong in girls than in boys.)

The prohibition against incest is only the first of a series of prohibitions which individuals are obliged to internalize, but it remains the prototype of all renunciations. Sexual renunciation is social as well as familial. By the time individual sexual development has progressed from infantile polymorphous perversity to adult heterosexuality (though it can be neurotically arrested at any of the intervening stages), prohibitions from other censoring sources will also have been internalized, so that most individuals will come to accept the sexual rules of the societies in which they live. (Or they will come to accept the sexual rules of the groups within the society to which they belong. Freud had a romanticized view of the sexual habits of the working class, regarding them as profligate with their sexual energy, less successfully repressed than the prudent bourgeoisie from which Freud and most of his patients came. This was a commonplace view until Kinsey.) The repression of sexual drives, and the censoring of the sexual wishes which are the forms which sexual drives take in their attempts to rush past the censor to take consciousness by storm, is never wholly successful. Freud's metaphor is unremittingly dynamic; drives, sexual energy, repression, libidinal pushing and shoving, are the stuff of the mechanical language of psychoanalysis. This 'economics of libido' (the phrase is Freud's own), of demand seeking supply, of gratification lying in wait for desire, lets a particularly nineteenth-century version of Newtonian mechanics into the unconscious to bring it under theoretical control, and it drives all Romanticism out. The unconscious is no longer the mysterious source of poetic and religious inspiration; it becomes as drearily predictable as any other system once the general laws of its operation become known. The unconscious repressed does try to make things difficult for its own bored censor and for the dismal scientist whose job it is to understand its workings. The unconscious repressed is infinitely devious; it codes its messages, or it uses a language that the censor is unlikely to be able to understand; it sometimes resorts to a kind of psychic invisible ink, but these are childish tricks, and they can always be found out. The unconscious is not so much chaotic as messy, and no matter what the lengths are to which it is prepared to go to deceive the censor or the analyst, in the end the exact nature of the devious game can be brought to the conscious attention of the patient in analysis. Freud puts the unconscious in its place by exposing its pretensions and the pretentious claims made on its behalf. In the Freudian version the unconscious is no longer the wild, conscienceless and fascinating thing it once had been.

Not the least of Freud's achievements was his success in narrowing down the idea of the unconscious to these theoretically manageable proportions, even though the unconscious lost a good deal of its charm in the process. A tart footnote in *Group Psychology* about Le Bon points up the difference between Freud's idea of the unconscious and other, less precise ideas of it: Freud notes that Le Bon's idea of the unconscious includes 'the racial mind' which 'as a matter of fact lies outside the scope of psychoanalysis' (*SE*, 18, p. 75, n. 1). Freud's view of the unconscious does not mean that orthodox psychoanalysis only has things to say about sexuality, and the later instinct theory from *Beyond the Pleasure Principle* (1920) onwards in fact posits a group of death instincts, Thanatos, in opposition to Eros, but Freud always insisted that what psychoanalysis had to say about more general cultural matters was only an application of psychoanalysis, and not a contribution to it. There was no question of, say, a psychoanalytical interpretation of religion, as in *The Future of an Illusion* (1927), being used to modify the basic Freudian picture of the unconscious, and, while Freud encouraged applied psychoanalysis, he was careful to confine it as far as possible to a separate journal, *Imago*. Freud never denied that there were things inherited or transmitted from a collective past which could be conceived of in national or racial terms, but he did maintain that psychoanalysis had to stick to what it knew, and to the theoretical basis on which it knew it, if it was to preserve its integrity as a psychological theory with claims to enlighten other aspects of human social living.

The banalization of the unconscious in psychoanalytic theory meant that by 1921 Freud was able to begin to unravel some of the puzzles which had bedevilled crowd theory ever since hypnotism had been imported into it in the 1880s to explain the extraordinary power which the leaders of crowds seemed able to exercise over the unconscious minds of their followers. All crowd theorists seem to agree that the 'heightening of affect' (emotional intensity) and the 'lowering of intelligence' are the 'fundamental facts of group psychology', and that 'rational' factors like intimidation, or the desire for self-preservation, are quite inadequate to explain the cohesion and unanimity of groups. Freud remarks that the magic of hypnotic suggestion in one form or another is always invoked to explain this central puzzle of group psychology. Le Bon relies on the 'mutual suggestion of individuals' in the crowd and on the 'prestige' of leaders, but this prestige of leaders is only recognizable by its capacity for provoking suggestion. Even Tarde, who deliberately avoids the word 'suggestion' in his preference for 'imitation', has been found out by his critics who have pointed out that imitation is simply one of the results of suggestion (*SE*, 18, pp. 88–9). The news of the sensational success of Charcot's experiments with hypnotism in the 1880s had quickly reached Viennese medical circles, and Freud himself, despite his rudimentary French, had travelled to Paris to witness them, and he was eventually to translate Charcot's *Leçons du mardi* into German. Psychoanalysis's flirtation with hypnotism did not last very long, partly because Freud himself was not a very good hypnotist, and partly because the technique of free association provided even better access to repressed material than hypnosis. Hypnotism itself had not been satisfactorily explained in the thirty years since Freud witnessed Bernheim's 'astonishing arts' in 1889, and the accepted opinion seems to be Bernheim's, that suggestibility is 'an irreducible, primitive phenomenon, a fundamental fact in the mental life of man' (*SE*, 18, p. 89). Freud thinks that a way out of this theoretical dead-end can be provided by the psychoanalytical theory of libido. He still had to be apologetic about the use of erotic concepts in 1921, but this cageyness about language cannot hide the ambitiousness of Freud's attempt to show that it is Eros which binds all human groups, from the hypnotic group of two, to highly organized formal groups like churches and armies.

The route which Freud takes to his explanation of hypnotism is not a direct one. He does not offer an erotic explanation of hypnotism and then apply it to the relationship between leaders and led. Rather, he begins from what he thinks is beyond question in crowd theory and in psychoanalysis and tries his hand straight away with the hypothesis that *all* groups are held together by love. Crowd theory shows above all else that the tie between leaders and led is strong, and psychoanalysis has shown the importance of Eros in a sense 'wider' than ordinary sexuality, so it seems sensible to try his fortune with the supposition that 'love relationships also constitute the essence of the group mind'. Perhaps these love relationships, or 'what would correspond to them', are 'concealed' behind the 'shelter, the screen, of suggestion' (*SE*, 18, pp. 91–2). The group is obviously held together by a power of some kind: 'to what power could this feat be better ascribed than to Eros, which holds everything together in the world?' If an individual gives up his 'distinctness' in a group and desires to be in harmony with others, 'perhaps he does it *ihnen zu Liebe* (for love of them, for their sake)' (*SE*, 18, p. 92).

The first groups that Freud tries out his erotic hypothesis on are churches and armies, 'artificial', not 'natural' groups. (Freud has a tendency to exaggerate the extent to which previous crowd theorists concerned themselves with 'natural', fleeting, not lasting groups, chance crowds, not what Tarde called 'corporations'.) Churches and armies are groups where formal constraints exist to prevent disintegration, but these constraints can only explain very inadequately why these groups remain intact; rather it is the illusion that a leader, Christ, or a commander-in-chief, loves each member of the group equally which explains the cohesion of churches and armies; the commander of a subordinate group in an army functions as a 'kind elder brother', a father substitute for the commander-in-chief; every captain loves every soldier of his company equally, and every sergeant loves every soldier in his section equally. In the highly organized formal group, the members are bound by a double emotional tie, to leaders and to the other members of the group, and this easily explains the 'alteration and limitation' on the individual's personality which crowd theorists have always remarked on.

It is not until Freud begins to look into the question of which of these two ties is the stronger, to leaders or to fellow group members, that the highly original thrust of his argument reveals itself, and we begin to realize why he begins from 'artificial' and not 'natural' groups. What Freud wants to argue is that the 'artificial' group, with its highly evolved structure of leadership, is more 'complete', in the sense of being more 'primitive', than the crowd which forms by accident and which only has a leader for a day (*SE*, 18, p. 100). Freud's argument for the primitiveness of the formal group comes from two directions, from the psychology of individuals, and from his conjectural psychoanthropology of origins. These two psychologies are not to be thought of as separate, but as confirming each other. They both tell the same story of the relationship of sons to fathers, and they both consist of untangling the complex and devious ways of Eros.

For Freud, everything that binds people together is erotic or has an erotic component, and psychoanalysis consists largely of sorting out the different forms which erotic ties can take. A form of the erotic tie is more 'primitive' in psychoanalytic language if it is formed early in the psychic life of an individual, and Freud, believing as he does with nineteenth-century biology and anthropology that ontogeny recapitulates phylogeny, would expect to find a confirming (and therefore confirmed) analogue for such an early erotic tie in the psychic history of the species. The earliest form of erotic tie which men form is identification with fathers, but this tie is not simple. Eros is usually thought of as being directed towards sexual possession, towards having and holding, but Freud thinks that identification is an even earlier stage of erotic binding. The boy-child wants to be his father even before he wants his mother. Identification fits well with the object-choice of the mother because part of being a father is having the mother, and because in its early stages Eros is anarchic, there can be a double erotic tie with the father – the little boy can want his father as well as wanting to be him. The Oedipus Complex develops out of these erotic entanglements by imposing a kind of order. Identification itself is ambivalent from the beginning because of the obvious contradiction between the choice of the father as a *subject* (I want to be him or to be like him) and the choice of the father and the mother as *objects* (I want to have him in the double senses of possession and of killing him, and I want to have her). This ambivalence occasions feelings of guilt in the boy-child, and the 'introjection' of those feelings of guilt as a conscience represents the first stage of a process in which some kind of institutionalized stability begins to impose itself on the erotic anarchy. The father's standards now become the standards of the little boy's own conscience. The father now says 'love and respect me, and respect your mother' from inside the little boy's own self, and so normal family life can safely begin.

Freud goes to considerable lengths to support his contention that the earliest form of libidinal tie is identification, because his whole theory of group formation will depend upon it. He finds confirmation for the primitiveness of identification in a phenomenon he calls 'regression', where sexual object-choice in adults regresses to father identification, as in the famous case of Dora, whose imitation of her father's cough showed that she no longer wanted to be possessed by her father, but to be her father. The most common form that regression takes is 'substitution' where the impossibility of ever possessing a loved object leads to the introjection of the loved object into the lover's own self, as happens in romantic and selfless love ('introjection of the object into the ego') where the idealized love-object becomes the lover's own 'I', the highest and purest part of himself, so that he sets out to live his life as She would want it to be. He is no longer himself, but lives at another's bidding; her wish is now his command. The most extreme case of identification is melancholia. In manic-depressives, the introjected ideal object 'casts a shadow over the ego'; the ego-ideal heaps bitter 'self'-criticism on the rest of the ego and creates depression; periods of elation come when that criticism is muted, or successfully tucked up in its own sphere, or manic intervals can also occur when the rest of the ego feels that it is living up to the standards which its introjected ego-ideal sets for it (*SE*, 18, pp. 103–8).

The tendency of those in love towards overvaluation and *idealization* of the objects of love (italics in original) provides the link between Eros, hypnosis and the leadership of groups. Crowd theorists and theorists of hypnotism had always been struck by the mindless compliance of hypnotized subjects. Hypnotized subjects lack initiative; the hypnotist is the sole object of their attention and they obey his commands in a dream-like way, and no part of the hypnotized subjects' minds seems to test for reality. These are the hypnotic phenomena which made the hypnotic model such an attractive way of explaining the leadership of crowds. Freud's sharp eye for the erotic even in its absence notes that the very absence of impulsions which are uninhibited in their sexual aims testifies to the extreme 'purity' of hypnotic phenomena; the hypnotic relation must therefore be 'the unlimited devotion of someone in love, but with the possibility of sexual satisfaction excluded' (*SE*, 18, pp. 114–15). The selflessness of the romantic and sentimental lover, the selflessness of the hypnotized subject, and the selflessness of the member of the psychological crowd all have the same cause. In psychoanalytic terms, libido, sexual energy, has been thwarted and redirected; narcissism diminishes with the diminution of self-love and self-esteem, and the love which aims at the possession of an object outside the self comes to accept that the loved object will never be possessed. Yet the dynamics of libido will not be denied; narcissistic love will find its release elsewhere, and it finds a way to satisfy itself deviously. The loved object is introjected and becomes part of us; one reason for the introjection and idealization of another might easily be that we want to find a substitute for some unrealized ego-ideal of our own. We attribute to the introjected ego-ideal the perfections which we have striven for in our own ego, and so we procure our own ego's perfection in a roundabout way through the perfection of the ego-ideal, and so satisfy our own narcissism (*SE*, 18, p. 112). Love's endless ingenuity in finding ways to satisfy itself led Freud to begin to wonder whether it might not be possible for identification to take place while the possibility of sexual possession remained intact. Perhaps an object of love could be both introjected into the ego as an ego-ideal and also not be so completely 'idealized' that it was beyond love's grosser clutches. In romantic and selfless love, the loved object as ego-ideal takes over the whole of the ego; it *becomes* ego, so that there is no ego left which could even contemplate sexual possession. Therefore, if it is to be at all possible that a loved object can be both introjected as an ego-ideal and still be an object of possible sexual possession, then it must also be possible that a loved object can be introjected into the ego without taking the ego over completely. This, in its turn, necessitates a change in the psychoanalytical theory of the ego itself. From *Group Psychology* onwards, psychoanalysis holds that the ego is not the unitary 'I' that it had once supposed; there must be a 'differentiating grade in the Ego', what was to become the classic Super-ego of *The Ego and the Id* (1923). There must be a difference between what we ordinarily mean by 'I' and something which, though it is part of the 'I', has been introduced into the 'I' from the outside, and perhaps these two parts of the 'I' operate according to different rules.

What is at issue in the distinction between Ego and Super-ego is still the selflessness shown in being in love, in hypnosis, and in crowds. (It seems sensible, now that the Super-ego has made its appearance, to give Ego, Super-ego and Id the capitals that translations of Freud always gave them after 1923.) Selflessness always implies some alteration or diminution of Ego. At first, Freud believed that there was a distinction to be drawn between two states of being in love, between 'fascination and bondage' on the one hand, and identification on the other; in identification he thought of the Ego as being 'enriched' with the (real or imagined) qualities of the loved object, while in the case of fascination he thought of the bound lover's ego as 'impoverished', his being the mooning and swooning kind of love which makes fools of us through the abjectness of our own Ego's surrender to another. Freud had no sooner put that distinction on paper than he realized that it was misconceived. Ego surrender and the introjection of the loved one's qualities into the Ego could obviously happen together, for there was no commonsensical reason why a lover could not devote himself selflessly to a loved one and at the same time accept her standards for his own in his own Ego. This possibility posed a very straightforward problem for Ego theory, because it was difficult to see how the same Ego could be something which I surrender to another ('fascination and bondage') and also something which I keep though it is altered (introjection and idealization). An Ego which is both not-mine and mine is a nonsense, and so the realization came very quickly to Freud in *Group Psychology* that if there were not to be two Egos, one of which is not-mine and so hardly an Ego at all, the Ego must be divided in some way, hence the distinction between Ego, and ego-ideal which was later to be renamed Super-ego. This distinction enabled Freud to begin to understand the business of 'being in love' in an entirely new way. 'Being in love' always involves some alteration or diminution of Ego function, and now 'being in love' could be understood according to whether the loved object takes the place of the Ego or the Super-ego, or of both (*SE*, 18, pp. 113–14). Freud's mind immediately went on to the interesting possibility that in 'psychological groups' very different things could be happening to Egos and to Super-egos.

Again, what is at issue is the selflessness of individuals in 'psychological groups'. All crowd theorists before Freud had emphasized the dualism of the ties which bind men in crowds. Individuals in the crowd were bound by ties to the leader and by ties to each other, but these ties were typically seen as being additionable because they were thought of as being basically of the same type. Explanations of crowd behaviour which relied on suggestion and imitation had never been able to make any clear distinction between the two; leaders suggested behaviour to the crowd, some members responded, and they in their turn suggested the same behaviour to the less responsive members of the crowd. The same process was broadly true in explanations of crowd behaviour based on imitation: leaders were imitated by followers and it did not much matter, theoretically speaking, whether members of the crowd imitated the leader direct or imitated other members of the crowd who had already imitated the leader. In both suggestion and imitation the same essential mechanism was at work which explained the relationship between leaders and led and the relationship between fellow members of the crowd. Yet there had always been something fuzzy about crowd theory here, and it became a real problem when leadership became crowd theory's leading concern. It began to look theoretically rather feeble to cry up leaders on the one hand, and on the other hand to say that what the leader did to the crowd was only an intensification of what crowd members did to each other, and what made it an intensification had still to be explained. Libido theory at last solves the mystery: '*A primary group of this kind is a number of individuals who have put one and the same object in the place of their ego ideal and have consequently identified themselves with one another in their ego*' (*SE*, 18, p. 116, italics in original). The erotic tie which binds the leader to the led is of a different type from the tie which binds followers to each other. The leader–led tie is a case of introjection, and internalization of the leader's own values as one's own, while the bond between followers is a case of the recognition that each man's case is identical.

The key word in Freud's exposition is 'consequently', by which he means that introjection and identification do not happen together by coincidence. Identification between members of the group happens *as a result* of introjection. Introjection, the internalization of what another wants as what we want, always takes place either before sexual object-choice, as in the case of the very young child, or as a substitute for sexual object-choice, as in the case of the adult. Aim-inhibited libido always finds an object if its natural object, sexual possession, proves to be beyond its reach, and introjection is one of the ways in which aim-inhibited libido finds this substitute satisfaction. Libido is to be looked upon as a quantity which is probably fixed, or, when it is 'spent', renews itself to its old level. It is this constant self-renewal which makes the erotic instinct so unruly. The easiest way to spend this erotic cash is orgasm, 'spend' being a cant term for orgasm, but where ordinary sexual release is not possible, other forms of sexual spending have to be found, otherwise the unspent libido can build up such a pressure that it becomes burdensome and leads to neurosis. In the case of the replacement of the Super-ego by the leader of crowds, the intensity of the feeling for the leader can be high, but the erotic spending can be low; lots of libido is left over to be deployed elsewhere, on to the other members of the group. Hence the identification of the members of the group with each other in their Egos. Submission to the leader is therefore necessarily accompanied by feelings of love (selflessness, absence of egotism, altruism, 'loving one's neighbour as one's self') for other members of the group. The leader cannot be possessed by each member of the group; each knows this, and the amount of libido this inhibition leaves unused finds its satisfaction in the identification with fellow group members. This is a 'cost' in the language of Eros, but it brings the benefit of the relief that one feels as a member of a group. All the old tensions which arise in ordinary life when we meet strangers, of different classes, races and religions, disappear, and we begin to value others as we value ourselves; our differences are submerged in the whole, and the group becomes one.

This analysis of the libidinal structure of groups also makes plain what it is about groups that is unconscious. Crowd theory before Freud made great play with the idea of the unconscious without being very explicit what it meant to say that the unconscious played a large part in group formation. At their least plausible, crowd theorists had talked as if the members of a crowd did not really know that they were in a crowd, in the same way that a hypnotized subject would not know that he was in hypnosis (and would 'forget' about it afterwards). Even as intelligent a thinker as Tarde could compare crowd behaviour with sleep-walking. There is no such difficulty in Freud's account of the crowd in *Group Psychology*. For Freud, the mechanisms of group formation are Ego mechanisms; they concern an 'I' and not a 'me'; they concern a subject, not an object, something I do, not something that happens to me. It is still no doubt true that the particular 'I's which happen to be involved in group formation do not understand exactly what the psychological mechanisms are which operate in group formation (not everybody understands psychoanalysis, or has even heard of it), but I still involve myself in the group; I know that I have internalized my leader's standards as my own, and I know that I feel altruistically about the other members of my group; I am neither hypnotized nor a somnambulist. Freud was in fact to revise his opinions about the relationship between the Ego and conciousness while he was writing *Group Psychology* and the revision was complete when he wrote *The Ego and Id* (1923). In *Group Psychology* Freud sometimes still talks as if all Ego functions were conscious, but the later position he held is that ego-ideal or Super-ego functions are unconscious. What this means for crowd theory is that after the internalization of the leader's standards as our own, they operate within us automatically like the unconscious Super-ego, but there is nothing mysterious about this in the old somnambulistic sense. The exchange of one set of internalized standards for another might happen behind consciousness's back, but only a fool could fail to realize that it had happened.

Freud's later position that Super-ego functions are unconscious opens the way for an explanation of the more horrific manifestations of crowd behaviour which had not been available to his predecessors. Crowd theorists before Freud had been interested in crowds because the crowd could become a mob howling for blood, but the crowd's bloodthirstiness had always been explained by very generalised references to instincts that men shared with animals, or by the bloodthirstiness of the suggestions of leaders, or, more generally still, by reference to the collapse of social restraints which necessarily accompanied the temporary madness of the mob. This kind of explanation of the mob's awfulness suited a particular kind of tempered Darwinian optimism well enough – the mob was a throwback; and it suited a pessimistic Darwinism very well indeed – the mob was a regression to a state of primal barbarism and animalism, not a chance 'survival' but a permanent threat. As an explanation, the Darwinian perspective was always vulnerable to the kind of objection put forward by Espinas, that animal societies were often models of organized altruism, or by Sighele, that there was something characteristically *modern* about the crowd, or by Tarde, who elegantly debunked the whole attempt to apply Darwinism to social matters in general and to the crowd in particular by pointing out that explanations of social facts based on imitation worked more simply without having to accommodate the whole evolutionary baggage. The Darwinian enterprise also had difficulties in easily accommodating ideas of nation and race because its emphasis on the preponderating influence of what had happened before human history even began could not live easily with the obvious and important differences of more recent date between different national crowds which all crowd theorists remarked upon. Either nation and race were much older than anyone thought (and there were nineteenth-century attempts without number, most of them ludicrous, to show that this was in fact the case), or national and racial factors in crowd behaviour were less important than the facts seemed to suggest. Freud's account of the Super-ego goes some way towards reconciling the regressive character of the behaviour of crowds with the fact of different manifestations of crowd behaviour in different societies, by suggesting the possibility that the Super-ego can function differently in different cultures.

The Super-ego is best thought of as a primal critic. It is primal because it begins its formation in individuals in identification, the first of all the libidinal bondings which occur in an individual's life. Little boys want to be their fathers before they want to possess their mothers; they identify with their fathers and take them as models for themselves; the desire for their mothers and the consequent desire to kill their rival fathers produces the first pangs of guilt, and this causes boys to internalize the standards of fathers as their own. Their guilt feelings harden into the taboo against incest, so that the fathers' prohibition against incest becomes the command of the boys' own conscience. The desire for mothers does not die, and an internal battle takes place between the Super-ego's prohibitions and the sexual instinct. With time, the Super-ego's criticisms of sexual wishes become stronger, but they also become routinized, and so less wounding, as sexuality moves on through its ordinary development towards adult heterosexuality. The formation of the Super-ego happens within the restrictions of the family, but its development takes place in the wider context of a society which adds criticisms and prohibitions of its own, until a human individual becomes a recognizably socialized member of it. The dynamic nature of the psychoanalytic view of personality sets great store by this repressive function of the Super-ego, and it follows that, in societies which give the Super-ego a heavy workload, the pressure building up under its burdens can be unreasonable, and in societies where the Super-ego works three shifts a day without stopping (even dreams are censored), we would expect a large number of neurotic casualties. Like Tarde and his criminal, Freud re-integrates the neurotic into society as the person in whom society is too successful. Like Tarde's criminal, the neurotic is not anti-social, but not anti-social *enough*; he cannot resist society's pressures; his Super-ego nags him day and night and he unconsciously takes upon himself such a burden of guilt that he develops neurotic symptoms (and perhaps physical symptoms, the 'actual' neuroses) so that he can no longer even live the 'normal' life that he has come to think his society expects of him. The neurotic's illness is not the revolutionary madness that nineteenth-century crowd thinkers were so fond of attributing to leaders and their crowds. The neurotic is testimony to society's success, an exaggerated version of what all of us are.

But Freud's group psychology also tells us that there is *something* dangerous about neurotics, or that there is something dangerous about the *other* Super-egos in the societies which produce neurotics. In groups, the Super-egos of individuals are exchanged for the desires and commands of leaders. The commands of leaders control the unconscious inner lives of followers, and it follows that the effectiveness of these commands depends on the strength of the Super-egos which the leader replaces *and not on what it is that the leader actually commands*. Leaders of a traditional kind, a Habsburg, say, or a Hohenzollern, steeped in the values of a society and seeking only to reinforce them, will command easily, and that can easily mislead us into thinking that it is the nature of their commands, and not the unconscious reinforcing commands of the Super-ego, which is at the root of the effectiveness of the commands of dynasts. When a new leader appears, of the kind predicted by crowd theory since the *Commune*, it is equally easy to think that he is going to have a hard time of it because, as a revolutionary, he has established leaders and established Super-egos to contend with. However, the Freudian theory of the crowd shows that in one important respect this is misleading, because established leaders and established Super-egos can easily become the victims of their own erstwhile success. When a 'psychological group' exchanges its Super-ego for a leader who commands the instinctual drives to liberate themselves and who also commands the individuals in whom these drives clamour for satisfaction to rise up against the institutions of the society in which these drives are denied satisfaction, then the internal and institutional mechanisms of repression connive at their own destruction, because the amount of the release of pressure consequent upon the change is bound to be proportional to the success of past repression. In very repressed societies there will be an explosion, because the greater the burden, the greater the release. (This is a truth instinctively recognized by children on rocky foreshores. They know that the heavier the stone, the nastier the creepy-crawlies underneath.)

Freud first thought of all instinctual life as sexual, but as psychoanalysis began to grow out of its original sexual vocabulary, he divided the instincts into two groups, one centred on Eros, 'the builder of cities', and the other on Thanatos, the slayer. The Great War had made him realize that the State had forbidden violence to its members not because it disapproved of violence, but because it wanted to monopolize it 'like salt and tobacco' ('Thoughts for the Times on War and Death' (1915), *SE*, 14, p. 279). War is a release, a liberation of pent-up instinctual energy which has been denied satisfaction. Long periods of peace need prolonged blood-letting and its accompanying barbarism, but wars between states are only one form that this release can take; the mob's own violence, or the violence of mob politics, can be a substitute for it. This meta-pyschological dualism of Freud's between Eros and Thanatos has proved to be too hot for the blood of the more staid of his followers, who have tried to distinguish, like Marxists

256

in reverse, between an early 'scientific' Freud and a late 'speculative' Freud (and this despite Freud's own repeated statements that he was only ever really interested in 'theory') without realizing that Freud's social theory is a commentary on and incorporates half a century's highly speculative theoretical work on crowd problems, and without realizing that Freud offers solutions to some of the more intractable problems of crowd theory. The theory of Super-ego replacement by leaders elegantly solves the problem of the apparent contradiction between the crowd's modernity and its primitiveness. It is the very success of the modern State and of the rigidity of modern social norms which *causes* the primitive barbarism of the crowd. After Freud, we are simply no longer entitled to ask 'How could it happen *here* of all places?', if by 'here' we mean highly ordered States and successfully repressed societies, because 'here' is where it is most likely to happen. Nor are we likely to fall into the simplifying error of supposing that crowd politics will be the same everywhere. The Super-ego is universal, but it is not everywhere the same. (I owe this argument in part to Herbert Marcuse's *Eros and Civilization*, Boston, 1966, *passim*.)

Freud's account of the crowd in the terms of the psychology of individuals could stand on its own without the phylogenetic confirmation it receives from his version of evolutionary anthropology, but Freud's was a mind formed at a time when almost any explanation, of almost anything, had to do more than nod in the direction of Darwinism. Freud introduced the required beat of distant tom-toms into psychoanalysis in *Totem and Taboo* (1913) with a discussion, centred round the concept of 'ambivalence', of 'some points of agreement' between the mental lives of savages and neurotics. The minds of savages and neurotics (and also children) were ambivalent because they could contain the opposed feelings of love and hate directed towards the same object without being troubled by, or even aware of, the contradiction. Freud was struck by the obvious ambivalence in totemism, where to kill the totem animal is the most terrible of all crimes, except once a year, when the totem animal is ceremonially killed and eaten, and he was equally struck by the extremely complex social structure of savage tribes which appears to be designed to make incest impossible. Freud goes on to consider whether the ambivalence of the savage mind, and the ambivalence which psychoanalysis has discovered in the minds of children towards parents, can be traced to a single source. Freud finds this source in a suggestion of Darwin's in *The Descent of Man* that in their most primitive social state men lived in hordes dominated by a single powerful male (*SE*, 13, p. 125), and from this conjecture follows Freud's celebrated (and much lampooned) account of the slaying of the primal father, the Ur-event whose memory hangs fatally over the psychic history of the human race.

257

The story of the Ur-slaying is simple enough. The domineering primal father monopolized the women of the horde. The frustrated brothers rebelled against their father's sexual tyranny, killed him and, being cannibal, they ate him. The period of liberation which followed was a period of fratricidal anarchy, because each of the brothers had taken part in the rebellion out of a desire to take the father's place, and not out of a spirit of fair shares for all. The brothers could not have rebelled out of a frustrated sense of justice, because before the Ur-slaying no sense of justice could exist while the father's law was imposed from the outside by force. The quarrels of the brothers, like the competition of Hobbes's men in the State of Nature, neutralized them as a social force (this may have been the period of matriarchy); like Hobbes's men trying to quit the State of Nature in which the future would be an endless re-run of the past, the brothers realized that they had much to gain by putting an end to the war of all against all, and they also realized that to make living together possible, each brother would have to renounce the women of the horde and seek sexual satisfaction elsewhere (for monogamy had yet to be invented), otherwise, there was always a possibility that the fratricidal war over the women would break out again. So the first social contract was an agreement to forbid incest. But a contract, rationalistically conceived, is not enough to turn a prohibition into a taboo, because a taboo is an internalized prohibition which each man carries within himself, not a ban policed externally by force. For a taboo to work, men have to be able to feel guilt, because taboos are self-policing. Guilt feelings had not existed in the primal horde in its original condition because its morality and law were externally imposed through the domination of the father. The original guilt feelings arose in the brothers during the period of the fratricidal war. During that time, the brothers used their many opportunities for solitary reflection to realize what they had done; it occurred to each of them that in their anger at their father, they had forgotten that they had loved him too. They began to wish that they had not killed him, longed nostalgically for his return, and this longing was reinforced by the prudent reflection that the fruits of their victory over the father were bitter, because the women he had enjoyed none could now enjoy. The contractual renunciation of the women was in effect the return of the father's authority in an internal form, because the brothers now added to it a reinforcing feeling of guilt. They felt that they had *wronged* their father by betraying their own love for him. They cast about for a way of making the father return so that they could re-declare their betrayed love; they displaced that love on to an animal, made it their totem, and made it taboo to kill it. Totem and taboo, taken together, constitute as complete a return of the father's authority as is possible short of reincarnation. But the original ambivalence towards the father as an object of love and hatred would not die. When they set up the totem as a re-declaration of their love for the father, the brothers remembered that they had hated him too, and the pain of the renunciation of the women reminded them why. Nostalgia for the father's return mingled uneasily with a nostalgia for the original rebellion which they now knew they must never repeat, so the brothers institutionalized the memory of the original revolt and procured a substitute satisfaction for it in the once-yearly totem feast, when the primal father is again killed and eaten, symbolically, as the totem animal (*SE*, 13, pp. 141–2).

Freud finds the origins of religion, morality and law in totem and taboo, and also the beginnings of the psychology of individuals. The ambivalence towards fathers is still clearly visible in the psychoanalytic theory of the Oedipus Complex, and in *Group Psychology* Freud begins to wonder whether there might not still be other traces of these horrific primal events in psychological groups. The regression theme is as old as crowd theory itself, but what put Freud on to the idea that ambivalence might be the clue to the mechanism of regression was an observation of Le Bon's that the group mind could believe in contradictory ideas with equal conviction, and that words seemed to exercise a 'magical power' over it. Freud compares Le Bon's description of the group mind with the account psychoanalysis gives of the mental lives of neurotics, and he is again struck by the fact that both the group mind and the neurotic mind are guided by the illusions of 'psychological reality' and not by ordinary reality. For instance, 'hysterics suffer mainly from reminiscences' (*SE*, 2, p. 7) in the form of compulsions to repeat remembered fantasies of experiences, and not real experiences; their repetitions are repetitions of unfulfilled wishes. (*SE*, 18, pp. 79–80)[2]. This comparison, combined with the regressive nature of the tie of the individual to the leader in the 'psychological group', is Freud's route to the startling thesis that the 'psychological group' is itself a repetition of the primal horde. Freud is careful to say that the account of the primal horde in *Totem and Taboo* is a Just-So story, or a hypothesis 'such as archaeologists use to lighten the darkness of prehistoric times', but he cannot help observing that the regressive quality of the mental life of groups is exactly the sort of quality you would expect to find in a primal horde (*SE*, 18, p. 122). From this hypothesis based on a hypothesis, Freud makes the spectacular leap to the further hypothesis that 'just as primitive man survives potentially in every individual, so the primal horde may arise once more out of any random collection' of individuals (ibid., p. 123). Just as the oldest psychology of individuals is the father-identification out of which the Oedipus Complex comes, so the psychology of the primal horde must be the oldest collective psychology of the human species.

The original psychology of the primal horde had its own primitive complexities. The brothers of the group were bound by ties to each other, which arose naturally out of the aim-inhibition of their libido, and by ties to the father, but 'the father of the primal horde was free'. His was the strong mind and will, giving away no more than was 'strictly necessary'; he was the superman that Nietzsche expected only from the future. Before the Ur-slaying, the father was an absolute individual, completely narcissistic, whose will needed no reinforcement from the outside, while the brothers were trapped in group psychology. The more the father dominated them, and the stricter the enforcement of the ban on sexual contact with the women of the horde, the more relentlessly the aim-inhibited libido of the brothers would find its substitute satisfaction by reinforcing the ties of group solidarity which bound them. The only way out of group psychology was through the act of love. The father was not immortal; he had to be replaced, and when he died or was killed, his place was probably taken by the youngest son, who could then give up his group ties by satisfying his libido direct. He would lose interest in his brothers and could allow his narcissism 'to rise to its full height' (ibid., p. 124). The primal father is loved by the brothers, but his own love is anti-social because, being directed towards a sexual object, or narcissistically towards himself, he has none left for the brothers. He is absolutely satisfied and self-satisfied, is obeyed, but owes no obedience; he is an erotic Hobbesian Sovereign, with the difference that he existed from the beginning by the strength of his own will. He is the original individual who subjected others to a rude natural equality. Unlike Hobbes, who saw the Sovereign as coming out of the frustrations of equality, Freud sees the frustrations of equality as arising from the domination of a Sovereign.

Freud's social theory does not begin with the postulate of a generalized atomistic individualism, so he does not have the problem of having to explain how stable collectivity comes out of the chaos of competing wills. His social contract comes after the original Sovereign has been deposed, when the frustrations of the attempt to break out from collective to individual psychology have become apparent to the brothers of the primal horde. The brothers can see no other solution to the problem of competing individual wills than to reinstate the father's authority in a permanent, institutionalized form. For Freud, individuality was only a moment in the history of the species; group psychology is the given, and it is individuality which has to be explained. Group psychology in recognizably human history is a recapitulation of the events of the primal horde, and the different forms which human living takes are the different forms available to that recapitulation. The illusion in churches and armies that the leader loves all followers equally is an 'idealistic' remodelling of the primal horde where the brothers were all equally persecuted by and equally feared the father. This recasting, 'upon which all social duties are built', is presupposed by the form of

260

society which succeeds the primal horde, the totemic clan, where all regard themselves as equals in the duties which totemism imposes, and so on to the human family, whose 'indestructible strength' rests on the possibility that the father really can love all the members of the family equally (ibid., pp. 124–5).

The human family is the point at which Freud's two accounts of group psychology meet, the Oedipal and the anthropological. Each human individual preserves within himself the imprint of his early Oedipal struggles in the form of his Super-ego; it is this Super-ego, reinforced and supplemented by the norms of the society in which he lives (or of the groups of which he is a member in that society), which he exchanges for a leader in a psychological group. It is because the love relationship with the leader must exclude the possibility of sexual satisfaction that the individual in the group has unsatisfied libido to spare for his fellow members of the group, so he comes to love them too. The development of the Oedipus Complex is itself a recapitulation of a family struggle much older than ancient Thebes; sons have been trying unsuccessfully to oust fathers ever since the original rebellion in the primal horde. Groups with leaders are in Freud's language more 'complete' and more 'primitive' because they contain two 'whole' psychologies, where 'whole' is to be understood as containing the whole development of both individual and group psychology. For Freud, the psychology of groups is therefore regressive in a double sense. In the terms of individual psychology, the leader–led tie is a recapitulation of 'identification', the earliest libidinal bond of which an individual is capable, and in the terms of group psychology, the leader–led tie is a recapitulation of the introjection of the father's authority after the Ur-slaying.

After this theorizing in the grand manner, Freud solves the original mystery of hypnotism almost as an afterthought by showing that it is not really a problem at all. If Eros is the bond in all groups, then the hypnotic relationship is a 'group formation of two members' (SE, 18, p. 115). It was no small thing for Freud to take up a problem that had been worrying the best minds in psychology and crowd theory for fifty years and to offer a solution to it at his first attempt. And that solution is a solution of the best kind because it turns a puzzle into a commonplace, by pointing out that hypnotism had only been a puzzle because the problem had been wrongly posed. The mistake all previous thinkers had made had been either to treat the capacity to be hypnotized too seriously, as a fundamental cause in the mind's life, or not seriously enough, as a trick or a game. In Freud's account, neither can be true; the capacity for being hypnotized is a consequence, not a cause, of group formation, but it cannot be a trick or a game in any trivializing sense because it is a special case of the regressive recapitulation of events in minds whose illnesses often arise from compulsions to repeat ancient events. One of the standard taunts against hypnotism since its music-hall days had been that it was too well-rehearsed. On Freud's account of it, hypnosis was genuine precisely because it was a rehearsal, but a rehearsal of events which were deadly serious because they came from further back in the lives of groups and individuals than any thinker before him had any idea of. The solving of the mystery of the riddle of the individual and the group solves the riddle of hypnotism, not the other way round. Hypnosis is not the clue to group formation previous thinkers had thought it was, because the hypnotic relationship is a special case of a group of two obeying the general law of the libidinal structure of groups.

The ambitious scope of Freud's theory of the libidinal structure of all groups, from highly formal groups like churches and armies, to the least formal like crowds in the streets, means that his group psychology, on the face of it at least, lacks the anti-popular thrust of nearly all of his predecessors in the crowd theory tradition. Previous crowd theorists had typically begun from a sense of horror at what the revolutionary or the criminal crowd was capable of, and they typically identified the lower orders as the social milieu out of which the crowd or the mob was likely to come. They had then gone on in a spirit of social pessimism to consider the wider question of whether anyone, regardless of class, might join the crowd if the circumstances were right, and after that crowd theorists went on, more optimistically, to consider whether there might not be other kinds of social group which, while they might display some crowd-like characteristics, might none-the-less be immune from the crowd's worst features. The conclusion most crowd theorists reached was that there is a sliding scale of groups, from the chance crowd in the street to the corporation, and while it was unfortunate that highly formalized groups at the top of the scale were not always immune from the heightening of emotional affect and the lowering of collective intelligence characteristic of crowds, none-the-less, the higher up the scale, the safer the group. Even this qualified optimism was always shaky, because organized corporation-like crimi-nal conspiracies like the Mafia, and conspiratorial revolutionary groups like the anarchists, should by rights have been high on the scale, but could hardly be regarded with propriety as safe, and the suspicion of *all* collectivities which this perspective necessarily implied meant that too much faith for comfort had to be placed in the individual-as-leader when it was also an article of doctrine that a crowd without a leader was a contradiction in terms; hence the rather feeble hope that if the right kind of leaders could be found for unsafe groups, all would be well.

Freud's highly original account of groups turns the scale upside-down. Previous crowd theorists had regarded the undifferentiated crowd as the paradigm, primitive case of the group, but Freud regards the highly organized group with a leader as the paradigm, primitive group. What his predecessors had called corporations are not for him variants and improvements on the crowd; rather the crowd is a less complete variant of the corporation. In Freud's view of it, when a crowd in the ordinary sense of the word finds ways of institutionalizing itself into some kind of permanent life, it does not jack itself up the rungs of the ladder of civilization; quite the reverse: it begins to recapitulate the events of the primal horde after the Ur-slaying. If a group's primitiveness is to be the criterion for our suspicion of it, as it was for all crowd theorists who worked in the evolutionist perspective (and as it also was for Gabriel Tarde who did not), then we have every reason to fear corporations like churches and armies, the very institutions on which crowd thinkers before Freud had placed their diminishing hopes of social peace. What is the mob compared to the army which is called in to save us from it? Combine this view of organized groups with Freud's account of the primitive psychic struggles in the family, and it completes an extremely dark picture of human collective living.

It was that picture which made Freud a conservative, because the original, failed rebellion of the brothers still exercises its fatal charm. It is important to recall exactly why that rebellion failed, and how over-complete the consequences of that failure were. The brothers rebelled against their father because each brother wanted to break out of group psychology to take the place of the father because the father, alone, enjoyed narcissistic and self-sufficient individual psychology, but after the slaying and eating of the father, the brothers came to realize that there had been a kind of justice in the father's rule by force because his equal persecution of the brothers had made collective life possible. After the period of the brothers' war, when it had dawned on them that the life which each brother lived was a solitary parody of the father's individuality they had all longed to imitate, the brothers voluntarily renounced the women of the horde, instituted the taboo against incest, and agreed to seek their sexual partners elsewhere. This contract, which made social living possible again, was reinforced by totem, the internalization of the most dreadful of all prohibitions, against the killing of fathers. It is conceivable that the brothers might have found other ways of solving the problem of the allocation of resources made scarce by the irruption of desire, by inventing monogamy for instance, or by resorting to homosexuality, but the guilt of parricide they could not escape, and the effect of that crime on the psychic history of the human race was permanent.

The totem feast is only one of the ways in which the memory of the original, failed triumph over authority is preserved. Each man carries the scars of his own private infantile battle with his own father, shoulders his own private burden of guilt, and passes it on to his sons. The mechanical vocabulary of psychoanalysis shows that Freud means us to think of guilt as a force, a quantity which can be increased or diminished, but which can never be reduced to zero. The thirst for obedience, and the consequent casting round for a Caesar, which had baffled crowd psychology into its too intense love-affair with hypnotism, is at last explained: the ousting of fathers compounds guilt, and out of compounded guilt comes a corresponding increase in the thirst for a return to obedience. The crowd's leader is thus a substitute father in two necessarily connected and additionable senses: the leader is a substitute for *my* father, and for the father-figure of authority in the society in which the crowd arises. If the leader of the crowd becomes a successful revolutionary, the old authority of the ousted father-figure becomes his authority, and it is reinforced by a new feeling of guilt internalized as a necessary consequence of this new instance of double psychic parricide. If the crowd turns on its leader, even if he was only a leader for a day, this further instance of psychic parricide still adds to the burden of guilt, which reinforces existing authority. The political lesson to be learned from Freud's thesis that all authority comes from fathers is very clear (though as a *political* thinker Freud himself is too timid to see it): all rebellions in the name of liberty are doomed; rebellions increase our capacity for obedience; the more complete the rebellion, the more abject our inner surrender to successful revolutionary leaders; much better, then, to put up with the old paternal authority than to submit to the new, because in principle there is no limit to the cravenness of human kind. So long live Franz Josef! Down with Karl Lueger!

The Habsburgs, and their rivals in Austrian politics, like Hitler's early role model Karl Lueger, leader of the anti-semitic Christian Social Party and rabble-rousing mayor of Vienna, do not come accidentally into the story of Freud's social theory, which is finely tuned to the politics of its own time. Lueger, and later Hitler, were new leaders of exactly the type of rival fathers intent on encroaching on, or replacing the authority of established paternalisms of which Franz Josef is the archetype. This fine-tuning is easily missed, because the very generalized language of *Totem and Taboo* and *Group Psychology* can give the impression that Freud's is a social theory written without serious contemporary reference. Freud's dependence on the Le Bon tradition of crowd theory, and on the now outmoded anthropological tradition of Frazer, Spencer, McLellan, Wundt and Robertson-Smith, show him comfortably at home in the intellectual currents of the day, but apart from the essay of 1915, 'Thoughts for the Times on War and Death', there is very little direct contemporary reference to politics in the major published works. If we add to this Freud's own mannered public stance as a detached *savant* (a stance faithfully supported by Ernest Jones in his very official three-volume *Life*), a picture can easily emerge of Freud as a man who 'followed the local news and politics of his time, but did not feel much involved in them' (Jones, 2, p. 436). However, some of the material in Jones's own *Life*, and Freud's published correspondence, tell a very different story, of a Freud who from a very early period of his life, was deeply interested in and deeply worried by mob politics, and by the anti-semitic mob in particular.

Freud's political anxiety began very early indeed, with his father's telling him of an occasion when his cap was thrown into the gutter by an anti-semitic thug; old Jacob Freud submitted without protest, picked up his cap, and went his way. The boy Freud vowed that he would never repeat what he saw as his father's cowardice, and the incident counted with Freud throughout his adult life (Jones, 1, p. 25). It is probably at the back of Freud's well-known interest in and identification with the semitic hero, Hannibal, whose father swore him to eternal hatred of the enemies of his race; the anti-semitism of his schoolfellows warned Freud always to be on his guard, and 'the figure of the semitic general rose still higher in my esteem. To my youthful mind Hannibal and Rome symbolised the conflict between the tenacity of Jewry and the organisation of the Catholic church' (*SE*, 5, pp. 196–7). Freud's interest in archaeology – he often expressed a preference for the 'pre-historic', and liked to compare the preserved layers of the mind to the different historical periods traceable in archaeological maps of ancient cities – naturally attracted him to Italy, but it was years before he actually got to Rome. Freud was a nervous traveller at the best of times, but he recognized that there was something 'deeply neurotic' in his 'longing for Rome' which he analyses half-jokingly in a letter to Fliess in 1897: 'It is connected with my schoolboy hero-worship of the Semitic Hannibal, and in fact this year I have no more reached Rome than he did from Lake Trasimene' (Bonaparte *et al.*, 1954, p. 236); Freud also know Grabbe's play *Hannibal* well enough to quote from it (E. L. Freud, 1960, p. 317). The form Freud's imitation of Hannibal took was to stand up to anti-semitism whenever he was confronted by it, and his courage in the face of the Gestapo in 1938 was the last of a series of such encounters. A letter to his wife from Leipzig in 1883 recounts his refusal to be intimidated by an anti-semitic mob on a train, and his dismissal of the incident as a 'silly story' cannot conceal a certain pride (ibid., pp. 93–4); Martin Freud, showing the pride in his father denied to Freud himself, tells how once on a family holiday Freud was returning to the hotel with his children when they were faced with a crowd shouting anti-semitic slogans; Freud deliberately made for the middle of the crowd, swinging his stick, and they readily dispersed to let the family through (M. Freud, 1958, pp. 70–1).

This concern for anti-semitism is not simply a matter of the family history of the Freuds. The invention of political mob anti-semitism in the 1880s seems to have been Vienna's contribution to the art of modern politics. The Pan-Germanist Georg von Schonerer (another of Hitler's heroes) and Karl Lueger realized at about the same time that mob anti-semitism was a exploitable political resource, Schonerer choosing to work the university and the intelligentsia and Lueger the streets. Freud's own student days were lived in an atmosphere of 'general bitterness' (ibid., p. 143). Anti-semitism was out in the open in Austrian politics from the time of the Röhling affair in the early 1880s onwards,[3] and, as in France during the Dreyfus Affair, the anti-semites covered the whole cultural market, seeking 'to justify anti-Jewish sentiment to the more open-minded men of the intelligent classes' as well as to 'inflame the instincts of the lower classes' (Bloch, 1923, p. 71). It was in this year, 1883, that we find Freud, chafing under the constraints of his long engagement to Martha Bernhays, writing about 'The Mob [which] gives vent to its appetites [while] we deprive ourselves to maintain our integrity . . . It would be easy to demonstrate how the people (das Volk) judge, think and work in a manner utterly different from ourselves. There is a psychology of the common man which differs considerably from ours' (E. L. Freud, 1960, pp. 65–6). The Paris that Freud was to visit two years later to listen to Charcot's famous lectures on hypnotism was still the Paris of the revolutionary mob, 'given to psychical epidemics, historical mass convulsions'; the city and its inhabitants struck Freud as 'uncanny . . . of a different species from ourselves; I feel that they are all possessed of a thousand demons, and instead of "Monsieur" and "Voilà L'Echo de Paris" I hear them yelling "A la Lanterne" and "A bas dieser und jener"' (ibid., p. 194). This was a state of mind easily carried over into Viennese politics in the 1890s when Karl Lueger's Christian Social Party was sweeping all before it; Franz Josef twice refused to ratify Lueger's election as mayor of Vienna, and Freud, engaged in one of his periodic attempts to give up smoking, famously smoked a cigar in the emperor's honour (Bonaparte et al., p. 133). Freud followed the Dreyfus Affair ('the disgusting behaviour of the French' (ibid., p. 245)) and again subjected the 'grande nation' to collective analysis: France 'cannot face the idea that it can be defeated in war. Ergo, it was not defeated; the victory does not count. It provides an example of mass paranoia and invents the illusion of betrayal' (ibid., p. 112).

Karl Kraus's remark that 'recent years have seen the sphere of Viennese Liberalism restricted to the parquets of theatres on opening nights' does not have to be taken literally to guess what effect Viennese anti-semitism had on Freud. If the choice was to be between the kings and the demagogues, Franz Josef would win over Karl Lueger every time. This psychic alliance between the Jew and the Habsburg could never be a comfortable one, but it would last for as long as the Habsburgs remained as a bulwark against those grossdeutschen aspirations which were fulfilled at the Anschluss. Allowing for the patriotic exaggeration of the moment, we should not be surprised that Freud remarked at the outbreak of war in 1914: 'All my libido is given to Austria-Hungary' (Jones, 2, p. 192).[4] Freud wrote his *Group Psychology* in the uncertain atmosphere of the defeated, Habsburgless Austria of threatening civil war and inflation (which came near to ruining him) after 1919, a time, as Freud's son Martin testifies, of 'insecurity, caused by an absence of discipline which permitted the mob to get out of hand, [which] was the hardest to bear' (M. Freud, 1958, p. 188). That sense of uncertainty pervades Freud's speculative essays of the late 1920s, *The Future of an Illusion* and *Civilization and its Discontents*. In them, Freud begins to wonder whether science will ever live up to its promise that it will help to overcome the regressively infantile illusions of religion, and he adds the sombre thought that civilization's cost in terms of instinctual renunciation may be so high that most men will continue to doubt that the effort was worth it. Freud certainly thought that the elite which was prepared to pay the price of instinctual renunciation was entitled to rule the masses to extract from them a kind of enforced saving of human energy which was to be civilization's future capital. Freud began to see the psychoanalytic view of mind as a metaphor for a civilization threatened with destruction. 'Our mind', he wrote in 1932, 'is to be compared with a modern State in which a mob, eager for destruction, has to be held down by a prudent and superior class' (*SE*, 22, p. 221).

It is tempting, in the face of this repoliticized picture of Freud, to say that the crowd of *Group Psychology* is the anti-semitic mob, and that Freud's group theory signals a shift in crowd theory away from the nineteenth century's concern with the criminal and proletarian revolutionary crowd on to the anti-semitic crowd of fascism, but that is far too simple a view because *Group Psychology*'s argument is a very general one which takes in all human groups. Fear of the anti-semitic mob is undoubtedly part of the story of how Freud came to write *Group Psychology*, but the scope of the work goes far beyond that. It is a measure of Freud's political pessimism that he has nothing good to say about *any* collectivity, and his stated intention in *Group Psychology* of giving an account of all groups, from churches and armies, to crowds, to show that organized groups are the most 'complete', has an ominous ring to it. Army and church, together with the bureaucracy and the police, were the characteristic institutions of Habsburg Austria, and the crowd is the Viennese anti-semitic mob; Freud seems to be saying that the emperor is to his institutions what the mob's leader is to the mob, the only difference being that the mob is a disturber of the emperor's peace, one of whose beneficiaries is Freud himself. Freud does not consider explicitly the possibility that the anti-semitic crowd might find ways of completing itself by acquiring those church- and army-like features which would give it a permanent life, that Lueger's crowd might turn itself into Hitler's.

Why Freud did not do that is a puzzle only if we accept the Freud-as-predictor-of-Hitler thesis in its most literal form. It is bound to be true that Freud and Hitler should share the same crowd concerns, but it is the fact that Freud's social theory is finely tuned to its own time which should be taken literally. Crowd theory had been predicting leaders like Hitler for fifty years, so that from the standpoint of a thinker in the early 1920s there was not really much that remained to be predicted, and the fact that leadership of the Hitler kind had been over-predicted probably accounts for the remarkable lack of jitteriness about the arrival of fascist leaders and their movements. Of course, predicting a thing is very different from experiencing the thing itself, but, seen from the perspective of crowd theory, it was always going to be hard to resist at least a theoretical sense of *déjà vu*, and it was always going to be difficult to think of fascist leaders as revolutionaries, or even as representing anything particularly new. Crowd theory since the *Commune* had hammered home the message that crowds and their leaders were regressive and given to violence; they could take things backwards, and they could threaten civilization, but there was nothing essentially *new* in that. As an old-fashioned liberal, Freud would see that the crowd and its leader posed a threat to whatever enlightened progress there had been in the world, but there was no particular reason why it should occur to him that fascism could institute a new political, social and moral order. Nor was fascism the only force in the modern world which threatened civilized progress as Freud understood it. The ominous 'experiment' in the land 'between Europe and Asia' after 1917, and general vulgarity and energy of American culture (an opinion kept quiet for the sake of American converts to psychoanalysis) could rank just as high on Freud's list of things he did not like about the world as those leaders who are coming too close to the masses. Besides, there was always that border between Germany and Austria which Adolf Hitler's father had once manned as a minor official of the Habsburg state.

Notes

1 References are to *The Standard Edition of the Complete Psychological Works of Sigmund Freud*, ed. J Strachey *et al.*, 24 vols, London, 1955–66.
2 It has commonly been taken as evidence of Freud's 'genius' (e.g. by Ernest Jones, *Life*, 2, pp. 5–6) that he was able to see this 'psychological' truth in the tales of infantile seduction which psychoanalytic practice commonly elicited. Infantile seduction just could not be as common as the reminiscences of it seemed to suggest, and so Freud realized that the

reminiscences of it must be based on fantasy. Some recent work on Freud (e.g. J. Malcolm, *In the Freud Archives*, London, 1936, *passim*) and on the extent of the sexual abuse of children has led to the suggestion that Freud twisted or suppressed the real truth about childhood seduction as a 'political' ploy to smooth the path for the acceptance of psychoanalysis in a world that did not care to hear direct any truths about its sexuality, let alone truths about the seduction and rape of children by parents and near relatives. However, from the point of view of psychoanalytic theory, it does not matter much whether more of the stories of infantile seduction are true than was once supposed, provided that some at least are fantasies, though it should make a great deal of difference to psychoanalytic practice.

3 In *The Talmud Jew*, Röhling, who was Professor of Hebrew Antiquities at the University of Prague, revived the ancient lie about Jewish ritual slaughter of Christian children by claiming that the Talmud specifically encouraged it. One of the forgotten heroes of nineteenth-century decency, Josef Bloch, a rabbi from Galicia, found out that Röhling could not even read Hebrew, managed to trap him into court in a libel action, found the rabbi whom Röhling had approached to teach him some Hebrew while the trial was pending, and published a reply to Röhling's pamphlet which ran to three editions and sold 100,000 copies in 1883 (J. S. Bloch, 1923, p. 27 and *passim*).

4 This enforced alliance between bourgeois Austrian Jewry and the Habsburg monarchy may lie at the root of Freud's admiration for kings in general. When Alfonso XII died in 1885, Freud wrote that 'he is the first sovereign of my own generation whom I have outlived, and his death has made a strange impression on me' (E. L. Freud, 1960, p. 197). (It should be added that Freud, who was superstitious about dates, shared a birthday with Alfonso.)

9

The Triumph of the Crowd: Adolf Hitler's *Mein Kampf* (1924–5)

The old equation of crowd theory: violence equals atavism, is implicit in Freud's social theory as a whole, and shows that his theory of the crowd is still firmly rooted in the concerns of the *fin de siècle*, when violence was a matter for *reflection*. When Sorel reflected about violence before 1914, he was doing far more than merely observing that civilized men thought they were living in societies where violence had decreased in the past and could be expected to decline in the future. What he was really interested in was what enabled people to think like that, which in its turn meant asking what the ideological configurations were which encouraged them to think like that. What was at issue was not just that men found the progressive decline in the evidence of violence encouraging; rather what was at issue was what made the expectation of further decline a matter of certain prediction, and therefore of smug self-congratulation. Sorel was enough of a Marxist always to smell ideology when an age begins to congratulate itself on what it thinks, and he was right to smell ideology in the age's view of violence. What Sorel points to is a world in which all social theory with any pretensions at all to being progressive, was writing violence out of its picture of the world and that world's future, and what angers him is that most socialists had by 1900 become part of the progressive consensus. What makes Sorel an original in his own time is his insistence that violence has a future. The violence that Sorel preached (the word is deliberate) was the necessary violence of class war, 'domestic' violence, not war between nations, but what he actually says about violence fits the case of international war equally well. For Sorel violence is not instrumental in the ordinary sense, not a means towards a specific end, because he realizes that if violence is only instrumental then in principle substitute means can always be found for it. Violence is still instrumental for Sorel, but its aim is to form the kind of revolutionary consciousness

270

which makes the determined pursuit of revolutionary ends more likely. Consciousness always interposes itself between violence and its object. The end which violence pursues does not have to be a 'real' end at all; it can be a fantasy or a myth; all that the pursuit of a mythologized end has to do is to energize revolutionaries; *real* revolutionary ends will come out of this violence-loaded energy.

The directness, the violence even, with which Sorel put his case, was a challenge to progressive assumptions where these were assumptions about the pacific tendency of the industrial order. At the root of these assumptions lay a single assumption, common to liberals and Marxists alike, that the industrial order would become a universal order (the old 'false universality' of Hegel), which would make war between nation-states less likely. This was the view of Spencerians (industrialism means co-operation, not force; therefore pacifism) and Durkheimians, and also of Marxists who emphasized the cosmopolitan aspects of industrialism, and saw violence as necessarily either revolutionary or counter-revolutionary, and therefore confined to the internal politics of individual nation-states. (I owe this argument in part to Giddens, 1985, pp. 22–31.) This was the violence for which, as Sorel pointed out, substitutes could always be found in states where democratic rights were coming to be widely enjoyed. The political programme of international peace conceived of in industrial terms was an extension of the Cobdenite free trade treaty, which could contain even national feeling within bounds. The free trade treaty was the perfect answer to problems of international peace because it elegantly combined two different kinds of law, positive law and the laws by which the mechanisms of economic harmony worked. Liberals since Adam Smith had always warned men to expect trouble when enacted law was at variance with economic laws; that had been the liberal case against mercantilism. Now, in so far as a treaty could be law, free trade was law between nations. The presumption could now be in favour of international peace, and this would take the sting out of the xenophobia of nationalism. International trade could now be the *form* which international rivalry would take, which in its turn would convert potentially hostile relations between the powers into the essentially pacific relations between buyer and seller. Let the buyer still beware, but what was being demanded was his money and not his life; a certain wariness was now all that was required, not going armed into the market-place.

It was assumptions like these which account for the notorious theoretical unpreparedness of European liberalism for the Great War, and the war itself can be regarded in part as the counter-revolution of aristocratic military elites against the liberalization of their own societies. Liberalism needed time to work its way through the governing institutions of the European states, and liberalism itself had never really given any convincing theoretical account of the possibility that essentially reactionary forces – reactionary because they were wedded to violence as a means of coping with domestic problems and of solving international problems – might see through liberalism's own game, and begin to play a counter-progressive game of their own. In part, this was no doubt due to a failure on liberalism's part always to distinguish clearly between positive and social law, and between the two kinds of force which were the expression of these laws in action. On liberalism's view of it, force which was the expression of the State's authority would give way to those evolutionary and progressive forces which social laws decreed would increasingly hold sway in modern societies, so that the State itself would become less authoritarian. This perspective had always assumed a rather supine attitude on the part of traditional military elites, who were expected either to submit to the progress of liberalism with high aristocratic grace, or to submit to the professionalization of military power under strict civilian and legal control, and become just another example of socially divided labour in a socially organic whole. As a part of the whole, the military was not expected to make any claims beyond its own specialism, certainly not those of an estate or a caste. What liberalism forgot – and it ruined Spencer's almost universal reputation as a social theorist in a generation – was that, anti-statist in a general sense though it was, liberalism had also created a modern state which was ripe for take-over by militarism. Even to use the expression 'take-over' implies the modern State as something separate enough from 'society' for it to be 'taken over'. The modern State's claim to modernity since Hegel, and more distantly since Adam Smith, lay in its claim to neutrality, as not being a king's cat's-paw, or aristocracy writ large and permitted to run amok in a servile peasantry whose only form of self-protection was revolt or shelter under the chartered liberties of a town. The modern State was to be separate in the sense of professional; the work of bureaucracy was to be labour divided, a separate calling, a world away from the essentially amateurish, localized rule of landowners; aristocratic ama-teurs of power were to be replaced by office-bound lovers of rules, barons replaced by red tape. (I mean to refer to continental European experience, in which red lords like Byron and Bertrand Russell have no theoretical place.) Part of this 'separate' State was its army. In Prussia a military caste had only to bide its time, acquire control of the conscript army which the modern State in Germany provided and of which it was the training cadre, wait for the moment of Bismarck's dismissal to end the balancing act by which civilian control of the military and military control of the civilians were embodied in one man, and the Prussianization of the German Empire and its foreign policy could proceed unhindered. And so to war in 1914.

Hitler's own account of his service in the poor bloody infantry (*der arme Frontschwein*) in the fighting in the Western Front is not primarily a military account. He is concerned to show that the First World War was for him a political experience, the violent continuation of the political education that he had been acquiring painfully in prewar Vienna. The descriptions of the fighting are curiously unreal, abstract even, but the account of a man who has found his first real home since childhood (Germany not Austria), and his *Fatherland*, in the army, ring truer. This enables Hitler to see the First World War as his war, and the defeat as a personal tragedy. By 1918, Hitler probably only felt at home in a trench or in a barracks (hence the later accounts of the rather contrived domestic life at Berchtesgaden); his lack of any life to go back to – no family, no home, no friends, no job – had set him apart from his comrades at the front, and it was natural for him to home in on an army camp in Munich when the war was over (he had served in the Bavarian List regiment). Hitler's account of the war is remarkable because of his close identification of his own aims with the aims of the High Command. Whether this was 'true at the time', or a later embellishment, does not greatly matter; what does matter is the sheer 'impersonality' of the account, which is at the same time deeply felt. Perhaps without knowing it, Hitler gives us an account of himself in the Great War which would have been instantly recognizable to the crowd theorists of the immediate prewar generation as the perfect crowd-man: his self-description is of a man who is a member of the army, pure and simple; a member of no other groups, familyless, therefore having no past of his own, wifeless and friendless, therefore having no libidinal ties outside the group; jobless and penniless, therefore classless, and therefore having no place to go outside the group. His only real experience is the experience of the group as a whole, an experience he shares with millions; he has no intervening loyalties which mediate between the collective experience and his own; his very ordinariness, his impersonality, means that he has shared the experience of the collectivity to the full, with nothing getting in the way. He has 'been through it all', so that the defeat and humiliation of 1918–19 is his own defeat and humiliation.

The crowd-man's experience of the defeat as *his* defeat leads Hitler to look round for somebody to blame for it, hence the 'stab in the back'. This leads to a sense of betrayal which is worlds away from the sense of betrayal to be found, say, in the works of the English First World War poets. There, the betrayal is in driving a whole generation of young men into the war in the first place, and then keeping them there to be slaughtered; there is the usual contempt for 'scarlet majors at the base', but the fault lies beyond them in the decisions and failures of foresight which allowed the war to happen at all. 'The stab in the back' view holds the opposite: there was nothing wrong with going to war – how could there be when its chief effect was to unite Germany now that the Austrian Germans were at last united in arms with their brothers in the *Reich*, and the shame of being on different sides at Sadowa could now be forgotten. What was criminal was pulling the army of all the Germans out of the war when the victory against the Slavs in the East had already been won and when the final victory in the West was within their grasp. In this view of it, what was *wrong* with the war was not the slaughter, terrible though that was, but the ending of it. The violence was something that had to be lived, and lived through, necessary even, but secondary. The psychological origins of the 'stab in the back' view have no doubt got something to do with the contempt of the front-line soldier for everybody who is not in the same position as himself, but Hitler's version of it leads him down a pseudo-Nietzschean path: theirs was the failure of will, not ours; we kept the faith and could have won through, they did not.

The attitude to violence with which Hitler came out of the First World War could not have been more different from the attitude of the victorious liberal-democratic powers, whose view of violence did not change at all. For them, the war had been a ghastly mistake, or the fault of German militarism or a combination of both; the war confirmed the blessings of peace and showed once and for all that war was a price too high to be paid for solutions to international problems. The pains of war could no longer be contained within the reassuring analogy with obstetrics; nor could the international order afford to tolerate the possibility of occasional, Cabinet wars of the nineteenth-century type, because the Great War had shown that limited war could no longer be contained by policy. The international order came to be seen as even more vulnerable to violence than the domestic order. Liberalism had realized its own dream that recourse to violence in society would one day become the exception to the rule so that society could live with its own level of crime, only to find the problem of violence still more acute in international affairs. The old liberal fear that if crime, especially collective crime, got out of hand it would turn into riot, and then into a revolutionary overthrow of the whole existing order, was now transferred to the society of nations. Then any aggressive behaviour by any state would quickly (quickly, that is, by the standards of pre-technological diplomacy and pre-nuclear war) involve other states, and there seemed to be no obvious limit to the extent of that involvement; perhaps next time war would really be world war. So some body had to be created which was analogous to the domestic state to plan the peace which was the domestic state's first, and some liberals would say only, aim. Hence the emphasis on international law, and hence the League of Nations. (I say 'analogous to' because even the most superficial reader of Hobbes would realize that, while it is possible for men to come together voluntarily to create a sovereign, a law-maker whose sword makes his own commands law, it is impossible for them to come together to make law which is binding; the League was certainly not meant to be the first, though it may have been the shadow of the illusion of the second.) Just as the only legitimate planning available to the liberal State was planning for social peace, so the international community would plan for its own peace. Of course, international violence would not stop altogether. The existence of a legal system in a society does not stop violence, but it is supposed to change the nature of violence, to outlaw it, to drive it underground, to make it less blatant, to make it ashamed of itself. So in the international order states were at least expected to pretend that they had renounced violence, to claim they were the victims of violence, not its instigators; they could be expected to lie about the extent of their armaments, claim their war-plans were defensive, and cover up. Whether this could have any effect other than to intensify the customary mendacity of diplomacy was a moot point, but it plainly had the intention of making it in the interest of knaves to act, or at least to talk, like honest men.

With hindsight, we can see that this was an extension to the whole world of the squeamishness about violence which Sorel had condemned in individual societies before 1914. It is based on the assumption which Sorel himself attacked, that any violence voluntarily committed, is never worth it; to commit oneself to violence as a first resort is the worst of all crimes against civilization; even *ultima ratio regis*, no matter how late in the day, is an admission of failure. That view of violence could mean nothing to a mind like Hitler's, which blamed Germany's failure to achieve her war aims on a failure of civilian strength of will, and which thought the casualty figures of the war a small price to pay for the comradeship in the ranks which he extrapolated into a sense of national and racial unity. Hitler's own conception of violence is a mixture of both the anti-liberal views of violence available in late-nineteenth-century Europe: on the one hand, the Sorelian view of violence as the instrument which creates a heroic crowd consciousness in its initiates, and on the other the older Bismarckian view of violence as the instrument of policy. But Hitler goes further: combine the two within one national state, then the internal violence of a crowd movement can be used to capture state power, whose violence can then be used in the pursuit of foreign policy ends; first the Party and the SA, and then the *Wehrmacht*.

That war comradeship which for Hitler stood for national and racial unity (*Volksgemeinschaft*) was to be the model both for the party that was to capture power in the *Reich* and for the *Reich* itself: it was both a means and an end. The question remained of how this scheme was to be put into operation, which meant that a technique of political mobilization had be be worked out which would work in the circumstances that Germany found itself in after the war. Hitler's description of postwar Germany, by accident or design, is a description of crowd society or mass society in a sense that would have realized the worst fears of Le Bon, and of the tradition on which Le Bon relied. Le Bon's description of what the individualism of the French Revolution did to French society could easily come from *Mein Kampf*'s description of the Weimar Republic as a society of lost souls. Individualism, Le Bon writes, isolated the Frenchman from 'his caste, from his family, from the social groups of which he was a unit, [and] left him delivered over to himself, and has thus transformed society into a mass of individuals, without cohesion and without ties' (*The Psychology of Socialism* (1899), p. 5). This was the kind of society which Le Bon had thought would be taken over by the crowd, and Le Bon's reasons for thinking that became what was later to be known as the theory of mass society (see above, pp. 207–9). However, Hitler adds a crucial twist to Le Bon by taking one part of Le Bon's theory, the 'Law of the Mental Unity of Crowds', to an even higher level of generality as a theory of mass psychology and gives to it a central place in his social theory. In Hitler's view, it is possible to separate crowd society from the crowd, so that the crowd becomes the solution to the problem of crowd society, not just its most obvious symptom. In Le Bon, and in the tradition which Le Bon summarized, crowd society was the general condition of a society which produced crowd politics; crowd society is the general cause of which the crowd, and the crowd as mob, is the particular effect. The relationship between crowd society and the crowd is taken for granted; the problem of crowd society for Le Bon is therefore the problem of crowd politics watered down. Neither is desirable; both are to be feared, hence Le Bon's elitist hope that leaders can be found for the crowd in crowd society who can steer that society's politics away from the atavistic barbarian which the crowd brings to civilization in all the epochs of human history. Hitler's view is different, because he takes the idea of mass society as crowd society much more literally, and he does this in a way which highlights what had always been a latent contradiction in the crowd theory of Le Bon and his predecessors in the crowd theory tradition.

There had always been something implausible in the contrast between the descriptions given by crowd theorists of crowd society on the one hand, and of their fascination with the crowd as mob on the other. Crowd society was seen as atomistic, as having lost its way, as lacking solidarity, formless, headless, having no will. The crowd, by contrast, was everything crowd society was not: united, with a sense of direction, single-minded, led by a leader who always resembled a Caesar, strong-willed. How could the single-minded energy of the crowd come out of such a flaccid, decadent society? *Where* did the crowd come from? Of course, it was precisely this contrast which interested crowd theorists from the beginning. The contrast was so vast, and the speed of the transformation of mindless crowd society into mob so sudden, that exotic-seeming explanatory mechanisms had to be found to account for it. Here was an example of sociological and psychological magic; a live animal was produced from the hat; hence the dragging of hypnotism out of the music hall to be dressed up in positivist clothes and produced on the scientific stage to account for the remarkable goings-on of the crowd. The trouble with explanations of collective life based on suggestion and suggestibility was that while they worked well enough for 'real' crowds with real leaders, they did not work so well for larger, physically non-proximate groups whose only thing in common was the vaguely shared 'mental state' induced by, say, reading the same newspaper. Either the mental state of newspaper readers was the same as the state of hypnotized people, in which case the contrast between the crowd and crowd society was not as vast and as interesting as it so obviously was, or the mental state of newspaper readers was such a watered-down version of hypnotism that the difference between it and hypnotism was so great that comparison between it and the hypnotic state was pointless. If the comparison was pointless, then the problem of the connection between crowd society and the crowd was left unexplained, and to leave it unexplained meant watering down crowd theory's whole claim for itself as being a social theory with high scientific pretensions to generalize which it had certainly become by the time Le Bon plundered Sighele and Tarde to sell crowd theory on exactly those terms to the expectant literate world.

What Hitler does in *Mein Kampf* is to make the latent tensions between crowd theory as the theory of mass society, and crowd theory as small group theory, a matter almost for theoretical separation. Separate them almost completely, make the generalizable aspects of crowd theory more generalized still, more 'abstract', less psychological and more social in Durkheim's sense, and make crowd theory as small group theory more precise, more truly psychological and less social, then the crowd in its primitive sense of throng can be theoretically (and socially) engineered into the vehicle for the re-energizing of crowd society. In this sense, crowd and crowd society become antitheses; crowd politics is not the *symptom* of crowd society, the crowd disease in its galloping form, acute not chronic; rather the crowd is the *solution* to the enervation of crowd society.[1]

Part of the strategy of energizing enervated crowd society was the use of violence and the symbols of violence; the Party and its military wings, the SA and the SS, were to be much more than a parody of an army. They were to be a substitute for the German army which had been all but banned by the Treaty of Versailles, and to show that they were a 'real' army they had to fight battles as well as looking smart in their uniforms. Above all, the Party had to march; Nazism was a movement, and its goal was the realization of the original party programme of *Mein Kampf* which Hitler insisted should never be altered, not even after 1934 when the quasi-Socialist elements in the Party were cowed by the massacre of the Night of the Long Knives and the Second (social) Revolution was firmly repudiated. The unaltered programme was left as a Sorelian myth with a vengeance. Street violence – "Possession of the streets is the key to power in the state" was a favourite slogan of the SA (cit. Bullock, 1962, p. 167) – or the threat of violence, was part of the propaganda appeal of Nazism, and was only incidentally a direct instrument of political success. The Nazis tended to show the more respectable side of their nature during elections; they were, after all, committed to a 'legal' acquisition of power, so it was important for them not to revive memories of their putschish past and to confine their more violent activities to attacks on their political enemies; the Social Democrats had a party army of their own anyway (the *Reichsbanner*), and the Communists were Bolsheviks who, despite their participation in elections, were committed to a violent revolution at some time in the future; attack them and leave the police alone, and above all, do nothing that could possibly give President Hindenburg an excuse for calling in the *Reichswehr* to restore order in what looked like civil war. The SA (there were 2–3 million of them by 1933, more than ten or twenty times the size of the regular *Reichswehr* (Bullock, 1962, p. 285)) waited for the *putsch* that never came, and after 1933 Hitler had to explain away their sense of betrayal by claiming that their victory had in fact already been won when their leader became Chancellor, so that they, unlike the German army of 1918, had not been betrayed at all; the SA had been a political army all along, and no definition of the crowd as a 'political army' could come closer to the spirit of Le Bon. That is precisely what crowd theorists (with the exception of Sighele) had feared before 1914; one is reminded of Tarde's description of the anarchists as 'the light cavalry of socialism'.

What had changed was not the idea, but the perception of the nature of the society in which the violence of the crowd occurred. What made crowd violence pernicious in liberal society before 1914 was that, according to the progressive consensus, societies were supposed to be becoming less violent, though crowd theory also showed that the individualism and democratization of liberal society laid it open to the danger of crowd politics. The crowd, like crime in general, was one of the problems with which liberal societies had to cope. The collection of causes of crowd politics later became mass society theory, but liberal society's tendency towards becoming mass society before 1914 was only a tendency for which antidotes might be found, of which the most famous was Le Bon's recipe for finding leaders for the crowd from outside the crowd. Of course, crowd theory's discovery that the crowd was potentially everybody was frightening, so that those who were prepared to take it seriously could talk themselves into a fairly acute form of terror, but they could if they wished take comfort in Le Bon's formulas, or begin to believe with Tarde that the crowd was a thing of the past which would be replaced by the more civilized, pluralistic world of reading and thinking 'publics' of which newspaper readerships were the paradigms and the most obvious examples. Certainly there was nothing to mobilize the masses as crowds in those societies remotely comparable to the massive mobilizations of the Great War. France and Britain, because they were the victors, would return to something like their old politics (though there is no telling what might have happened if they had lost), but Germany, which had been the least liberal of the Western states anyway, could not. She had liberalism thrust upon her by the victors, all at once, with the burdens of war-guilt, a 'criminal' constitution, reparations, in a country where millions had gone through the violence of the war and who continued to think about their betrayal by politicians while they kept their old uniforms neat or talked things over with old comrades in the queues of the unemployed. What could the old liberal distaste for violence mean to them? Joining the Nazi Party would easily appear to them to be a new kind of mobilization, a form of 'voluntary' conscription back into the army in a country which had thought of its army as the soul of the nation since the founding of the German Empire and beyond, and which was denied all but a pitiful remnant of an official army by the *Diktat* of Versailles. In the terms of crowd theory, the party was an institutionalized crowd, a Tardean corporation in the making, with a hierarchy and a leader. In the new world of the 1920s, where the liberal consensus was outlawing all violence, internal and international, where the new Bolshevik regime was being treated as a pariah, and where violence was being pushed underground, Nazi violence, and the threat of violence, was a supreme propaganda weapon; it was neither obstetric nor furtive; it was open, 'honest', straightforward, and it showed that Nazis were like no others on earth.

Again, it has to be stressed that it was not the perception of the nature of the crowd that had changed, but the perception of the society in which the crowd appeared, a society which was not going to be shocked by the crowd, but which would welcome it. No doubt, Hitler exaggerated the extent to which Weimar was a crowd society, just as crowd theorists had exaggerated it before 1914; in many ways Weimar society was just as bourgeois as Wilhelmine society had been, and Hitler recognized that too, hence the pride he took in saying that other political forces in Germany with which he had to deal would always misunderstand the nature of Nazism to the Nazis' advantage: *they* would always regard the Nazis as bourgeois because they themselves were bourgeois, and would be taken in by the fact that the Nazi Party played the legal, parliamentary game. When the Nazis' thuggishness showed through their frock-coat respectability, the politicians who thought they were using Hitler could always reassure themselves with the thought that office would tame Hitler in much the same way that in Italy Giolitti had thought that bringing the fascists within the constitutional arch would cool Mussolini down. When the Nazis were safely sharing power in a government of the right, they could make good their claim to being a party which stood for order by becoming part of the existing order. Then three birds could be killed with one stone: the parties of the left would be branded as the real threat to social peace, the government of the right would acquire a mass Nazi following, and high office in the state would exercise its soporific magic on the Nazi leaders. What was the unfortunate necessity of having Hitler as Chancellor, and a few Nazis in the Cabinet, compared with these? Hitler always knew what 'reactionaries' like Hindenburg and Papen really thought of him, and he never forgot Hindenburg's Junker dismissal of him as perhaps fit to be a Minister of Posts, but definitely not Chancellor material. He was half-educated, a rowdy from out of town (he did not become a German citizen until just before he stood against Hindenburg for the Presidency in 1932), who happened to be necessary for the electoral defeat of the left-centre Weimar coalition, and who therefore had to be paid the price of his hire. Hitler realized that his paymasters never understood the lit-eralness of Nazism, any more than they were capable of understanding his 'artistic' temperament – that was left for simpler folk. Nazism's lack of scruple, its love of action, its instinctive drive to violence as a first resort could easily appear to its patrons as bluff, as mere showmanship, as mere propaganda, useful perhaps, and occasionally nasty, but not fundamentally serious. What they had not realized was that the violence which had been held in check before Hitler became Chancellor could be used ruthlessly afterwards; that office was not to be the occasion for throwing in the violent hand, but for playing it; and that office had given Hitler all the wild cards. The Reichstag Fire in 1933 was simply the opportunity and Hitler's own comment, recorded by Rauschning, sums up the matter exactly:

> The reactionary forces believe they have me on the lead . . . they hope I will achieve my own ruin by mismanagement. But we should not wait for them to act. Our great opportunity lies in acting before they do. We have no scruples, no bourgeois hesitations . . . They regard me as an uneducated barbarian. Yes, we are barbarians. We want to be barbarians. It is an honourable title.
>
> (cit. Bullock, 1962, p. 276)

That pride in the title of barbarians tells the whole story of the final political victory of the crowd and its leaders. Since Taine's first, tentative account of the psychopathology of political regression, crowd theorists had added positivist gloss after gloss to the elitist commonplace that every appearance of the crowd in politics was a new barbarian invasion. The later a theorist comes in the tradition of crowd theory, the more the idea dawns upon him that the idea of invasion from the outside is misplaced and the more he begins to think with Nietzsche that the barbarians are already inside the walls, that we are all potential barbarians; when Le Bon summarized the fears of a whole generation of crowd thinkers in 1895 by proclaiming the Era of Crowds as the new barbarian age, he was again reiterating the old elitist commonplace, but by then it was a positivist commonplace which had all the authority of the latest psychological, sociological and evolutionary-biological thinking behind it. It was no less commonplace for that, but its nature as a commonplace had changed; it was still cant, but now it was scientific cant. Before 1914, the direct-action of the crowd appeared to be barbarous because its childish refusal to accept any mediation between the thought, the desire and the *action directe*, threatened to destroy the high degree of social differentiation which evolutionary-biological theory had taught a whole generation of social thinkers to regard as the hallmark of social progress. Social energy flowed through millions of highly evolved social channels, each minutely and beautifully connected to each other, and the whole organism worked, but its very beauty, and the fragility of its constituent parts, made it vulnerable to brute ignorance in action, an energy which was not social in any recognizably evolved sense at all, therefore primitive, barbarous and regressive. But this anti-social, barbarous energy, which thinkers like Sorel had already begun to see as an antidote to the decadence of the *fin de siècle*, could be positively beneficial in an enervated crowd society, and that was certainly Hitler's view of it. Hitler is remarkably close to Le Bon in his view of how the crowd is different from all other, competing, social institutions. Le Bon talks about crowd society as if there were nothing between the individual and the State except the crowd and in this he follows in the tradition which derives from Taine and Tocqueville, and more distantly from Montesquieu, which puts a high value on intermediary and mediating institutions which protect the individual from the State, and which protect the State from the dynamism of popular legitimization. Of course, even Le Bon, crude though he is as a political sociologist, recognizes that social institutions do not disappear overnight in crowd society; what in fact happens to them is that they lose their old force, become ossified, less corporation-like, and either

281

themselves come to resemble crowds or they die off. The socio-logical structure of crowd society, if it accepts crowd theory as its own self-understanding, comes to be seen as a collection of groups which, because they begin to lose their force, find them-selves increasingly incapable of ordering their relations with other groups on their old basis; they become isolated, look round for alliances, but find their allies in the same sorry state as themselves, hardly alliance-worthy at all. In societies like Weimar, the other available theory of self-understanding was Marxism, whose homogenizing threat to universalize the proletariat had acquired a new, threatening urgency since the Bolshevik Revolution. In the face of that, Hitler's party as corporatized crowd could easily appear to be a saviour. The great traumatizing events – the war, the inflation, the economic troubles following the Wall Street Crash – would shake some people right out of their traditional sociological categories; they would find themselves on the streets to be swallowed up into the Party. Others would remain, fearful of Marxism, within their traditional groups, but would look to Nazism to protect their groups from the left and to breathe some life into them to prevent them becoming empty shells. In these circumstances, Nazism's rude barbarian energy was not just the price that had to be paid; it was the means by which Germany could reawaken.

Mein Kampf itself lacks most of whatever precise sociological sophis-tication is necessary to put things quite so clearly as this, and it might appear that it was left to later mass society theory to put the matter in these terms, or in something like them. I insist on using the term 'crowd society', or on using it interchangeably with the term 'mass society', when discussing Le Bon and Hitler because the political sociology of *Mein Kampf* – and it is there if you dig for it – is not a *prefiguring* of the later mass society theory; rather, both the later mass society theory, and the political sociology of *Mein Kampf* are plain to see in Le Bon, where you don't have to dig for it. Much ink has been spilled in attempts to show that Hitler must have read a translation of Le Bon in one or other of the lending libraries that he frequented when he was down on his luck in Vienna before 1914; certainly, some of the phrases in *Mein Kampf* look like borrowings from a German translation, and the celebrated account of the techniques of political propaganda is a summary of which Le Bon, himself the master summarizer, might have been proud, but that is to miss the whole point of the Le Bon phenomenon as a widespread ideology (see above, Chapter 7), and of crowd theory as a prevailing theory of social explanation at the beginning of the twentieth century. After the First World War, you had no more to read crowd theorists, or even Le Bon, to be a crowd thinker, any more than you had to read Darwin in the late nineteenth century to be a evolutionist, Marx after

1917 to be a Marxist, or Rousseau before 1789 to believe in the virtues of the people and approve of the fall of the Bastille.

The question does remain: Did crowd theory, as Hitler received it, actually work? Hitler is the great adept of crowd theory; Canetti calls him a great 'empiricist' of crowds (Canetti, 1979, p. 147); Bullock calls him 'the greatest demagogue in history' (Bullock, 1962, p. 68). There seems to be general agreement that the ideology of Nazism, that rag-bag of the volkish sense of German national destiny, anti-semitism, anti-Bolshevism, the cult of the leader, and so on, was derivative, and Bullock speaks for the consensus when he says Hitler's ideas were 'entirely unoriginal' (ibid., 1963, p. 44); in contrast Bullock describes the chapter on War Propaganda in *Mein Kampf* as a 'masterly exercise' (ibid., p. 55), and a few pages later he tells us that 'The pages in *Mein Kampf* in which he discusses the techniques of mass propaganda and political leadership stand out in brilliant contrast with the turgid attempts to explain his entirely unoriginal political ideas' (ibid., p. 69). Bullock then goes on to summarize Hitler's summary: the receptive powers of the masses are very feeble, so the content of effective propaganda must be cut to the bone and cast in easily and constantly repeated formulas; when you lie, tell big lies; never hesitate and never qualify; never concede an inch to opponents, so all the good is on your side and all the bad on theirs – black is black and white is white; vehemence, passion and fanaticism will win every time; just as the spoken word will always win over the written word so the voice, and the presence, is mightier than the pen, while the sword impresses and attracts people against their own will (ibid., pp. 64–71), but Bullock's own summary only serves to emphasize how obviously derived from earlier crowd theory Hitler's account is. This might not appear to matter very much, though it is useful to set the record straight. What does matter is that the mistaken contrast, between Hitler as a mediocre political thinker and as someone who has something masterly to say about political propaganda, tends to obscure the obvious fact that, because Hitler was a crowd theorist in the tradition of crowd theory, the ideological content of Nazism *had* to be derivative if it was to succeed at all. Crowd theory's message about ideology had always been that the masses were fundamentally conservative; even the urban mob were peasants at heart. From its very beginning in Taine's attack on Michelet's version of the fall of the Bastille as the act of the whole revolutionary people armed with the Rights of Man, crowd psychologists had plundered the whole science of man from physiology to anthropology in the search for arguments to show that the people, or the masses, or the lower orders, could never be revolutionary because popular revolutionary action would always take a crowd form, and what the psychology of the crowd showed above everything else was that the crowd mind regressed to a state of primal barbarism; revolutions only lead backwards, so better not make revolutions at all. (In later crowd theory, a crowd of anybody, *savants* even, regressed too, but the implication was always there that a proletarian crowd would regress further, or at least quicker; they had nothing to lose, and on the evolutionary scale, they had less far to go to reach geological bottom.) The release of brutal instincts in the crowd, its revolutionary madness often literally conceived, its hallucinations, its collective hypnosis, all pointed inexorably to the same theoretical conclusion: the revolutionary crowd could change things, but it could only usher in a future which would be a repetition of a barbarous, anthropological and even zoological past. Crowd theorists were, on the whole, progressives; progress was possible, but only through the largely undirected, and certainly not centrally directed, evolutionary process of the social division of labour as societies became ever more complex and differentiated wholes; social biology of the Espinas kind as popularized by Spencerism was both progressivism's scientific basis and its sustaining metaphor; progress and the destructive energy of the crowd were theoretically as far apart as it was possible to be.

A view of the essential conservatism of human instinct, and of human nature in general (for nineteenth-century social theory had yet to grow nervous about such a generalization, however much it would be prepared to qualify it in specific instances) would hardly fail to come out of this style of theorizing; human nature was conservative and backward-looking in every possible sense except the evolutionary-biological. What is really surprising is that most crowd theorists could think like this and remain progressives, however massively qualified their social optimism was; for them, progress was still natural, but natural progress now meant something biologically specific; and the recognition that in the course of evolution taken as a whole almost all mutations, and almost all changes in physical environment, had been fatal to species, taught progressives that progress could not be engineered, and that even tinkering with social processes was fraught with danger. (Thinking like this, it is inconceivable that in economic matters crowd theorists could have been anything except free-marketeers.) This meant that periods of popular disturbance, let alone periods of revolutionary upheaval, were, properly speaking, periods of potential or actual dissolution, crimes against civilization. Of course, such dissolutions were always accompanied, perhaps even in a sense were caused by or made possible by, very fair-sounding rhetorics of liberation, invented by discontented would-be elites, which filter down to the masses in the form of easily remembered and repeated slogans, all of which have the Rights of Man for their original. What crowd theory asks us to see behind the slogans and the furore is the operation of imperatives inherited from a national culture, or from a race, or from ancestors whose prehistory only evolutionary theory can trace. The crowd loves its ideas, but it loves them too well to offend them by thinking about them. (The best recent example of thoughts so loved are the *Thoughts of Chairman Mao*, which came bound in a plastic cover so that they could be waved in the rain.) It follows that the crowd's natural ideology would be the one best suited to its own atavism: nationalist, racist, brutal, and brutally simple-minded. Sighele began to see that just before the Great War, and Le Bon realized it during the war, and both tried to turn it to their own country's military advantage, but Hitler understood it best of all. Looked at from the point of view of crowd theory, Hitler was being entirely orthodox in believing that an entirely unoriginal 'derivative' ideology was the natural content with which to fill up the crowd mind. The derivativeness of Nazi ideology is simply the connection between the crowd's own atavism and political action. The *Volk's* first triumph had been the defeat of the Roman Empire in the West, and Western history since then had been the story of the vicissitudes of *Volk's* heroic attempts to realize its own destiny. The Third Reich would represent the final, millennarian victory over its own internal and external enemies, the corrupt and corrupted within and the internationalists without. That vision sat easily with a tradition of German nationalism going back at least to the middle of the eighteenth century, and it could easily accommodate different strands within that tradition (Herder *and* Hegel); it enabled the Nazis to claim to speak for all Germans, the living and the dead, while the Social Darwinist theme of a people struggling for life, and for the room to live it in, tied Nazi ideology to the received nineteenth-century idea that social theory could be conceived as an extension of evolutionary biology. (I say 'sat easily with' and 'tied' for the very obvious reason that the connections are arbitrary; but they are not accidental. Crowd theory might even be said to make them necessary, granted much of crowd theory's own grounding in evolutionary theory, its concern for natural 'organic' groups, and its tendency to think in evolutionary time-scales.) Nazi ideology may still be a rag-bag, but it begins to look like a rag-bag which in crowd theory's terms is not only familiar, but predictable. Hitler did not just take a part of crowd theory and use it as a technique of political propaganda which would work; he also took from it a complete idea of what kind of ideology the crowd mind needed for the propaganda to work.

If crowd theory worked in Hitler's hands, it worked in the service of ends which would have shocked crowd thinkers before 1914. The technique was no doubt the same, but the ideology which it was the technique's function to propagate and exploit was the kind of ideology which elitist crowd thinkers feared that the crowd, if left to itself, would take for its own. This complete crowd, operating according to its own psychological laws and with an ideology in accordance with those laws, was precisely what was to be feared. (Something like the complete crowd could be encouraged in times of national emergency, like war, but strictly on a hostilities-only basis, to be demobilized afterwards.) Crowd theory's qualified hopes for the future had depended on it being possible to separate the crowd from its own ideology and its own leaders, so as to be able to impose on it leaders from the outside who would use the ordinary technique of crowd leadership to manipulate the crowd in the service of elitist ends which would likewise to imposed from without. From this point of view, there was plainly something going wrong in the Nazi case, and it is easy, with hindsight, to see what it was: Hitler was the crowd's own authentic leader, perhaps the first the crowd ever had.

The Nazi cult of leadership answered a question which had bedevilled crowd theory since Taine: Was the leader of the crowd genuinely a member of the crowd, or was he something rather special? Crowd theory had agonized over that problem for fifty years (see above, pp. 237–9), so that by the time Freud wrote his *Group Psychology* in 1921 it had become crowd theory's central concern. Nazism solved the problem by showing that it was not a problem at all; the crowd's leader *was* the common man, albeit in an intensified form, but that intensification only made him more authentically the crowd's leader. Ortega y Gasset's *The Revolt of the Masses* (published in 1930, but in the making since the date of Mussolini's March on Rome, 1922) is the classic account of the character the common man gives to his age. Ortega's focus is the politics of southern Europe (he does not even mention Hitler) but there is something uncanny in the way that his picture of the common man making the world his own fits Hitler to the life. Ortega is a liberal elitist; the great achievement of the nineteenth century was what sociologists have come to call 'industrial society' in its Western version; its two organizing principles are liberal democracy and the technical knowledge which is the basis of modern industrial progress; this has raised the level of the common man far above anything he could have imagined before; he no longer feels the 'veto' of the world outside himself, and so he loses his sense of 'limitation, obligation, dependence; in a word pressure [or] oppression' (Ortega, 1930, p. 43). The common man looks upon this new world as a given, regards his prosperity and his political liberty as rights, and never spares a thought for the political and scientific elites who created his world and who are still necessary to that world if it is not to stagnate and to regress (ibid., ch. 7, 'Noble Life and common Life, or Effort and Inertia', *passim*). Mass man is therefore self-satisfied; he admits of nothing outside himself which can lay down the law to him; the mass is 'hermetically enclosed', and therefore 'indocile', because in its self-sufficiency the mass can no longer be led from outside by elites (ibid., pp. 50–1). Ortega might have added that therefore it will only tolerate the leadership of one of its own.

In that remarkable little book Ortega unwittingly provides the key to the long autobiographical first section of *Mein Kampf*, and to the reason why the title of the whole work is so apposite. Hitler's account of his own life is ordinary, everyman's struggle to free himself from the limitations imposed by Austrian society before the First World War; after 1918, the Party's effort to establish itself in and eventually to destroy the bourgeois democracy of Weimar Germany, is a continuation of that same struggle. A biography of Hitler like Bullock's tells the same story. Of course Hitler felt the slights any half-educated corporal would feel in a society where social prestige was handed out with the army commission and the doctor's degree, and it may also be true that he never entirely overcame his sense of his own inferiority. And that high Wilhelmine disdain continues in the huge Hitler literature whenever the question is asked: How could a man like *that* come to rule a country like ours? It must have been accidental; he must have mesmerized us; occult powers must be at work here; black magic. But that ground had all been covered before in the crowd theory of the previous fifty years. Explanations like these do not have to be invented to explain the Hitler phenomenon, because by the time of Le Bon's *The Crowd* in 1895 they had already become commonplace, so commonplace that they *should* have been used to predict the emergence of a politics and leadership of the Hitler type.

Hitler made crowd politics work. The struggle was real, and it took a long time, and because crowd politics was by its very nature public, noisy and violent, the question still has to be asked: Why did so many, for so long, not realize what was happening and what the dangers were? Crowd theory had been complete since Le Bon; there was universal agreement that the First World War was a great trauma which had altered the nature of the German economy, society and politics, and it had been no secret since 1895 that the Era of Crowds would come in societies where ruling groups and ruling ideas began to lose their force. And what was it that people could be expected to predict? Not perhaps, the full horror of the Second World War and the Holocaust but certainly the rise of a crowd movement which crowd theorists had been predicting since 1870 would destroy everything that liberalism stood for, and everything that liberal society was supposed to embody, and, to alter Nietzsche slightly, 'without liberalism all things are possible'.

The blindness can be partly explained by the circumstances of the Nazi rise to power. The party's struggle was long, but its rise to national prominence out of Bavarian provincial politics was very sudden (1929–31); the men who called Hitler to the centre to provide mass backing for a right-wing government could only see a demagogue in Hitler, one of Ortega's common men who could still be used for its own purposes by an elite. Hitler and his Nazis would be domesticated by that same parliamentary *embourgeoisement* which had already worked on leaders of the erstwhile revolutionary Social Democracy, now the most law-abiding party in continental Europe. The elite's hesitations before it allied itself fully with the Nazis, and the Nazis' own efforts to tidy up their image in their dealings with the elite ('legal', 'a party of order') show that the elite knew it was taking a risk. What made that risk worth taking? The usual answer is fear of a civil war, which the left would win as a prelude to the Bolshevization of Germany, the Nazis and the Communists being alternatives between which a choice had to be made. (A whiff of this thesis still remains in the now well-known description, by a member of the royal family, of a part of the SS as a body of noble Silesian huntsmen who disagreed with the aims of Bolshevism.) That was certainly a widespread fear in the Weimar Republic during the economic crisis following the Wall Street Crash when the two extremist parties, the Nazis and the Communists, were the parties which consistently gained ground (and there were even moments when it looked as if the two anti-bourgeois parties might make common ground and fight a civil war on the same side if not actually in alliance), and politics become increasingly violent. It has become something of a cliché that in these circumstances the established right would be expected to make common cause with the rabble-rousing right, and that the supporters of the centre would rush to the right too, for fear of being caught in the middle of a battlefield, thus making Sorel come true; violence, and the threat of violence, even in a country with a loyal and solid army, created a divided society. But it was not the violence of the Nazis which put off their potential allies, however great their distaste for rowdiness might be. The Versailles army was jealous beneath its contempt of the SA and the SS; the *Reichswehr* was the historically legitimate monopolizer of violence in the German state, while the politicians of the right and their industrialist paymasters (who fastidiously laundered most of the money they paid to the Nazis through the respectable Nationalist Party) knew what they were buying. What rather appears to have put them off most were the populist and socialist aspects of the Nazi programme. This was part of the oldest fear of the crowd; the choice between the left and the Nazis was a choice between two different versions of crowd politics; because socialist crowd politics was the more frightening, the Nazis were the safer choice.

The fact that this was a choice between two different forms of crowd politics tends to be obscured by the fascist form that crowd politics took in the 1920s and 1930s. Nothing is easier to accept than the orthodox Marxist contrast between the class solidarity of socialism and the falsely conscious mob-spirit of fascism. It is equally easy to forget that all crowd theorists up to and including Le Bon expected crowd politics to be socialist, and that Sighele's conversion to the crowd was in the name of 'proletarian nationalism'. Part of the case against the crowd was its equality; that equality, as homogeneity of mind, was part of what made the crowd atavistic; barbarism was undifferentiated, and differentiation was what the whole of history, evolutionary and human, had achieved. The social division of labour was advanced, therefore socialism was primitive; no wonder that the first state calling itself socialist had been established in the only half-European East (and what relief when Stalin proclaimed 'socialism is one country'). Up to 1934, Nazism's socialism was in the orthodox tradition of crowd theory, as ideologically atavistic as its anti-semitism and its volkish nationalism.

Those who saw politics through eyes like Le Bon's could still see the crowd in the Social Democrats, no matter how respectable they might appear to be, or in the Communists, no matter how disciplined; the success of the Nazi Party was enough to show how solid the crowd could become if it could institutionalize itself around a leader (or what Canetti would call a 'crowd crystal'). It might even have been possible not to see the Nazis as a crowd at all by seeing the 'real' crowd in the politics of the left, the lineal descendants of the crowd which had (at least in imagination) stormed the Bastille in 1789, and the Winter Palace in 1917; it would certainly have been in the mainstream of crowd theory still to regard the really dangerous crowd in 1930 as the left-wing crowd, and it would have been much clearer after 1934, with the Nazis installed as a party of the existing order and with the Second, socialist, Nazi Revolution off the party agenda for ever.

The left's failure to see the dangers inherent in Nazism as the fulfilment of the worst fears of half a century's worth of crowd theory is easier to explain, and it is perhaps easier to forgive. The left in Germany, and especially the Communist left, was very late in seeing that Nazism, and fascism in general, had a future because it could strengthen the State. The left's failure to understand came partly from the insistence of Comintern orthodoxy that fascism was one of the possible last forms that the State in capitalist society could take. Marxism, in its orthodox Leninist variant, had always expected the capitalist State in its last stage to be vicious – as the class struggle intensified the State, as agents of the bourgeoisie, would resort increasingly to violence as the social order became more ragged at the edges, but Marxist orthodoxy was equally insistent that the increasing resort to violence should not be equated with an increase in State power in any long term. In *The Eighteenth Brumaire of Louis Bonaparte* Marx himself had said that in times of intense class conflict contending classes might cancel each other out, so to speak, as they had done during the French Revolution of 1848, so that the State could *appear* as independent and autonomous – hence the Empire of Louis Bonaparte, the seeming autonomy of whose regime came about because it was not directly dependent on either of the two great contending classes, the bourgeoisie and the proletariat; the Second Empire came to power with the support of the lumpenproletariat, the support of the peasantry kept it in being, and sections of the bourgeoisie eventually came round. There was no equivalent in Weimar of France's peasant majority in 1851 to keep Hitler in power as it had kept Louis Bonaparte, so mainstream Marxism missed its opportunity of extending its analysis of Marx's own lumpenproletarian riff-raff into a theory of crowd politics, though there were exceptions. Clara Zetkin, August Thalmeir (who was excluded from the German Communist Party in 1928) and the Austro-Marxist Bruno Bauer (who returned to the orthodox Communists himself in 1938) did go some way towards understanding fascism as a variant of Bonapartist plebiscitary crowd despotism, and so, from the point of view of the Freudian theory of crowd leadership did the English Marxist Reuben Osborn (*Freud and Marx: A Dialectical Study*, 1937, pp. 263–7 and *passim*) but the Comintern view, which reached its final form in the Dimitroff definition two years after Hitler became Chancellor, that fascists ruled as agents of the capitalist ruling class, prevailed. (For a summary of the Marxist interpretations of fascism and Nazism in the 1930s, see I. Kershaw, 1985, pp. 24–6.) This theoretical opportunity missed by Marxists since the *Eighteenth Brumaire* was the same opportunity seized upon by crowd theorists after 1870, and although no crowd theorist quotes it, Marx's own description of the lumpenproletariat which formed the hard core of Louis Bonaparte's *coup d'état* is a perfect description of a crowd formed from ideal crowd material, and the importance of Caesarism in the development of the theory of crowds needs no stressing. The only Marxist to take crowd theory at all seriously was Sorel, but he was too much of a maverick to count; his dismissal by Lenin was too authoritative, and Sorel could too easily be seen as giving aid and comfort to the enemy – Mussolini was liable to say of him, as he was of Le Bon, that he was the only writer who ever influenced him. Shils is perhaps correct when he says that mass society theory is the standard *ex post facto* 'quasi-Marxist' way of explaining the role of Nazism in Weimar Germany (see above, pp. 207–8), but the early version of mass society theory in crowd theory going back to at least 1870 gave Marxists ample opportunity to come to terms with the crowd, but they did not. Perhaps they should not be blamed for that too much, because the proceedings of a symposium on *The Crowd* published in Paris (the home of crowd theory in both the political and the intellectual senses) in 1934 still treats the crowd as a revolutionary, that is left-wing, phenomenon, and fails to mention fascism at all, so well had crowd theory taught its lesson that the crowd would be socialist (Bohn *et al.*, 1934).

The one thing which still stands in the way of the interpretations of Nazism as the triumph of the crowd is that Hitler actually came to power by a back-stairs intrigue, the method of traditional 'high politics', and the very antithesis of the victory of the leader of the crowd. By 1930 Hitler had all the required qualifications of a crowd leader, and the SA had always expected, and had been allowed by Hitler to expect, that there would be a Nazi revolution to seize power. The way Hitler came to power by the invitation of those bourgeois and reactionaries whom Nazism was intended to supplant, was something which had to be lived down. The Nazi Dr Goebbels, minister of propaganda, understood that very well. After the Nazi accession to power, propaganda by film, wireless and newspaper treated Hitler *as if* he was the leader who had been swept to power by the crowd from the outside. Goebbels used the state control of media of mass persuasion to complete the portrait of Hitler as the kind of leader that crowd theory had always predicted. Of course, this was to a degree fraudulent, the cart having come before the horse. Crowd theory was being used not only as a means, but also as an *ex post facto* justification. This was the true sense in which the Nazis drew a technique of political persuasion out of crowd theory, but they did not thereby relinquish the rest of it, least of all the theory of crowd leadership. What Goebbels did after 1933 was to use one part of crowd theory, its techniques of persuasion, to persuade Germans that another part of crowd theory, its expectation of charismatic leadership, was realized in the person of Adolf Hitler. *Then* the Führer principle could itself be used as a technique to bind the people to its leader.

Hitler's own attitude to the masses, like Lenin's, was a mixture of revolutionary expectation and effective contempt; Hitler could wax lyrical at one moment about the volkish soul of the masses as the agent of German salvation, and at another dismiss them with Caesarist disdain: 'the great mass of working-men want only bread and circuses. They have no understanding for ideals of any sort whatsoever' (cit. Bullock, 1962, p. 157). What had changed since Caesar's day was that Caesarism had been so thoroughly psychologized by the whole tradition of crowd theory that it amounted to no less than a theory of totalitarianism. The depth psychology which since Taine had been applied to the mind of crowds, and which reaches its most refined expression in Freud's *Group Psychology*, had let the crowd's leader right into the depths of each man's soul. Disenchanted liberals and individualists as most crowd theorists were, that is what really terrified them, and that is what they tried so hard to warn their fellow men against. When crowd theory discovered that all men could become crowd men, that all men really wanted to be crowd men because the demands

291

of civilization were too much for them, that being led by a great hypnotist–Caesar–father fitted perfectly with an inner psychological need of a fundamentally conservative and unthinking human nature, then the theoretical foundations for totalitarian leadership of Hitler's kind were complete.

It must again be said that this is the age of fascism's own psychological and social theory, not something invented later to explain Nazism. It has a familiar ring to it because something very like it was reinvented late in the Weimar day, and after 1945, to explain Hitler. The theory of mass society in its late, 'quasi-Marxist', form which Shils mistakes for all mass society theory (see above, pp. 207–8), the 'fear of freedom' and 'authoritarian personality' themes associated with Erich Fromm and with the Frankfurt School, and more generally the debate about totalitarianism, were all later theoretical responses to the rise of Nazism, but these were all theoretical concerns thoroughly worked out before the world had even heard of Hitler, and most of that working out had taken place well before 1914, and all of it had been worked out by the time Freud's *Group Psychology* was published in 1921. It has to be said again that men have only got their own era's psychology to understand themselves with, and their own age's social theory to understand their own age's society and politics in, and crowd theory was one of the prevailing psychological and social theories. Above all, crowd theory was up to date: it was the latest social theory; it was comprehensive, and its basis was scientific in all the appropriate senses; and it went to the *heart* of the matter. How much of that theory remains intact is a moot point; what is undoubtedly true is that crowd theory prepared the way for Nazism; the Nazis exploited it as a technique of mass persuasion but more importantly, they fulfilled its doom-laded prophecies about the barbarous Era of Crowds simply by taking them literally.

Notes

1 I exaggerate slightly the originality of Hitler's insight here to point out the new departure in crowd theory in *Mein Kampf*. Sighele, in the later stages of his theoretical development at the time of the Libyan War of 1912, comes very near Hitler's position (see above, p. 171–2). The point is that Hitler begins from a position that Sighele only reaches after many twists and turns.

10

The Sanity of Crowds and the Madness of Power: Elias Canetti's *Crowds and Power* (1960)

Canetti's *Crowds and Power* is the only masterpiece of crowd theory. The triumph of crowd politics with the rise of National Socialism in Germany enables Canetti to survey the *whole* experience of the crowd from its anthropological beginnings, and to re-work the whole tradition of crowd theory. In Canetti, crowd theory is completed in a sense that was not available to his predecessors whose crowd theory could only be complete as prediction. In Canetti, the whole crowd experience itself is complete; the crowd and its leaders have come to power out of a decayed civilization; in the form of Nazism the paranoid delusions of a leader of crowds became 'the creed of a great nation, leading under a "Mongol Prince", to the conquest of Europe and coming within a hair's breadth of the conquest of the world' (*CP*, p. 447).[1] Impressive though crowd theory was before 1914, there was not much in it to predict the casualty figures of the Great War, and there was certainly nothing in it, or in the crowd theory of the 1920s, to predict the heap of corpses left by Hitler's war. Canetti accepts that all the important events of the modern world, inflations, revolutions and wars, are crowd phenomena (*CP*, p. 183). All have barbarous consequences, but Canetti avoids the 'atavistic–evolutionary' style of crowd explanation of his predecessors in the crowd tradition because 'It is not for a European of the 20th century to regard himself as above savagery' (*CP*, p. 411). The evolutionist perspective was only possible in a civilization still capable of believing in its own superiority over all the cultures of the past, and over all those contemporary cultures which were not yet up to its own mark; being superior put it in a position to feel threatened by the crowd as a throwback to an earlier stage of evolutionary progress. The era Canetti deals with begins with the Great War and ends with the

293

threat of the nuclear holocaust; its masses are on the move, and they leave masses of the dead behind them; the superiority of evolutionary distance is no longer available. Canetti dismisses all Darwinism (*CP*, p. 384), not because he thinks Darwinism is untrue or because he is unaware of the existence of 'pessimistic Darwinism', but because he wants to put as much distance as he can between his own crowd theory and the progressive biology on which so much of the crowd theory tradition rested.

Canetti's own biology derives not from Darwin but from Pasteur. All crowd theory is concerned about numbers; crowds number in thousands, and the masses in millions; crowd theory in its modern form would have been unnecessary, and perhaps impossible, without an awareness of the teeming life of large cities, of a world increasingly populated and pressed for space. Canetti thinks that the origin of this 'million magic' goes beyond urbanization and population growth to the discovery (which is recent: Pasteur died the year after Le Bon's *The Crowd*) that the world is already overpopulated to an unimaginable degree by masses of hostile bacilli which fight men for their sustenance in the countryside (diseases of crops; Pasteur and phylloxera) and for their lives in the towns (epidemics);[2] human life itself begins with the suicide of the 200 million who accompany the surviving spermatazoon (*CP*, p. 47). Living now is living with uncounted millions; crowds are everywhere and demand the attention of the sciences, while in the past the crowd was 'never taken quite seriously' (*CP*, p. 21). (Le Bon, who had a nose for everything, began to play with the analogy between crowds and microbes in his discussion of the growth of the crowd by contagion, but he did not take the matter very far.)

Now that it is possible to construct the history of man as a completed crowd history, it would be ridiculous for Canetti to distance himself from the crowd in the way that his predecessors did. Canetti is remarkable as the first autobiographer of crowds. He is the first to have a sense of what being-in-the-crowd is like and to describe it. Other crowd theorists had felt the crowd's menace, Freud in Vienna, for instance, or Taine frightened for his wife's safety and of his Paris apartment being set on fire during the *Commune*, or Gibbon in London during the Gordon Riots, but Canetti's account of the crowd of his student days in Vienna (15 July 1927) is an account of a *shared* experience.

There had been shooting in Burgen and workers had been killed. The Court had acquitted the murderers. The judgment was designated, no, trumpeted as a 'just verdict' in the organ of the government party . . . From all parts of the city the workers marched in closed processions to the Palace of Justice, which with its sheer name embodied injustice for them. It was a completely spontaneous reaction, I personally, felt just how spontaneous. Taking my bicycle, I zoomed into the city and joined the procession. The workers, usually well disciplined, trusting their Social Democratic leaders, and content that Vienna was ruled by them in an exemplary fashion, were acting *without* their leaders on that day. When they set fire to the Palace of Justice, Mayor Seitz standing on a fire engine, tried to block their way with his right hand raised high. His gesture was futile; the Palace of Justice was *burning*. The police were ordered to shoot, ninety people were killed.

That was forty-six years ago, and the excitement of that day still lingers in my bones. It was the closest thing to a revolution that I had physically experienced. A hundred pages would not suffice to describe what I saw. Since then, I have known very precisely that I need not read a single word about what happened during the storming of the Bastille. I became part of the crowd, I dissolved into it fully. I did not feel the least resistance to what it did. I am surprised that I was nevertheless able to grasp all the concrete details occurring before my eyes.

(*CW*, pp. 205–6)

In that confession of a crowd man for a day – 'the workers, usually so well-disciplined . . . were acting *without* their leaders on that day' – there is an important hint of the direction in which Canetti's crowd theory will go. In *Crowds and Power*, Canetti will do all he can to force a theoretical separation between crowds and leaders, because it is only through that separation that Canetti can establish equality as the fundamental attribute of the crowd. Canetti knows that the authority of two-and-a-half thousand years tells us to look at the crowd as the demagogue's creation. Traditional crowd theory raises the crowd's leader so far above the crowd that by comparison with leaders the members of the crowd can seem all to be the same, because the differences between them are nothing when compared to the gap which separates them from their leader. It was this sameness among followers which had led to the idea of group mind, that mindless homogeneity upon which so many crowd theorists had poured their elitist contempt. The group mind was at once the leader's creation and his source of power, because he could fill it with any content he wished; it became *his* mind, to do with as he pleased. This explained the extraordinary closeness of the bond between the leader and his crowd; the leader knew instinctively what the crowd wanted because the crowd, being *his* crowd, and its mind being *his* mind, would always want what he wanted. Of course, there is a kind of equality in the traditional picture of the crowd, but it is the equality of equal slavishness. The crowd is there to do its leader's bidding; it does nothing for itself. Crowd men only have two alternatives, either to continue to live in society and be subject to its patterns of authority, or to join the crowd and become subject to the authoritarian commands of a leader. In both cases, authority is a given, the only difference being that in ordinary society authority is more complex because it emanates from more than one source and is embodied in more than one set of rules, whereas in the crowd all is simplicity because there the leader is the single, visible source of command. Nothing really changes *in* the crowd, though crowd men can begin to acquire a taste for being in the crowd, and they can begin to see their ordinary society and the crowd as alternatives. A society in which this happens is a mass society on the way to some very nasty politics.

Crowds and Power is written very largely to unravel that received account of the crowd. Canetti wishes us to see the relationship between crowds and power as always being problematic, and his way of doing that is by making the crowd's first 'attribute' its equality. A crowd does not become a crowd until its members lose their 'burdens of distance', differences of rank, status and property (*CP*, p. 17). Canetti calls the moment of equality the 'discharge', and he means us to take very literally his assertion that the crowd is not a crowd until the discharge happens. The promptings of a demagogue can be the occasion for a crowd to gather, but it is not those promptings which make the crowd a crowd. Rather it is the loss of the fear of being touched (*CP*, p. 15), which leads to the loss of the burdens of distance, which makes the crowd. The crowd, through the loss of the fear of being touched, makes itself; this it can do whether it is acting with leaders or without them, and so the crowd cannot be the leader's creation. These can seem to be mere quibbles. It might be said that it makes very little difference whether you say that the crowd is a crowd as soon as they gather to listen to a leader, or whether you say a crowd is not a crowd until the moment of discharge, but Canetti thinks it matters a great deal because it is not until you make a distinction of this kind that you can even begin to see that crowds and power can be alternatives. The power that comes from crowd leadership is not a necessary power for Canetti, and he is not even sure that power *can* come from crowds. He denies, for instance, that a crowd's leader can command the crowd as a whole (see below, p. 298). What he is certain of is that power in all its forms, whether it is the legitimate power of a king by hereditary descent or the power of a leader who has come to power with the crowd, goes looking for crowds. Far from being a source of power, the crowd for Canetti is part of the scope for power, the field of its exercise, and this applies no matter how the power which feeds on the crowd itself originated.

That distinction, between the power which *comes* from crowds and the power which *feeds* on crowds, is not a quibble. Crowd theory had always seen an antithesis between the illegitimate, threatening power of crowds and the legitimate, established patterns of power in orderly societies, and crowd theory had always insisted that civilized living depended on the uninterrupted exercise of legitimate power against the barbarous power of the crowd. Canetti thinks that antithesis between crowd power and legitimate power has diverted attention from the crowd aspects of all power. For him, the power which comes from crowds, in the received sense of demagogic power, is only a single case of power feeding on the crowd, and it is by no means the most important one. Crowd theory's focus on the crowd as an alternative power base arising to challenge established power, and crowd theory's long love-affair with the leaders of crowds, have obscured the fact that all power, whether we choose to call it legitimate or not, feeds on crowds. For this to be properly understood, we have to shift our attention away from crowd theory's ancient focus on the crowd as a means to the acquisition of power, and on to what power does with the crowd once power has been acquired. Canetti will say that the crowd is power's victim, the instrumentality not of power's acquisition but of its aggrandisement.

It is not until one reads *Crowds and Power* that one realizes how implicitly Hobbesian all other crowd theory was. It was always assumed that when the crowd comes together it creates power for its leader. In received crowd theory, the crowd in its ideal type is made up of discrete, atomistic individuals who have been shaken out of the social categories of a collapsing social order. These atoms, heterogeneous by their social origins, but now homogeneous in their isolation, come together in the crowd to produce a leader and to put power into his hands. Crowd theory since Le Bon had largely concerned itself with untangling the psychological mechanisms of this creation and transfer of power. The questions addressed were of the type: Does the crowd *cause* the leader, or does the leader *cause* the crowd? Does the leader *come from* the crowd? Is his psychological make-up the same as the psychological make-up of the typical crowd member, or does the leader come from outside the crowd and is therefore very different? These, and similar questions, are the stuff of Sighele, Tarde and Le Bon, so that by the time of Freud and Hitler, crowd theory had effectively become leadership theory. 'No leader, no crowd' is the motto of almost all crowd theory up to Canetti. Canetti shows us how glaringly Hobbesian the assumption is which lies behind this way of looking at crowds. Hobbes's own language can be used without parody to express it: the unity of the thing is in its representer, not in the thing represented; the crowd is its leader and has put the sword into his hand; take the sword away and the crowd returns to the atomistic condition which Hobbes calls the State of Nature.[3]

Canetti's strategy for dealing with received crowd theory's obsession with the leaders of crowds is to make his readers wait a very long time before he *even mentions* crowd leaders in any very serious way, and then only after his treatment of the crowd is substantially complete. The first two hundred pages of *Crowds and Power* consist of an elaborate typology of crowds (*CP*, pp. 15–93), a corresponding typology of packs as the lineal ancestors of crowds (*CP*, pp. 93–127), followed by a section on 'The Pack and Religion' (*CP*, pp. 127–69) and a section on 'The Crowd in History' (*CP*, pp. 169–203). The demagogue, and the received crowd theory in which the demagogue plays such an important part, do not make their appearance until p. 310, by which time they are separated from the crowd by a distance of over 200 pages, and when the demagogue is produced he is immediately cut down to size. The demagogue may think he commands the crowd in the same way that a military commander gives orders to his troops, but he is mistaken, and so too are those crowd theorists who have flattered demagogues as demagogues flatter themselves. The demagogue may actually address his commands to the crowd, but *in fact* he only commands one man who, if he listens, begins to spread that command 'horizontally' in the crowd (the old crowd theorists' 'mutual suggestion'). The spread of command can happen 'instantaneously', so creating the illusion that the crowd as a whole obeys its leader, but Canetti insists that this appearance of collective obedience is simply another instance of the renowned quickness of crowds. The demagogue is command's point of origin only, and he is no more important than the man who first listened to his command and began the process by which the command was spread right through the crowd. Of course, it may be true that the demagogue wanted a crowd to form, and it may be true that his command is in fact the command which the whole crowd eventually obeys, but this does not alter the fact that in the crowd there is an equality of command because everybody gives commands to everybody else. It can even be said that the crowd has really taken advantage of the demagogue because crowds 'want' their moment of discharge to get rid of their burdens of distance; far from demagogues exploiting crowds, crowds exploit them (*CP*, pp. 310–13). This is by no means a quibble. Traditional crowd theory had treated with high seriousness the question of how the crowd comes to act as a single unit, but it had never given a satisfactory answer to the question of whether the leader addressed his commands directly to the crowd as a whole, or whether he addressed them to some members of the crowd who then passed them on to others. Of course, it had not mattered much to traditional crowd theory which was true, because crowd theory before Canetti assumed that everything important about the crowd came from leaders, so the question of whether it came direct or not was a matter of secondary importance. Not for Canetti, who sees in this conundrum another opportunity to separate crowds from their leaders.

It follows that if the demagogue, whatever he may think he is doing, does not command the crowd, he cannot do the crowd any lasting damage. The traditional fear of crowd theorists that men in the crowd would acquire a taste for the authoritarian commands of leaders, so that a society's politics would increasingly take on a Caesarist character, is shown to be groundless. Far from being the school of authoritarian command, the crowd for Canetti becomes the only refuge from *all* commands. This freedom from command is implicit in the crowd's loss of its burdens of distance which is Canetti's starting point in *Crowds and Power*, but he waits until p. 324 before stating explicitly that 'part of those burdens of distance is made up of the stings of command accumulated in every individual'. These stings of command are to be thought of as the psychological effects in individuals of the commands coming from all the sources of authority to which men are subject. Canetti wants us to look upon commands as alien, and as leaving a barb in us after they have been carried out. The revolutionary crowd (Canetti calls it a *reversal* crowd) comes together specifically for the purpose of ridding itself of the accumulated stings of command which its members are no longer capable of getting rid of on their own (*CP*, pp. 327–8). Crowds in general are an escape from the patterns of authority existing in social life, but reversal crowds are a means of actually beginning to dismantle social and political power. The revolutionary crowd gets rid of its stings of command by passing them on to the crowd's enemies, the givers of commands, so that even if the revolution fails, the members of the crowd are less amenable to commands when they return to normality. There is no question here, as there is in Freud, of failed revolutions compounding the desire for obedience. The revolutionary crowd may take its suggestions indirectly from a leader, but it does not thereby acquire an increased taste for authority, because the commands of the leaders of crowds leave no stings behind because they are immediately passed on through the crowd. Even failed revolutions may be worth it.

Canetti's hugely intricate classification of crowds comes between his original assertion of equality as the crowd's fundamental characteristic, and his treatment of demagogues, command, and what he calls The Dissolution of the Sting. He wants us to see that a complete typology of crowds can be constructed without ever referring to the leaders of crowds. This can sometimes lead him into absurdity, as when he offers a complete typology of packs (*CP*, pp. 93–158) without mentioning that there is such a thing as the leader of the pack, but he plainly thinks that leadership theory has colonized crowd theory so thoroughly that any strategy is justified which will make us think again about crowds and their leaders.

An important part of that strategy is to ignore Le Bon, who does not even rate a mention in the whole of *Crowds and Power*, and almost the whole tradition that Le Bon fed on is excluded from *Crowds and Power*, apart from a summary of it in a few paragraphs (*CP*, pp. 310–13). Only Sighele even makes it into Canetti's very full bibliography, and he does not appear in the text or the accompanying notes; and there is no Taine, no Tarde, none of the Freud of *Group Psychology* (though Freud is mentioned elsewhere as a meddler in the case of Schreber (*CW*, p. 25)). What is most conspicuously absent from *Crowds and Power* is any serious reference to the hypnotic model of crowd leadership, so there is no Charcot, no Bernheim, and no Liébault, the psychiatric sources on which all serious crowd theorists, with the exception of Taine, relied. The exclusion of hypnotism gives Canetti's game away. The hypnotic model, without which late crowd theory could hardly be said to exist at all, is the psychiatric disguise in which an implicitly Hobbesian assumption about power appeared in the theory of the crowd. In banishing it, Canetti banishes the most authoritarian of all psychological crowd models.

When Canetti does draw eventually on the world of psychiatric medicine, he recruits from it a hero of the resistance to command, the schizophrenic, to replace the victim of command, the hypnotized subject. Command is a 'sting'; it is always alien, something which implies aggression from the outside; stings leave their barbs behind, and men would naturally get rid of them if they could. There is nothing in this of the implied complicity between hypnotist leader and subject, none of the 'rehearsal', practice-makes-perfect, it-gets-easier-as-you-go-along undertones of hypnotism, in Canetti's account of command. The stings of command 'accumulate'; they become more painful the greater their number; in two particular cases, the soldier and the schizophrenic, accumulated stings of command become the major determinants of personality, though the soldier and the schizophrenic cope with command in different ways, the soldier by obedience, the schizophrenic by resistance. Accumulation of stings of command is called discipline in military life: 'in a soldier, these stings must accumulate to a monstrous degree because each command he carries out – and they are innumerable – leaves a sting behind in him' (*CP*, p. 315). The soldier lives in 'constant expectation of commands' (*zu Befehl*), hence Prussian 'rigidity'. The only way open to a soldier to rid himself of his stings of command short of mutiny is by promotion; then he gives the orders. The duplication of the situation is almost uncanny; it is as though it had been invented for the needs of his stings of command. He strikes others with what formerly struck him (*CP*, pp. 315–16).

All of us carry 'a multitude of stings'. Their persistence is remarkable: 'nothing sinks so deep into human beings and nothing is so indissoluble'. In extreme cases, as in schizophrenia, a man 'can become so completely riddled with them . . . and except for them can feel nothing . . . defence against new commands becomes a matter of life and death'. The subject tries not to hear new commands, or refuses to understand them, or if he is made to understand them he flagrantly evades them by doing the opposite of what he is told to do. This evasion of command is called *negativism* in the literature on schizophrenia. This isolation of the schizophrenic from commands contrasts strongly with his other typical state where he exhibits 'suggestion-slavery' in which he exaggerates his performance of whatever is asked of him in a manner which often appears ridiculous. Canetti thinks that 'normal' people (the italics are his) exhibit these contrasting attitudes. The soldier on duty, for instance, is in an 'artificial state of negativism'; he will let nothing tempt him from his post, but 'on his superior's command . . . he can be turned from a state of negativism into behaving in a manner as officiously compliant as the schizophrenic in *his* alternative state' (*CP*, pp. 322–3). The schizophrenic is cunning. He either negates commands or, in his alternative state of extreme suggestibility, acts as a member of a crowd would. It is only the fact that psychiatric medicine confronts the schizophrenic in isolation which stops us from realizing that, from his own point of view, the schizophrenic may feel as though he were in a crowd: 'He is a fragment broken from a crowd' (*CP*, p. 324).

It is only after he has completed his account of the schizophrenic's double evasion of commands, through negativism and through imagining himself part of a crowd, that Canetti begins to make clear why he has spent so much time on it. He reminds us that right at the beginning of his theory of crowds he had said that in crowds men lose 'the burdens of distance', and he now adds that 'part of these burdens of distance is made up of the stings of command accumulated in every individual' (*CP*, p. 324). In the crowd nobody commands by right, and in the crowd no new stings of command are formed but all the old ones are got rid of for the time being. Like the ordinary man in the crowd, the schizophrenic does not feel his stings because he has the illusion of being in a crowd and because he has a sense of being linked to others again. No one 'is more in need of the crowd than the schizophrenic, who is crammed with stings and feels suffocated by them. He cannot find the crowd outside and so he surrenders to one within him' (*CP*, pp. 323–4).

Canetti's view of the crowd as an escape from command stops the received crowd tradition in its tracks. Canetti's schizophrenic implicitly struggles with the hypnotized subject for the crowd's resistance to command, and for its equality. Suggestibility (Canetti scrupulously avoids the word 'hypnosis') appears in *Crowds and Power* only as an aspect of schizophrenia, and is denied all independent existence. We begin to realize that close attendance to the italics in the passage from *The Conscience of Words* where Canetti describes his own crowd in his student days (quoted above, p. 294–5) might have given the whole game away: 'the workers . . . were acting *without* their leaders on that day'.

Canetti's own classification of crowds can also be seen as an implicit attack on another of the main facets of the crowd theory tradition as exemplified by Le Bon. Le Bon's critics never tired of pointing out that Le Bon stretched the category 'crowd' much too wide and it was pointed out in Chapter 7 above that Le Bon did this deliberately to frighten his readers into buying *The Crowd* and with it the elitist ideology which Le Bon was also trying to sell. On the face of it, Canetti might seem to be doing the same thing in his very comprehensive typology of crowds, and, like Le Bon, Canetti believes that the most important events in 'our modern civilization' are crowd events (*CP*, p. 183); again like Le Bon, Canetti realizes that the spectacular modern increase in population and in the size of cities has 'more and more often' given rise to the formation of the crowd; the crowd now forces itself on political and theoretical attention, while in the past it was 'never taken quite seriously' (*CP*, p. 21). What, then, is the difference between Le Bon and Canetti? Canetti's procedure is in fact the reverse of Le Bon's. Le Bon begins with the most frightening contemporary crowd he can find and proceeds to hunt down that same crowd in history to show that the crowd is always the same. The crowd is always atavistic, no matter what historical period it makes its appearance in; even in the remote past, the crowd was still a throw-back, and the only difference now is that in the modern world the atavistic crowd appears more often. What Le Bon's critics never saw clearly enough was that in stretching the crowd net very wide, Le Bon actually kept the category 'crowd' constant and found the *same* crowd everywhere. Canetti's procedure is the reverse; he offers a highly differentiated classification of crowds as a universal history of man out of which modern crowds *emerge* as types for which precedents exist, but they do not have to be the *same* crowds as crowds of the past, so they do not have to be throw-backs.

Canetti's classification of crowds works like this: all crowds have four essential attributes: growth, equality, density and direction; there are four opposed pairs of types of crowd: *open* and *closed* crowds, *rhythmic* and *stagnating* crowds, *slow* and *quick* crowds, and *visible* and *invisible* crowds; and there are five types of emotional content available to crowds, producing five different types of crowd depending on which type of emotion predominates: *baiting, prohibition, reversal, feast* and *double* crowds. This classification is meant to be complete in a sense that is recognizably Aristotelian, because crowds, like states in Aristotle's classification of them, rarely exist in their pure forms. Crowds are never likely to be completely open or completely closed, entirely visible or entirely invisible, and the volatility of crowds means that they can easily swing from one emotion to another. Canetti's classification of crowds produces 280 different types of crowd if they are classified according to pure forms and purity of emotional content alone. When the possibilities of impure emotional contents are added, as in a theatre audience which can cover the whole range of emotional content during a single performance (*CP*, p. 40), the number of possible different types of crowds becomes so large that it is advisable to use a calculator to find it. It is not necessary to follow the arithmetical implications of Canetti's system of classification in detail. Canetti himself does not play mathematical games with it and is content for us simply to grasp what the numerical possibilities of different types of crowd are. He guides us through the typology to the revolutionary, war and inflation crowds which really interest him, but he does mean us to take seriously the classification's claim to being comprehensive.

It is obvious that Canetti takes the differences between types of crowds much more seriously than any of his predecessors, and by the time his classification of crowds is complete we begin to understand that, in Canetti's title *Crowds and Power*, 'crowds' in the plural is meant to show up the absurdity of the singular in Le Bon's *The Crowd*. In Canetti, crowds are scrupulously differentiated in a way which would have been literally unthinkable for those who worked within the evolutionary–atavistic perspective. (Even Tarde, the least evolutionist of crowd thinkers, who distinguished between crowds and more civilized 'publics', hardly differentiated when compared with Canetti. Sighele, who thought even crime might 'evolve' (more brain, less brawn), none the less came to admire the crowd of proletarian nationalism because it remained primitive, therefore heroic.) Canetti's differentiated crowds show the absurdity of the Le Bon equation: the crowd = the mob = the masses = the end of any civilization, and when that equation is shown to be false, much of the ideological plausibility of Le Bon's view of the crowd and its place in history is shown up for the rhetoric that it is.

What, then, is to *replace* the evolutionist–atavistic hypothesis? What is the connection between crowds past and present? Canetti's answer is simple: man, from his earliest beginnings, *wanted* to be a crowd; only the smallness of his numbers when he lived in packs has obscured the simple truth that man always wanted '*to be more*' (*CP*, p. 107). This wanting to be more is how Canetti thinks 'he really became man' (*CP*, p. 108). The pack must always have felt the dangers of its smallness; the original form of pack, the *hunting* pack, and its extension, the *war* pack, arose from vulnerability; out of these comes the *lamenting* pack to cope with the fact of death; these were the 'simplest' forms of the pack, 'central' to the existence of primitive peoples (*CP*, pp. 94–107). *Increase* packs are 'more complex'; 'In the enormously long period of time during which he lived in small groups, [man] as it were, incorporated into himself, *by transformation*, all the animals he knew. It was through the development of transformation that he really became man; it was his specific gift and pleasure' (*CP*, p. 108). Canetti's evidence for this process of transformation-increase comes from 'the secret of the totem' (his source is the anthropology of Australian aborigines): kangaroos always outnumbered man; the incorporation of the kangaroo in the totem feast increases the numbers of man; he desires *their* increase and at the same time desires his own: a tribe 'which consists of many totems has appropriated to itself the increase of them all' (*CP*, p. 110). Once this desire of the pack for increase has been fixed as a precise shape it 'can be cultivated as a tradition'; there is no reason why totems should always be animals: clouds, rain, wind, grass, burning grass, fire, sound, the sea and the stars are all to be found as totems among primitive people (*CP*, p. 110). These increase totems from anthropology become the *crowd symbols* of history. Crowd symbols are names given to 'collective units which do not consist of men but which are still felt to be crowds'; each of them comprehends 'some of the essential attributes of the crowd' and each 'recalls the crowd and stands as symbols for it in myth, dream, speech and song' (*CP*, p. 75). Canetti gives a list: fire, the sea, rain, rivers, forests, corn, wind, sand, heaps and treasure (*CP*, pp. 77–88), and treats them in a way which seems irritatingly oracular until we realize that these symbols form one of the two connecting links between the life of the pack and modern crowds.

Canetti is the first crowd theorist to take the mind of the crowd seriously, and to provide it with a content of its own. The crowd is not just seen from the outside *as* something – the crowd spreads 'like fire'. The crowd itself feels *as* something. This becomes clear in Canetti's chapter on national crowd symbols in the section 'The Crowd in History'. Nations, when they go to war, go *as* crowds and see themselves as crowd symbols. 'What they are fighting *for* is proclaimed often enough, but what they fight *as* is unknown' (*CP*, p. 169). Canetti then lists the 'concrete contents of their national claims, the real ideologies behind them': the English, when they go to war, see themselves as the sea, the Dutch as a dyke withstanding the sea, the Germans as a marching forest, the French as the crowd storming the Bastille, the Swiss as mountains, the Spaniards as a bullfighter ('Everyman is at once the knight who slays the bull and part of the crowd which acclaims him' (*CP*, p. 176)), and the Jews as the Exodus from Egypt (*CP*, pp. 171–9). Italy alone is denied any settled symbol of self-conception; 'all its cities are haunted by greater memories' and 'the crowd-buildings of ancient times stood there, empty'; St Peter's is full, but a rival. 'Fascism attempted what appeared the simplest solution, which was to dress up in the genuine antique costume', but the toga did not fit (it was too big), the *fasces* 'aroused only the hatred of those who were beaten' and 'fortunately for the Italians, the attempt to impose a false symbol on Italy was a failure' (*CP*, pp. 177–8).

Canetti's list contains no surprises, but in providing the crowd mind with a content he deals a final blow to the Le Bon tradition which had always insisted on the empty-mindedness of the crowd. The group mind which came miraculously into existence in the crowd to be manipulated by its leader was always a *new* mind in the sense that it *came* into existence, and it always waited to be filled by suggestion with any content that the leader wanted to fill it with. Ever since Enrico Ferri suggested to Sighele that the crowd was an exception to Spencer's law because the workings of its mind could not be explained in the terms of how its component individual minds worked, crowd theorists (Tarde is the exception) in the evolutionist tradition had decided that this new mind was also the oldest of all minds because the only way they could explain how it came to exist *at all* (*ex nihil nihilo*) was to say that it had *always* existed. The very fact that the group mind was undifferentiated *proved* that its mind must be very low down on the evolutionary scale. Of course, as a mind it could not be *entirely* empty, because evolution does not square easily with the *tabula rasa*, so whatever it did contain was bound to be very primitive and, by implication very nasty, or at least, not very advanced, where advanced is a synonym for civilized. Hence the great leaps across whole millennia of the atavistic theory of the crowd; centuries' worth of the 'bank and capital of nations' (the phrase is Burke's, but it fits) could be wiped out or set at a discount whenever the crowd foregathered and reproduced the original of all minds. There was always something silly about that way of looking at the crowd, but great efforts, and successful efforts too, were made to cover up its fundamental implausibility. But if the mind of the crowd has a content whose genealogy can be traced as Canetti thinks it can through crowd symbolism and totemism, through historical times to the earliest life of the pack straining itself psychically to turn itself into a crowd, then the way is clear to saying *both* that the mind of the crowd is very old *and* that the atavism theory of the crowd is nonsense. The empty single-mindedness of the crowd gives way to many crowds with many minds.

Of course, received crowd theory had not ignored national traditions, but it had put them in the opposite side of the balance from crowds. The crowd and national tradition came to be seen as opposites because the crowd was a mob only fit for destruction. Taine, for instance, follows Burke in seeing political institutions as the sole repository of inherited national wisdom, so that when the revolutionary crowd attacks institutions, it obliterates its own national past.[4] Tarde takes a similar line: societies alternate between periods where the spirit of crowd-imitation creates new fashion crazes, and periods where the calmer tradition-conscious spirit of the family and the corporation predominates. Le Bon follows the same line. In his early period (up to *The Psychology of Socialism*) he will allow only two determining categories of social explanation, race and crowd; by race he means national culture, which creates the organizing institutions in men's lives, and by crowd he means primal, undifferentiated barbarism; in periods of upheaval ('eras of crowds') the crowd mind wins over the spirit of the race, so that in 1914 the racial spirit has to be *put back* into the minds of the French masses from the outside if they are to defeat the Germans. Before Canetti, only Sighele and Hitler saw clearly that nationalism *is* the crowd's atavism.

The crowd crystal is the other, reinforcing, 'institutional' link between modern crowds and the ancient pack. The pack is a crowd crystal without a crowd. The pack cannot grow though 'its fiercest wish is *to be more*'; it is never big enough for the individual to lose himself in as completely as in a modern crowd because 'in the changing constellation of the pack . . . he will again and again find himself at its edge'. Not being a 'multitude', they 'have to make up in intensity what they lack in actual numbers' (*CP*, p. 93). Packs are 'very determined' (*CP*, p. 116); they can survive over 'tens of thousands of years' (*CP*, p. 94) by 'repetition'; by doing the same thing again and again the pack is always *there*, and it is this repetitiveness of their life 'which explains how they can still be made to play a part in more complex civilizations' (*CP*, p. 116). They survive as crowd crystals, whenever there is a need for the quick formation of crowds, though they can survive in their pure form as in English fox-hunting, and lynch mobs (*CP*, pp. 116–17). Canetti's crowd crystals are easily recognizable as Tardean corporations, and he gives the same obvious examples as Tarde, religious and military orders. Their 'historical permanence' makes them a *constant*; life outside the crystal does not count for them; unlike the crowd, the crowd crystal is 'all limits'; they can go on living for long periods without contact with the outside world; they are not 'restless', even in the midst of the crowd, and they lack 'all spontaneity' (*CP*, pp. 73–4). In the same way that the Tardean sect of the anarchists stalked the socialist movement in France at the end of the nineteenth century, Canetti's crowd crystal is the ancient pack lying in wait for its crowd in the twentieth.

In writing atavistic evolutionism out of the crowd's psychic and institutional genealogy from primitive times to the present day, Canetti at last frees the crowd from the absolute empire of Le Bon. With Le Bon out of the way (and Sighele's criminal crowd imprisoned in his bibliography), Canetti can allow the crowd a fresh start in his great classification of crowds, and as that classification of crowds unfolds, all the great crowds of the crowd theory tradition are assigned to their places. The crowd's four attributes, growth, equality, density and direction ('a crowd exists so long as it has an unattained goal' (*CP*, p. 29), exist in any crowd (*CP*, pp. 16–29). The destructiveness of the crowd 'which is often mentioned as its most conspicuous quality', but which is often only 'discussed and disapproved of' but 'never really explained', is not a fundamental crowd characteristic; it is a derivative of the crowd's desire for growth and for equality; it is not the fragility of objects which attracts crowd violence (the crowd is not brutal), but rather the noise of broken glass, which represents 'fresh life'; windows and doors are broken by the crowd as 'boundaries', obstacles to growth; houses are destroyed because the crowd fears it will be shut up again; 'To the crowd in its nakedness everything seems a Bastille'. The crowd loves especially to destroy 'representative images', the symbols of hierarchy and of its 'burdens of distance'; above all else, the crowd loves fire; as long as fire spreads, everything will join it; fire attracts crowds and fire itself is the most powerful of all 'crowd symbols'; after the fire, fire and the crowd die away (*CP*, pp. 19–21). With the crowd's famous 'criminality' dismissed, and the leaders of crowds ignored, Canetti goes on to divide crowds into types according to which of the four attributes predominates and according to how they manifest themselves. This produces three contrasting pairs: *open* and *closed* crowds; *rhythmic* and *stagnating* crowds; *slow* and *quick* crowds (*CP*, p. 30); Canetti later (*CP*, p. 42) adds a fourth pair, *visible* and *invisible* crowds, which will be of great importance when he comes to discuss power.

The *open crowd* is the natural crowd, and is what people ordinarily mean when they speak of a crowd; its goal is inside itself, 'the blackest spot where most people are gathered'; it is 'everywhere spontaneous', except for its 'innermost core', '5, 10 or 12 people' (the exact number does not matter to Canetti provided it is more than 1, for Canetti wants the natural crowd to be leaderless); the natural crowd recognizes no limits and suspects those who hide from it. Like all crowds, the open crowd *becomes* a crowd at the moment of *discharge*, when the differences (of rank, status and property) between men disappear; the equality which comes about when men shed these burdens of distance, which include the accumulated 'stings of command', is an illusion 'because eventually everyone returns to their normal workaday selves', but while the crowd is on the streets its equality is real. Only 'true conversion' leads men to give up their old terms of association; the true converts are the crowd crystals of the future (e.g. the monastic orders). The open crowd puts all its hopes on increase, and just as it originates, so it disappears (*CP*, p. 16). By contrast, the *closed crowd* hopes to survive by *repetition*; it accepts limits and desires to fill its own space; it loves its density, and its boundaries protect it 'from outside influence which could be hostile'; these boundaries prevent 'disorderly increase' and keep the closed crowd from *eruption*, the transition from the closed to the open crowd which sets the closed crowd on the path to increase in the place of repetition; eruption has typically taken the form of rebellion against 'traditional ceremonial' in the history of religions (Reformation), of which the most obvious modern example is Methodism. The history of Europe since the French Revolution has culminated in

a spate of such eruptions; they have engulfed even wars, for all wars are now mass wars. The crowd is no longer content with pious promises and conditionals. It wants to experience for itself the strongest possible feelings of its own animal force and passion and, as a means to this end, it will use whatever social pretexts and demands offer themselves.

(CP, pp. 17–22)

The difference between *rhythmic* and *stagnating* crowds refers to equality and density. The stagnating crowd 'lives for its discharge': the crowd waiting for a public execution, or for a concert to begin, or 'standing on Arafat' at the climax to the pilgrimage to Mecca ('the most impressive case')' or waiting for the Last Judgement, is a patient crowd (CP, pp. 35–9). It feels certain of its discharge and puts it off, and it requires a long period of density to prepare for it. The stagnating crowd begins with density and *reaches* equality; contrast the rhythmic crowd of the dance, where density and equality are there at the beginning; as in the haka of the Maoris, the rhythmic crowd ends only in physical exhaustion (CP, pp. 30, 32).

The distinction between the *slow* and the *quick* crowd refers exclusively to the goal of the crowd. Quick crowds, 'the political, sporting and warlike crowds' which 'form such an essential part of modern life' are conspicuous for their *direction*; these are impatient crowds, in contrast to the slow crowds of religion whose goal is heaven, or the crowds of pilgrims, whose goal is remote – heaven, Jerusalem, or a far-off country. We only see the 'tributaries' of the slow crowd which 'sees itself as permanent in a far distance' (CP, p. 30); no discharge is permitted in the slow crowd until the goal has been reached; the Children of Israel are a crowd as long as they believe in the Promised Land; we see the 'network of streams' of the pilgrimage to Mecca; the goal of the slow crowd can be 'invisible' – the Promised Land is unseen, and the slow crowd can be itself invisible – the pilgrims may not know each other (CP, pp. 39–41).

Canetti adds *visible* and *invisible* crowds to complete the typology of pairs. Crowds in the ordinary sense are visible, but they may not always be visible to a single glance. The important invisible crowd is the crowd of the dead. The idea of the crowd of the dead is found all over the world (in Africa, Siberia, among the Celts of Scotland, in Alaska, Valhalla, among Jews, in India) and is not confined to those societies we are pleased to call 'primitive' – witness the modern, invisible crowds of bacilli and spermatozoa. The 'serious thought' given to invisible crowds in the middle ages is shown in the attempts made to count the number of devils (variously computed at 44; 635; 569; 11 billion) (*CP*, pp. 42–71). The true significance of the crowd of the dead will not become apparent until Canetti comes to deal with survivors, political power, and mass destruction; the leader–survivor will above all else wish the crowd of the dead to grow.

The classification of crowds according to fundamental attributes and 'physical' characteristics says very little about the emotional content of crowds. The five types of the emotional content of crowds, *baiting, flight, prohibition, reversal,* and *double* crowds, 'make a very early appearance; their history is as old as that of humanity itself'; in two cases, baiting and flight crowds, the emotion is 'even older', because in baiting and flight crowds men experience their emotions as animals (*CP*, p. 48). The *baiting* crowd is the murderous crowd, a quick crowd which forms to kill; it is cowardly, being itself in no danger and always superior to its prey; ideally it looks for a single victim: 'A murder shared with many others, which is not only safe and permitted, but indeed recommended, is irresistible to the great majority of men' (*CP*, p. 49). The baiting crowd 'goes back to the most primitive dynamic unit known among men, the hunting pack' (*CP*, p. 50), and the hunting pack is still to be found in the baiting crowd's crystal. All forms of public execution are connected to the old practice of collective killing; the crucifixion crowd chose its own victim; medieval slow baiting crowds waited patiently for drawn-out executions to begin, but in revolutionary periods the impatient quick baiting crowd wants its executions speeded up; in the French Revolution the executioner took a pride in his rate of dispatch. *Flight* crowds are the most single-minded in the old Le Bon sense; the threat which puts it to flight makes no distinctions; all are equally affected, it is the quickest of all crowds, and it is also the quickest to disintegrate when its goal is reached, for example the Grand Army after the retreat from Moscow, or the flight from Paris in 1940 (*CP*, pp. 53–5). The *prohibition* crowd is *negative*; it obeys a sudden, self-imposed prohibition; the most obvious example is a workers' strike; its great moment, celebrated in workers' songs, is the standstill, the moment of discharge when all become equal (*CP*, pp. 55–6).

The *reversal* crowd is the revolutionary crowd; the execution of a king turns a baiting crowd into a reversal crowd: the right of execution which used to be his is now theirs (*CP*, p. 52). In *reversal* crowds the sheep find they have teeth and eat the wolves: 'Their numbers have to make up for the experience in viciousness which they lack' (CP, p. 58). Reversal crowds presuppose a stratified society, so the reversal crowd is the revolutionary crowd attempting to rid itself of its 'stings of command' (CP, pp. 58–9). Canetti is playful here in the deadly manner of Nietzsche's aphorisms: 'the French Revolution is usually considered to have begun with the storming of the Bastille. It actually began earlier with a massacre of hares' (CP, p. 59). He cites Camille Desmoulins (itself a name at the same time innocent-sounding and smelling of blood) on the slaughter of the royal hares by Breton peasants under the eyes of the game-wardens on the plain of St Germain. The lowest of the hierarchy of privilege are massacred first: 'Before they dare attack the wolves the sheep turn against hares' (CP, p. 59). Reversal proper happens at the storming of the Bastille. The Bastille crowd executed the Governor and his assistants, and also thieves; it killed some and spared others; the crowd thus showed that justice in its two aspects, punishment and mercy, had been taken over by the people. Reversal crowds form in the most diverse circumstances: in slave revolts, mutinies and race wars. Canetti is careful to distinguish between *quick baiting reversal* crowds and *slow open reversal* crowds in revolutions. Baiting crowds are on the 'surface' of revolutions; they hunt down single victims and kill them, with or without trial, and they quickly attain their goal. They are by no means the whole of revolution, which is the spread through a whole society of the reversal crowd as the people with its future in its own hands (CP, pp. 59–60). The quick reversal crowd is also to be found in religious revivalism, where the crowd revises its attitude to God's commands; the reversal is preceded by 'a kind of death' (everyone falls to the ground), then all rise reborn in God's obedience; the slow religious reversal crowd expects 'the last shall be first' only in heaven (CP, pp. 60–1). (The *feast* crowd is a prohibition crowd in reverse; it celebrates the removal of prohibitions on gastronomic and sexual self-indulgence; it is slow, dense and tedious (CP, pp. 62–3).)

The *double* crowd is one of the ways available in which the crowd can prolong its life. Often the *only* way a crowd can preserve itself is to exploit the existence of a second crowd to which it is related; thus they must both be roughly equal, otherwise the weaker will become a flight crowd. This *two-crowd structure*[5] takes the form of three pairs: men and women; the living and the dead; friend and foe. Only the last are normally thought of as opposing crowds, but anthropology produces examples of opposing crowds of men and women in the dance (CP, pp. 64–6), and of the conflict between the living and the dead in the rituals of death: the living do not give up one of their number easily, though the dead always prevail. The warrior crowd of the Amazons links the two-crowd structure of men and women with the really interesting case of double crowds in war (*CP*, pp. 66–7).

War crowds are Canetti's route to the politics of the twentieth century. His normal technique is the reverse of didactic, and he does not overburden his readers with modern instances. In his own way he plays Le Bon's game, but much more skilfully. Canetti knows that we are interested in the great crowd events of the twentieth century, the Great War, the rise of Nazism, the Second World War and the Holocaust, but in *Crowds and Power* he makes us wait (a slow crowd of readers waiting for its discharge), until he deals specifically with power to reveal his true originality as a theorist of crowds *as victims*. Canetti himself is a natural victim of the Holocaust, who somehow escaped; survival is the central theme of twentieth-century politics, and the natural survivors are the wielders of power. Crowds have always existed, but they are more easily available in the modern world as the scope for the exercise of power. In the past, it was difficult to mobilize subjects, and even the most frightened nineteenth-century crowd theorist never dreamt how easy it would be to mobilize the masses in the twentieth century and what the scale of the resultant carnage would be. Mob was the word for the crowd when it threatened civilized living; crowd was the word for the mob while it gathered its strength between riots; civilization was the word for what the crowd threatened; rule was the word for what kept the crowd from becoming a mob; riot or revolution the word for the mob's own life. Even when the crowd was seen to be manipulated by its leaders for their own ends, it was always typically concern for the victims of those ends, and not for the crowd itself, which predominated. (What compassion there was, was reserved for those hapless, mindless folk who had been easily led into collective crimes, against the better judgement they did not possess.) Canetti has to tread carefully here because the crowd has connived at all the twentieth century's great disasters. Canetti's crowd is mindful of itself, but it has never understood power; the price the crowd pays for the self-understanding which Canetti attributes to it is that the wielders of power have their own view of the crowd, which does not differ much from Caligula's when he wished that it had only one neck so he could chop it. Canetti packs two vocabularies into the language of the crowd; the crowd still looks for its own victims, and the crowd is itself a victim of the leader as survivor ('The moment of survival is the moment of power' (*CP*, p. 227).

The crowd begins to dig a pit for itself in war. Nations go to war as crowds conscious of themselves as national crowd symbols. The Germans went to war in the 'well-attested' euphoria of 1914 as a marching forest, and it was this crowd-feeling which provided Hitler with 'his decisive experience, the one moment at which he himself honestly became part of a crowd. He never forgot it and his whole subsequent career was devoted to the re-creation of this moment, but *from outside*' (*CP*, p. 181). War is 'astonishing' because the formation of belligerent crowds has not hitherto been satisfactorily explained. The usual explanation for war is defence: 'I can be killed, therefore I can kill this man'. Canetti thinks this is a sham. The purpose of war is killing; the aim is to 'transform a dangerous crowd of live adversaries into a heap of dead'; all wars are aggressive and the danger to oneself is a consequence of war, not a cause: 'I want to kill this or that man, therefore I can be killed'. Nor can wars be caused by the military; the soldierly character, being rigid, waits for command *in* war (see above, p. 300). Wars must therefore be caused by civilians and connived at by crowds. The secret of war is a crowd secret, and it is revealed by the suddenness of civilian clamour for war as an *eruption of two crowds*. Wars can be prolonged to provide a definite duration of life for the crowd; aggressive wars therefore satisfy two fundamental human desires, the desire to forestall one's own death by killing another, and the desire to act like a crowd (*CP*, pp. 67–72).[6]

It is this self-annihilating desire to survive others and to be part of a crowd which explains why Germany was not sick of war by 1918, and it also explains why Nazi propaganda was able to make so much out of the *Diktat* of Versailles. In the 'crowd structure' of Germany, the army as a marching forest was the crowd symbol of the nation; the army was a closed crowd through which conscription made sure that everyone passed; its crowd crystal, the Junkers, were its 'order of chivalry', or its 'hereditary orchestra, thoroughly familiar with the music with which it has to infect its audience'. The whole German people became an open crowd round this crowd crystal in 1914, and it led the nation to war. The terrible mistake of the Treaty of Versailles was that, by disbanding the closed crowd of the army, it caused the army to erupt into German society as a whole because 'Every closed crowd which is dissolved by force transforms itself into an open crowd to which it imparts all its own characteristics'. The Nazi Party replaced the Junkers by coming to the rescue of the army. The Party 'had no limits set to its recruitment from within the nation; every single German – man, woman or child, soldier or civilian – could become a National Socialist'. A civilian was probably more anxious to join if he had not been a soldier before because, by joining the party, he achieved 'participation in activities hitherto denied him'. The *Diktat* of Versailles did not mean defeat for Hitler, because defeat had simply not happened; Nazism was the 'undoing of Versailles' by putting Germans back in uniform (*CP*, pp. 179–83).

Hitler was also able to exploit the inflation as a crowd phenomenon, and to turn it to the service of the most notorious anti-semitism known to history. Routine nineteenth-century anti-semitism had contented itself with the proclamation of Jewish inferiority. Jews were somewhere *down there* with other races whose claim to humanity was inferior but never absolutely denied. Nazism's peculiarly murderous twist was to push Jews down so far on the scale of biological life that it became possible to deny that Jews were human at all. Canetti thinks that a period of rapid inflation is the ideal opportunity for the degradation of human beings; the fall of the Bastille was nothing to the French aristocracy compared to what the fall of the mark was to the Jews of Europe.

Inflation, Canetti thinks, is 'a crowd phenomenon in the strictest and most concrete sense of the word'; transformation is its 'concealed history': 'apart from wars and revolutions, there is nothing in our modern civilizations which compares in importance to it' (*CP*, p. 183). Populations and paper money are measured in millions ('The modern treasure is the million'). During inflation, 'The unit of money suddenly loses its identity. The crowd it is part of starts growing and, the larger it becomes, the smaller becomes the worth of each unit. The millions one always wanted are suddenly there in one's hand, but they are no longer millions in fact, but only in name' (*CP*, pp. 185–6). The process of sudden *increase* is what we call 'runaway' inflation; it has the character of a flight which seems to have no end because money can be devalued downwards to any depth; this is the same urge to rapid and unlimited growth which characterized the crowd, but here 'the growth negates itself; as the crowd grows, its units become weaker and weaker'. The identification of the individual with his mark is broken; it changes hourly, is no longer 'fixed and stable'; it becomes degraded, and he feels its degradation as his own; he is like the million he always wanted – he becomes nothing. All inflation can be called 'a witches' sabbath of devaluation' where men and their money 'have the strongest effects on each other'; the one stands for the other, men feeling as 'bad' as their money; 'together they are all at its mercy and all feel equally worthless' (*CP*, p. 186). The individual feels devalued in the *unit* of money, and the crowd feels devalued in the *million*. The equality felt by the crowd during inflation is no illusion. The 'inflation crowd' really does cancel out social distances; the wage-earner and the *rentier* are equally affected, and neither ever forgets his humiliation. The crowd looks round for a scapegoat, and finds the Jews, who alone now are 'on good terms with money', but traditional anti-semitism is no longer enough. What is now required is a dynamic process of humiliation – something must be treated in such a way that it becomes worth less and less, as the unit of money becomes devalued during the inflation. This process must be continued until its object is reduced to a state of utter worthlessness: 'Then one can throw it away like paper, or repulp it' (*CP*, pp. 186–8).

The degradation of Jews to the status of less than human is also the most obvious modern example of the ages-old corruption of power.

One of traditional crowd theory's unfulfilled promises was to provide a genuine psychopathology of power, and it is easy to see with hindsight that crowd theorists before Canetti failed to provide a convincing psychopathology of power because they were, by and large, conservatives, who wanted to see crowd leadership as a very special case of the dangers of political power, and to contrast it with the 'normal', institutionalized, power of civilized societies. Being antithetical to crowd power was what institutionalized power was *for*, so that before Canetti (the exception is Freud) there was a certain reluctance to generalize from models of crowd leadership to answer questions about why it is exactly that men want power, and what psychological forms that wanting takes. In this, as in so much else, crowd theory was hampered by the psychiatric models available to it, because so long as the hypnotherapist stood in for the leader of crowds, and the hypnotized subject stood in for the crowd, it was difficult to shake off the assumption that the leader of crowds was 'well' while the crowd itself was 'sick'. From there, it was the easiest of all steps to assume that the only difference between the medical practitioner and the leader of crowds, was that the doctor treated the patient in the patient's own interest for a fee, while the leader of crowds manipulated the crowd in his own interests for which the pay-off could range from the capture of state power, through profit from the crowd's crimes, to simple notoriety. There were hints that something more than this was going on between leaders and crowds, that the leaders which the crowd threw up were of a special type, nervously excitable perhaps, or in Tarde's treatment of Rousseau, actually mad, but the consensus seemed to be that these were special cases, and all the crowd theorists would have agreed with Le Bon that it was possible, at least in principle, to substitute other, perfectly 'normal', leaders for any leaders, however mad, that the crowd might find, unaided, for itself. The leader of crowds introduced from the outside could 'cure' the crowd madness in a sense that is stronger than mere analogy, and the simple truth is that in its compulsion to fit the crowd mind into a received psychiatric vocabulary, the madness of leaders fell by the wayside. The mental health of leaders was certainly not *improved* by contact with crowds, just as doctors, if they were not careful, might succumb to *folie à deux* – and all psychiatrists are a little mad, but there the matter rested.

Perhaps what happened in the crowd theory tradition can be made to stand for the history of political science in general. Apart from Plato's account of the tyrant's blood-lust, and certain elaborately coded passages in Machiavelli, it is hard to think of any major political thinker who takes seriously the question of why men want power and what goes on inside their heads when they want it. There is no lack of moralizing precept about the dangers of power, and of advice on how to prevent power's aggrandisement, and from Suetonius onwards there has been an abundance of horror stories about the quirks of tyrants as clues to public policy, but the consensus seems to be that power is an available human good like any other, though not everyone would go as far as Hobbes in assuming that any fool would grab at power if it came his way. When the crowd gets into the story of power at all, it typically gets in as the instrument by which power is grabbed. The anxiety of the ancient oligarchs on the lookout for the tyrants who would come to power on the backs of the crowd is still the anxiety of conservatives, quick to see the heirs of Caesar in too popular leaders, and looking round from time to time for a Caesar of their own. Canetti is less interested in the power which comes into its own with the crowd than in the power which *feeds* on the crowd. Neither of the two examples he gives of power-madness, Muhammad Tuglak, a fourteenth-century Sultan of Delhi, and Schreber, the celebrated paranoid schizophrenic memoirist, is a crowd leader. Muhammad Tuglak succeeded to the throne of his ancestors, and Schreber was a judge in a Dresden court before he went mad, so each exercised the least crowd-like power. So the question is: Why did Muhammad Tuglak or Schreber *need* crowds? And by extension, why did Hitler, whom Canetti invites us to see as a combination of Tuglak and Schreber, need the crowd *after* he came to power? Canetti's answer to that question takes us into the 'entrails' of power, and into a lunatic world in which the crowd becomes part of the *illness* of power. Canetti transfers the traditional 'madness of the crowd' into the wielder of power's own mind; Muhammad Tuglak is obsessed by crowds and Schreber's illness is caused by them; paranoid schizophrenia is an illness of power in which the crowd becomes the victim's victim. Power itself is the survivor's obsession to outlive the crowd, to be left in solitary contemplation of a crowd of the dead numbered in millions. Canetti's argument, baldly stated, can itself sound mad, but what is remarkable about it is the unhurried scrupulosity of its stages and the concreteness of its detail, so that by the time he has finished we come very close to being convinced that 'crowds in the head' are 'normal' in the wielders of power.

Canetti's treatment of power proceeds, like his treatment of crowds, from the fear of being touched. Seizure of another's body is power in the raw. Cannibals *incorporate* their captives to degrade them by turning them into excrement (CP, p. 209). Anyone who wants to rule men soon discovers the secret of degradation; he tries to degrade them to the status of animals, and the worse he treats them, the more he despises them; when they are of no more use to him 'he disposes of them as he does of his excrement, simply seeing to it that they do not poison the air of his house' (CP, p. 210). Degradation justifies power, but only surviving the deaths of others can make power satisfying.

Confronted with his victim, the killer feels a 'special kind of strength'; the heroism of heroes increases indiscriminately as they survive enemies and comrades. Satisfaction in survival can be achieved by proxy, as when rulers direct others in war (*CP*, pp. 227–9). Leaders always pretend they will be the first to die, but, like Josephus at the siege of Jotapata, they grow stronger with the death of each of their comrades, 'feeding on the deaths of those whom they have led, and living on with an enhanced sense of their own lives' (*CP*, pp. 234–42). 'Nobody knows what Napoleon's real feelings were during the retreat from Moscow' (*CP*, pp. 230–1). Despots are notoriously hostile to other survivors: Muhammad Tuglak was a messenger-killer (*CP*, p. 242) and the Zulu king Shaka would not be survived by a son (*CP*, p. 245).

Despots live only to command, and each command is either a sentence of death or carries with it the threat of death. 'Power discharges commands like a hail of arrows; those who are hit must surrender themselves. The command wounds them and also surrounds and guides them to the seat of power' (*CP*, pp. 303–5). Commands also 'recoil' on their originators, because not all the arrows of command hit their mark, and those which miss give rise to the Anxiety of Command because those who were aimed at threaten vengeance. With each escape from a death sentence paranoid anxiety increases, and a new dimension is added to the despot's need to dissemble. He already has to wear the mask of benevolence, and now he must hide the anxiety of recoil which, after a life-time, can suddenly manifest itself as madness, as with certain Roman emperors (*CP*, pp. 241, 308, 309).

Like Machiavelli's prince, Canetti's despot is always on stage. He must act his part, conceal his own 'inner malevolence', and control his anxiety; others must act their parts too, because the despot knows that there are always some who do not acknowledge him and regard themselves as his rivals (*CP*, p. 377). The despot's moment of greatest danger comes when he begins to believe in his own benevolence. He must deny himself the *transformation* into what he is pretending to be, and keep alive within himself his sense of hostility to others, or his guard is down (*CP*, pp. 370–3). The weapon the despot uses against others is The Power of Unmasking. He waits for the right moment 'to tear the mask from their faces' and behind it finds the 'malevolence he knows so well in himself'. Unmasking is the exact opposite of transformation: to the despot the wealth of appearances is suspect, and the power of unmasking enables him to make everybody the same. His sense of his own power depends on suppressing transformation in himself and controlling transformations in others. Only he can raise others up and put them down: 'a ruler wages continuous warfare against spontaneous and uncontrolled transformations'. The resemblance to paranoia is obvious; paranoiacs are notoriously clever at concealing their own disease (what psychiatrists call *dissimulation*), and their urge to unmask appearances and discover enemies 'becomes a kind of tyranny' (*CP*, p. 378).

The case of the paranoid ruler which Canetti cites (his source is the fourteenth-century Arab traveller, Ibn Batuta) is carefully chosen. Muhammad Tuglak is no Caligula. He has many excellent qualities. He was generous, cultured and learned, delighting in the conversation of philosophers whose dogmas 'had a powerful influence over him'; he was a pious Muslim, courageous in war, a prince of 'brilliant qualities'. But outside his door was 'the platform where the executioners sat'. Anyone approaching the palace 'would come first upon corpses'. His fear of his enemies led him to empty the capital (but he paid the full price for all the houses). One night he climbed to the roof of his palace and looked over Delhi 'where there was neither fire, nor smoke nor lamp, and said "Now my mind is tranquil and my wrath appeased"'. This was in only the second year of his reign. His main delusion was to bring the whole habitable world under his rule. It required colossal armies and more and more money; by pious sophistry he extended the number of capital crimes in the Koran: 'I punish the people because they have all at once become my enemies and opponents'. Muhammad Tuglak's is a mind 'dominated by four kinds of crowd: army, treasure, corpses and court (and with it his Capital)' (*CP*, 424–33).

Canetti knows that the report of a fourteenth-century traveller, however well informed, cannot let us far enough into the mind of Mohammad Tuglak for us to be able to say that the mind of Tuglak and the mind of Hitler are the same, but it is Hitler's mind that Canetti's whole treatment of power is intended to elucidate. The connecting link is the case of Schreber, whose *Memoirs of my Nervous Illness* (1903) give us a complete account of what goes on inside a paranoiac's head, and we are to assume that what went on inside Schreber's head also went on inside Tuglak's head, and in Hitler's. Schreber's confessions 'lay bare the inner process of power, though in a man who, fortunately, only possessed it in his delusions' (*CP*, p. 434). Like the case of Muhammad Tuglak ('the purest case of a paranoiac ruler' (*CP*, p. 433), the case of Schreber is carefully chosen. Schreber's delusions contain a system of politics 'of a disturbingly familiar kind' (*CP*, p. 443): the bitter winter of 1870–1 was a deliberate move on God's part to turn the Franco-Prussian War in the Germans' favour; the Germans therefore have now replaced the old Jews, the Russians and the Graeco-Romans as God's chosen people; the chosen people naturally have enemies who plot against them: Slavs, Jews and Catholics; therefore it is Protestant Germany which has been chosen and which is called upon to defend its 'racial honour'; in Schreber's view of it, it is by no means certain that the Germans are altogether up to the struggle; Schreber himself might become a 'Mongol Prince' to indicate that 'all the Aryan peoples had shown themselves unfitted to be pillars of God's realm'; the apocalyptic struggle would begin in the year 1894 (*CP*, pp. 445–7). (Schreber got the date wrong, and the role of Mongol Prince would fall to another.) Schreber's hostile crowds are increase crowds: 'No-one has a sharper eye for the attributes of the crowd than the paranoiac or the despot who – as will perhaps be more readily admitted now – are one and the same. But the only crowds which he (to indicate both with the same pronoun) is concerned with are those he wants to attack or rule; these all have the same features' (*CP*, p. 447); Schreber's Mongol Prince is Genghis Khan and he is fascinated by the Mongols' 'pyramids of skulls' (*CP*, p. 448).

The crowds which Schreber produces from his own head are crowds of diminished particles. As Schreber himself grows to fill the whole of time and space, and the 'great souls' like Goethe and Bismarck lose their identity, the hostile crowd of his enemies ('I could cite here the names of hundreds, if not thousands'), of other souls, of his subjects and even of the stars, grow *smaller*. Schreber the ruler's people do not just stand assembled around him, they *diminish*; their ruler's contempt is 'annihilating' (*CP*, pp. 435–40). This annihilated crowd is the point at which Canetti's treatment of crowds and his treatment of power meet. This is the crowd of the scope of power and the illness of power, which causes its leader to see everything outside himself, friend and enemy, as hostile. This hostility finally takes a biological form; the hostile crowd is a crowd of vermin. Canetti wants to explain what has become one of the central problems of the politics of the twentieth century: How did it come about that a whole people could be the target for genocide? What was it that turned the endemic anti-semitism of nineteenth-century Europe into a murderous microbiology which pushed Jews so far down the scale of biological life that 'the Jewish question' would become a matter of racial hygiene, social medicine, and finally a technical problem of vermin extermination in a scientifically based programme of public health? No doubt, the evolutionism which had been commonplace in social theory since the mid-century helped. They playing of the theme of social progress up the evolutionary scale that we find, for instance, in Espinas and Sighele, could be played just as easily back down the scale, as it was by crowd theorists looking for evolutionary causes of the crowd's barbarism, and images of crime and criminals as social antibodies were commonplace in the most scientifically advanced criminology. But something else was required to make the short, homicidal, and finally genocidal step from targeting groups as *carriers* of a lethal disease to targeting groups *as the bacilli* of a fatal disease.[7]

We have already seen what part Canetti thinks the flight crowd in runaway inflation played in the process of degradation when it transferred its sense of its own regressive degradation on to Jews as a way of preserving its own self-esteem (see above pp. 312–13), but that does not account for the part played by the paranoid leader of the crowd, for it is he who produces the crowd as vermin *from out of his own head* and transfers the idea to a real human group. Canetti is aware that this is a startling thesis, so he is very careful in marshalling the evidence to support it, and he calls the state of mind in which a man feels himself to be surrounded by tiny hostile creatures the 'Lilliput effect' to remind us that the idea at least is familiar enough to the averagely literate child.

The basis of the Lilliput effect is what Canetti calls *transformation*, the process by which a person transforms himself or others into something else; the tyrant guards against his own transformation into a benevolent despot while his contempt for his subjects transforms them into animals which he can use or dispose of at will. Transformation is the basis of slavery and of the tyrannical state: 'Once men had succeeded in collecting large numbers of slaves, as they collected animals in their herds, the foundations for the tyranny of the state were laid. Nor is there the slightest doubt that a ruler's desire to own a whole people like slaves or animals grows stronger as their numbers increase' (*CP*, p. 384). Metamorphosis, especially to escape danger, was a commonplace with the ancients whose categories of god, man and animal were notoriously unstable (*CP*, pp. 342–8), and it has remained a staple of folk-tales and children's stories. Canetti is especially interested in transformation which involves *increase*, and he finds its origins in the increase myths of Australian aborigines (his source is Strehlow's *Aranda Traditions*) in which an ancestor produces a living mass of the totem animals from his own body. This *self-increase* 'gives birth to crowds'; 'Every cell in the body of the original ancestor is either a living animal or a living human being' (Canetti, quoting Strehlow (*CP*, p. 353)). The increase crowd of the Aranda is friendly, unlike the swarms of vermin felt on the skin in *delirium tremens*; in cocaine delirium the crowd of microscopically small creatures 'has some resemblance to a dissociation of the body into its component cells' (*CP*, p. 362). Canetti's aristocrat of mental illness is the schizophrenic with *delirium tremens* (Bleuler, *Lehrbuch der Psychiatrie*, 1924): his crowds and crowd symbols – forests, rivers, oceans, droves of spirit figures, vast workshops of production, angelic choirs proclaiming him – 'scarcely [omit] any of the crowd phenomena we have discussed'; even the double war crowd makes its appearance as two armies fight each other with himself as the spoils of victory, or rather his dead body (*CP*, pp. 366–9). This sensation of being attacked by a 'numberless host of tiny aggressors' has become 'increasingly marked' in the course of human history; mosquitoes, locusts and ants have always been crowd symbols, and being buried alive in an ant-hill is an ancient punishment; now bacilli stand for the teeming millions, and modern man feels himself more 'isolated' than before. The Lilliput effect is

> one of the central myths in the history of human thought. Man easily persuaded himself to see as vermin everything which opposed him . . . the despot who reduces men to animals and only manages to rule them by regarding them as belonging to a lower state, reduces to vermin all who do not qualify even to be ruled and ends by destroying them by the million.
>
> (CP, p. 363)

There is no reason in principle to restrict the examination of the phenomenon of power to the cases where power is achieved, and there is every reason in practice to distrust the historians' accounts of power. A kind of collusion exists between the tyrants and their historians. The eulogists of power (some modern Indian historians of Muhammad Tuglak (CP, p. 434); the vindicators of Caesar's and Napoleon's 'passion to survive great crowds of fellow beings' (CP, p. 231)) have yielded to the fascination of the despots 'while honestly sifting the facts', and, by thinking themselves into an age, they have absorbed some of the fear that real contemporaries had for the ruthlessness of the power-wielders (the school of Dilthey, though Canetti does not name him). There is also a 'more noble motive', of which 'even great thinkers were not free' (presumably Hegel); they cannot admit that such large numbers of people died for nothing so they invent a historical 'meaning' for the heap of corpses, and so dignify what is really *shameful*: 'the crux is a private passion of the power-wielder'. The actual substance of this power is 'the desire massively to survive other people' (CW, pp. 21–2). When we admire 'greatness' we do no more than admire poor, solitary Schreber, the survivor in his own deluded universe, 'standing in an immense field of corpses'; it is not only as a paranoiac that he reveals himself here. 'To be the last man to remain alive is the deepest urge of every real seeker after power' (CP, p. 443).

'Paranoia is an *illness of power* in the most literal sense of the words.' What Schreber imagined, others have attained, and there is nothing far-fetched about this; all meat-eaters are in their own way successful ('here each of us is a king in a field of corpses'):

> A conscientious investigation of power must ignore success. We must look for its attributes and their perversions wherever they appear, and then compare them. A madman, helpless, outcast and despised, who drags out a twilight existence in some asylum, may, through the insights he procures us, prove more important than Hitler or Napoleon, illuminating for mankind its curse and its masters.
>
> (CP, p. 448)

The rulers of mankind are not *like* paranoiacs; rather paranoia and politics are the two forms that power can take; all rulers are rulers of crowds; some rulers come to power with the crowd, some rulers achieve power in other ways, and some rulers have to settle for the loneliness of delusion. The case of Hitler is simply the case of Muhammad Tuglak with Schreber's mind; Schreber's is the case of a power delusion 'which found only one adherent' (*CP*, p. 465).

Canetti's assertion of the essential sickness of great leaders is a far cry from the rather over-heated discussions of the leaders of crowds in late-nineteenth-century crowd theory, just as his own theory of crowds is much more sophisticated than the 'one-crowd' theory of his predecessors like Le Bon. What is remarkable about Canetti's treatment of the crowd is the sheer diversity of the types of crowd and crowd-like groups available to the leaders of crowds. In the Hitler case, the crowd crystal is the Party faithful; the Party at large was recruited from the open crowd which formed when the closed crowd of the army erupted into the nation after the Treaty of Versailles; the inflation divided Germany into two crowds, the degraded inflation flight crowd and the degraded crowd of Jews on to whom the inflation crowd transferred its own sense of the worthlessness it felt in the devaluation of its money; recruits to the party formed a closed crowd round the crowd crystal, an army by any other name; the degraded Jews became the crowd of hostile bacilli fit only for extermination; the *Wehrmacht* formed part of the double crowd structure of war; and all the time Hitler as the leader–survivor intended to survive even larger numbers than he had survived in the First World War. The crowds were all remarkable for their *increase*: more members of the Party; more millions in the Reich; more millions in the conquered territories; millions killed in the war; millions slaughtered in the Holocaust; million after ghastly million. What were the worries of nineteenth-century crowd theory compared with these?

Crowds are the consistency of Nazism. From the one moment when Hitler felt himself part of the crowd in the war euphoria of 1914 right to the end, when as Schreber's Mongol Prince, he determined that the German people were not going to survive *him*, the story of Hitler is the story of the crowd. After he came to power, Hitler still *needed* crowds. In the chapter on Hitler, it was argued that Hitler felt he had to present himself as the great leader of crowds which crowd theory had always predicted, to compensate for the rather squalid way he in fact came to power by intrigue. The crowd propaganda was not the instrument by which the leader came to power; rather it was designed to show the German people what *kind* of leader they had got. Canetti adds a much more sinister layer of duplicity: behind the propagandist crowd leader there lay the real leader of crowds, and his real crowd was the crowd of the dead. In his review of Speer's *Inside the Third Reich*, Canetti plays Procopius, linking the buildings Hitler planned to the secret life of the leader of crowds. Hitler planned to build massive amphitheatres, vast 'crowd containers' to outdo the Egyptians and the Romans in the impressiveness of his public architecture; his native city, Linz, was to be made bigger than the Vienna where he had been rejected; he had a 'superstitious veneration' for his own rise through the crowd (Canetti ignores the intrigue), and crowd containers were a way of making *his* crowd permanent, so that he could bequeath it to his successor, for even Hitler knew that eventually he would die. His Arch of Triumph was to be twice the size of Napoleon's, and on it were to be carried the names of the 1,800,000 war dead of the Great War, whom *he* had survived; it is *his* Arch of Triumph: 'The feeling for the crowd of the dead is decisive in Hitler. It is his *real* crowd' (*CW*, pp. 147–55).

It needs no emphasis that Canetti's message for mankind in the age of nuclear weapons is very bleak indeed. War as a means to the rapid increase of the ruled crowd of the living is now played out; the Germany of National Socialism was the scene of its final eruption in its primitive form. One can safely assume [Canetti was writing in 1960] that never again will war be waged for this purpose. The urge to increase now takes the form of increased production; the world is divided into several very large 'centres of increase', and capitalism and socialism now play the same game; they no longer want to destroy each other but to *surpass* each other; today, countries are more anxious to protect their productivity than their peoples. East and West are 'armed to the teeth and rivals for the moon', but war for increase is unthinkable on any rational consideration of the matter (*CP*, p. 466). War can, in fact, be replaced by other systems of double crowds; in ancient Rome, sport 'replaced war as a crowd phenomenon', and there is something of that in the televising of sport. War is dying, 'and its end could be predicted as imminent, but for the fact that we still have to reckon with the *survivor*' (*CP*, p. 467). The static, double crowd structure of nuclear confrontation leaves only the crowd of the dead as the means of increase; war as a means of rapid increase of the crowd of the living may be dead, but the survivor 'is not yet extinct'; few can look upon a survivor like Josephus 'without some feeling of disgust', but in other guises he has 'been glorified as a hero and obeyed as a ruler, but fundamentally he is always the same'. The Bomb means that a single individual can easily destroy mankind; he could survive 'more human beings than could generations of his predecessors'; 'Today there is only a moment between decision and effect, and, measured by our potentialities, Genghis Khan, Tamerlane and Hitler seem pitiful amateurs' (*CP*, pp. 467–8).

The pilers-up of heaps of corpses work by giving commands to executioners. History's butchers' assistants are not difficult to understand. In despotisms the executioner is the only contented man. The despot has his anxiety of command to contend with and his subjects quail in the expectation of commands, each one of which carries with it the threat of a sentence of death; these stings of command bite deep; commands accumulate, and the same command can find its mark in them from many different angles. To get rid of a sting of command, it is necessary for the circumstances of the original command to be repeated, but *in reverse*; at first, he who is struck by a command and carries it out (only the carrying out of a command leaves a sting) has an exact recollection of the original circumstances of the command, but with time, and the accumulation of stings, the 'original situation has become obscured'; he can no longer picture to himself what it was like; one meaning overlays another, and he cannot distinguish between stings; they feel like a single burden to him; he wants to get rid of it, but it is hopeless; 'Alone he is no longer capable of freeing himself from his burden' because it 'can no longer be broken up into its elements' (*CP*, pp. 327–8). Only the executioner is contented, because he is the only one who immediately passes on his own sting: 'It is important to be quite clear about this; official killers are contented in proportion as the commands they are given lead directly to death.' The warder who delivers up the victims is not so happy, but he survives the victim and so some of the prestige of the survivor accrues to him; besides 'He finds himself a wife, has children and leads a normal family life', and this compensates for the contentedness of the executor which is denied him (*CP*, pp. 330–1).

The butchers do not feel the least responsibility for what they have done. Men who act under orders are capable of the most appalling deeds; they will deny that they did them, and they can only with difficulty be made to admit that they *really* did them. This is not to be dismissed simply as the guilty denial which anyone accused of terrible crimes might make, for the denial is often persisted in in the teeth of the evidence. When that evidence becomes overwhelming, they 'search themselves for traces of the deed and cannot find them'. Otherwise they are perfectly ordinary and normal, capable of judging *their* actions; they would never kill, or torture; the life they lead afterwards really *is* another life. 'But for us it is no longer a riddle'; the sting of command is always alien; the more foreign it is to a man's own nature, the less it appears to be his; the sting is 'his permanent witness that it was not he himself who perpetrated a given wrong. He sees himself as its victim and thus has no feeling left for the real victim.' He may feel 'astonishment' that he was once so at the mercy of command, but even this stirring of insight is worthless, because it only comes when it is all over, and it relates only to the past. What has happened once can easily happen again, and they remain just as defenceless as before in the face of commands. Fortunately, few carry this to its logical conclusion – 'with them command becomes destiny and they make it their pride to surrender to it blindly, as though it were particularly manly to bind oneself' (*CP*, pp. 331–2).

So what are we to do in a world where the commands of the survivors could destroy mankind? Canetti answers: Resist commands! How is this to be done? Canetti answers that we must 'face command boldly and search for means to deprive it of its sting' (*CP*, p. 470). In the whole of *Crowds and Power* there are only three genuine resisters to command: the schizophrenic, the solitary, and the member of a *reversal* crowd. Of these, the schizophrenic is only half a resister, and 'creative solitude' which earns immortality for itself is, 'by definition', available only to a few (*CP*, p. 469). (And command is not necessarily absent from even that. Kien, the solitary scholar-hero of Canetti's novel *Auto-da-Fé*, gives orders to his books, and on one occasion turns them into a crowd by turning their spines inwards.) There are hints that it may be possible to learn how to evade command, or to 'stand against it and break its tyranny', so that the stings that man suffers 'become burrs which can be removed with a touch' (*CP*, p. 332), but we are never told how. That only leaves the *reversal* crowd.

We saw at the beginning of this chapter how careful Canetti is to avoid the 'psychology of the crowd', where that means using the traditional hypnotist/leader model of crowd leadership. He does this partly to break away from the Le Bon tradition, and partly to preserve the crowd as a refuge from commands. The distinction he draws between armies and crowds serves the same end: the soldier and the man in the crowd have different psychologies, whatever Le Bon or Freud might say. The crowd which forms for the specific purpose of getting rid of stings of command is the *reversal* crowd, which is the revolutionary crowd. It is not a pretty sight, and the baiting crowd operates on its surface, but the reversal crowd is the only means that a man has to rid himself of stings of command which have accumulated to the point where he cannot himself even distinguish between one sting and another; they are all the same to him, a burden which he would shed if only he knew how. Reversal must be exact; only precise repetition of the original circumstances of the command in *reverse* will do, and the reversal command must be carried out, because only commands which were themselves carried out leave stings. A reversal crowd unites 'to turn on some group of other people whom they see as the originators of all the commands which they have borne so long'. For soldiers, any officer will do; for workers, any employer; caste or class 'cease to be mere concepts and become reality' as all the members of each group 'act as equals': 'The lower class, which is in revolt, forms a single, cohesive crowd; the higher one, which is threatened and outnumbered and surrounded, forms a series of frightened packs, bent on flight'. The people attacked by the crowd present a number of possible targets for 'every individual sting'; none of the targets needs actually be the originator of the stings which are now reversed against them, but they 'stand for them', and they are treated as if they were. 'What the crowd experiences is clearest in the most concentrated case of this kind: when it is a single individual such as a king that the revolt is directed against'; the king is the 'ultimate source of all commands'. The crowd obliterates the distance between themselves and the king by forcing its way into the palace, and the process it begins does not stop: the process of getting rid of stings proceeds now there *is* a crowd: 'One must remember how much will have been done to these people to keep them obedient; how many stings they will have accumulated in them in the course of years.' The real threat which hung continually over their heads was death, so they kill the king. Not all revolts become revolutions, but 'For that period at any rate they were free of stings and so will look back to it with nostalgia' (*CP*, pp. 328–9).

The revolutionary crowd is back with a vengeance in Canetti, but he does not celebrate it in the way that Michelet did, or denigrate it like Taine and all those who followed him. There is some hope to be found in the fact that commands are unnatural and alien ('there is no man who does not turn against a command imposed on him from outside' and who does not reserve the 'right to vengeance and rebellion', the contented executioner always excepted), but the longevity of the stings of command in everyone (they lie buried, stored up 'for years and decades') means that Canetti erodes all revolutionary enthusiasm: 'the free man is not the man who rids himself of commands after he has received them, but the man who knows how to evade them. But the man who takes longest to rid himself of them, or who never achieves it, is undoubtedly the least free' (*CP*, p. 306). None the less Canetti does admit the likelihood that the process of getting rid of the accursed stings of command can be cumulative. He has none of that nineteenth-century pessimism, which reaches its depths in Freud, which would have us believe that the revolutionary crowd necessarily takes civilization downwards and downwards, with the possibility of ever climbing up again getting fainter and fainter with every step down on the evolutionary ladder.

Notes

1   The Seaburg/Continuum edition of Canetti is the standard edition in English (the dates of the original German publication are in brackets): *Crowds and*

Power (1960); *The Human Province* (1973); *The Conscience of Words* (1976); *The Tongue Set Free* (1977).

2 This makes towns liable to double-sieges in war: the enemy outside the walls and cholera inside. J. G. Farrell captures that sense of double-siege brilliantly in the triple-battle of his Indian Mutiny novel, *The Siege of Krishapur*: a collection of besieged English people are attacked by cholera and divide over the question of what causes it to spread, inhalation or drinking-water; the debate obsesses them, and they hardly notice when the siege is raised; the battle against cholera wins.

3 In *Leviathan*, Hobbes does not mention any special qualities which would attract attention to a potential Sovereign in the State of Nature; there is no princely man in Machiavelli's sense. Hobbes appears to think that any man on'whom the choice fell would do as a Sovereign, and that any man chosen would accept. Perhaps Hobbes thought that, just as any man could become part of the crowd, so any man could become the crowd's leader. This, if it is true, is a startling proposition, reassuring in 1651 neither to a Sovereign-to-be, like Charles II, nor to a Sovereign-in-place, like Cromwell. Much clearly needs to be done on Hobbes as a crowd thinker.

4 It is eloquent testimony to the success of Burke's *Reflections* that the antithesis between 'revolution' and 'tradition' has lasted for so long, and that despite the fact that the phrase 'revolutionary tradition' has almost, but not quite, entered the language. Part II of Paine's *Rights of Man* shows how traditional (in the sense of accumulated) revolutionary demands can be; they do not come out of a new crowd mind, or 'out of the air'.

5 This may appear to be jargon. *Crowds and Power* is remarkably jargon-free, and we do well to remember that 'structure' was still a respectable English word in 1960.

6 Nietzsche's aphorism 'The deadly but true nihilism of Darwin' captures the sense of Canetti's idea of survival: for the fit to survive, the unfit have to *perish*; an echo of that sense remains in American Social Darwinism: 'It's not enough to win; somebody has to *lose*'.

7 *Mein Kampf* (especially pp. 230–4, on syphilis) should be required reading for those who use the language of moral 'health' in the discussion of social problems connected with the spread of a disease, and it contains much useful instruction for those who are inclined to proceed from observations about the incidence of disease, like AIDS, to making recommendations about policy in matters of public health.

AFTERWORD:
Safety from Numbers

Canetti's *Crowds and Power* is aptly named because the whole crowd theory tradition accepts that there is a connection worth exploring between the crowd and the structure and exercise of political power. The crowd is never a simple throng; something else is always going on in the crowd. That something else is almost always regarded as being sinister, which is why the initial human response to the crowd is nearly always fear and why the initial theoretical response is nearly always contempt. Yet the crowd has notable champions in Machiavelli, Michelet, Sighele, Sorel, Hitler and Canetti. How can this be, if they saw the same thing that the anti-crowd theorists saw when they saw the crowd? The easy answer to that question is to say that they saw different crowds, or that they saw different aspects of the same crowds, but that will not do because the great connecting theme of crowd theory is the belief of almost all crowd theorists that they were in fact talking about the same thing. The tradition of crowd theory is extremely self-conscious of itself as a tradition. Its internal debates are meticulous even when mud is being slung, and the fact Le Bon could summarize the tradition in glib formulas shows that there was considerable agreement about which crowds mattered and what the problems of crowd theory were. Another simple answer to the question of why the crowd divides its theorists for and against is to say that theorists brought different judgements of value to the crowds which they treated, but that will not do either, because no crowd theorist really likes the crowd, and by 1900 it had dawned on crowd thinkers that the crowd is everybody, so that the idea of *bringing* judgements of value to bear on the crowd is by no means a simple one. There is no *them* to which *we* can apply our judgements. We may judge the crowd part of ourselves by another part, our unreason by our reason, our darkness by our enlightenment, but that is an exercise fraught with difficulty, acutely vulnerable to straightforward objections of the kind ordinarily associated with the untrustworthiness of introspection. How can we know which part of us is which?

327

The real dividing line between crowd theorists is a particular attitude to the crowd's violence, or rather a particular attitude to the connection between crowd violence and social order. If the crowd is seen only as the random, casual source of violence in a society, intermittent though always a possibility, then the crowd can be treated as an exaggerated case of criminality. Crime in the ordinary sense can be frightening, so that the crimes of crowds are more frightening because the scale of their crimes is larger. That would be true even in societies where neither the prevention nor the punishment of crime were very efficient, and these would be the societies in which one would expect ways to be found for accommodating the crowd, as medieval societies did. These would be the kinds of society whose attitude to violence, from a progressive, nineteenth-century point of view, would appear to be primitive in the sense that there would be a widespread acceptance of violence in the ordinary course of life. Violence would be unremarkable in the relationships between superiors and inferiors, and violence would have to be very remarkable indeed where it was the deterrent violence of public executions or war. In societies like these, it would be very difficult to see violence and public order as the clear antitheses on which so much of late-nineteenth- and twentieth-century crowd theory was based.

So what was it that made that antithesis: violence/order possible? In part, the answer clearly lies in the invention of the modern State, which, by claiming to monopolize all legitimate violence, attempted for the first time to distinguish between legitimate and illegitimate violence, with the State also claiming for itself the right to say what was legitimate violence and what was not. At least in principle, every violent act which took place in a modern State was the authorized violence of an agent of the State, was permitted or not forbidden by the State, or was a crime. Of course, this was a view which took time to make itself felt even in the most modern of the modernizing States; it was a programme rather than an accomplished fact, and in practice there was bound to be a very wide toleration of older practices, but a process occurred by which tolerated acts of private violence came increasingly to be seen as private in a sense not available before. Hence the distinction between violence which was orderly and violence which threatened order.

That distinction was still frank in its acceptance of the necessity for violence, and that acceptance was based until well on into the nineteenth century on versions of the doctrine of original sin. Recourse to violence in pursuit of sinful ends was a permanent part of the nature of fallen man; the State's violence was regrettable too, but it was better than private violence because, being lawful, it served the godly end of social peace; and even wars could be just.

The evolutionist perspective did not differ very much in its view of violence from the old Augustinian doctrine, and it is easy to see why there could not have been much of a conflict on the level of social theory between Christianity and the pessimistic Darwinism of crowd theory. Both stressed the primacy of events as distant in the collective past as it was possible to be. No doubt, the myth of Eden could not really compete with evolutionary time-scales in the race for antiquity, but no very great effort of mental gymnastics was required to transfer belief from the one theory of the primacy of origins to the other. When a crowd theorist asked his readers to see long inherited animal passions at work when a mob was on the loose and recruited criminals from the goals, it took no imagination at all to remember that the crowd in Jerusalem had freed Barabbas. Crowd theory showed above everything else just how double-edged evolutionism was as the basis for social theory. The crowd was at the same time very modern and very ancient, and the more crowd theory advanced its claims to be the social theory of the modern world, the more problematic modernity's own claim to be progressive became. The crowd was the great blot on the progressive landscape, and there was no covering up the fact.

It was unfortunate for democracy that crowd theory and the extension of the franchise happened at the same time. There was something indecent in the haste with which crowd theory became part of the anti-democratic argument almost before democracy became an accomplished fact. Crowd theory had been lying in wait for democracy ever since the storming of the Bastille. Any view of the modern world which emphasized the importance of the French Revolution was at least implicitly a crowd view, and the easiest of all antitheses was the one between the Age of Reason and the barbarism of the revolutionary crowd. Modernity began in riot, only to be told by crowd theory that it was not modernity at all. All popular sovereignty came to be seen as psychologically equivalent to the mob, and when the mob itself came to be seen not as a physical threat but rather as a particularly irrational and regressive mental set, then it was easy to begin to see elections as a form of psychic riot. Mature crowd theory added its own twist to the story by asserting that it did not matter who the electors were; just being an electorate was enough to make it into an electoral crowd. Earlier crowd theory had tended to equate the crowd mentality with the class consciousness of the lower orders, but as time went on it became increasingly difficult to square that elitism with the realization that crowd consciousness was no respecter of persons. Class consciousness was always one form which the crowd mentality could assume, but it became absurd to argue that one form of class consciousness was superior to another when the formative

329

psychological mechanisms of group consciousness were the same in everybody. Suspicion of all collectivities seemed to be the obvious moral to be drawn from crowd theory, but it was a suspicion which was not able to be balanced by any real faith in the individual. All crowd theorists believed that individualism was a cause of the crowd, and it could hardly be the crowd's antidote as well. Modern crowds came out of atomized societies where individualism meant the lowest common denominator of sameness which remained after the weakening of traditional group and institutional loyalties, and it was that sameness which was at the root of the irrational group mind of the crowd. The more evolutionarily minded crowd theorists even doubted if there was, properly speaking, such a thing as a human individual, preferring to believe that man was an interim aggregate between the true individual, the cell, and the wider aggregate of a whole society. From that point of view, a whole society had just as much right to call itself an individual as a single man.

So where was there that was safe from the crowd? In crowd theory's own terms, there was nowhere, because, before Canetti, crowd theory's emphasis was always on *the* crowd, and the success of crowd theory seemed to depend on its ability to show that the crowd was a universal category which applied to the hypnotic group of two at one end of the scale and to all of us at the other. There was always something gleefully self-destructive about crowd theory in the grand manner, a delight in showing just how crowd-like cherished institutions and practices really were. There were human collectivities which were less crowd-like than others, sects, corporations of all kinds, conspiracies, any group which was hierarchically organized and which had strict criteria for membership, but the problem here was that groups like these were often either wicked, like the Mafia and the anarchists, or frankly reactionary, like the Jesuits or the Prussian General Staff. There was in fact a good deal of nostalgia for the corporations of the *ancien régime*, hence the bitter enlightened irony of Freud's argument in *Group Psychology* that churches and armies are more completely crowd-like than the chance crowds of great riots. For those prepared to take crowd theory seriously, the choice was stark, because on the one hand there was the enormous weight of the tradition which proclaimed that the crowd was a threat to everything that civilization was supposed to stand for, and on the other hand there was the unmistakable implication that anyone who stood apart from the crowd was liable to become one of the crowd's victims. The crowd was itself unsafe, but it was also unsafe to be left outside the crowd; that choice was at its starkest in the politics of facism. Nineteenth-century crowd theory had toyed with the idea that crowd leaders could be found who would keep their distance from the crowd's own tarnished soul, but there was never any very clear idea about where those leaders were to come from, and it was always more likely that the crowd's leaders were going to be those morbidly excitable, half-mad, manipulating types which crowd theory had been warning against for so long. And so it proved.

Or did it? There is a great danger in using an age's own social theory to explain that age's politics and to say that what crowd theory predicted actually happened. It would be odd, to say the least, if that were true of crowd theory when social theory in general is a notoriously bad predicter, and the Hitler case, where a deliberate attempt was made to show that crowd theory *had* come true, is enough to raise doubts. My guess is that, by the 1930s, thinking in the style of crowd theory had become so commonplace that almost anything that could have happened could be explained in crowd theory terms. More than that, I would say that the form crowd theory had inherited from before the Great War was a victim of its own theoretical success. Its concerns had taken it so far from the 'real' crowds of the French Revolution that it was no longer very clear exactly what the crowd was that was being talked about. Crowd theory paid the price of its own theoretical ambition to become a theory of all human groups. It had really become a matter of numbers, the faceless crowd of mass society which could never be a 'real' crowd until parts of it were energized by a leader. This 'real' energized crowd was the crowd with which the orderly crowd of a parliamentary electorate could never compete, though the electoral crowd might be a substitute for it when nothing very fundamental was at issue and when feeling did not run high. Without realizing it, crowd theory returned to something like the form it took before the French Revolution, when, with notable exceptions, it was a vehicle for loading contempt on the generality of mankind. The crowd became everybody again, and a destructive mob was what we would all become if given the chance by unmindful authority. Faint echoes of a more ancient view of the crowd, which would have been familiar to Machiavelli and Montesquieu, continued to be heard from the modern State's conscript armies when they returned from the wars, or when they mutinied towards war's end, becoming Livy's crowd in modern dress.

Now that it has been demobilized and disarmed, possesses democratic rights, and has access to a modest affluence, it is hard, Canetti apart, to see what the moral case for the crowd in the West now is, except perhaps in emergencies. Those emergencies have changed their nature. The crowd is no longer called in to save the State, or to advance the cause of opposition, or to restore the vitality of a decaying civilization. If there is a permitted crowd, it is the crowd which is called upon to confront the State's own violence, or the institutionalized forms which violence takes in Western societies, the civil rights crowd, or the crowds of anti-Vietnam protest, or the crowds of nuclear disarmament. These crowds are the anti-violent crowds of the milder forms of civil disobedience, caught between a lawful acceptance of the State's monopoly of violence in principle, and an abhorrence of some of the forms which that violence takes in practice. These crowds are suspicious of leadership, though they have had notable leaders, and they are reluctant to place their leaders in positions of power which are analogous to the State's own positions of power, preferring stewards, marshals and chairmen. Crowd theory explains why this should be so. The last thing these crowds want to be is crowds in crowd theory's traditional conception of them. They do not want to go down the road of regressive barbarism at the command of leaders because they see the State's own leaders taking that same road – witness the threat of nuclear holocaust which would excite the envy of Tamerlane or Genghis Khan. The anti-violent crowd turns the tables on crowd theory by making *us* the repository of social and human peace and by making *them*, the legitimate forces of order and defence, the threat to peace. It is the traditional antitheses reversed; *they* are no longer the *we* which they once were, that which has to be protected from the crowd; *they* are the crowd and *we* need protection against them.

There is nothing far-fetched about this, nothing anarchistical, no quasi-Marxist inversion of subject and object. Rather, it comes naturally out of orthodox crowd theory itself, one of whose central insights it is that the more perfect a crowd becomes, the more it comes to resemble an army. Le Bon was perhaps the first to understand that properly. The single-minded group, automatically obedient to a leader, unselfish and with a feeling of invulnerability and invincibility, ever on the lookout for an object to attack, violent in its essence, was the perfect image of a military unit at the charge. Patriot that he was, Le Bon put his discovery at the service of his country in the Great War. After that war, Freud drew out the implications of Le Bon's insight for all groups, arguing that armies and churches were the most primitive in his special sense, and certainly more primitive than unorganized crowds, because the psychic structure of armies and churches was the most primitive psychic structure that psychoanalysis could discover. For those prepared to believe it, that argument put paid to the most ancient image of order, where the disciplined force of an army confronts the disorderly force of the crowd. In Le Bon's and Freud's terms, crowd simply confronts crowd, and if it is the primitiveness of a crowd, where primitiveness means a compulsion to violence, which makes it an object of terror, then we should be more frightened of the army than of the crowd which that army confronts. (The same would also be true, though to a lesser degree, of the police.) In political terms, power confronts power, and that confrontation is a confrontation in a very exact sense. The power of the crowd is power in the raw, power that cannot be negotiated with, and therefore power which exists outside the normal power relations between groups in the society in which the crowd arises. The crowd is very difficult to make deals with, especially when it is suspicious of its own leaders. Established power looks for the crowd's leaders, and sighs with relief when the crowd has specific demands; established power waits for the crowd to go away and hopes to negotiate with its leaders, thereby turning the crowd into a constituency and socializing its leaders into the established power game whose rules are already fixed and in which established leaders are already adepts. Crowds know this, disperse with reluctance, and agree to meet again as much to keep tabs on their own leaders as to continue the struggle for the cause. Indeed, not having leaders in the traditional sense *is* the crowd's cause, because the anti-violent crowd assembles precisely because it thinks that traditional leaders are the trouble-makers, the ringleaders in violence's own conspiracy and the contemporary anarchists by the deed.

That impasse of crowd theory, in which the crowd of order and the crowd of disorder confront each other, is the starting point for Canetti's attempt in *Crowds and Power* to unravel the whole crowd theory tradition. Canetti realizes that, in the most developed form of crowd theory, 'crowd' has come to mean almost any group, so that the question: 'What is distinctive about the crowd?' has to be reformulated. Canetti attacks received crowd theory at the point it had reached when the realization had come that an army was just a particularly perfect form of crowd. Canetti never makes it clear exactly whose version of the army-as-crowd theory he is attacking, so we are to take it that he is attacking all the versions of that theory, and also the whole development of crowd theory which led up to it. When Canetti has finished constructing his very elaborate classification of crowds without giving any weight at all to the part played by leaders in the formation and behaviour of crowds, we begin to realize that he is intent on rehabilitating the crowd by showing that, appearances to the contrary, armies are not crowds, but their opposite. Armies are characterized by their rigid structures of command; crowds are self-commanded, the self-delusions of demagogues notwithstanding. To show this, Canetti has to overcome the awkwardness of the fact that the demagogue's pedigree is already two-and-a-half millennia old, not to mention the commonsensical fact that crowds do sometimes, if not always, have leaders. Add to that the fact that some of history's most lethal crowds have had particularly murderous leaders and we begin to see the dimensions of the theoretical and historical problem with which Canetti's revisionism presents him.

Canetti's route to the theoretical separation between the power of leaders and the crowd is implicitly anti-Hobbesian. The crowd is not to be thought of as the amalgamation of discrete, atomistic particles coming together by chance or choice to put power into the hands of a sovereign or a temporary king. By showing that the crowd is a refuge from command and also a way of undoing the psychological effects of command in individuals, Canetti is attempting to undermine the theory of the Caesarism of crowds which was already familiar to the nervous oligarchs of ancient Thebes. If Canetti is right, then the image of the crowd commanded by its Caesar, or, in a more recent idiom, manipulated by an elite, can never be an image of the State, ancient or modern. If Canetti is right about that, then it follows that most of the crowd theory tradition is an invitation to a false understanding of huge chunks of Western European politics from its very beginnings because the crowd could not have been what most crowd thinkers have said it is.

The question remains: If this is so, then how could it happen that the crowd has been so consistently misunderstood? The simple answer is in the ancient world the persuasiveness of Plato, with all the subsequent glosses on the Caesarist theme down to the end of antiquity and beyond, and in the modern world, the French Revolution's origins in riot. The crowd theory of the nineteenth century was mainly an attempt to explain how a riot had been allowed to get out of hand to usher in those aspects of modernity which some crowd thinkers applauded and others detested. The evolutionist dimension to crowd theory was the source of nearly everything that anti-crowd theorists feared. Evolutionism caught them in a double bind from which escape was very difficult, because evolutionism on the one hand taught that the crowd was the agent of regression to a primal barbarism, but on the other hand to be an evolutionist was to put oneself on the side of the very latest scientific and social thought. Just to be progressive as a social thinker seemed to involve thinking that there was one aspect of modernity, the crowd, which threatened all the others. As the category 'crowd' was spread wider to take in a very large number of social groups, it was easy to begin to doubt whether modernity was all that it was cracked up to be. From there it was a very short step indeed to begin to wonder whether in the future regression and not progress might be all that humanity had to look forward to, and it was no step at all to begin to see that the future was the crowd's, to jettison all the progressive baggage which had been the Enlightenment's gift to the nineteenth century, and to cash in on the crowd's promise to rejuvenate a decaying civilization with its rude barbarian energy.

The fear which still attends manifestations of the crowd, especially but not exclusively when the crowd is violent, shows that that perspective, or something very like it, is not yet dead. The fact is that crowds are capable of frightening societies which by pre-modern standards are models of social control, where officials stay at their desk and where armies and policemen are loyal and conscientious. Unless one is oneself directly threatened by a crowd, it is hard to see why one should be frightened, and frightened for the whole social order, unless one thinks of the crowd as the very thick end of a theoretical wedge which owes a great deal to the tradition of crowd theory. It was once said that the theory of mass society was the one social theory which every sociologist accepted, but it now appears that mass society theory has had its day. It may now be said that crowd theory has been the most tenacious of all the social theories which have been invented since the French Revolution raised the problem of how to achieve safety from numbers.

Bibliography

Aristotle, *The Politics*, ed. J. A. Sinclair (London, 1962).
The Augustan History, ed. Birley (London: Penguin, 1983).
Aulard, A., 'Taine, historien de la révolution française', *Revue d'Histoire Moderne et Contemporaine*, 50, i (1906), pp. 193–220.
Aulard, A., *Taine, historien de la révolution française* (Paris, 1907).
Bagehot, W. *Physics and Politics* (London, 1876).
Barker, E., *Political thought in England from Herbert Spencer to the Present Day* (London, 1915).
Barker, E. *Principles of Social and Political Theory* (Oxford, 1951).
Barrows, S. *Distorting Mirrors: Visions of the Crowd in Late Nineteenth Century France* (New Haven, Conn., 1981).
Becker, C. L. *The Declaration of Independence* (New York, 1922).
Beloff, M. *Public Order and Popular Disturbances, 1660–1714* (Oxford, 1938).
Berlin, I., *Vico and Herder* (London, 1980).
Bloch, J. S., *My Reminiscences* (Berlin and Vienna, 1923).
Bohn, G. *et al.*, *La Foule* (Paris, 1934).
Bonaparte, M. *et al.* (eds), *S. Freud, The Origins of Psycho-Analysis. Letters to Wilhelm Fliess, Drafts and Notes* (London, 1954).
Bosanquet, B., *The Philosophical Theory of the State* (London, 1899).
Bourget, *L'Action Française*, 3, 32, 1900.
Boutmy, E., 'La Jeunesse de Taine', *Revue Bleue*, 4th series, vol. XVIII, no. 9 (1902), pp. 257–64.
Brogan, H., *Longman History of the United States of America* (London and New York, 1985).
Brown, P., *Society and the Holy in Late Antiquity* (London, 1982).
Browning, R., 'The riot of AD 387 in Antioch', *Journal of Roman Studies*, vol. XIII (1952), pp. 23–30.
Brunt, P. A., 'The Roman mob', *Past and Present*, vol. 35 (1966), pp. 3–27.
Bullock, A., *Hitler: a Study in Tyranny* (London, 1962).
Burrow, J. W., *Evolution and Society* (Cambridge, 1966).
Bury, J. B., 'The Nika Riot', *Journal of Hellenic Studies*, vol. 27 (1897), pp. 90–119.
Cameron, A., *Porphyrius the Charioteer* (Oxford, 1976).
Cameron, A., *Circus Factions* (Oxford, 1976).
Cameron, A., 'Images of authority: elites and icons in late 6th century Byzantium', *Past and Present*, vol. 84 (1979), pp. 3–35.
Canetti, E., *Crowds and Power* (New York, 1978).
Canetti, E., *The Human Province* (New York, 1978).
Canetti, E., *The Conscience of Words* (New York, 1979).
Canetti, E., *Auto-da-Fé* (New York, 1982).
Canetti, E., *The Tongue Set Free* (New York, 1983).
Carlyle, T., *Sartor Resartus, Lectures on Heroes, Chartism and Past and Present* (London, 1888).

Carlyle, T., *The French Revolution*, 2 vols (London: Everyman, 1966).
Clark, T. N. (ed.), *Gabriel Tarde: On Communication and Social Influence* (Chicago, 1969).
Cobb, R., *The Police and the People: French Popular Protest, 1789–1820* (Oxford, 1970).
Cobban, A., *Aspects of the French Revolution* (New York, 1968).
Cohn, N. *The Pursuit of the Millennium* (London, 1970).
Conway, M., 'Is parliament a mere crowd?', *Nineteenth Century,* vol. LVII (June 1905), pp. 898–911.
Craddock, P. B. (ed.), *The English Essays of Edward Gibbon* (Oxford, 1972).
Crèvecoeur, J. H. St J. de, *Letters from an American Farmer* (London: Penguin, 1981).
Davis, M. M., *Psychological Interpretations of Society* (New York, 1909).
De Castro, J. P., *The Gordon Riots* (London, 1926).
Dickinson, H. T., *Liberty and Property* (London, 1977).
Dimier, L., *Les Maîtres de la contre-révolution au dix-neuvième siècle* (Paris, 1906).
Espinas, A., *Des Sociétés animales* (Paris, 1878).
Finley, M. I., 'Athenian demagogues', *Past and Present*, vol. 21 (1962), pp. 2–24.
Finley, M. I., *Democracy Ancient and Modern* (New Brunswick, NJ, 1973).
Freud, E. L. (ed.), *The Letters of Sigmund Freud, 1873–1939* (London, 1960).
Freud, M. *Sigmund Freud, Man and Father* (New York, 1958).
Freud, Sigmund, *The Standard Edition of the Complete Psychological Works of Sigmund Freud*, ed. Strachey *et al.*, 24 vols (London, 1952–66).
Geiger, R. L., 'Democracy and the crowd: the social history of an idea in France and Italy, 1890–1914', *Societas*, vol. 7, i (Winter, 1977), pp. 47–71.
Geyl, P., *Encounters in History* (London, 1963).
Gibaudan, R., *Les Idées sociales de Taine* (Paris, 1928).
Gibbon, Edward, *The Letters of Edward Gibbon*, ed. Norton, 3 vols (London, 1956).
Gibbon, Edward, *The Decline and Fall of the Roman Empire*, 6 vols (London: Everyman, 1960).
Giddens, A., *The Nation State and Violence* (Berkeley, Calif., 1985).
Giner, S., *Mass Society* (London, 1976).
Hamilton, A. *et al.*, *The Federalist Papers* (London: Everyman, 1961).
Hartz, L., *The Liberal Tradition in America* (New York, 1955).
Hibbert, C., *King Mob* (London, 1958).
Hitler, Adolf, *Mein Kampf*, (ed. D. C. Watt, London, 1969).
Horowitz, I. L., *Radicalism and the Revolt against Reason* (London, 1961).
Jefferson, Thomas, *Papers*, ed. Boyd, 19 vols (Princeton, N.J.: 1950–74).
Jones, A. H. M., *Athenian Democracy* (Oxford, 1957).
Jones, E., *Sigmund Freud: Life and Work*, 3 vols (London, 1953–7).
Keegan, J., *The Face of Battle* (London, 1976).
Kershaw, I., *The Nazi Dictatorship* (London, 1985).
Kornhauser, W., *The Politics of Mass Society* (London, 1960).
Le Bon, G., *The Crowd: a Study of the Popular Mind* (reprint of the second English edition) (Dunwoody, Georgia, n.d.).
Le Bon, G., *La Psychologie politique et la défense sociale* (Paris, 1910).
Le Bon, G. *The Psychology of Socialism*, ed. J. L. Stanley (New Brunswick and London, 1982).
Lefebvre, G., *La Naissance de l'historiographie moderne* (Paris, 1971).
Lindsay, A. D. (ed.), *The Socratic Discourses of Plato and Xenophon* (London: Everyman, 1910).
Lively, J., *The Social and Political Thought of Alexis de Tocqueville* (Oxford, 1962).

Livy, *The Early History of Rome*, ed. Selincourt and Ogilvie (London: Penguin, 1971).

Lukes, S., *Emile Durkheim* (London, 1973).

McClelland, J. S. (ed.), *The French Right: From De Maistre to Maurras* (London, 1970).

Machiavelli, *The Prince and the Discourses*, ed. Lerner (New York, 1950).

Mackrell, J. Q. C., *The Attack on 'Feudalism' in Eighteenth Century France* (London, 1973).

MacMullen, R., *Enemies of the Roman Order* (Cambridge, Mass., 1967).

de Maistre, J., *Works*, ed. Lively (London, 1965).

Malcolm, J., *In the Freud Archives* (London, 1986).

Marcuse, H., *Eros and Civilization* (Boston, 1966).

Markus, R., Review of P. Brown, *Society and the Holy in Late Antiquity*, *Times Literary Supplement* (22 October 1982), p. 1157.

Mason, S. M., 'Livy and Montesquieu', in T. A. Dovey (ed.), *Livy* (London, 1971).

Mendell, C. W., *Tacitus* (New Haven, Conn., 1970).

Michelet, J., *Histoire de la Révolution Française* (Paris: Editions de la Pléiade, 1952).

Michelet, J., *History of the French Revolution*, ed. Wright (Chicago, 1967).

Miller, J. C., *Sam Adams: Pioneer in Propaganda* (Stanford, Calif., 1936).

Montesquieu, *Lettres persanes*, ed. Faguet (Paris, 1951).

Montesquieu, *Considerations on the Causes of the Greatness of the Romans and their Decline*, ed. Lowenthal (New York, 1965).

Montesquieu, *The Spirit of the Laws*, ed. Neumann (New York, 1966).

Moore, J. M. (ed.), *Aristotle and Xenophon on Democracy and Oligarchy* (London, 1975).

Nye, R. A., *The Origins of Crowd Psychology: Gustave Le Bon and the Crisis of Mass Democracy* (London and Beverly Hills, 1975).

Ortega y Gasset, Y., *The Revolt of the Masses* (London, 1961).

Osborn, R., *Freud and Marx: a Dialectical Study* (London, 1937).

Peel, J. D. Y., *Herbert Spencer: the Evolution of a Sociologist* (London, 1971).

Picard, E., *Gustave Le Bon et son oeuvre* (Paris, 1909).

Plato, *The Republic*, ed. Lee (London: Penguin, 1962).

Plutarch, *Lives*, ed. Clough, 3 vols (London: Everyman, 1914).

Plutarch, *Fall of the Roman Republic*, ed. Warner and Seager (London: Penguin, 1972).

Pocock, J. G. A., *The Machiavellian Moment* (Princeton, N.J., 1975).

Polybius, *The Rise of the Roman Empire*, ed. Walbank (London: Penguin, 1979).

Pons, A., 'Vico and French Thought', in G. Tagliacozzo and H. White (eds), *Giambattista Vico, an International Symposium* (Baltimore, 1969).

Procopius, *Works*, ed. Dewing, Vol. I (London, 1935).

Revue Blanche, 'Quelques opinions sur l'oeuvre de H Taine', vol. 13 (1897), pp. 263–95.

Rosca, D. D., *L'Influence de Hegel sur Taine théoricien de la connaissance* (Paris, 1928).

Rudé, G., *The Crowd in the French Revolution* (Oxford, 1959).

Rudé, G., *Wilkes and Liberty* (Oxford, 1962).

Rudé, G., *The Crowd in History* (London, 1964).

Shackleton, R., 'Montesquieu, Bolingbroke and the Separation of Powers', *French Studies* (1949), pp. 25–38.

Shackleton, R., *Montesquieu* (Oxford, 1961).

Shils, E., 'The theory of mass society', in *Centre and Periphery: Essays in Macrosociology* (Chicago, 1975).

Sidis, B., *The Psychology of Suggestion* (New York and London, 1927).

Sighele, Scipio, *Psychologie des sectes* (Paris, 1898).

Sighele, Scipio, *La Foule criminelle*, 2nd edn (Paris, 1901).

Sighele, Scipio, *Littérature et criminalité* (Paris, 1908).

Simon, W. M., *European Positivism in the Nineteenth Century* (Ithaca, N.Y., 1963).

Slaughter, T. P., 'Mobs and crowds, riots and brawls: the history of early American political violence', unpublished MS article.

Sorel, Georges, 'G. Le Bon, *Psychologie des Foules*: Revue critique', *Le Devenir Social*, vol. 1 (1895), pp. 765–70.

Sorel, Georges, *Reflections on Violence*, ed. E. Shils (New York, 1961).

Stanley, J. L. (ed.), *From Georges Sorel* (New York, 1976).

Stanley, J. L., *The Sociology of Virtue: the Political and Social Theories of Georges Sorel* (Berkeley, Calif., 1981).

Stein, A., 'Adolf Hitler und Gustave Le Bon', *Gesichte in Wissenschaft und Unterricht*, vol. 6 (1955), pp. 362–8.

Abbot Suger on the Abbey Church of St-Denis, ed. Panofsky (Princeton, N.J., 1946).

Swain, J. W., *Edward Gibbon the Historian* (London, 1966).

Syme, R., *Ten Studies in Tacitus* (Oxford, 1970).

Tacitus, *Historical Works*, 2 vols (*The Annals* and *The History*, etc (London: Everyman, 1908).

Taine, H., *Sa Vie et sa Correspondance*, 4 vols (Paris, 1891).

Taine, H., *De l'Intelligence*, 2 vols (Paris, 1948).

Taine, H., *The Origins of Contemporary France*, trans. Durand, 6 vols (Boston, 1962), *The Ancient Regime* and *The French Revolution*.

Taine, H., *History of English Literature*, trans. Van Laun, 2 vols (London, n.d.).

Tarde, Gabriel, *L'Opinion et la foule* (Paris, 1901).

Tarde, Gabriel, *Underground Man*, intro. H. G. Wells (London, 1905).

Tarde, Gabriel, *Introduction et pages choisies par ses fils* (Paris, 1909).

Tarde, Gabriel, *Penal Philosophy*, trans. Howell (Boston, 1912).

Thayer, J. A., *Italy and the Great War: Politics and Culture, 1870–1915* (Madison, Wisc., 1964).

Thompson, E. P., *The Making of the English Working Class* (London: Penguin, 1968).

Trotter, W., *The Instincts of the Herd in Peace and War* (London, 1923).

Vico, J.-B., *Principes de la Philosophie de l'Histoire*, ed. Michelet (Paris, 1963).

Vile, M. J. C., *Constitutionalism* (Oxford, 1969).

Villehardouin, *Chronicles of the Crusades: Joinville and Villehardouin*, ed. Shaw (London: Penguin, 1976).

Walbank, F. W., *Polybius* (Berkeley, Calif., 1972).

Weber, E., *The Nationalist Revival in France, 1905–1914* (Berkeley, Calif., 1959).

Whitfield, J. H., 'Machiavelli's use of Livy', in T. A. Dorey (ed.), *Livy* (London, 1971).

Whyte, L. L., *The Unconscious before Freud* (New York, 1960).

Wiener, M. J., *Between Two Worlds: the Political Thought of Graham Wallas* (Oxford, 1971).

Wills, Garry, *Inventing America* (Garden City, N.Y., 1978).

Wilson, H. Schütz, 'Carlyle and Taine on the French Revolution', *Gentleman's Magazine*, vol. 277 (1894), 341ff.

INDEX